# Voices of the Race

*Voices of the Race* offers English translations of more than one hundred articles published in Black newspapers in Argentina, Brazil, Cuba, and Uruguay from 1870 to 1960. Those publications were as important in Black community and intellectual life in Latin America as African American newspapers were in the United States, yet they are almost completely unknown to English-language readers. Expertly curated, the articles are organized into chapters centered on themes that emerged in the Black press: politics and citizenship, racism and anti-racism, family and education, community life, women, Africa and African culture, diaspora and Black internationalism, and arts and literature. Each chapter includes an introduction explaining how discussions on those topics evolved over time, and a list of questions to provoke further reflection. Each article is carefully edited and annotated; footnotes and a glossary explain names, events, and other references that will be unfamiliar to English-language readers. A unique, fascinating insight into the rich body of Black cultural and intellectual production across Latin America.

Paulina Laura Alberto is Professor of History, Spanish, and Portuguese at the University of Michigan. She is the author of *Black Legend: The Many Lives of Raúl Grigera and the Power of Racial Storytelling in Argentina*.

George Reid Andrews is Distinguished Professor of History at the University of Pittsburgh. He co-edits, with Alejandro de la Fuente, the Afro-Latin America book series at Cambridge University Press. He is the author of *Afro-Latin America: Black Lives, 1600–2000*.

Jesse Hoffnung-Garskof is Professor of History and American Culture and Director of the Immigrant Justice Lab at the University of Michigan. He is the author of *Racial Migrations: New York City and the Revolutionary Politics of the Spanish Caribbean*.

# Afro-Latin America

**Series editors**

George Reid Andrews, *University of Pittsburgh*
Alejandro de la Fuente, *Harvard University*

This series reflects the coming of age of the new, multidisciplinary field of Afro-Latin American Studies, which centers on the histories, cultures, and experiences of people of African descent in Latin America. The series aims to showcase scholarship produced by different disciplines, including history, political science, sociology, ethnomusicology, anthropology, religious studies, art, law, and cultural studies. It covers the full temporal span of the African Diaspora in Latin America, from the early colonial period to the present and includes continental Latin America, the Caribbean, and other key areas in the region where Africans and their descendants have made a significant impact.

*A full list of titles published in the series can be found at:*
www.cambridge.org/afro-latin-america

# Voices of the Race

*Black Newspapers in Latin America, 1870–1960*

Edited and translated by

**PAULINA LAURA ALBERTO**
*University of Michigan, Ann Arbor*

**GEORGE REID ANDREWS**
*University of Pittsburgh*

**JESSE HOFFNUNG-GARSKOF**
*University of Michigan, Ann Arbor*

CAMBRIDGE
UNIVERSITY PRESS

# CAMBRIDGE
## UNIVERSITY PRESS

University Printing House, Cambridge CB2 8BS, United Kingdom

One Liberty Plaza, 20th Floor, New York, NY 10006, USA

477 Williamstown Road, Port Melbourne, VIC 3207, Australia

314–321, 3rd Floor, Plot 3, Splendor Forum, Jasola District Centre, New Delhi – 110025, India

103 Penang Road, #05–06/07, Visioncrest Commercial, Singapore 238467

Cambridge University Press is part of the University of Cambridge.

It furthers the University's mission by disseminating knowledge in the pursuit of education, learning, and research at the highest international levels of excellence.

www.cambridge.org
Information on this title: www.cambridge.org/9781316513224
DOI: 10.1017/9781009063791

First published 2022

*A catalogue record for this publication is available from the British Library.*

*Library of Congress Cataloging-in-Publication Data*
NAMES: Alberto, Paulina L., editor. | Andrews, George Reid, 1951– editor. | Hoffnung-Garskof, Jesse, 1971– editor.
TITLE: Voices of the race : Black newspapers in Latin America, 1870–1960 / edited by Paulina Laura Alberto, George Reid Andrews, Jesse Hoffnung-Garskof.
DESCRIPTION: Cambridge, United Kingdom ; New York, NY : Cambridge University Press, 2022. | Series: Afro-Latin America | In English. Articles translated from Spanish and Portuguese. | Includes bibliographical references and index.
IDENTIFIERS: LCCN 2022007777 (print) | LCCN 2022007778 (ebook) | ISBN 9781316513224 (hardback) | ISBN 9781009073318 (paperback) | ISBN 9781009063791 (ebook)
SUBJECTS: LCSH: Black newspapers – Latin America – 19th century. | Black newspapers – Latin America – 20th century. | Black people – Latin America – Intellectual life. | Latin America – Intellectual life – 19th century. | Latin America – Intellectual life – 20th century. | BISAC: HISTORY / Latin America / General
CLASSIFICATION: LCC PN4930 .V65 2022 (print) | LCC PN4930 (ebook) | DDC 079/.808996–dc23/eng/20220627
LC record available at https://lccn.loc.gov/2022007777
LC ebook record available at https://lccn.loc.gov/2022007778

ISBN 978-1-316-51322-4 Hardback
ISBN 978-1-009-07331-8 Paperback

*To the writers and readers of Latin America's Black press –*
*past, present, and future*

# Contents

# Figures

Cover image and credit: Benedicto Ferreyra, in 1908, holding what appears to be an issue of his paper, *La Verdad* (Buenos Aires, Argentina). Credit: Argentina. Archivo General de la Nación. AGASo1. Acervo Gráfico, Audiovisual y Sonoro. Departamento Documentos Fotográficos. Repositorio Gráfico. Fotografía en papel. 1824. 953660 (1908).

# Acknowledgments

From 2016 to 2018, the three of us participated in the preparation of an edited volume that included, among others, a seminal essay by Frank Guridy and Juliet Hooker on Black political and social thought in Latin America.[1] As they sketched the broad outlines of that body of writing, Guridy and Hooker also noted, with regret, how little of it was available to English-language readers. That observation struck a very strong chord with each of us. Having spent years doing research on Black newspapers in Argentina, Brazil, Cuba, and Uruguay, we knew what a rich and concentrated lode of cultural and intellectual production they contained. And so the idea arose of introducing North American readers to those newspapers by translating a selection of their articles and features. Much work still remains to be done to make the words of Afro-Latin American thinkers accessible beyond their national languages and contexts, including within Latin America itself.

Little did we know, when we began this project, how many debts we would accrue along the way. Even with the widespread digital availability of most of our sources, this book would never have materialized without the generosity and support of countless individuals. Our absolute dependence on the goodwill of friends, colleagues, acquaintances, and strangers became especially clear as the original project to select, translate, and annotate these articles from Latin America's Black press generated a parallel project to identify and locate the descendants of many of these authors in the search for permissions. Even as the scope of that second project expanded to daunting dimensions (exacerbated by the difficulties

[1] Guridy and Hooker, "Currents in Afro-Latin American Political and Social Thought."

xiv

of travel and communication in a global pandemic), it afforded us the opportunity to be in touch with many of the descendants of these writers and with scholars and activists. These individuals not only mobilized to lend a hand at an immensely difficult time for their families and societies, but their responses stirred our hope that this book would help further the anti-racist struggles joined by Afro-Latin American authors in decades and centuries past. We would like to express our deepest gratitude to all the people named here, as well as many more who surely collaborated behind the scenes without our knowledge.

For Argentina, Lea Geler shared her expertise and her remarkable digital collection of Afro-Argentine newspapers (which she also donated years ago to Argentina's Biblioteca Nacional for scholars to consult), and María de Lourdes Ghidoli provided transcripts of a rare collection of *La Raza Africana* held at the Universidad de Córdoba. For Uruguay, Hernán Rodríguez shared his digital collection of *El Progresista*, William Acree and Alex Borucki answered specific queries, and Gustavo Goldman, Tomás Oliveira Chirimini, and Beatriz Santos Arrascaeta searched for information on several Afro-Uruguayan writers. For Cuba, Andrés Montalván Cuéllar and Nicolás Hernández Guillén, of the Fundación Nicolás Guillén, generously agreed to our permission requests. Ivor Miller and Alejandro de la Fuente were instrumental in locating the descendants of several prominent Afro-Cuban writers. Alejandro de la Fuente also temporarily parted with a trove of his own annotated photocopies of impossible-to-find Afro-Cuban papers so that we might work with them, and Cary Aileen García Yero, Marial Iglesias Utset, Adriana Chira, María de los Angeles Meriño Fuentes, and Aisnara Perera Díaz kindly shared or helped to produce digital images or transcriptions of complementary collections. José Fusté generously shared his own translation and interpretation of several idiomatic expressions.

For Brazil, the search for information on Black writers' descendants benefited from the efforts of numerous people and organizations. Amilcar Pereira, Petrônio Domingues, Flávio Gomes, Miriam Nicolau Ferrara, Flávio Carrança, Mário Augusto Medeiros da Silva, Márcia Lima, Ana Cláudia Castilho Barone, Maria Cláudia Cardoso Ferreira, Teresa Malatian, Maria Cecília Felix Calaça, Henrique Cunha Júnior, Valquíria Pereira Tenório, Luiz Paulo Lima, Keila Grinberg, João José Reis, and Ana Flávia Magalhães Pinto – and through them, Milton Barbosa, Flávio Jorge, Oswaldo de Camargo, and Márcio Barbosa – all went to great lengths to help us identify and contact possible heirs. Sueli

Carneiro of GELEDÉS, Nabor Jr. and Luciane Ramos Silva of *O Menelik 2° Ato*, the Brazilian Studies Association (BRASA), and H-LatAm graciously ceded space in their organizations' social media pages for our public postings in search of potential heirs. In the United States, Marc Hertzman, Dale Graden, Marisol Fila, and Kim Butler steered our search in productive directions, and Keisha Blain, Herrick Chapman, Matthew Delmont, Eric Jennings, and Eric Zolov generously responded to questions on topics outside our areas of expertise. For their willingness to allow us to republish the works of their ancestors and loved ones, warmest thanks go to Elisa Larkin Nascimento of IPEAFRO, Cláudia França dos Santos Antonio, Adriana Moreira, and to Philon Carneiro, whose untimely death, shortly after we had the pleasure to correspond with him, we profoundly lament.

At Cambridge University Press, Cecelia Cancellaro and Alejandro de la Fuente (as Editor and Series Editor respectively) provided unflagging encouragement, guidance, and feedback as this project took shape. We also wish to thank the two anonymous readers whose insightful and generative comments helped us make this book useful and appealing to as wide a range of readers as possible.

All royalties from *Voices of the Race* will go toward supporting Afrodescendant organizations in those four countries.

# A Note on the Text

Throughout this book, readers will find explanatory footnotes for people, places, concepts, and events that may be unfamiliar. Terms that appear in more than one article are rendered in **boldface** on first appearance within each headnote and article. Full definitions for these terms can be found in the Glossary at the end of this book. Many Spanish and Portuguese racial terms, left untranslated and set in italics throughout the book, are also explained in the Glossary.

# Introduction

This book introduces English-language readers to the historical (1870–1960) Black newspapers and magazines of Argentina, Brazil, Cuba, and Uruguay. In Latin America, the violence of enslavement, limited access to primary education and the world of publishing, and exclusion from regional archives and libraries make documents and texts produced by Afrodescendants themselves extremely rare.[1] The majority of the abundant documentary evidence of the participation of Africans and their descendants in the region's history was created by state and Church officials and institutions, lawyers, policemen, foreign visitors to the region, journalists, scientists, and others, most of whom were not themselves of African descent. Yet in their own periodical publications, Afro-Latin Americans eloquently expressed their thoughts on a host of social and political issues: slavery, race and racism, democracy, civic and social equality, gender, African-based culture, economic development, literature and the arts, parenting, and others. Those newspapers and magazines are the richest and most concentrated venue for Black voices in Latin American history.

Afro-Latin American newspapers are the direct analogue of, and were occasionally in dialogue with, the African American press in the United States. Yet they are virtually unknown in the English-speaking world and are in any case beyond the reach of audiences who do not

---

[1] For examples of historical texts by Black authors, see McKnight and Garofalo, eds., *Afro-Latino Voices*; de Jesús, *The Spiritual Diary*; Acree and Borucki, eds., *Jacinto Ventura de Molina*; Manzano, *Autobiography of a Slave*; Batrell, *A Black Soldier's Story*; Leite and Cuti, *... E disse o velho militante*; Castillo Bueno, *Reyita*.

read Spanish or Portuguese.[2] These barriers have deprived readers of access to an invaluable source of Afro-Latin American thought, as well as a wealth of detail about Black community life and political activism across these diverse local contexts. *Voices of the Race* brings English-language audiences a translated and annotated selection of articles from those papers, and through them, fuller access to the community life and the intellectual production of people of African descent across Latin America.

As readers may have noticed, we use "Black" interchangeably with "Afro-Latin American" or "Afrodescendant" to designate people who were regarded by themselves and others as having some visible degree of African ancestry, indicated by skin color or other features. In so doing, we follow the present-day consensus among scholars and activists in both Latin America and the United States. Yet these were not necessarily the preferred terms of self-identification of the writers or readers of these newspapers. Indeed, the naming or not naming of racial communities, the different contours of these communities across different places and times, and the various ways that Black writers engaged with their respective nations' guiding ideologies of race are at the heart of the story about Latin America's Black press: what it is, where and why it emerged, who wrote and read it, and what forms it took.

## WHAT IS THE BLACK PRESS OF LATIN AMERICA?

The Black press of Latin America consists of newsletters, newspapers, and magazines produced by Afrodescendant writers and directed primarily at a Black readership.[3] These publications were not designed to be a principal

---

[2] Recognizing the importance of this unique source, historians started researching the Afro-Latin American press in the 1960s and 1970s, and in recent years numerous monographs have been largely or partially based on the papers. Those monographs provide a clear sense of the content of the Black papers and of the themes of greatest interest to the men and women who wrote them. But owing to the constraints of monographic writing, they offer only brief snippets of the thought and writing contained in the papers. For early works utilizing the Black press, see Pereda Valdés, *El negro en el Uruguay*; Andrews, *The Afro-Argentines of Buenos Aires*; Deschamps Chapeaux, *El negro en el periodismo cubano*; Ferrara, *A imprensa negra paulista*; Ferrara, *Imprensa negra*. For examples of more recent work, see Alberto, *Terms of Inclusion*; Andrews, *Blackness in the White Nation*; de la Fuente, *A Nation for All*; Rodríguez, *Mbundo malungo a mundele*; Pinto, *Imprensa negra*; Santos, *Raiou a Alvorada*; Pappademos, *Black Political Activism*; Fernández Calderón, *Páginas en conflicto*; Brunson, "'Writing' Black Womanhood"; Poumier, *La cuestión tabú*; Butler, *Freedoms Given, Freedoms Won*; Domingues, *Uma história não contada*; Hoffnung-Garskof, *Racial Migrations*; Geler, *Andares negros*; Goldman, *Negros modernos*; Alberto, *Black Legend*; Ramos and Pinto, eds., *A imprensa negra*.

source of news and commentary. They were what scholars call a "complementary" press, meant to be read alongside broader-circulation local and national newspapers (often called the "mainstream" press). Writers and editors in the Black press were deeply engaged with periodicals edited primarily by White colleagues (as they were with other Black publications and colleagues), often quoting them extensively or writing in direct response to their coverage. Indeed, Black publications frequently addressed a broader public, including White journalists and politicians, in the name of a racial community. Black newspapers and magazines sometimes announced themselves as the "organs" or "defenders" of "the **class of color**," "the Black race," or "our community," and sometimes they did not.

Brazil is the country with the most extensive, oldest, and best-known Black press in the region. It is also the country with the longest and most extensive experience of slavery in the Americas: slave traders brought more African captives to Brazil than to any other New World society, and it was the last country in the region to abolish slavery. Enslaved people toiled in almost all areas of Brazil's economy, from booming plantations (primarily sugar and coffee) and mines to domestic work and street vending. Brazil remains the country with the largest Afrodescendant population in the hemisphere. At the time of the 2010 census, over 96 million Brazilians (just over half the total population) identified as *preto* (Black) or *pardo* (brown), confirming Brazil as a majority Afrodescendant country. By comparison, in the 2010 census of the United States, 39 million people identified as African American, about 13 percent of the population.[4]

The first Afro-Latin American newspapers appeared in the newly independent Empire of Brazil in the 1830s (roughly contemporaneously with the first African American papers in the United States).[5] But the Brazilian Black press expanded especially rapidly after the abolition of slavery in

---

[3] Writers in some countries occasionally used the term "Black press" (*prensa negra* in Spanish and *imprensa negra* in Portuguese) in relation to their publications. But the term emerges most frequently as a descriptor in academic works from the mid twentieth century onward, especially by scholars based in the United States, where a self-described Afro-American, African American, or Black press has been historically robust and visible. Danky and Hady, eds., *African-American Newspapers and Periodicals*; Vogel, *The Black Press*; Delmont, *Black Quotidian*.

[4] For Brazil, see https://biblioteca.ibge.gov.br/index.php/biblioteca-catalogo?view=detalhes &id=793; for the United States, see www.census.gov/prod/cen2010/briefs/c2010br-02 .pdf.

[5] *O Homem de Cor* (The Man of Color), published in Rio de Janeiro in 1833, appeared only six years after the first African American newspaper, *Freedom's Journal* (New York, 1827). Pinto, *Imprensa negra*, pp. 23–24; Foster, "A Narrative of the Interesting Origins."

1888 and the replacement in 1889 of the monarchy with a republic. Black writers and editors were particularly active in the cities and towns of the southeastern state of São Paulo, where Black Brazilians lived in spaces increasingly dominated by European immigrants.[6] Many Black publications began as newsletters associated with neighborhood-based social clubs for the "**class of color** (*classe de cor*)," and much of the coverage in papers like O *Bandeirante,* O *Baluarte,* O *Kosmos,* and others from the era focused on community or club events. Editors adopted variants of the phrase "organ of the men of color" on their mastheads, and called for Black Brazilians to assert full political, civil, and dignitary rights. They noted that the equality promised by republican laws was constantly threatened by racist ideas and practices. Many White writers in this period described Brazil as a unique "racial paradise" where, despite legacies of slavery and colonialism, three races (White, Black, Indigenous) lived in harmony. Black writers often invoked this shared ideal of interracial fraternity to support calls to remove real barriers to full Black citizenship.[7]

By the mid 1920s, a new generation of Afro-Brazilian writers in São Paulo city and state created publications increasingly aimed at discussing and combating racism directly and asserting the existence of a national (and often Afro-diasporic) racial community linked by a shared past and destiny. Political involvement in these years reshaped editors' sense of mission. Toward the end of the decade, for example, the editors of O *Clarim da Alvorada* (The Clarion of Dawn), initially a "literary, scientific, and humorous" publication, helped create the **Centro Cívico Palmares** in an effort to amalgamate the city's disparate Black associations. After this experience, they declared O *Clarim* a publication "in the interest of Black men" and dedicated to "struggle [*combate*]." In the 1930s, the **Frente Negra Brasileira**, a civic organization that briefly gave rise to one of the region's few Black political parties, further cemented the relationship between activism and São Paulo's Black press. The Frente Negra distributed thousands of copies of its newspaper, *A Voz da Raça* (The Voice of the Race), throughout Brazil. During Brazil's turbulent

---

[6] Similar papers appeared in other southern and southeastern Brazilian states: e.g., in Rio Grande do Sul, O *Exemplo* and A *Alvorada*; and in Minas Gerais, A *Raça.* Santos, *Raiou a Alvorada*; Pinto, *Imprensa negra*, pp. 137–71.

[7] On this ideal, see Alberto, *Terms of Inclusion,* chapter 2. The discussion of the early Paulista (from São Paulo) Black press in this paragraph and the next also draws from Andrews, *Blacks and Whites*; Butler, *Freedoms Given, Freedoms Won*; Domingues, *Uma história não contada*; Domingues, "A insurgência de ébano"; Gomes, *Negros e política*; Ferrara, *A imprensa negra paulista*; Graham, *Shifting the Meaning of Democracy.*

1930s, the Black press expanded to occupy the full spectrum of political positions between fascism and communism, but fell largely silent with the onset of the **Estado Novo** dictatorship (1937–45), which shut down political parties and heavily censored the press.

In Brazil's capital, Rio de Janeiro, fewer Black publications appeared in the first decades of the twentieth century. But in the wake of World War II, as Brazil's government returned to democracy and as Black activists re-organized, influential new publications emerged there. *Quilombo,* dedi-cated to the "Life, problems, and aspirations of the Black man," joined journals like *Alvorada* and *Senzala,* published in São Paulo (the latter with contributors from Rio and other states), as spaces for Black cultural criticism, political activism, and civil rights advocacy. The Black press of this era faced distinctive opportunities and challenges. On the one hand, the restoration of Brazil's democratic institutions brought hope that the country might begin to fulfill its promise as an inclusive and egalitarian multi-racial state. On the other hand, fulsome celebrations of Brazil as a singular **"racial democracy"** to be emulated the world over threatened to undermine the work of Black writers by declaring racism a non-issue. Indeed, while some White Brazilians backed Black writers' anti-racist demands, many others used the idea of racial democracy to represent Black organizations and publications as "reverse racists" who refused to subordinate their particular identities to the national whole.[8]

In Argentina, journalists created a Black press in a society with a much smaller and less visible Afrodescendant population. In 2010, only about 150,000 Argentines identified as Afrodescendant, out of a total popula-tion of more than 40 million inhabitants, though the number of Argentines with unacknowledged African ancestry is surely much higher.[9] Yet the Black population had historically been much more significant, if never as large as Brazil's. Buenos Aires had been one of the principal ports for the trade in African captives to Spanish America, and about one-third of the city's population, and higher proportions of some

---

[8] Alberto, *Terms of Inclusion*; Guimarães, *Classes, raças e democracia*; Graham, *Shifting the Meaning of Democracy.*
[9] For census figures, see https://sitioanterior.indec.gob.ar/nivel4_default.asp?id_tema_1=2&id_tema_2=21&id_tema_3=100. On alternative population counts, see Andrews, "Epilogue"; Lamadrid, Lamadrid, and Cirio, "Primer censo autogestionado." Preliminary test cases for the 2010 census, targeting areas of known Afro-Argentine residence in the cities of Santa Fe and Buenos Aires, registered between 3.5 percent and 4.3 percent of respondents with acknowledged African ancestry. Stubbs and Reyes, *Más allá de los promedios.*

interior provinces, was Afrodescendant when Spanish colonial rule came to an end in the early nineteenth century. The territory that became Argentina had relatively little plantation agriculture, with most Afro-Argentines, free and enslaved, working in domestic service, trades, ranching, and small-scale manufacturing.[10]

The earliest known Afro-Argentine publications appeared in Buenos Aires in 1858, under the titles of *La Raza Africana, o sea El Demócrata Negro* (The African Race, or the Black Democrat), and *El Proletario*. Slavery had been abolished in 1853 (except in the province of Buenos Aires, where abolition came in 1860), and free Afro-Argentine men, many of whom were veterans of the military campaigns of the previous decades, were fully enfranchised as citizens and voters. Those two papers were short-lived, however. The bulk of Argentina's Black press dates from the 1870s and 1880s, when the first generation of Argentines to benefit from a massive expansion of state-sponsored education came of age. Even as this small but dynamic Afrodescendant press flourished and found readers among a robust Black urban community, it was becoming difficult to know how many people of African descent lived in Argentina. After independence, and increasingly after midcentury, census officials and many other record-keepers stopped recording race or color categories (perceived as holdovers of a hierarchical colonial past) in the name of the nation's guiding principles of liberal racelessness, universal citizenship, and legal equality.[11]

Citizenship without regard to race was a value that many Black Argentine men and women embraced, and for which many had fought. Indeed, this second generation of Afro-Argentine editors avoided references to race in their newspapers' titles and descriptions, taking advantage of the openings that purportedly raceless liberalism appeared to offer to assert their belonging as full Argentine citizens. Mastheads announced these publications as the "organ of the working class" or a "weekly newspaper of general interest." Yet the papers still largely reported on and directed themselves toward Afro-Argentine readers. In 1881, the editors of *La Broma* (The Jest) reflected on that newspaper's evolution as it balanced its readers' general concerns as Argentines with their specific

---

[10] Borucki, *From Shipmates to Soldiers*; Andrews, *The Afro-Argentines of Buenos Aires.*
[11] The 1887 municipal census of Buenos Aires recorded a total of 8,005 people of "other colors" than White, under 2 percent of the total population of 433,000. The 1869 and 1895 national censuses offered no information on race or color. Andrews, *The Afro-Argentines of Buenos Aires*; Guzmán, "¿Quiénes son los trigueños?"; Alberto, *Black Legend.*

concerns as Afro-Argentines. Though originally a satirical paper, they noted, in the course of reporting on several major incidents of racial injustice, *La Broma* had become "a space for airing issues of great social importance." The editors added that "it is well understood that [*La Broma*] is the true and genuine organ of the humbler classes, the true interpreter of the beneficial social developments of the so-called people of 'color'."[12] Editors' forthright identification with Buenos Aires' "humbler classes," like their use of "so-called" or their placement of "color" in quotation marks, illustrates the reticence many in this generation felt toward racial identifications, and their aspiration to become unmarked Argentines (or ones marked at most by their identities as working people).[13]

Yet if in the 1870s and 1880s, some Afro-Argentines expressed a hope that liberal principles of colorlessness would abolish racism and ensure full respect and recognition for people of African descent, the events of the next decades proved disappointing. The liberal practice of omitting race in population counts led, by the end of the nineteenth century, to repeated assertions among White Argentine writers and statesmen that Afro-Argentines had all but disappeared, victims of wars, disease, and inter-mixture with the European immigrants who began arriving in waves.[14] At the turn of the century, moreover, discourses of racelessness faded as Argentine elites increasingly equated Argentineness with Whiteness, and anti-Black racism became particularly virulent, backed by the era's **scientific racist** discourses. In the first decades of the twentieth century, as Argentine elites remade Buenos Aires into the "Paris of Latin America," urban renewal projects pushed Afro-Argentines out of the central neighborhoods they had inhabited since colonial times to outlying marginal areas.[15] Afrodescendant writers and readers did not disappear – a few Black papers (lost to researchers) emerged in the first decades of the twentieth century (see Figures 0.1, 0.2), while some veterans of the

---

[12] "Porqué se llama 'La Broma'?", *La Broma* (Mar. 20, 1881), 1.

[13] On these themes in the nineteenth-century Afro-Argentine press, see Andrews, *The Afro-Argentines of Buenos Aires*; Geler, *Andares negros*; Ghidoli, *Estereotipos en negro*; Cirio, *Tinta negra en el gris de ayer*; Platero, *Piedra libre para nuestros negros*; Alberto, *Black Legend*.

[14] Andrews, *The Afro-Argentines of Buenos Aires*; Geler, *Andares negros*; Frigerio, *Cultura negra*.

[15] On the recrudescence of racism in turn-of-the-century Buenos Aires, see Andrews, *The Afro-Argentines of Buenos Aires*; Geler and Ghidoli, "Falucho"; Alberto, *Black Legend*; Frigerio, "'Sin otro delito'"; Helg, "Race in Argentina and Cuba." On geographic displacement, Geler et al., "Constructing the White City."

FIGURE 0.1 The editor (identified as "Mr. Terreiros") and administrator of the Argentine newspaper *La Ortiga* in the paper's offices. From Juan José de Soiza Reilly, "Gente de color," *Caras y Caretas* (Nov. 25, 1905).

Black press went on to join labor or mainstream newspapers, or published books of their own.[16] But as the bonds of racial community dissolved through dispersion, state-enforced practices of assimilation, and shifting racial identifications in a nation that elites increasingly declared

---

[16] These publications include the weekly *La Ortiga* and the biweekly *La Verdad*. The latter was founded by **Benedicto Ferreyra** (see front cover) in the early 1900s, ceased publication sometime after 1915, and was reissued by his son **Oscar Ferreyra** in the early 1930s. On these early twentieth-century papers and the community that sustained them, see Alberto, *Black Legend*, chapter 3. For the publications of Afro-Argentine writers, see Ghidoli, *Estereotipos en negro*, chapter 6.

FIGURE 0.2 **Oscar Ferreyra**, second editor of *La Verdad*, in his home office, preparing to reissue the early twentieth-century *La Verdad* (founded by his father, **Benedicto Ferreyra**) after a hiatus. From Martín Martirena, "Periodismo de color," *Caras y Caretas* (Apr. 25, 1931).

homogeneously White, the Afro-Argentine press went silent for the rest of the century.[17]

Uruguay shares borders with both Brazil and Argentina, and the history and dynamics of its Black press combine key features of those of its neighbors.[18] In the national household survey of 2006 and the national census of 2011, 8–9 percent of Uruguayans identified themselves as having some African ancestry.[19] Like Buenos Aires, Uruguay's capital, Montevideo, was a major entry point for African captives in the Spanish colonial period and was home to a substantial Afrodescendant minority when Uruguay became independent in the early nineteenth century.

[17] Argentina's Black press is reemerging in the twenty-first century; see *El Afroargentino* (est. 2014), the publication of DIAFAR (Diáspora Africana de la Argentina).

[18] Information in the following paragraphs based on Borucki, *From Shipmates to Soldiers*; Andrews, *Blackness in the White Nation*; Rodríguez, *Mbundo malungo a mundele*.

[19] Bucheli and Cabela, *Perfil demográfico y socioeconómico*, pp. 14–15; Cabella et al., *La población afro-uruguaya*, p. 15.

Afrodescendant editors began publishing newspapers in the 1870s, three decades after the abolition of slavery (1842) and in the context of universal manhood suffrage. Frustrated by the patronage systems that tied Black voters to the two entrenched political parties and military factions, papers like *La Conservación* and *El Progresista* argued that education and constitutional and civic values were crucial for the advancement of the "interests of the society of color." As in neighboring Argentina, Uruguay's very high literacy rate helped support a flourishing Black press, one that paid close attention both to national- and local-level events affecting the Black community.

Like counterparts in Argentina, by the end of the century, White Uruguayan statesmen congratulated themselves on the success of their project to "Whiten" the nation through immigration. Yet White immigration to Uruguay never reached the levels seen in Argentina, nor did Afro-Uruguayans become statistically, socially, and culturally invisible after 1900 as they did in that neighboring country. Well-defined Black communities persisted in Montevideo and in Uruguay's northern departments, which bordered Brazil and had close ties with Black communities across the border. Indeed, migration from the north replenished and reinforced Black communities, identities, and institutions in Montevideo. In this context, Afro-Uruguayan writers, like their Brazilian counterparts, produced one of the most prolific and long-lived Black presses in the region. By the 1920s and 1930s, Black newspapers had developed new forms of political radicalism that incorporated Marxism, anti-fascism, and anti-colonialism, while also articulating a strong sense of racial solidarity within Uruguay and with Black people in other parts of the Americas and the world. The editors of the newspaper *Nuestra Raza* (Our Race), which appeared regularly from 1933 to 1948, supported the unionization of female domestic workers. They also led an initiative, in 1936, to create the **Partido Autóctono Negro** (Autochthonous Black Party), focused on the rights of Black workers within a broader working-class coalition.

In the 1940s, Black journalists focused on racial discrimination in education and employment, which kept Afro-Uruguayans out of the growing middle class. As in neighboring Brazil at the same time, some White journalists joined this denunciation of racial discrimination, while others denied that any racism existed, blaming Afro-Uruguayans for their supposed failure to take advantage of equal opportunity. The Uruguayan Black press also worked to promote the visibility of Afro-Uruguayan culture, especially **Carnival** parades, in the national public sphere. A new appreciation for Black culture, writers reasoned, would reduce the disdain that White Uruguayans expressed towards their Black compatriots. This goal inspired extensive coverage of Black cultural production in the United States, Cuba, and elsewhere.

The Black press in Cuba emerged at roughly the same time as its counterparts in Argentina and Uruguay, but in a very different political, economic, and social context. Cuba remained a colony of Spain, with an economy dominated by plantation agriculture, until 1898. Beginning in 1868, a multiracial independence movement waged a sustained military insurgency against Spanish rule. At the time, official censuses counted about one-third of the population, roughly half a million people, as "of color." Hundreds of thousands were still held as slaves. In the territory controlled by the revolutionaries, Afro-Cuban leaders and White allies successfully advocated for the abolition of slavery and full civil rights. The first nationalist insurrection was defeated in 1878, but the colonial government granted new freedoms of association and press, and shortly thereafter, the gradual abolition of slavery across the colony. This opening allowed for the proliferation of "societies of color," many with their own publications. *El Pueblo* (1879), for instance, was first published at the headquarters of a newly created educational and recreational society in the city of Matanzas. By the middle of the 1880s, Afro-Cuban activists had begun an effort to coordinate these societies through a national civil rights organization, the **Directorio Central de las Sociedades de la Raza de Color**. Newspapers published by activists in this movement, most notably *La Fraternidad* in Havana, supported the effort to build solidarity among Black organizations affiliated with different political factions and located in the many cities and towns across the island.[20]

The evolution of the nationalist independence movement offered the opportunity for Afro-Cuban editors to participate in partisan publications. Black journalists served as editors-in-chief of nationalist publications in Key West, Florida, New York City, and Veracruz (Mexico), where substantial Cuban exile communities existed. But the nationalist ideal of a movement that would erase racial divisions, and the persistent accusation that Black Cubans sought to make war on Whites and establish another Haiti, also discouraged the naming of Black organizations and publications as such. In Havana, *La Fraternidad,* which announced on its masthead its commitment to the "defense of the interests of the race of color," ceased publication. A nearly identical set of writers immediately

---

[20] Ferrer, *Insurgent Cuba*; Lanier, *El directorio central*; Deschamps Chapeaux, *El negro en el periodismo cubano*.

began publishing *La Igualdad,* which called itself simply a "democratic newspaper. " While the pressure not to name publications in racial terms was certainly a constraint, Black editors also affirmatively demanded the right to speak in the name of the whole nation, rather than only for a racial community. **Rafael Serra** asserted, in response to accusations of racial division, that his *La Doctrina de Martí* was a "Cuban newspaper, nothing more."[21] Still, both *La Igualdad* and *La Doctrina de Martí* continued, as did the organizations affiliated with them, to speak to and in the name of Cubans of African descent.

By the early twentieth century, slavery had been abolished, universal manhood suffrage had been instituted, and a national constitution declared equal citizenship without consideration for race, thanks in large part to the efforts of Black soldiers and Black journalists over the preceding decade. As in Brazil, Argentina, and Uruguay, the Cuban government embarked on a successful project to encourage mass European immigration and "Whiten" the population. Nonetheless, Black Cubans were a substantial portion of the electorate, and several of the most successful Black journalists won elected office or received government jobs. They continued to face considerable pressure from White politicians not to create independent publications or organizations, which, as in Brazil several decades later, risked accusations of racial separatism and undermining the project of national unity. In this context, many continued the tradition of contributing to or editing party newspapers, including some that also functioned as Black newspapers, such as *El Nuevo Criollo.* *Previsión,* the official publication of the **Partido Independiente de Color** (PIC, Independent Party of Color), a Black political organization established in 1908 to compete in elections and exert pressure on the mainstream parties, was a clear exception. Accused of racism, *Previsión* ceased publication due to government repression in 1910, and its editors were killed in state-led repression of the PIC two years later.[22]

Afro-Cuban writers in subsequent years lived in the shadow of that repression, while also participating in new ways in the broader field of Cuban publishing. In the 1910s and 1920s, Black journalists began editing regular, Black-themed sections in mainstream newspapers, a practice that

---

[21] "Para que se sepa," *La Doctrina de Martí* (July 15, 1897).
[22] de la Fuente, *A Nation for All*; Portuondo Linares, *Los Independientes de Color*; Helg, *Our Rightful Share*; Pérez, "Politics, Peasants, and People of Color"; Fernández Robaina, *El negro en Cuba*; Scott, *Degrees of Freedom*, pp. 225–52; and the essays by Bronfman and Ibarra Cuesta in Heredia et al., *Espacios, silencios y los sentidos de la libertad.*

expanded in later decades. In the 1930s and 1940s, Afro-Cuban journalists also took on editorial roles in communist publications as well as in leading literary, general interest, and academic periodicals.[23] As Afro-Cuban editor Carlos A. Cervantes noted in 1938, "other individuals of the race of color have directed newspapers, and direct them still, but they are not, strictly speaking, publications of a specific ethnic character."[24] Yet many of these same writers also responded to the insufficient space granted by mainstream publications, creating their own literary and social magazines. They came together to contribute to *Minerva* and *Labor Nueva* in the 1910s, *Adelante* in the 1930s, and *Nuevos Rumbos, Atenas* and *Amanecer* in the early 1950s. Afro-Cuban writers did not adopt the increasingly assertive or combative names for these publications that were common in the Brazilian and Uruguayan Black presses in these years. Nonetheless, these magazines were venues for writing about community activities, racism, politics, and sophisticated criticism of Cuban arts.[25]

### WHERE WAS THERE A BLACK PRESS?

In the period covered by this volume, a sustained Black press developed in only four of the twenty Portuguese- and Spanish-speaking countries of Latin America. In all four, most Black newspapers and magazines were published in cities with White majorities – cities like São Paulo, Montevideo, Havana, and Buenos Aires.[26] Although governments across Latin America launched projects to Whiten local populations and cultures through European immigration, they achieved greatest success in these

---

[23] de la Fuente, "La 'raza' y los silencios de la cubanidad"; Robaina, "La bibliografía de autores de la raza de color."

[24] Carlos A. Cervantes, "Publicaciones de la raza de color (aporte bibliográfico)," *Adelante* (Mar. 1938), 10.

[25] Of forty-six Black publications that appeared in Cuba between 1912 and 1938, Cervantes identified twenty-seven as magazines and only six as newspapers. Cervantes, "Publicaciones de la raza de color."

[26] It is important to note that the major collections of Black newspapers and magazines, on which scholars necessarily depend, are most complete for these larger cities. Scholarship has begun to emerge on the many lesser-known Cuban and Brazilian Black periodicals produced outside these cities, but much more is needed. See for instance, Sartorius, *Ever Faithful*, on Cienfuegos, Cuba, and Castilho, "A 'Gallery of Illustrious Men of Color'," on Recife, Brazil (see also n6, above).

four cities. For Black writers and readers, the role of race in shaping opportunity and inclusion in these cities was sharply evident and racial identities were highly salient.

At the same time, establishment newspapers, or what one Afro-Cuban writer called the "White" press, granted Black writers "very limited space for maneuver."[27] The mainstream press in these countries was not wholly White; in fact, Afro-Latin Americans often worked as typesetters, printers, copyeditors, or journalists and engaged deeply as readers.[28] But it did little or no reporting on events in Black communities and organizations; when such reporting did appear, the tone was often condescending or derisive. Nor could Afro-Latin Americans typically appear in those papers' social columns. Black newspapers allowed Black journalists to cover those topics, to build social and political networks, and to speak more freely about issues of race and racism.

Anti-Black racism permeated the world of publishing in all corners of Latin America, so other factors must be considered as well in explaining the rise of a Black press during the period covered in this book. One was almost certainly literacy. The emergence of Black newspapers depended on the presence of a substantial Black reading public whose subscriptions or appeal to advertisers could sustain the costs of publication. This may explain why a Black press did not develop in some predominantly rural parts of Latin America with Afrodescendant majorities or with Afrodescendant minorities far larger than those found in Argentina and Uruguay, such as the Dominican Republic, Venezuela, or northeastern Brazil. The need for a substantial readership may also explain why, with the exception of the English-language press developed by West Indian migrants on the Caribbean coast of Central America, there was no Black press in Mesoamerican and Andean countries, where majorities were Indigenous or of mixed Indigenous ancestry. Afrodescendant intellectuals and writers were not absent in these various settings, but they tended to publish their work in contexts other than a Black press. The Afro-Peruvian ethnomusicologist Nicomedes Santa Cruz, for instance, published extensively in a wide range of Peruvian newspapers and magazines, addressing a largely non-Black Peruvian audience. Afro-Costa Rican writer Quince Duncan and Afro-Colombian Manuel Zapata Olivella

---

[27] Lino D'ou, "Surge et ambula" (item 3.9 in this volume).
[28] On Afrodescendants in publishing, see Castilho and Galvão, "Breaking the Silence"; Godoi and Pratt, "Printers, Typographers, and Readers"; Geler, *Andares negros*, pp. 255, 271–74; and the sources in n29, below.

published books of fiction and non-fiction that reached readers and critics beyond their respective countries more freely than a Black press would have.

The case is somewhat more complex in the region's many cities and towns with Afrodescendant majorities or significant minorities. In the towns of Puerto Rico and along the Atlantic Coast of Colombia Afrodescendant typesetters and journalists contributed to and edited labor and partisan newspapers throughout the nineteenth and early twentieth centuries. Afrodescendant intellectuals took part in the broader development of publishing in Santo Domingo, Rio de Janeiro, and Salvador da Bahia as well.[29] But writers in these contexts did not typically create explicitly Black publications. In part, this may have reflected what one scholar has called a "deracialized consciousness that precluded ethnic self-affirmation" in some settings with Afrodescendant majorities or large minorities.[30] Yet the absence of an avowedly Black press is not necessarily a mark of the absence of Black racial identifications. As other scholars note for nineteenth-century Brazil, the paucity of explicitly Black newspapers "should ... not be seen as reflecting a lower degree of Afro-racial consciousness, but as perhaps more a reflection of the dominant modes of public politics" – politics that often enforced racial silence.[31] In these contexts, especially within nations that idealized racelessness, racial harmony, or racial democracy, success within the field of journalism required Afrodescendant writers to build public identities that did not emphasize their Blackness.

On the other hand, the substantial space for self-expression, professional advancement, and even anti-racist advocacy afforded by liberal, socialist, and communist publications in many of these locations also helps explain why some Black writers in Latin America did not feel the need to create distinct Black publications. Black writers in labor and partisan publications in Puerto Rico and Colombia, for example, sometimes took up themes that would have been familiar to readers of the Black press elsewhere. Some writers published translations from the Black press in the United States. Others wrote for non-Black publications in their own

---

[29] Flórez-Bolívar, "Opino, luego existo"; Hoffnung-Garskof, "To Abolish the Law of Castes"; Ramos Perea, *Literatura puertorriqueña negra*; Pinto, *Escritos de liberdade*. In Salvador, see the case of Manuel Querino, who wrote for *A Gazeta da Tarde* and other publications, and published two short-lived papers of his own, *A Província* and *O Trabalho*. Leal, *Manuel Querino*, p. 91.

[30] Torres-Saillant, "The Tribulations of Blackness," 1096.

[31] Castilho and Galvão, "Breaking the Silence."

national contexts, while contributing to the Black press in other countries.[32] Since the 1970s, Black periodicals have emerged in Ecuador, Colombia, Peru, Bolivia, and Panama.[33]

The Black press represented in this volume, then, though the richest vein of Black intellectual and textual production in the region, was but one very particular formation in a much broader spectrum. These publications reflect the particular political and social contexts of Montevideo, São Paulo, Havana, and Buenos Aires, their respective national narratives of race, and the pressures and incentives these contexts offered for naming or not naming Blackness at different times. Yet these cities and contexts were by no means wholly unique, and their differences with places that did not produce a Black press were more of degree than of kind. The conditions that gave rise to these Black presses were familiar and recurring components of ideologies, experiences, and expressions of Blackness shared across Latin America. And while principally national in scope, the Black presses of Cuba, Brazil, Uruguay, and Argentina contributed to networks of Black thought and conversation far beyond those confines.

## WHO PRODUCED THE BLACK PRESS?

In the early years, most of those who participated in the production of Black newspapers were self-taught journalists, editors, and contributors. They were overwhelmingly men, although women's presence as readers, and as occasional contributors, was visible between the lines in the early papers and became increasingly so over time. The female editors who

---

[32] The Dominican Lorenzo Despradel (Muley) lived in Cuba for several decades, contributing to the Black press (see, for instance, his nine contributions to *Minerva* between 1910 and 1915) and to Liberal Party newspapers before moving to Santo Domingo, where he contributed to and edited various non-Black newspapers. Vallejo de Paredes, *Apuntes biográficos y bibliográficos*, pp. 383–85. Colombian Jorge Artel and Puerto Rican Tomás Carrión Maduro each appeared in the Cuban Black press – see "Haiti" (item 7.4 in this volume) and "Conferencia de Artel," *Atenas* (Sept. 1951), 12. In the very different context of late nineteenth-century Buenos Aires, when the leading Afro-Argentine newspapers were shuttered, some writers found outlets in the Black press of neighboring Montevideo (see, for instance, **Benedicto Ferreyra**, "Solicitada," *La Propaganda* [Jan. 20, 1895, and Feb. 3, 1895]). Spanish speakers from the Caribbean contributed to and read Spanish-language columns in the *Negro World* and the *New York Age*. Goldthree, "Afro-Cuban Intellectuals," 41–58.

[33] For example, *Boletín Afro-Boliviano* and *Raíces* (Bolivia), *D'Palenque* and *Bongó* (Peru), *Africamérica* (Venezuela), *Palenque* and *Cuadernos Negros Americanos* (Ecuador), *SAMAAP News* (Panama). On an earlier, primarily Anglophone Black Press in Panama and elsewhere along Central America's Caribbean coast, see Putnam, *Radical Moves*, 131–32.

helped to found the Cuban magazine *Minerva* in 1888 were an important exception to this rule (see Figure 0.3). As we will see, women were central to organizing, running, funding, and fundraising for the clubs and organizations that supported the early publications.[34]

Uruguayan and Argentine writers and contributors benefited from more extensive public education systems in the last quarter of the nineteenth century than did their Brazilian or Cuban counterparts. In all cases, however, publishing these community papers was a labor of love. Writers

URSULA C. DE VALVERDE,
*Redactora fundadora.*

FIGURE 0.3   Original caption: "**Úrsula Coimbra de Valverde,** Founding Editor." Photograph published in *Minerva* (Sept. 1911).

[34] See Chapter 5, "Women."

and editors in Latin America's Black press were rarely, if ever, able to rely on journalism for economic survival. Most depended on their income as craftsmen, musicians, municipal employees, office workers, and other working-class jobs.

By the early twentieth century, Cuba became an exception to this rule. Some of the most prominent Black journalists – **Martín Morúa Delgado, Juan Gualberto Gómez, Rafael Serra, Lino D'ou** – held elected office, were appointed to government jobs, or had important positions within party structures. Journalism did not itself necessarily produce enough income to support these men. But Black journalism was embedded in the broader field of politics and patronage in ways that did support a lucky few.

By the 1930s and 1940s, a growing number of writers in the Afro-Cuban press, and a few in the Afro-Brazilian press, held university degrees as lawyers, architects, engineers, sociologists, or other professions. Some of the women who wrote in the Cuban magazine *Adelante*, or the Brazilian magazine *Quilombo*, had professional degrees and careers as educators or social workers. Although some writers expressed socialist or communist sympathies, they nevertheless thought about racial questions from a relatively privileged class position.

## ANATOMY OF THE BLACK PRESS

The formats of the papers tended to be similar across the region. In the nineteenth and early twentieth centuries, almost all Black periodicals were small weekly, biweekly, or thrice-monthly publications. They were usually four pages in length, frequently consisting of a single large sheet, printed on both sides and folded in half. Below a masthead, front pages typically contained editorials commenting on community affairs or on national or international events that affected the Black population. Text in these early publications was generally arranged in four columns, occasionally embellished with more sophisticated design elements, illustrations, or photographs of writers and editors (see Figures 0.4, 0.5).

The middle pages offered news of local social clubs, civic organizations, and cultural events, and extensive social notes on weddings, births, deaths, travel, and parties. These pages often also included letters from readers or regular correspondents in other cities or overseas, and, not infrequently, poems, short stories, or a serialized work of fiction or non-fiction. The final page or two was usually devoted to advertisements, both from Black-owned businesses and from

FIGURE 0.4 Front page from the Brazilian newspaper *O Menelik* (Jan. 1, 1916), featuring a standard four-column layout and an inset poem, and decorative line drawings throughout.

businesses targeting a Black clientele, sometimes in the form of a directory with names and addresses of businesses and clubs (see Figures 0.6, 0.7). In many cases, this page was reproduced from edition

FIGURE 0.5 Front page from the Brazilian newspaper *O Clarim da Alvorada* (Jan. 25, 1925), featuring a standard four-column layout with portraits of the two founding editors as well as other decorative elements.

to edition with few changes, which undoubtedly saved time and resources for typesetting.

FIGURE 0.6 Advertisement page from the Argentine newspaper *La Broma* (Oct. 26, 1882).

Very few of the Black papers achieved lasting financial stability. While a number of African American papers in the United States became successful business enterprises, virtually all of the Afro-Latin American newspapers lost money; indeed, fundraising campaigns and appeals to

FIGURE 0.7 Front page from the Cuban newspaper *La Igualdad* (Feb. 14, 1893), which unusually featured advertisements on its front page rather than its back page.

subscribers to please pay their overdue bills were regular features in the papers. Some ceased publication after only a handful of issues; very few lasted more than four or five years.

Beginning with *Minerva,* a ladies' magazine produced in 1910s Cuba, some editors shifted from a newspaper format to a magazine layout. In Cuba, the literary and general interest magazines *Labor Nueva, Adelante, Atenas,* and *Amanecer* all adopted similar formats, featuring visually arresting covers and including many more pages with less text on each page (Figures 0.8, 0.9). The Cuban magazines also dedicated more space to advertising, which was interspersed throughout the publications. These included advertisements for mass-market commercial products, such as condensed milk or beer. Uruguayans made a similar transition in the 1930s, choosing a twelve-page monthly magazine layout for *Nuestra Raza* and *Revista Uruguay* (Figure 0.10). Brazilians made the transition several decades later, after World War II. *Quilombo,* a twelve-page magazine laid out in five columns, included extensive coverage and images of theater and film, lending it the look of a show-business magazine (Figure 0.11). The magazine format, and shifting technologies, allowed for many more illustrations and photographs, which lent greater visibility to a community of Black editors, writers, readers, and members of associations, and played an important role in the aesthetic valorization of Blackness (Figures 0.12, 0.13, 0.14, 0.15; see also Figures 5.1 and 5.2). In the twentieth century, the Cuban Black press often included sports coverage, with special attention to baseball and boxing.

## THE ORGANIZATION OF THIS BOOK

To compile this volume, we surveyed thousands of articles in a wide array of publications. Those included the eight newspapers published in Argentina, forty in Brazil, and seventeen in Uruguay for which full or partial collections exist, either in public libraries and archives or in private hands. Digital facsimiles of many of these are freely available online (see the Appendix on Black Periodicals in this volume). Cuban newspapers and magazines, most housed at the Biblioteca Nacional de Cuba José Martí, are more difficult for researchers outside of Havana to consult. Of the forty-six titles that appear in available library catalogues, we were able to survey thirteen, thanks to digital images or photocopies shared by colleagues and to digital or microform collections available in the United States (see Appendix).

As we considered articles to translate, we followed two main criteria. First, we chose articles that addressed themes or topics that appeared

FIGURE 0.8 Cover from the Cuban magazine *Minerva* (Apr. 15, 1911), showing both the use of photojournalism and art nouveau illustration in the new magazine format.

frequently in the papers, even (or especially) if the perspectives on those topics differed substantially from article to article, publication to

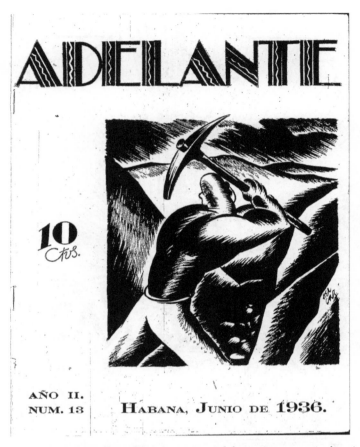

FIGURE 0.9 Cover from the Cuban magazine *Adelante* (June 1936), showing the influence of social realism.

publication, country to country, and over time. Second, we chose articles that we believe will engage readers and make them want to read more. Our hope is that readers will find the articles sufficiently compelling to warrant further exploration, either through the work of the historians who have researched the newspapers or perhaps even by looking at the papers themselves, most of which are available in digital form through the national libraries of Argentina, Brazil, and Uruguay.[35]

[35] See previous footnotes in this chapter, and the Appendix on Black periodicals.

FIGURE 0.10 Cover from the Uruguayan magazine *Nuestra Raza* (Jan. 1934).

We have organized our selection of 113 articles into chapters reflecting the most prominent themes that emerge from Latin America's Black press. Chapter introductions provide guidelines for reading the selected articles along thematic lines, briefly situating the pieces in their geographic and temporal contexts. The discussion questions at the end of each chapter introduction encourage readers to make deeper connections among the articles and to engage in comparison and contrast. The articles in each chapter proceed in chronological order.

FIGURE O.II Cover from the Brazilian magazine *Quilombo* (July 1949), showing the juxtaposition of news coverage (the nomination of African American scholar and diplomat Ralph Bunche for a Nobel Prize) with content and design reminiscent of a show-business publication (a staged photograph of the actress Ruth de Souza).

FIGURE 0.12 A "Social Chronicle" spread from the Cuban magazine *Minerva* (Oct. 15, 1912) illustrates the enhancement of this regular feature of the Latin American Black press through the inclusion of photography.

FIGURE 0.13 Caricatures from the literary page of *Minerva* (June 1, 1912) show Black critics expressing opinions on the work of illustrious White authors.

Los componentes del «Artigas» posando sonrientes para NUESTRA RAZA

De izquierda a derecha, (de pie): Claudio Silva. Julián Miguel Alamo (hijo), Luis Cardozo, Juan Emilio
Piriz y Héctor Liñán; (sentados): Julián Miguel Alamo (director), Teresa Silva, Paulita Liñán, Carmen
Silva de Liñán. Isabelita Liñán e Ismael Arribio.

FIGURE 0.14 Photograph from *Nuestra Raza* (Jan. 1934). Original caption: "The members of the Artigas [Drama Club] pose smiling for *Nuestra Raza*."

Although we have chosen this thematic grouping as the book's main organizing principle, no article can be said to address only one theme, as readers will quickly perceive. Questions of race, gender, citizenship, politics, aesthetics, diaspora, family, and community life were experienced as entangled and simultaneous, or, in today's scholarly terms, as intersectional and co-constitutive. Individual headnotes thus situate each piece and its author more precisely in their time and place, while suggesting thematic connections within and across chapters and national cases.

## LOS REDACTORES DE "NUESTRA RAZA"

FIGURE 0.15 Photographs from *Nuestra Raza* (Jan. 1934). Original caption: "The editors of *Nuestra Raza*."

# CHAPTER I

# Politics and Citizenship

## INTRODUCTION

These writings on politics and citizenship suggest the breadth of Black people's political thought and experiences in Latin America, and the depth of their commitments to political involvement.

National independence (achieved in the 1810s and 1820s in Argentina, Brazil, and Uruguay, and in the early twentieth century in Cuba) offered the opportunity to break with colonial rule and construct new national political orders. All four countries seized that opportunity to overturn colonial racial laws and write the principle of full civic and legal equality into their national constitutions. But as the Black newspapers repeatedly argued, constitutional ideals of egalitarian citizenship were consistently undercut and eroded by everyday racism and prejudice.

In nineteenth-century Argentina and Uruguay, Black writers denounced the racial barriers that severely limited their ability to take part in electoral party politics (1.1, 1.3, 1.4). Black publications in Brazil raised the same issue while simultaneously debating whether the country was better served by constitutional monarchy (1.2) or by republicanism (1.6). In Cuba, writers discussed how to reform their society while still contending with the very recent memory of slavery (1.5; see also 1.6); a civil rights movement based in the **Directorio Central de las Sociedades de la Raza de Color** fought to overturn colonial caste laws (1.7) and, once independence had been won, to reform governmental institutions in ways that would guarantee racial equality (1.8).

Finding the mainstream political parties unresponsive to their demands, between 1900 and 1940 groups of Black activists and intellectuals created new racially defined parties in Cuba (the **Partido Independiente de Color,**

1.9), in Brazil (the **Frente Negra Brasileira**, 1.11, 1.12), and in Uruguay (the **Partido Autóctono Negro**, 1.10). The Partido Independiente de Color was violently repressed in 1912, the Frente Negra Brasileira was banned by the national government in 1937, and the Partido Autóctono Negro dissolved in 1944 after a disappointing electoral showing.

During the 1930s, the Black papers debated the gathering confrontations among fascism, communism, and liberal democracy (1.10, 1.11, 1.12, 2.10, 6.4, 6.6, 7.11). As Brazil emerged in 1945 from an eight-year period of authoritarian rule, Afro-Brazilian writers celebrated the return to democracy and urged readers to support socialist or populist parties based in the country's labor movements (1.13, 1.14, 1.15). Black newspapers in Cuba adopted a similar orientation, and after **Fulgencio Batista**'s seizure of power in 1952, protested the return to authoritarianism after an extended period of electoral democracy (1.16).

### DISCUSSION QUESTIONS

- The creation of specifically Black political parties in three of these four countries speaks eloquently both of Afro-Latin Americans' high expectations for political involvement and their nations' persistent institutional failures to meet them. Yet race-based political organizing was only one avenue for political involvement. Others included constitutional monarchy, republicanism, liberal democracy, socialism and communism, fascism, feminism, or staunch political independence. On what grounds did different writers advocate for their particular political ideology? What seemed to be the affordances and limitations of each of these political ideologies and systems, as defended by these writers, for addressing the gap between ideals of full civic equality and realities of under-representation or political marginalization?

- In all four countries, Black writers faced the persistent coexistence of equality on paper with discrimination and exclusion in practice. They also faced the challenge of highlighting racial discrimination and advocating for specifically Black rights without seeming to place racial loyalties before national ones – something that often earned them accusations of "separatism" or reverse "racism" from White co-nationals. How did Black writers in different times and places navigate these shared challenges? How did their specific national and historical contexts shape or limit the kinds of political claims they made?

- For much of the period under discussion, access to voting was restricted by literacy requirements, property requirements, or gender, in addition to age. Most adult Afrodescendants in the region were subject to at least one of these limitations until the middle decades of the twentieth century. At the same time, it was relatively rare for Black candidates to appear on major party tickets. How do the writings of these Black thinkers seek to expand Black political representation within those confines or challenge them altogether? What areas of their nations' political systems and public life did writers identify as sites of urgent intervention, and on what grounds did they justify Black people's right to elect and be elected?
- Not all politics are electoral politics. How did different writers define political involvement? What did it mean to be a citizen, concretely and symbolically?
- As they wrote their impassioned appeals about politics and citizenship, Black writers wrote most immediately for Black readers. But they hoped to reach, and influence, broader national conversations. To do so, and to defend the righteousness of their cause, these writers used diverse rhetorical strategies: from classical references or invocations of world-historical events, to comparisons to the contemporary experiences of Afrodescendants elsewhere. How did writers mobilize these rhetorical strategies in support of their political goals? What did these rhetorical choices say about these individuals as authors, and about their intended audiences?

## 1.1 "THE WHITE MEN AND US," LA CONSERVACIÓN (MONTEVIDEO, URUGUAY: OCT. 27, 1872)

*During the 1800s and most of the 1900s, politics in Uruguay revolved around intense competition between the* **Colorado** *and* **Blanco** *parties, the former based largely in Montevideo and the smaller cities of the interior, the latter in the countryside. Both parties drew electoral support from networks of local political clubs, and in 1872 an Afro-Uruguayan club in Montevideo, the Club Defensa, proposed one of its members, José María Rodríguez, for a place on the Colorado list of candidates to the General Assembly. The party initially signaled its willingness to include Rodríguez on the list but subsequently withdrew its approval, provoking this angry response from* La Conservación, *one of the first Afro-Uruguayan papers. The article cited both the Uruguayan constitution and the record of Afro-Uruguayan military support for the Colorados in Uruguay's recurrent* *civil wars as justifications for Black men to be included in party lists. (Rodríguez was himself a sergeant major in the armed forces.) The paper proposed that, if the mainstream parties refused to nominate Black candidates, then Black voters should withdraw their support and form their own electoral lists – a forecast of the **Partido Autóctono Negro**, founded in 1936 (1.10).*

White men will always be the same, as much as they try to disguise their aversion toward us by claiming liberal and democratic sentiments.

We are seeing the proof of that in what is happening today with the Club Defensa, which believed that it would be enough to be faithful to the [**Colorado**] party for which men of color shed so much blood in all its struggles: the party which they support, and have supported, for such a long time, above all in the immortal siege of the New Troy,[1] where our race, with undeniable courage, performed prodigious feats that are some of the most glorious pages of our history.

[The Club Defensa] believed, I repeat, that that party would not be ungrateful. [But] now that our race is claiming the reward for its services, the most precious of the rights of man, which is the right to equality – now those men [of the Colorado Party] are afraid to be stained by having men of color as their equals!

A fatal contrast:

The Empire of Brazil, where aristocracy and slavery reign, grants men of color the right to equality.

The great Argentine Confederation admits men of color into its legislature.

But: the Republic of Uruguay cannot admit men of color in its legislature.

Why is this? Are men of color legal citizens of the Republic, or not?

I think so; when the country is in the greatest peril, it calls to its defense all its sons, with no distinction of color.

Are men of color not sons of Adam and Eve, like the Whites?

I think so, given that Europe, the mother of civilization, considers us to be her brothers.

If all the civilized nations give men of color the right to equality, why doesn't the Republic of Uruguay do so as well?

---

[1] The Siege of Montevideo (1843–51) during the Guerra Grande (1839–51), a prolonged civil war between the Blanco and Colorado Parties.

Because men of color have not realized that in this republic, White men, regardless of the [political] opinion to which they belong, are enemies of our race.

In order to conquer our rights, let's forget **Blancos** and Colorados and think just that we are free citizens, and that by uniting we will triumph.

The Club Defensa must stop being the vassal of a party, and must call to its breast all the men of our race, to form lists [of candidates] dictated by their consciences. By uniting we will obtain what we will never achieve if we wait for the enemies of our race to help us.

### 1.2  "RECIFE, MARCH 9, 1876," O HOMEM (RECIFE, BRAZIL: MAR. 9, 1876)[2]

*The topic of Black military service appeared frequently in the nineteenth-century Black press. Black service to the nation in past and current wars was a powerful argument for civil and legal equality; and high military rank bestowed significant political and social stature, along with some measure of economic well-being, on its holders. O Homem thus raised a pressing question: why had high-ranking (and even low-ranking) Black and brown officers disappeared from the ranks of Pernambuco's National Guard? They were abundant during the first half of the 1800s; now, half a century after independence, they were nowhere to be seen. How had this happened, and what did it say about Brazil's model of constitutional monarchy, supposedly based on full racial equality?*

*The article then pivoted to address a second, related concern: the future abolition of slavery. Speaking to, and on behalf of, Pernambuco's large free Black population, the paper predicted that "sooner than some might think, there will be no more slaves in Brazil." British pressure on Brazil to end the country's Atlantic slave trade, and the recent abolition of serfdom and slavery in Russia and the United States, respectively, had made clear in which direction the global winds of freedom were blowing. But slavery was so deeply entrenched in Brazilian life that some extraordinary measure would be required to achieve final abolition, and the paper called on Brazil's emperor, **Dom Pedro II**, to take that step.*

---

[2] Though this article was published anonymously, Celso Castilho and Rafaella Galvão attribute it to O *Homem*'s publisher and editor, Felipe Neri Collaço (1815–94). Collaço was a schoolteacher, journalist, and committed abolitionist. Castilho and Galvão, "Breaking the Silence."

*When final abolition eventually took place, twelve years later, it was through a hastily approved act of parliament, duly signed by **Princess Regent Isabel**; the Emperor was traveling in Europe at the time.*

In our previous issue we showed who was the great Henrique Dias,[3] and how the Portuguese government honored him not just during his life, by naming him governor and regimental commander (lieutenant colonel) but after his death by ordering that his body be buried at the expense of the Royal Treasury.

Elsewhere in this issue readers will find other documents produced by the same government with the same goal of honoring the Pernambucan hero.

His Black color was not an obstacle to such distinguished honors being bestowed upon him. And as we will show in future issues, it was not only toward this distinguished Brazilian that the aforementioned government thus acted; it named others of Black and brown color, in recognition of the service they provided, to be colonels, lieutenant colonels, majors, captains, etc., etc.

In all of the province of Pernambuco today, show us a single colonel, a single lieutenant colonel, a single major of the National Guard who is brown.

Show us a single captain, a single lieutenant, who is Black!

In days gone by, we had militia battalions of brown and Black men, all commanded by citizen officers belonging to the same **classes**. We still know a colonel named Joaquim Ramos, a Black man who lives on the Praça da Boa Vista, and a lieutenant colonel named Joaquim de Siqueira Varejão, a brown man, who lives in the street that abuts the main church in that neighborhood, and son of Colonel Gregorio de Siqueira Varejão, of the same color. Our elders used to tell us about various others belonging to the same classes, as well as a large number of officers of less elevated rank. All of that is now ended.

Could it be because the men of these classes have degenerated from their progenitors? That during the centuries of darkness, under the rule of absolutism, those classes could produce superior men, and now under the reign of freedom, the opposite is occurring?

No, the cause lies elsewhere.

---

[3] Henrique Dias (?–1662) commanded Black militia troops in Pernambuco during the war against the Dutch occupation of northeastern Brazil (1630–54). Today he is recognized as a hero both of Brazilian military history and of Afro-Brazilian history. Hebe Mattos, "Henrique Dias," in Knight and Gates, *Dictionary*, vol. II, pp. 341–43.

Whatever it may be, we will ask: What did the men of color gain, personally, from the proclamation of independence and the Empire, for which they sacrificed so much?[4]

Of what use is it to them that the constitution says that every citizen can hold public civil and military office without any distinctions other than those of their talents and virtues, if they find themselves excluded from high military and civil office, there not being in this province, as we said above, *a single one* who is a colonel, lieutenant colonel or major of the National Guard, *a single one* who is head of a state agency?

Is that how equality before the law should be understood?

Will there be in this regard a true society, or merely a fiction of a society?

The lion of the fable also formed a society to hunt, but once the prey had been caught, instead of dividing it equally among his partners, he took all of it for himself, saying that he deserved one part by right of being a member [of the society], another by right of being the strongest, another by right of being king, and not having any other right to cover the fourth part, he said: if anybody touches it, I will strangle them immediately.

Is this the point to which one wishes to arrive?

Oh! Slavery has to end some day, either peacefully or through revolution. We are convinced that this outrage against the laws of humanity cannot last many more years, and that whatever it may cost, equilibrium will be re-established.

Yes, sooner than some might think, there will be no more slaves in Brazil.

We owe the first step toward the future regeneration of Brazilian men of color to the direct intervention of **England**, against which those involved in the infamous [slave] trade protested so strongly.

Had it not been for that, we might still be witnessing today the clandestine arrival of African slaves to our country's soil.

The second step we owe to the moral influence of public opinion in Europe, to the glorious examples provided by the two largest nations of the Old World and the New – Russia emancipating its serfs after the Crimean War, and the United States freeing its slaves – and perhaps even indirectly to the war that we fought against Paraguay.[5]

---

[4] Independence was declared in 1822; the Empire was the system of constitutional monarchy that governed Brazil from 1824 to 1889.

[5] Serfdom was abolished in 1861 in Russia; slavery was abolished in 1865 in the United States. Between 1864 and 1870, Brazil fought alongside Argentina and Uruguay in the **War of the Triple Alliance** against Paraguay. Thousands of enslaved Brazilians won freedom through military service, and one year after the end of the war, in 1871, parliament

Thanks to the beneficial effects of these powerful causes, no more slaves are being born in Brazil!

The final extinction [of slavery] will come, not as some expect, through regular means, but rather through extraordinary means. Slavery is a knot that cannot be untied, it must be cut. The gangrenous limb must be amputated lest the entire organism be corrupted. And yet, happy is the country in which that operation is not left to the convulsive hand of some audacious speculator who puts himself at the head of the angry masses!

Wisdom counsels that before that comes to pass, a skilled practitioner with a steady hand should take on the necessary operation, and among us, that practitioner can be none other than **Dom Pedro II**.

Not for nothing did the nation confer on him the so meaningful title of *eternal defender of Brazil.*

Let him imitate, then, the glorious examples provided by Czar Alexander of Russia and President Lincoln of the United States, let him complete the work that he began with the **Free Womb Law**, and his name will go down to posterity as the greatest of the Brazilians.

## 1.3 "OUR RIGHTS," LA BROMA (BUENOS AIRES, ARGENTINA: NOV. 20, 1879)

*Across Latin America, Black writers and thinkers were keenly aware of the rights enshrined in national laws and constitutions. They invoked them frequently to celebrate the political evolution of their nation and rally fellow Afrodescendants to make the fullest use of their legal guarantees. Here, an editor of Buenos Aires'* La Broma *took another common approach, denouncing the coexistence of laws proclaiming equal rights with a "law of custom" – a set of entrenched, habitual practices and prejudices – that sanctioned the unequal treatment of Afrodescendants.*

*As was common in the Black press across Latin America, the author substantiated what he called "the legitimacy of our aspirations" to equal rights and full citizenship by pointing to Black military service (see 1.2, 6.4). Rarely, however, was the thorny theme of a nation's collective debt to its Black citizens – and the condemnation of White ingratitude – phrased so pointedly as in this editorial. In an Afro-Porteño press in which outright denunciations of the shortcomings of liberal republicanism were*

---

approved the Rio Branco Law (referred to later in this article as the **Free Womb Law**), under which children of slave mothers were born free, thus guaranteeing the eventual end of slavery.

*infrequent, as was the explicit naming of "Whites" and "Blacks" as discrete and oppositional groups, this author denounced, and finally damned, White Argentines for their condescension, pride, and selfishness toward their Black co-nationals, and for their failure to recognize past sacrifices with present-day political rights.*

In our earlier article, we intended to demonstrate the legitimacy of our aspirations by maintaining that all who, in the business of life, inhabit Argentine territory are free and equal in responsibilities and rights.

We also affirmed that the law of custom continues to tyrannize people of humble backgrounds, with all the capriciousness of fashion.

They mock for the mere *luxury* of it.

They scoff for the *pleasure* of it.

They lord it over others *because they can*, because *they feel like it*, without observing the fatal consequences this can bring.

It beggars belief that a society as learned, decent, [and] refined as ours would not know how to pay homage to the glorious traditions that the battalions of Blacks and ***mulatos*** etched with their blood onto the battle-fields of Maipú and Chacabuco, during our war of independence![6]

Yes! Because those who today scoff at them [Blacks and *mulatos*] owe the very liberty they enjoy not to themselves, but to the heroic, self-denying sacrifice of that indomitable race that carried its gigantic courage to the snowy peaks of the **Andes**!

What sad rewards have been given to that race . . . !

How boundless is human pride!

Ingrates!

You, Whites, de facto aristocrats, who boast so much of being free and independent, do tell: To whom do you owe your freedoms and your independence?

To yourselves?

No!

You owe them to those who, at every moment of danger faced by the Fatherland, shoulder their weapons and fill their hearts with that generous sentiment harbored by noble and brave souls; [to those] who look not to the ingratitude of the future, but to the dangers of the present; [to those]

---

[6] The Battle of Chacabuco (February 12, 1817) and the Battle of Maipú (April 5, 1818), both near Santiago, Chile, were decisive battles in the wars of independence between the patriot Army of the Andes (led by Argentine General **José de San Martín** and composed of Argentine and Chilean troops) and Spanish forces.

who cast not a backward glance to the home and the family they abandon, but raise their sights to the lines of the bayonets and the mouths of the cannons that wish to rob them of that patrimony that God has given all men: the liberty of their Fatherland and freedom of conscience!

I am sure that if a pretentious *White* [man] were to read these lines, a smile of pity and scorn would alight upon his face, because mankind's pride overpowers all nobility, all sentiments, all abnegations, and – let us say it, to [mankind's] great shame – overpowers even the infinite greatness of God himself!

Yes, because there are men in this world who humiliate everything, mistreat everything, forget everything in the interests of that miserable selfishness that lives inside miserly and sickly hearts, which fail to heal because it would seem that the very blood in them had frozen.

Ah! Human selfishness be damned, damned be those who forget that they owe their freedom and independence to those they insult with the most cynical insolence.

## 1.4 "THE CANDIDATES AND THE BLACKS," LA BROMA (BUENOS AIRES, ARGENTINA: MAR. 21, 1880)

*In Argentina (as in neighboring Uruguay, see 1.1), the early onset of gradual abolition and the establishment of comparatively broad male suffrage meant that Afrodescendant men participated energetically in electoral politics during the nineteenth century, as voters and as candidates for low-level posts. Through the press, political clubs, and networks of sociability and patronage, they also worked as mobilizers and recruiters of other Afro-Argentine voters. This article articulated a sharp criticism of the ways that party leaders, in the run-up to elections, courted and flattered Black political clubs and their members, citing republican and Christian notions of racial equality and fraternity. Yet once the elections passed, elected officials forgot or cast aside their commitment to constitutional principles, repaying Black support with "scorn," "contempt," and discrimination. "Only during electoral contests," this author wryly noted, "are we treated and looked upon, in accord with the constitution, as citizens." This denunciation was not, however, a wholesale repudiation of electoral politics. As was frequently the case in such writings, the general critique of White politicians helped marshal support for a specific political patron, whom this writer vociferously (and strategically) claimed would be different.*

(Special contribution [anonymous])

According to our National Constitution there are no distinctions of caste or of race on our Republic's soil;[7] but [this principle] exists only in theory and not in practice, for our race is always scorned, and none remember that it has contributed with its blood to winning the independence and freedom that this country enjoys today.

We have always been and are [still] scorned by those whom we have helped to ascend to power. They have used us like rungs with which to climb up the ladder of public offices, and once arrived [at their posts], they have repaid us with contempt and even by snatching away from us our rights as citizens.

Every time an electoral contest arises we see certain individuals who seek us out with great determination and lavish us with tender solicitousness. And what for? Because they need our vote to benefit this or that candidate.

In these cases, it is common to see scenes like the ones we will narrate here:

In [political] club A or B, attended only by the *aristocracy* of money (for our country does not recognize the aristocracy of parchments and of blood), where a Black man was barred from entering, we see him against whom the doors were until then closed received courteously and even regaled (by the same individual who, in any other occasion, would be debased from his *hierarchy* by deigning to speak with a Black man), and [we see] the following dialogue ensue:

- Mister C., we have eagerly awaited you, because a man of your virtues is the very soul of our party, and without you our work cannot begin.
- Sir, I am undeserving of such praise; you flatter me.
- Not at all, I speak only the truth.
- No sir, my talents are not so great as to deserve such words from your lips.
- None of this modesty, you deserve much more; you are a man of renown, and that bodes well for our party's triumph.
- It would make me happy if I and my friends could contribute to placing in power those men who, through their talents and good judgment, will bring about the happiness of my country, which is my only aspiration.

---

[7] The writer refers to Article 16 of the Argentine constitution of 1853: "The Argentine Confederation admits no prerogatives of blood or of birth; it recognizes no privileges or titles of nobility. All of its inhabitants are equal before the law and admissible for employment with no other consideration than their aptitudes." The previous article abolished slavery.

- With a man like you we shall achieve it, my friend. And when we find ourselves holding the reins of power we shall not forget you.
- I ask nothing for myself. I only desire that our foundational charter [the constitution] be strictly obeyed; for if it is obeyed, we will be citizens and not poor Blacks, disdained by those who have White faces.
- It is true that part of our society feels a certain repugnance toward Blacks, but those who behave that way are not republicans, and not even Christians, for Jesus Christ said that we were all God's children, all brothers.

At this point, the dialogue is interrupted by the arrival of another character who must deliver important news.

The [club] president calls the meeting to order and each of them goes to occupy his seat. They reserve the best spot for our hero, Mister C. The [club] secretary recounts all the work undertaken so far, most of which was done by C. All [club members], upon hearing this, congratulate C., who finds himself stunned by the praise heaped upon him by those gentlemen, and knows not what to say. Finally, to his relief, the session ends and each person abandons his seat to devote himself with renewed zeal to finding voters, which is what the work of the clubs comes down to.

Things continue in this vein. The day of the election arrives. The candidate that C. supports wins. He rises to power, and once there, he forgets C. and all the Blacks who contributed to his election, and instead of ensuring that they receive respect as the citizens they are, he is the first to scorn them.

This is how all those who aspire to power keep their promises.

We are citizens, they fête us, they treat us as equals as long as they need our vote, so as to climb the rungs of power, and once they arrive there, they scorn us and even deny our rights as free men. For if a Black man goes before any authority to bring a suit against a White man, even being in the right, they pay him no heed, and the first thing they say [is]: he is Black.

As if a Black man did not have the same prerogatives, the same rights as a White man.

[As if] because he was born with a Black face, he should remain, for the duration of his days, in that abject and disgraceful life.

No, and a thousand times no.

Only during electoral contests are we treated and looked upon, in accord with the constitution, as citizens; but once those moments pass, we return to the abjectness to which they have condemned us.

No!

We want our foundational charter to be strictly obeyed, and in particular as it pertains to our race. That is why from the columns of this humble newspaper – which, although small in form, is colossal in its noble sentiments – we invite our brothers to cooperate with their canvassing energies and to contribute with their vote to elevating to the Presidency of the Republic the worthy and distinguished Dr. Bernardo de Irigoyen.[8] For the name of this appealing figure, the pride of **Porteños** and of the republic as a whole, harbors none of the miseries and maliciousness that, until now, have been thrown in our faces.

Yes! Under that name and that of the great party that holds him aloft, made up of men who applaud peace because they love their country, is inscribed in indelible characters the motto:

EQUALITY BEFORE THE LAW.

Let us bow before it.

### 1.5 ÁFRICA C. CÉSPEDES, "TO CUBA," MINERVA (HAVANA, CUBA: MAR. 16, 1889)

*In 1888, two years after the process of gradual abolition came to an end in Cuba, a group of Black women led by* **Úrsula Coimbra de Valverde** *helped to launch* Minerva, *the first publication in Latin America dedicated specifically to "the woman of color." The magazine was administered and edited by men, many of the same writers and activists who edited* La Fraternidad *at the same time. The pages were full of articles by these men voicing their opinions on women's issues. But the editors also expressed their commitment to "offering a vehicle where our sisters who have studied literature can evolve a definite literary vocation [and] bring their efforts into the public eye and thus encourage our women to pursue further studies."[9] Coimbra and a handful of other female writers contributed letters, poems, and articles to every issue until the magazine shut*

---

[8] Bernardo de Irigoyen (1822–1906) was a lawyer, diplomat, and politician who ran (unsuccessfully) as one of several candidates of the Partido Autonomista Nacional in the presidential elections of 1880. He later became one of the founding members of an opposition party, the Unión Cívica Radical, and ran for president on its ticket.

[9] Cited in Montejo Arrechea, "*Minerva*," 34.

*down in July of 1889. When the magazine reopened in 1910, again with male editors, a new generation of women writers contributed regularly. Minerva is quite simply the richest known repository of Afro-Latin American women's writing from both periods.*

*During the first era (1888–89), a small number of essays signed by África Céspedes*[10] *were notable for their assertive style and sharp political edge. In this one, Céspedes offered a reflection on the abolition of slavery that began with a powerfully evocative reflection on the experience of women in bondage. Céspedes did not say whether she herself had been enslaved. But her account is clearly that of an "eyewitness." Such vivid and horrifying memories were difficult to leave behind, she wrote, and the transition to freedom sometimes seemed like a dream or an illusion. Although she accepted that the new decrees of freedom and rights for Black Cubans had redeemed "the fatherland," she did not hesitate to remind readers that these measures had come "late," and that, until recently, some of Cuba's sons had "groaned beneath the cruelest servitude." Céspedes emphasized that freedom, for women, generally meant leaving behind jobs that were antithetical, she believed, to women's constitutions, such as field labor, and taking up what she saw as their natural domestic roles. Some later writers in* Minerva *saw things differently. To them, intellectual pursuits on equal footing to men represented freedom, while domestic chores were drudgery.*[11] *It is worth noting that writers and readers of* Minerva *were relatively better-off than other Black Cubans. Most Afro-Cuban women did not enjoy either the financial security necessary to dedicate themselves wholly to domestic tasks in their own homes or the educational opportunities necessary to become writers.*

If, after the events that have taken place in our hospitable Cuba over four hundred years, we had been born in the middle of the twentieth century, when the shameful period of slavery through which we have passed will be almost completely forgotten, and, leafing through the history books we

---

[10] Very little is known about this writer. Mirabal suggests that África Céspedes was a pseudonym. *Suspect Freedoms*, 119–23. The geographical term "Africa" was by no means a common first name in Cuba and, combined with Céspedes, the surname of one of the most hallowed leaders of the Ten Years' War, would be a richly symbolic *nom de plume*. It may also have been her given name, which Helg takes as evidence that some Black Cubans "chose to name their children after their origin, no doubt as a mark of respect for the African continent." *Our Rightful Share*, p. 40.

[11] María Risquet de Márquez, "Impresiones y reflexiones," *Minerva* (Havana, Cuba: Nov. 1, 1910).

were to discover in their pages that the woman of color had served as a strong, necessary element for the ascent of ignominious capital – whether watering the fertile fields of our wretched Cuba with the bitter sweat of her brow, engaged in hard agricultural tasks, from clearing and tilling the fields to harvesting the fruit; whether serving as laborers for masons or carpenters in the construction of buildings, or as assistants at the forges of master smiths, or in the most taxing occupations in the sugar mills during the time of harvest; in sum, in all those tasks that are suitable for men and clearly in conflict with women's constitution – we would not have believed it. But as eyewitnesses to these dangerous labors, the painful reality disconcerts us with its terrible eloquence.

For this reason, it seems to me a dream that the word slavery has been erased from our laws and replaced with the word liberty; that the Black race and those originally from Africa have been given the inalienable rights that had for so long been usurped; that [these groups] have been restored to the civil status that, by law and by right, has always been their due, as an integral part of the human family.

We women who, approaching midnight in the outbuildings of the sugar mills, have heard the fearsome crack of the overseer's whip following upon the tolling lament of the swinging bell or of the piercing steam whistle, signals that the extended work hours [of the harvest season] had begun; and who have seen, in almost military formation, men and women covered in filthy rags (it seems that not even the twenty-hour work shifts in the sugar mills and fields were enough to provide clothing to the work crew) in the interminable, harsh, winter nights, the women carrying their newborns on their backs in bundles of henequen or palm leaves, the product of illicit loves,[12] and in their hands the short-handled hoe or the machete or some other instrument of work or production, beginning their march toward the fields and the outbuildings, to work by the weak light of the waning moon; while the inhuman slave-driver sinks his lash into the backsides of his victims on the merest whim – for us, it is difficult to cast off the dream, the nightmare, the perception that such an important transition may be an illusion.

---

[12] By adopting the euphemism "love" to refer to sexual liaisons, Céspedes creates ambiguity. Does she mean willing encounters with enslaved men that are illicit because they are prohibited by plantation owners, or forced encounters with overseers and enslavers? Céspedes had written about the sexual abuse of women under slavery in a previous article about unjust representations of Black women as depraved and immoral. "Reflexionemos," *Minerva* (Feb. 28, 1889).

But we must cast off this nightmare, this illusion, this dream and wake up satisfied by the just, if late, redress for so many injustices committed against the race that seemed to be condemned to eternal servitude.

Some compensation was bound to reach the Black family for the heroic sacrifice of generous blood spilled by so many martyrs, as an offering to the fatherland in the epic of the **Ten Years' War!**

The day was fated to arrive when Cuba would become the pure and immaculate virgin who would erase the stain which, like a shameful stigma, she wore stamped on her innocent brow!

The day was fated to arrive when you, my dear fatherland, would become the crucible that would purify, with the fire of reason and conscience, the fool's gold that debased the purity of your birth!

Now – thank God! – women can, whatever their background, dedicate themselves with complete liberty to the tasks that are suitable for them and enter, with the logical requirements of the modern legal system, in the civil status that will elevate them to the category of consideration and respect.

Today, Cuba, your poets will be joyfully inspired by the magnificent expression of your bountiful nature, which harbors a people comprised of free colonial subjects; today they can sing praise, in complete freedom, to the thousand enchantments bequeathed to you by Providence.

And the sparkling waters of your mighty rivers and your notable lakes, as clear and crystalline as a brilliant mirror, reproduce in its purest expression the vault of your bewitching sky in the temperate nights of flowery May. Your forests of giant palms confide whispering melodies to the morning breeze; your birds, with their brilliant feathers, sing in satisfaction that you are a mother and not a tyrant to your sons; the sun that illuminates you is clearer, purer, more splendid and, in sum, all that surrounds you is gratified that you are a worthy daughter of that most democratic nation of the Old World, whose name is Spain.[13]

From today onward, Cuba, you will be blessed for all eternity, because those sons who groaned beneath the cruelest servitude, now free in the embrace of your loving bosom, will be, after a few years of constant study, men of worth to their families, to society, and to the fatherland.

---

[13] It is unclear whether this endorsement of Spain as a democratic society, or the earlier phrase "free colonial subjects" (the word she used, *colonos*, can also be read as "settlers" or "colonists"), were intended to be ironic. There were Black writers in this period who were Spanish loyalists; see Sartorius, *Ever Faithful*. The editors of *Minerva*, however, were ardent proponents of Cuban independence (citizenship rather than subjecthood) and fierce critics of Spanish monarchism.

África C. Céspedes

Manzanillo, February 1889.

Author's note: This article was written in response to the publication of the Royal Decree that brought about the total extinction of slavery.[14]

## 1.6 IGNÁCIO DE ARAÚJO LIMA, "RIO DE JANEIRO," A PÁTRIA (SÃO PAULO, BRAZIL: AUG. 2, 1889)

*In the year-and-a-half after the abolition of slavery (1888), conflict intensified in Brazil between supporters of the monarchy and those who favored a republican system of government. In this article, Ignácio de Araújo Lima, a leading São Paulo abolitionist, saluted the formation in Rio de Janeiro of the Club Republicano dos Homens de Cor.[15] Writing during the final months of monarchical rule, Araújo Lima presented the Republic as a more likely (than the monarchy) guarantor of Black rights and wellbeing. Since the Republic did not yet exist, that argument was largely theoretical; not in the least theoretical was the article's vivid depiction of the sufferings of slavery, abolished just fifteen months earlier. The article is also striking for its fervent embrace of the African parents and grandparents of Brazil's Black population, who had suffered so atrociously under slavery, and for its expressions of pride in "the African blood coursing through our veins." As we will see in other articles (6.3, 7.5), during a period in which* **scientific racism** *condemned both racial mixture and non-White racial ancestry, not all writers in the Black press were willing to identify so strongly and firmly with their enslaved African ancestors.*

To the Republican Club of the Men of Color.

> Hosanna, hosanna, let us sing to the day
> On which this news announced to us
> That, united by the idea, you are there,
> Ready to combat tyranny
> And those others who scorn our race.
> Let us avenge our parents.

[14] The Royal Decree of October 7, 1886, ended the period of forced apprenticeship (*patronato*) two years earlier than stipulated in the gradual abolition law of 1880. Scott, *Slave Emancipation in Cuba*.

[15] On the Club Republicano dos Homens de Cor, see Pinto, *Escritos de liberdade*, pp. 334–41.

Yes, men of Rio, your idea was sublime, your means majestic!

Could we, the men of color here in São Paulo, receive in silence the news given by the Rio newspapers, and reproduced by the São Paulo press, which filled us with pleasure? No. We who yesterday raised our weak voice against the organization of the projected Guarda Negra, here in São Paulo we have nourished for some time a hope that has the same basis, the same goals.[16] Your idea, which you publicly express, is the same as ours, and do you know why? They call us Paulistas because our cradle was in the city of São Paulo, legendary and heroic for the brilliant deeds of its children, yet we can only say: Here in this part of South America we had our cradle, but where is our country? This question we cannot answer, for now.

It has been more than three and a half centuries since the discovery of Brazil; in each single century, in each single year, in each single month, in each single week, in each single minute, in each single second, you have the pages of history of three centuries and many years, in which was written the martyrology of the unhappy children of Africa who were enslaved in Brazil. We found the tyranny and evil of the Brazilian Torquemadas and Dezas[17] in the owners of the **Bastilles** of slavery, the plantations, where those depraved beings nourished the soil with the bodies of our grandparents and parents, and watered it with their blood and with their tears! Well might we wish to seek punishment for so many crimes; but it is late, very late.

The mission that we must take on is even more difficult, but also more noble and more honorable.

Yesterday they gave freedom to the enslaved, but they forgot that the freedman, who has become a citizen, has a right to, and needs to have, a country. Yes, who more than he has a right to the soil on which he walks?

Meanwhile here he is, hushed and timid. No one hears the echo of his voice; he is the statue of Contemplation and Hope, built on the pedestal that is the passage of time and faith in the future. And we, what attitude should we assume in the face of this sad picture before us, the legacy left to us by slavery? We, who feel African blood coursing through our veins, we

[16] The Guarda Negra was an informal militia, organized by abolitionist **José do Patrocínio** and based in Rio de Janeiro, that supported the monarchy and opposed the Republican movement, at times in violent street confrontations. The group disbanded after the overthrow of the monarchy in November 1889. Gomes, *Negros e política*, pp. 12–26.

[17] Tomás de Torquemada (1420–98) and Diego Deza (1444–1523) were Grand Inquisitors of the Spanish Inquisition.

who take pride in belonging to that race, the first to penetrate the virgin bosom of the earth and to return laden with gold and precious stones, fruits that our race gathered that were then transformed into cloaks that hid so many crimes and even today exist in the coffers of the powerful; an exiled and enslaved race that, for well over three centuries, labored only to fill the treasuries of kings and emperors with gold and precious stones? The passing of time demands our conciliation so that together we can combat the darkness in which many of yesterday's freedmen are still immersed, educate them, and guide them toward the majestic idea of the Nation and the Republic.

So let us go forward full of faith and courage to conquer the country for the freedman. What do sacrifices matter? Our grandparents and our parents succumbed to sacrifices and excruciating pain, not on the battlefield of aspirations or ideas, but under the blows of a whip cracked by powerful arms, in the broad courtyards of the plantations, surrounded by an enormous multitude of men and women, enslaved wretches, mute witnesses, who attended the sad spectacle. There they saw the flesh ripped off a man's body, the fragments of that body falling on the blood-soaked ground, where later also fell the skeleton of that fleshless body breathing an ay, or a muffled groan, a final goodbye to his brothers and sisters, his work-gang companions! And with that groan, ay, or sigh, the soul of one more martyr set off to seek the bosom of the Creator.

We know well that we are small compared to the majesty and power of the great, but we are also the descendants of that race that for three centuries was martyred, extorted, and vilified; destroy the atom, dispute the fact. And where we will find Country and Freedom, if not in the sun of the Republic, because the tears of misfortune, the blood from so much torture, the sweat of so much anguish, are the trophies of glory that our grandparents and our parents left us. Let us guard those trophies in the reliquary of our hearts, and for those [grandparents and parents] who remain, old and broken, let us seek for them and for us the complement of Freedom, Fatherland, and Rest. To achieve our aspirations, we need audacity and courage, so let us apply all of our energy and efforts toward evolution and revolution. Does it matter which? Revolution? Here is how two great writers consider it: Revolution is the distillation of the times; Revolution is the Jurisprudence of God.[18]

---

[18] We do not know who Araújo Lima was quoting here.

Saluting you from here, the staff of *A Pátria* sends you a fraternal embrace, and leaves you with these parting words: each one of you represents an idea, and in that conjunction of ideas exists an ideal; on that ideal raise up the Goddess of the Republic. Only with her will we have rest for our parents in the remaining days of their existence, under the empire of democracy, of government by the people for the people, in a country truly free.

### 1.7 "THIS IS HOW HISTORY IS BEING WRITTEN," LA IGUALDAD (HAVANA, CUBA: APR. 4, 1893)

*The* **Directorio Central de las Sociedades de la Raza de Color** *was an umbrella organization for Black clubs and associations in Cuba, created in 1886, the year that slavery was fully abolished. By the early 1890s, under the leadership of the journalist* **Juan Gualberto Gómez**, *it had developed into an island-wide civil rights organization. The Directorio petitioned the colonial government, with some success, for the expansion of public schooling, the elimination of racial discrimination in criminal sentencing, the elimination of separate birth and death registries and identity cards based on race, the right to the honorific titles don and doña, the enforcement of laws against discrimination in cafés and theaters, and an end to municipal ordinances requiring people of color to give way to White people on sidewalks and restricting access to public parks. Gómez and the Directorio also sought to pressure the political parties to come out in support of equal civil and political rights for Black Cubans. Opponents, most notably writers aligned with the Autonomista Party, accused the Directorio of sowing racial division and hatred, of being a first step toward a Black political party, and of fomenting race war. This unsigned article in the newspaper* La Igualdad, *edited by Gómez and his supporters, employed scathing sarcasm to point out the absurdity of these accusations. It provides a clear example of the ways that writers in the Black press used irony to address the claim that racial prejudice did not exist in Cuba (see also 8.4).*

It appears that before the **Directorio Central de las Sociedades de la Raza de Color** was founded, the idea of race did not exist in this country. All of its inhabitants lived in the most perfect unity, absolutely unaware of any idea of race or color. No differences among them were recognized, other than the ones that can be seen in countries like France, Germany, Italy,

Spain, England, etc., where people associate or separate according to the affinities or differences created by social position and education.

Everywhere the sentiment of fraternity shone forth. Blacks and Whites gathered together for all social functions. It never occurred to the White man to think himself, simply because of the color of his skin, the superior of the Black man. And he [the Black man], in turn, never felt in the least humiliated by being made the victim of any sort of prejudice.

In other countries this had happened. But not in Cuba. In other countries it had come to pass that slavery separated Whites from Blacks, making the former into the higher class and the latter into the lower. It was natural, in the places where this had happened, that with the passage of time, this idea that one race was superior should give rise to prejudices against the other, and as those who considered themselves disadvantaged began to educate themselves, this state of humiliation, imposed upon them only because of their color, seemed less tolerable. But none of this happened in Cuba. Here it had come to pass that, despite the enslavement of the Blacks, their ignorance, their intentionally being held back, there were no prejudices; to such a degree that the most perfect unity among the members of both races had always and constantly been observed in all aspects of public and social life.

Who can remember the existence of any prejudices keeping Whites separated from Blacks five or six years ago? Was it not the case that everyone was equal? Surely there was no such thing as an aggravating circumstance in the Penal Code?[19] Can it be that Municipal Schools were divided into schools for Whites and for [people of] color?[20] Can it be that any distinctions were made in public establishments, or was everyone served equally?[21]

No: these things were unknown in Cuba, until the "Directorio Central" of the **class of color** was founded.

---

[19] Article 10 of the Penal Code, specifying higher penalties for criminal acts "committed against a White person by one who is not" remained in effect until the ratification of the 1901 Constitution.

[20] At the time, Cuban municipalities were allowed to exclude Black children from schools attended by White children but were supposed to create separate schools in which to educate them. In practice, schools for Black children, where they did exist, were frequently neglected.

[21] Among the Directorio's victories were a government decree that overturned local ordinances segregating parks and public ways, and several judicial decisions against owners of cafés, restaurants, and theaters who denied service to Black Cubans. But the colonial administration did not require local authorities to abide by these rulings, so they went unenforced.

This was a diabolical idea. In view of the fact that Black men were not accepted in the Club, in the new Lyceum, the Caridad del Cerro,[22] it was all well and good that they should create educational and recreational associations that were only for themselves. This did not smack of separation. But what has seemed very bad is that all of these societies should band together in a "Directorio Central," while still retaining their autonomy, in order to achieve their common goals. This has brought with it, as a consequence, the separation of the races.

Since the "Directorio" was founded, the [Penal] Code was modified to add the aggravating circumstance of color. Since then, distinctions that did not previously exist were put in place in public establishments. Since then, theaters began prohibiting people of color from occupying decent seats. And since then, but only since then, the municipal schools were divided into schools for Whites and [children] of color. In a word: the Directorio has [moved the country] backwards, because it has caused the Whites to feel prejudices that they had never felt before, or even heard of.

It is evident that the "Directorio" has brought all of these things to a country where they were unknown. But it is much more evident that the majority of the country ought not to believe in the Directorio's baneful actions and that only a small group of distinguished spirits, who have always thought and worked in the same way, has the glory of seeing the matter clearly, and sufficient virtue to shout hoarsely day after day, telling others, in vain, that they should break away from the Directorio.

In view of the fact that the majority has insisted in believing that divisions existed, and that what the Directorio proposes to do is precisely to eliminate the basis of all prejudices and to bring unity and brotherhood – those distinguished individuals are voices crying in the wilderness.[23] They blame the Directorio for wrongs that, in the judgment of its supporters, it seeks to right, which many imagine to have existed since time immemorial in this land, where the Blacks were slaves and therefore despised by the race of their masters.

This is how history is being written ... by some historians!

---

[22] A Havana social club that hosted elite literary events as well as gatherings of the Autonomista (Liberal) Party.

[23] A reference to John the Baptist, who is described in the New Testament as "a voice crying in the wilderness," a phrase drawn from the Old Testament Book of Isaiah.

1.8 RAFAEL SERRA, "TO THE HOUSE OF REPRESENTATIVES,"
EL NUEVO CRIOLLO (HAVANA, CUBA: JAN. 21, 1905)

*The journalist and politician* **Rafael Serra**, *who had been a close ally of* **José Martí** *in the independence movement while both men were in exile, won a seat in the Cuban House of Representatives in 1904. He continued to edit his newspaper* El Nuevo Criollo *while in office. Here, in an article addressed to other legislators, Serra described several incidents of injustice dispensed by the local police courts that had been established under United States* **occupation**. *He offered the account in support of a bill that he had drafted along with another Afrodescendant congressman, Antonio Poveda y Ferrer. The "Poveda Bill," which was never passed, would have created a commission to draft reforms to the courts with the goal of reining in judicial discretion, regularizing sentencing to eliminate inequities, reducing bail, and preventing arbitrary or unnecessary pre-trial detention of alleged offenders.*

*Having participated in a decades-long movement to remove distinctions of race from Cuban public life (1.7), and familiar with the constraints on independent Black organizing within the Cuban political system, Serra chose not to frame the need for these reforms in terms of racial justice. He did not even mention the race of the man whose unjustified imprisonment is at the center of his account, instead highlighting the rights of all citizens and the abuse of the poor. He closed with the argument that the corrupt justice system was at odds with Cuban "capacity for self-government," a reference to the justification United States officials frequently used for their intervention in Cuban affairs.*

Very esteemed and distinguished comrades,

Without prejudices of any kind, without partisan artifice, but rather, as loyal spokesmen for the mission that all in our chamber ought to fulfill, we address this august body, created to govern or regulate the destiny of a people, to frankly set forth, without ridiculous partisanship or bad blood, the painful, sad, and insufferable evils of which a great part of our honorable citizens are the defenseless victims, everywhere on the island; and equally because of our zeal as men of equity and justice and because we carry, to a high degree, the task of representing our people, we must prevent at all costs the aggressive rise, with all of its iniquitous horrors, in the bosom of this Republic which was won at such a high price and which we love so much, of that tremendous tyranny that, in the form of Correctional Courts, has already sowed discontent, terror, and a lack of confidence in all of the homes of our working classes, which suffer and endure the excesses of a branch [of government] that, in the name of morality and justice, must be reined in.

It must be made known that these Correctional Courts, which, as their name establishes, should stand for justice and correctness, have an abundance of exactly the opposite: abuse by judges. In many parts of the island, far from the austere procedures necessary for the sacred profession that they profane, the judges go so far as to practice the most reprehensively brazen form of *mockery* (if you will pardon the phrase) against the victims of their excesses and venalities. The victims of a judge who perverts justice, after suffering injurious ridicule at the hands of those who are entrusted with administering justice, are fined in irregular fashion and without a chance to appeal. And if this is how we are to begin to build a nation, sapping its vigor by constructing a citizenry from elements that have been degraded by the same men of laws; if we must create a people out of fearful and servile men, accustomed to enervating abuses, it is sad to say it, but our Republic is in doubt. And for the same reasons, it may happen that in moments of danger for our nationality, our enemies will feed off the indifference of our popular masses who, wounded in the most noble and delicate aspects of their dignity, may understand that they should not sacrifice even a single drop of their blood for a Republic that is hostile to meeting their moral needs; for a Republic that is as burdensome and useless as it is ungrateful and offensive. For all of these reasons, and because both prudence and justice suggest it, it is imperative that just, discreet, and vigorous action by the legislative branch restrain, as soon as possible, the insufferable acts of contempt for public respect and against the rights of people by none other than those who are responsible for keeping watch over the well-being of honest people and for administering evenhanded justice, which should not have one yardstick for people who are poor and another for those who are not.

For the moment, and while a general reform of all the machinery of the correctional system is completed, Order Number 213 should be repealed in the name of morality and justice.[24] That a policeman, out of an excess of zeal or for personal vengeance, should arrest an individual for an offence and throw them, without distinction of sex, to sleep in a *vivac*,[25]

---

[24] The Correctional Courts were created by Civil Order 213, issued by US occupation authorities.

[25] The Vivac (Bivouac) was the name given to the holding cells at the Castillo del Príncipe Fortress in Havana.

for no cause other than vengeance, is unjust. And it is immoral too, because some have turned all this into a hub of transactions, where some duty officers are suspiciously interested in helping with bail.

We know of innumerable exploits of these Correctional Courts, which we will publish when appropriate, but we will not fail to set down, now, one of the most edifying of these, which took place in Santiago de Cuba.

For in that city, we are presented with a model case for the study of the aggressive and injurious corruptness of a Correctional Judge.

The event takes place in the market square. An honest artisan, needing to buy a hen for his wife, who has just given birth to an infant, crosses paths with a seller and buys one of his many hens. The purchase completed, he is headed towards home, satisfied and in a hurry, when he is stopped by an individual who is determined to take the recently purchased hen from him. The stranger claims that it is his and had been stolen from him. The assaulted man resists and soon the intervention of a police officer becomes necessary, resulting in [the officer] taking the man to the police station and then to the famous Correctional Court. Once the accusation is made, the judge interrogates the accused, who maintains that he has bought the hen in the market. It is ordered that the accused go to the market, in the custody of a police officer, to find the seller. But as the row has been quite public, of course, the man they are looking for has had time to disappear. Without success in the objective, the detainee is again brought to the Court, where he is condemned to three months in prison for stealing a hen. In vain the accused protests, suffering bitterly for two reasons: both because he found himself unjustly convicted of robbery and because of the bad effect that such unpleasant news would have on his wife, who has just given birth. He might resign himself to suffering through his imprisonment, but to endanger his wife's recovery from child-birth was painful, unjust, and sad, and he could in no way resign himself. But he had to go to jail. And here is a Correctional Judge, one of those in charge of constitutional guarantees, at his most wicked. A few days into the prison sentence of the alleged hen thief, a new prisoner arrives. The man recognizes at once the one who sold him the hen in the market. He questions the other man in front of witnesses, and the other man does not deny the facts. A petition is made to the Correctional Judge to hear and resolve the matter. The Magistrate attends, and when the second accused man maintains that yes, he had sold the hen to the first, the Judge becomes irritated and condemns him [the seller] to six months for stealing hens. How overjoyed must the innocent man have been to see himself rehabilitated! But, oh, what a bitter disappoint-ment! When he requests a speedy release, by virtue of this proof of his innocence, the Judge tells him: You, Mr. So-and So, have to serve your three months.

In another part of that same province [Santiago de Cuba], only a few days ago, another curious event took place. It happens that the banned sport of cockfighting is tolerated in that place; and we are told that a local official breeds fighting cocks, and knowing that his cocks were losing a fight that was taking place was motive enough for [him to order] the match to be raided and the gamblers fined.

All of this is sufficient material for our Chamber to make haste, either by approving the Cué bill[26] or the Poveda bill, in the matter about which we write. Because it is greatly at odds with our democratic sentiments, our civilization, and our capacity for self-government.

For to govern is neither to oppress nor to corrupt.

## 1.9 "INDEPENDENT PARTY OF COLOR – PLATFORM," PREVISIÓN (HAVANA, CUBA: FEB. 25, 1910)

*In 1908, after a fraudulent election and brief uprising known as the August Revolution, Cuba was under United States* **occupation** *for a second time. Looking back at their first experiences as participants in partisan politics, Black writers and politicians made several attempts to regroup.* **Rafael Serra** *and* **Juan Gualberto Gómez**, *longtime allies who were now in opposing political factions led by White men, proposed the reconstitution of the* **Directorio Central de las Sociedades de la Raza de Color** *to set a unified agenda and exert pressure on the parties.* **Evaristo Estenoz**, *leading a group of Black veterans of the independence wars and the August Revolution, took a different approach, creating the* **Partido Independiente de Color** *(Independent Party of Color, PIC). The party had little success attracting support from Black voters in 1908. Then, as new elections approached in 1910, the governing Liberal Party leveled familiar accusations of "racism" against it (see 1.7). In 1910, Liberal Senator* **Martín Morúa Delgado** *proposed, and the legislature passed, a law outlawing parties "constituted exclusively by individuals of one race or color, which pursue racist ends." Estenoz and his allies were imprisoned and tried. In advance of the 1912 elections, the Independientes staged an uprising modeled on the August Revolution.*

---

[26] Pedro Cué Abreu and several other representatives had proposed a thorough restructuring of appointments in the municipal justice system in 1902.

*The Liberal government accused them of waging a "race war," a pretext for a brutal racial repression and massacre.*

*These accusations aside, the Party's "Platform," published multiple times in its organ* Previsión, *offered a clear accounting of a wide range of policy goals. Of these, only those having to do with education, immigration, and public employment dealt explicitly with the elimination of racial discrimination. Projects such as the eight-hour day, a labor tribunal, land reforms, and hiring preferences for Cuban workers (reminiscent of similar measures in Brazil, see 1.12) would benefit all island-born workers. Like the supporters of criminal justice reform in the House of Representatives (1.8), the Platform presented trial by jury and the end of the death penalty as questions of modern civilization, rather than racial justice.*

*The document closed with the controversial issue of strategy. Estenoz did not propose to campaign for exclusive control of the government, but rather to create an apparatus with which to take part in governing coalitions. Given the failure of the mainstream parties to create racial harmony and treat Black members with dignity, independent party organizing was a necessary step for resisting "dangerous manifestations of isolation" and "separationism."*

The **Partido Independiente de Color,** national in character, is [hereby] constituted in the whole territory of the Republic in order to maintain the balance among all the Cuban interests, to spread love of the fatherland and of Cuban nationality, so that all of those who are born in this land may participate equally in our public administration.

The Republic, equal, sovereign, and independent, with neither racial prejudices nor social antagonisms, will be our motto.

We will propose that all Cubans who are worthy to serve should figure in the Diplomatic Corps, and that citizens of the race of color should be appointed as a matter of preference and of urgent necessity, so that the Republic may be represented as it really is.

We favor trial by jury in all matters of justice that take place in the Republic. Jury service should be obligatory and unpaid.

We will advocate for the abolition of the death penalty, and for the creation of penitentiaries that correspond to the needs of modern civilization.[27]

---

[27] Anti-racist journalists in Cuba noted the tendency of Cuban presidents to commute death sentences for White defendants but not for Black defendants.

The creation of modern Justice in our Laws and Tribunals will be the reason for all of our activity, for it will not be possible to live in accord with progress if there is not Justice in fact and in law.

[We call for] the creation of Training Ships to serve as reformatories for those young people who, according to the law, cannot receive a higher sentence.[28]

Free and obligatory education, including trades and crafts.

University instruction offered to all without charge, being public and national.

The regulation of private and public education under the care of the state, so that the education of all Cubans will be uniform.

The creation of Naval and Military academies.

The open and fair admission of the Ethiopian race in military, administrative, governmental, and judicial service, so that all of the races are represented in the service of the state.

Immigration should be free to all the races, without making preferences for any. Free entry for all individuals who, while meeting sanitary requirements, come in good faith to contribute to the growth and development of the public weal.

The repatriation at public expense of all those Cubans who wish to return from foreign shores to their native land and who lack the necessary resources.

The creation of a law that guarantees the hiring of Cuban employees, in preference to foreigners who have not yet been naturalized, in public service and in all public companies, whether they be incorporated in Cuba or abroad, and preventing new companies established in Cuba from being incorporated abroad.

We will work so that in the whole territory of the Republic a workday is understood to last eight hours.

The creation of a Labor Tribunal to regulate the differences that may arise between capital and labor.

The promulgation of a Law to prohibit the immigration of minors and of women unless they arrive as part of a family.[29]

---

[28] Training ships provided hands-on education for naval recruits or entry-level workers in the merchant marines. The PIC imagined this kind of rigorous, coercive job training as a tool for progressive juvenile justice.

[29] It is possible that this was intended as a measure to protect women and children from human trafficking. Or it may have been designed to prevent employers from recruiting immigrant women and children, displacing or undercutting adult male Cuban workers.

The distribution as colonies of public lands, or lands acquired for this purpose, among Cubans who lack resources and wish to dedicate themselves to agricultural labors, with a preference for those who are unprepared for jobs in public service.

As a moral question, we will work for the review and audit of all the land titles that have been put into effect, conceded between the first American intervention and the present.[30]

Approved and signed by all the members who belong to the Party and by all those who may join.

[We declare] constituted a National political Grouping, capable of the defense of the moral and political interests of the race of color; in order to thus assist all governments that may be established in the Republic and to share with them the responsibilities, whether in [times of] danger or prosperity.

In forming, in constituting a party of the race of color of Cuba, with the name Agrupación Independiente de Color (Independent Grouping of Color),[31] we do so with neither personal nor utilitarian aims. No, we do so rather for the most special reason that we, as much as anyone, love the independence and democratic institutions that Cuba has bequeathed itself through its legendary revolutions, by virtue of which it is now a free and sovereign Nation.[32]

The seed of the togetherness, harmony, and comingling of which we have made ourselves deserving has not yet been able to sprout, not even within political groups with shared tendencies, for the childish reason that the Blacks have not been able, even with our efforts and sacrifices, to earn the moral and material consideration of those who, being our compatriots, born beneath the same sky, shared the same sadness during the struggle but forget about us in victory.

For all these reasons, and because of the understanding obtained in the period elapsed since the implantation of the current regime,[33] it has become evident that we need to counteract dangerous manifestations of

[30] Under legal rules established under the US occupation and enforced by subsequent Cuban and occupation governments, thousands of small farmers in Eastern Cuba, many of whom were Afro-Cuban, lost their land. Meanwhile, investors from the United States consolidated large holdings. Pérez, "Politics, Peasants, and People of Color."

[31] This was the original name of the organization that became the Partido Independiente de Color.

[32] These revolutions refer to the three anticolonial rebellions of the nineteenth century, 1868–78, 1879, and 1895–98, but also likely to the August Revolution of 1906.

[33] The presidency of the Liberal José Miguel Gómez, elected and installed during the second US occupation.

isolation, of separationism, if you will, with a resistance based on dignity. This should in no way become an impediment to observing the deepest respect for other constituted political groups, among which public opinion is divided, and to working in concert and without respite to make our Nation into a stable Republic with a wide democratic base, in which all can live in prosperity and satisfaction without condemning the Black to a world apart.

The moment is not only paramount but opportune for this patriotic endeavor, and great is our responsibility before God and History.

[This is] all the more so, given the internecine nature of the problems whose solution demands our preferential attention toward the goal of preserving the nation's equilibrium and its power to unify as the only means of satisfying our moral and material needs. Blacks and Whites created a fatherland, Blacks and Whites fought for it on the field of battle, all together shedding our blood for its flag should anyone dare stain its glory and splendor, raised at the cost of so great an effort.

For these reasons the men of the Partido Independiente de Color, fulfilling an obligation that is among the most natural for all human beings – the instinct of self-preservation – and forced into action by the necessity of satisfying the demands of thousands of Cubans who are excluded, against all Natural and Political Law, from any participation in public affairs, band together, congregate, and express solidarity in order that they will wake from their lethargy and say with Socrates, to the government of the Nation,

"I exist, therefore I am."

That is, I was born in Cuba, I, the Black man! Therefore I am a citizen, the same as you, oh White man! Having said that which has not seemed absolutely necessary to say, we will end our Platform swearing that we are Cubans first, but this [our loyalty to the nation] is not a barrier that will make us resign ourselves to live the life of the old slave and to be condemned to a World apart.

We would never accept this, because it is not the republican equality for which [**Antonio**] Maceo and [Guillermo] Moncada fought.[34]

Our rule will be to demonstrate our culture and capacity for the free exercise of politics at the same time that we show that we are conscious of our duties.

---

[34] Guillermo Moncada (1841–95) served in all three independence wars as one of the highest-ranking Black commanders.

We will point out injustices wherever we may find them, whoever the perpetrator may be – as well as the unjustifiable measures that may continue to be used against the race of color to keep it submerged in misery and to inflict its disappearance, such as precipitous emigrations.[35]

Convinced as we are of what we can do, of who we are, and of what is rightly ours, let us say it very loudly so that we are heard everywhere: we want to take part in the public affairs of the Republic, so that we are governed well, but without ever being interested in the Blacks alone having control over the Government. This [the government], rather, should be equal, based on the legitimate equity that should unite men in the gigantic twentieth century, where the preservation of caste is an absurdity, and to signal a different path to the Black would be reckless, a negation of Christian morality, of modern science, of all that comprises the beautiful and admirable ensemble of civilization, and of that God who, at the summit of Golgotha, to the astonishment of the ancient sages and of ancient theodicy, proclaimed this terrible word which has operated in all revolutions: Equality!

## 1.10 "THE INITIATIVE OF NUESTRA RAZA, JUSTIFIED AND BRILLIANTLY DEFENDED BY THE EMERGENCY COMMITTEE," NUESTRA RAZA (MONTEVIDEO, URUGUAY: JUNE 1936)

*In preparation for the Congressional elections of 1938, the writers and activists associated with* Nuestra Raza *decided in 1936 to create the* **Partido Autóctono Negro** *(Autochthonous Black Party, PAN), Uruguay's first and only Black political party. The goals of the PAN were to elect Afro-Uruguayan representatives to parliament, and, by offering Black voters an alternative to the* **Colorado** *and* **Blanco** *Parties, to put pressure on those parties to respond to Black demands. As the article suggests, those demands centered on the full enforcement of constitutional provisions guaranteeing equality in the country. "Prejudice is still far from disappearing" in Uruguay and was particularly visible, the paper argued, in the area of state employment, where hiring and promotion depended on "the greater or lesser pigmentation of [one's] skin."*

*In addition to racial justice, the PAN sought larger goals of social justice as well. In keeping with* Nuestra Raza's *Popular Front orientation, the party positioned itself as pro-worker, anti-fascist and anti-imperialist,*

---

[35] Over the first decade of Cuban independence the government promoted European immigration to Cuba as part of a project to "Whiten" the population.

*"in favor of the disinherited and against the opulent, in favor of the oppressed and against the oppressors." Party leaders called on the country's Black social clubs and cultural organizations to hold benefits to raise money to support the party's electoral campaign; members of the executive committee were expected to make personal contributions as well.*

The campaign in favor of a candidate for the National Parliament, belonging to the Black race, marches forward. Despite the efforts of the defeatists – very few, to be sure – who conspire to make this initiative fail through odious obstructionisms, even if they have no solid arguments, revealing clearly the base hatreds that their small spirits feel for the creators of this initiative – despite those efforts, the campaign stands tall and is growing by leaps and bounds through the generous adherence of worthy people within and outside our social and political sphere.

As previously announced, on May 23 there was an assembly at the meeting rooms of the Asociación Fraternidad, attended by about thirty people. Opening the session, the provisional chairs, Mr. **Mario R. Méndez** and Mr. **Elemo Cabral**, informed those present of the motive for the meeting. After a thorough presentation by Dr. **Betervide**, the meeting approved a motion by Mr. Pablo García to appoint an Emergency Committee charged with drafting a report laying out the basic points on which the electoral campaign will be based, and proposing means to finance it.

The Committee has issued the following report:

Gentlemen of the Assembly: Complying with the charge given to us by the Assembly on May 23, we present to you the following report that states, in general outline, the formal ideological character of this initiative of the magazine *Nuestra Raza*, to elect to the National Parliament, under conditions of the strictest and most absolute autonomy, representatives of the Black race.

We will lay out what have been the principal and valid reasons that give birth to this, in our opinion, more than auspicious initiative, which in and of itself demonstrates the proof that in the core of our collectivity, in its marrow, throbs the hope and lives the longing for a better future, one more in accordance with our rightful place in society on the basis of our numbers but mainly because of our beautiful history of work and sacrifice.

First, it must be established that it would not be necessary to argue in any sense to justify this longing for improvement, which is more than just, if in isolation our contribution to society and to progress is logically more than certain and effective. By joining together our common efforts in a struggle that is obviously noble, that contribution will increase, determining a tightening of the ranks and obliging us to organize in the necessary way so that our rights may be recognized in all their absolute fullness. At the same time, we give absolute assurance of complying exactly with our duties.

But it is necessary to establish that, notwithstanding the logic of this explanation, of course clearly simplistic, there are fundamental reasons that justify this initiative from every point of view, and even more, that require all conscientious men of the race to fight for its realization, obeying a categorical imperative of collective existence.

It is quite certain that, legally and constitutionally, the equality of all citizens is fully recognized, and that if we observe with the attention that is customarily applied to collective problems – as concerns respect for rights and the application of those norms of equality – we seem to be perfectly respected in the application of those ruling norms. But if we pause for a moment in our critical spirit, if we try to determine the actual truth of this situation of apparent equality, we will see after digging only a little that prejudice is still far from disappearing.

Any of us knows perfectly well that in more than one hundred cases, the promotion of an employee or the appointment of a state official has depended not on the greater or lesser fitness of the candidate, or on his motives for seeking the promotion, but rather on the greater or lesser pigmentation of the skin of this person or that.

On this point we sincerely believe that we need not insist any further.

But even more so, outside these situations in which vested interests play such a preponderant role, we note in the thousand circumstances of daily life the existence of a certain lack of consideration that does not square with the so oft-mentioned equality expressed so clearly in our laws and our Constitution.

The undeniable existence of these facts obliges us to seek, through the decisive exercise of our rights, the means of struggle necessary to establish, in all exact points, the picture of equality that in theory all accept without discussion.

We sincerely believe that, more than the possibility or the necessity of struggling for our own candidates, the race has the obligation to do so.

And it is of course indispensable that the struggle take place through the creation of our own party, autonomous, completely dispensing with the existing parties, given that those parties are incapable of interpreting the problem in its true reality.

The current political panorama clearly demonstrates that there are too many bad habits and too much ill will in those parties, for them to redirect their attention in the least degree to situations other than their political interests and the achievement of their respective programs.

In the interests of creating an independent party, we must take into account that, once the fundamental points of our ideological orientation have been determined, we remain at absolute liberty to work with any of the afore-mentioned tendencies [parties] when reasons of justice so advise.

We do not believe that setting the basic points that will orient the work of the new party is a task that it falls to us to take on; but we do declare with absolute unanimity of opinion and as absolutely fundamental for the smallest effort to take place, that we must take stock of the situation. We will fight tirelessly and intervene inexorably in all social problems, orienting our action in favor of the disinherited and against the opulent, in favor of the oppressed and against the oppressors, in favor of attaining true social justice, which, sadly, humanity is somewhat far from achieving but which it surely will achieve, because it deserves to. And we will also fight tirelessly against all those more or less new currents that, under the labels of warlike fascism or imperialism, threaten the existence of Democracy and Rights.

These two points, we repeat, are basic and are the only ones that give our struggle reason to exist, without setting aside of course our conviction of a veiled but real struggle of races, or at least the denial of our full rights.

This Report Committee recommends the creation of a National Executive Committee as the directing authority of the movement, with the following sub-authorities: fiscal, advisory, administrative, and resources.

The fiscal authorities will be in charge of the party treasury. The advisory authorities will be in charge of studying laws already created and those that will be created, and of advising the party officials, whenever such advice is requested. The administrative authorities will be in charge of financing the [electoral] campaign and of overseeing the committee on resources, which would be a direct dependency of the administrative committee.

RESOURCES: The committee on resources will be in charge of gathering funds to pay the expenses of the aforementioned campaign. To that effect we advise [the committee] to direct itself to all the organized social centers[36] so that they lend their cooperation by holding festivals to benefit

---

[36] Black social and cultural organizations in Montevideo and other cities.

our party, which itself may also hold festivals or fund drives, issue solidarity bonds, etc. Obligatory personal contributions from all members of the Committee, and soliciting voluntary donations in money or in kind from all persons who sympathize with our cause.

Montevideo, June 15, 1936

DR. SALVADOR BETERBIDE, MARIO R. MÉNDEZ,
ELEMO CABRAL, **PILAR E. BARRIOS**, SANDALIO
DEL PUERTO, JOSE SILVEIRA, TRIFÓN MACEDO

1.11 PEDRO PAULO BARBOSA, "THE RED DANGER," A VOZ DA RAÇA (SÃO PAULO, BRAZIL: NOV. 1936)

*Five years before the* **Partido Autóctono Negro** *was launched in Uruguay, the* **Frente Negra Brasileira** *was founded in São Paulo, Brazil, in 1931. Initially conceived as a combination of civic organization and mutual aid society, the Frente ran candidates for election to the national Constituent Assembly in 1933 and the São Paulo city council in 1934; in 1936 it was officially certified as a political party.*

*The Frente Negra was deeply enmeshed in the local, national, and international political turmoil of the 1930s. Locally, it clashed with Black socialists, who organized the Clube Negro de Cultura Social and the Frente Negra Socialista. Locally and nationally, it was aligned with the fascist-inspired* **Integralist** *movement and was intensely anti-communist; at the international level, its paper,* A Voz da Raça *(The Voice of the Race), wrote approvingly about Italian fascism and German Nazism (2.10).*

*In this article, Pedro Paulo Barbosa, commander of the Frente's militia organization, the Green Shirts, denounced communist infiltration of Brazil. Barbosa was writing a year after a failed communist uprising among army units in northeastern Brazil and in Rio de Janeiro (see also 7.11). He was also responding to efforts by communist activists to make inroads on the Frente's membership and compete actively with the Frente for Black political support.*[37]

It is necessary to combat the danger of communism.

It is the red danger!

It is the abominable, violent danger, in which men are solely instruments, or better said, machines of production.

---

[37] Graham, *Shifting the Meaning of Democracy*, pp. 49–52.

And Russia is the example, unworkable in every way, so much so that the telegraph announces mass shootings.

It falls to the world, as brothers, to be on guard against such a terrible evil.

The tricks and stratagems employed by Moscow's agents – who are scattered around the world – are the most cunning in every way. The salary that they receive obligates them to everything: thus you see them infiltrate the peaceful milieu of the working class, inciting it to the general strike.

It is necessary that those who have the responsibilities of government promote a tenacious and persistent campaign against those who, in exchange for money, attempt to subvert the order in which we live. Society needs to rid itself, once and for all, of these infamous assassins of women and children. Of these betrayers of national tradition, because communism, which is unachievable on the face of the earth in every way, does not respect the family, the glories of the past, and even less the traditions that adorn and influence the character of peoples.

We think that alongside other means, such as the radio, the press, the classroom, etc., the campaign against the red danger must be based first and foremost on the education of the people. And the people not just of the city, who have everything at hand, but the true weight of the full population, including the descendants of the Indian, who live dispersed across the miles, and even in another civilization.

At the risk of appearing pretentious, we would propose the urgent, immediate necessity of sending out caravans of preachers of Democracy, scrupulously serving Brazil in the best way possible and avoiding any question of political parties. At the present time, just one flag, one standard, one pennant should wave over the heads of the Brazilian people. The flag that ennobles, the standard that dignifies, and the single pennant for which ... we wish ... to die!

In this moment of communist attacks in the Americas, our Magna Carta [constitution] should be much, but really much, more disseminated in the heart of the people. The masses need to absorb its contents. It is a right! The Brazilian needs to know himself, learning the Constitution! Unfortunately, in Brazil there is the fixed idea that only university graduates talk about laws and legal codes. This does not happen with peoples in other parts of the world, notably the Japanese, who in their middle schools and high schools impart more knowledge.

We apply here the old lesson: Talking about economics with economists achieves nothing. Talking about economics with those who need economics, that is what is more rational!

The elites guide themselves, but the masses need to be guided, molded for the common goal.

Let's educate ourselves, let's take precautions against the great evil that threatens us!

The terrible, nefarious red danger!

The fratricide of all peoples!

### 1.12 FRANCISCO LUCRÉCIO, "THE BLACK IN THE FACE OF THE CURRENT SITUATION," A VOZ DA RAÇA (SÃO PAULO, BRAZIL: NOV. 1937)

*On November 10, 1937, President* **Getúlio Vargas** *suspended Congress and imposed a new constitution on Brazil, greatly increasing federal authority and instituting the* **Estado Novo**, *an authoritarian regime inspired by Portuguese and Italian fascism. During his two terms in office (1930–37), Vargas had instituted a number of policies that benefited Afro-Brazilians: the 1933 Nationalization of Labor Law, which reserved two-thirds of the positions in large firms for native-born Brazilian workers (as opposed to European or Japanese immigrants); state promotion of national industries; government support for workers and their unions; and the expansion of social programs for poor and working-class people. In this essay, Francisco Lucrécio, Secretary General of the* **Frente Negra Brasileira**, *expressed the organization's support for the new regime, which he hailed as the "reaffirmation of Brazilianness." Despite Lucrécio's hopes for the Estado Novo, the new government banned all political parties, including the Frente Negra, which formally disbanded in 1938.*

We are now living under the impulse of a new constitutional charter, which was so opportunely promulgated by His Excellency, the President of the Republic. Commerce, industry, and even Brazilian souls, received the balm of calm, through the influence of the new atmosphere that rules across the entire land since the day of November 10, 1937.

November 15[38] was commemorated in the entire country with rare brilliance, demonstrating that there still exists civic spirit allied to love of

---

[38] November 15 is the Day of the Republic in Brazil, marking the overthrow of the monarchy in 1889 and the proclamation of the First Republic.

country. The country saw that day the current generation paying homage to the glorious founders of the Brazilian Republic, appropriate expressions of rejoicing and recognition of those men's heroism in greatening everything we have. For that reason, the most representative members of the Nation swore allegiance to the [new] regime.

And the Black! What is the position of the Black element in the face of the current situation? In the intellectual circles of the race, the expressions of support for the current state are the best possible. Except for some impetuous little groups carried away, for certain, by the customary sly promises of some politicians, there was no major shift among Black people, because the most authoritative [Black] newspapers did not take a position on this and maintained an unwavering equidistance from the parties and the candidates.

The day consecrated to the Brazilian flag![39] Yesterday we attended the expressions of rejoicing paid to our flag by the armed forces, the cultural associations, the class-based associations, and by the people. It is the reaffirmation of Brazilianness, it is the veneration of our great figures, it is our nationality that speaks, and it is Brazil that is reviving within its glorious traditions. The Black was present, as he was always present, on all the occasions necessary for the common good.

In the face of these affirmations and recognition of what is ours, we are certain the legislators, conscious of their high responsibilities, will not leave unnoticed at the margins the Blacks who have given so many benefits to the country and want to continue to give them. Our people need schools: elementary and vocational schools, and social services, to be educated and reeducated from every point of view, from the artistic to the intellectual to the civic, in order to assist more effectively in the great work of national reconstruction.

With all the strength of our Brazilian hearts, anxious to see the Fatherland sovereign and free, let us give sincere homage to the Most Excellent Chief of the Nation, and to the National Army and Navy, for the brilliant act of profound patriotism and love for the land of Brazil, pulling it out of the disorder and tumult in which it found itself and guiding it down the road of prosperity, progress, and tranquility, which is the strong desire and pride of its sons and daughters.

[39] November 19 is National Flag Day in Brazil.

## 1.13 LUIZ LOBATO, "WARNING," SENZALA (SÃO PAULO, BRAZIL: JAN. 1946)

*In October 1945,* **Getúlio Vargas' Estado Novo** *was overthrown by the armed forces, opening the way for a return to civilian democratic rule. This political juncture could have provided an opportunity to resurrect the* **Frente Negra Brasileira,** *but in this article Luiz Lobato, a schoolteacher and occasional contributor to the Black press, argued strenuously against such a project. Never mentioning the Frente by name, Lobato railed against Black "false leaders" who created "racist" organizations that sought to divide Afro-Brazilians from the rest of Brazilian society, and by so doing to create a strategic position for themselves as mediators between the Black population and the political system. (For similar arguments in Cuba, see 1.16.) Lobato was deeply opposed to the Frente's alignment with fascism and Nazism and to what he saw as its orientation toward racial separatism. A member of the Communist Party during the 1930s and one of the founders in 1947 of the Partido Socialista Brasileiro, he argued that Black people should organize not along racial lines but as part of a broad national movement against socioeconomic inequality and exploitation. Deep and thoroughgoing social and economic reform, he argued, would be far more effective than racial separatism in combating race prejudice and inequality in Brazil. With the return to electoral democracy, many Afro-Brazilians did join those movements, helping to account for the electoral successes both of the Communist Party and of the Partido Trabalhista Brasileiro (Brazilian Labor Party).*

The year 1945 was a very fertile one for Congresses and Conventions of political parties. But there were also meetings, Congresses, and Conventions of elements of the Black race.

Well- or ill-intentioned and -oriented, the Black leaders of São Paulo mobilized, renewing the struggle that our ancestors initiated with the campaign for Abolition. Once again "the enlightened ones" emerged in our milieu, seeking to provide an immediate and opportunistic solution for the Black problem. Others, of typically racist and reactionary tendencies, thought that they could revive the racial struggle, believing that through those means they could return to the positions they had previously enjoyed. This time, however, the situation was different from the one to which "the historic militants" were accustomed. Understanding his real role in Brazilian society, the Black did not let himself be bewitched by the racist speeches that once drew so much applause from the Blacks. To the contrary, in these meetings, conventions, and congresses we note that the Black element was settling accounts with its leaders, leaving them at times in a difficult position with those who were meeting in good faith.

As Brazil takes large steps toward industrialization, the social classes will have to clearly differentiate themselves, and the lower strata will sense more strongly and more easily their exploitation. As part of the most exploited stratum of the proletariat, the Black man, regardless of his particular demands, cannot fail to be aware of this phenomenon, the awareness of which was revealed in that tremendous revolt against class and race privilege. Often disoriented, and distrustful of false leaders, the Black nevertheless participated in the struggle for the re-democratization of the country. And we noted something curious: every time that racist tendencies emerged, either in camouflage or openly, they were repudiated. The Black element's capacity for struggle, and its previous experience in this very state [São Paulo], allied them to another form of resistance: the resistance for democratic principles.

This enlightenment to which we have referred, with respect to democracy, made us better understand the real aspect of the struggle against color and racial prejudice. In a lecture I gave in Piracicaba last September 28,[40] I had the opportunity to analyze how color prejudice and race prejudice are a technique of domination that in our days was used and abused by Nazi Germany. That is why we are frankly disappointed when we encounter a Black person with fascist or Nazi tendencies, given that that ideology would bring them no benefit. To the contrary: if that regime were to be established in the world, the Black would be the most persecuted, perhaps surpassing the persecution that the Jews suffered in occupied Europe, from the Germans. In this present day, the great role of supporting democracy in Brazil falls to the Black, because we are potentially a very great force within the national population. And also because it will be impossible to struggle for social, economic, and political advancement unless we take into consideration the general situation of the Brazilian people. Therefore, alongside our own particular demands, we have to raise the battle flag of the exploited class.

The false Black leaders, who desire only their own personal advancement and have nothing in common with the general situation of the Black

---

[40] September 28, 1871, was the date when the Rio Branco Law (also known as the **Free Womb Law**), mandating the eventual abolition of slavery, was signed by **Princess Regent Isabel**. During the mid 1900s it was celebrated by Black organizations as the Dia da Mãe Preta, the Day of the **Black Mother**.

element, sought and still seek the impossibility of an effective struggle against color prejudice and for the resolution of many problems toward which we are striving, if we have a clearly mass-based orientation. That attitude is perfectly understandable, if we consider the interest that those leaders have in seeing the Black separated from communion with Brazilian society, so that they can usurp [the role of] being interpreters of our thinking, which will be expressed through their own personal thinking, with no consultation whatsoever with the great and weighty mass of Blacks. We must put an end to these self-appointed leaders. Accomplishing this requires the participation of the Black element in everything that concerns them, discussing, accepting, or opposing, in public or in meetings, the decisions taken in their name. The Black must lose the fear of saying what he thinks, to not displease Mr. High-and-Mighty. The Black is no longer the tutee, and his capacity for work, for reasoning, and for struggle has been put to the test. Whoever possesses those qualities has no need for self-interested tutors or guardians.

During these times through which we are passing, it is easy for "Black Whites" to emerge, who in our meetings trace their genealogical history to prove that one of their great-great-grandfathers was Black. But when they arrive at the door of a casino or an elegant party, they do everything to show that their ancestors were English, French, Italian, or Greek, of pure blood. Or when they can't deny what their color proclaims, they say that they are descendants of [Indigenous] Tupi Guarani. On the other hand, there emerge from the heart of our community the "perpetual defenders of the Blacks," playing the demagogue with their own race, demanding things that are stupid and with no real consequence. For example, there are those who demand land for the Blacks, which at first looks correct. But analyzing it further, what do we find? Everything, except for the actual struggle to reach the objective. For example: what Black man, living in a major capital city, even if he were hungry, would accept some acres of land in the states of Mato Grosso and Goiás?[41] If he accepted them, would he go to cultivate them? Where would be the means of production?[42] Could it be that the Confederation of Industry, which did everything at the Petrópolis convention to take land away from the farmers, would provide the means of production to the Black man? Could it be that the federal government would deliver the means of production to the Black element,

---

[41] Mato Grosso and Goiás are states in central Brazil. In 1946, they represented the remote frontier, far distant from the coastal states where most Brazilians lived.
[42] Tools, infrastructure, seeds, financing, etc.

in response to Black pressure? Frankly, given the interests involved, this issue will only bring concrete results through a mass movement demanding the distribution of land to the people, transforming large properties into small ones, with the State guaranteeing the means of production. That distribution must be broad and wide, also reaching the regions near the great industrial centers. That struggle would allow for the people's political education, in the sense of wiping out, culturally and psychologically, color prejudice in Brazil.

As we can see, the solution to the Black problem does not lie in the demagoguery of pitting Blacks against Whites, using the Blacks of the United States as an example – I consider such demagoguery to be psychological exploitation of the Black element. Nor does it lie in the act of simply handing over ownership of land, without taking into account the general level of the people and unless the means of production are provided. It lies, first and foremost, in an unceasing struggle against the exploitation of man by man, against social inequality, in the practical and effective struggle for a democratic regime, which will provide the solution to Brazil's Black problem.

May the Blacks be alert to and cautious of the easy promises of the present moment, and may they seek to participate more actively in the questions that concern them, so as not to allow their demands to serve as stairways for those claiming to be their leaders but whose interests are exclusively personal.

## 1.14–15 TWO ARTICLES ON DEMOCRACY AND RACE IN MIDCENTURY BRAZIL

*Brazil returned to democracy in 1945, in the wake of the Allied victory in World War II, a moment when international organizations, journalists, and academics across much of Europe and the Americas argued that both totalitarianism and state-sponsored racism had been discredited. In Brazil, Black thinkers and writers enthusiastically greeted the return of democratic institutions – freedoms of speech and assembly, free and democratic elections – and used the language of democracy to reframe ongoing claims to racial equality. It was in this era that many Black and White Brazilians and foreigners began referring to Brazil as a **racial democracy**. In its most famous iteration, that phrase portrayed Brazil as a model of a harmonious, socially egalitarian multiracial society – a beacon of hope for a world traumatized by Nazi genocide. Black thinkers and writers, along with many of their White counterparts,* *sometimes espoused this celebratory vision of Brazil's racial inclusiveness (2.16, 6.3, 7.5). At other times, as in these two articles, Black thinkers deployed a more critical idea of the connection between democracy and race, making racial equality the test of Brazil's democracy.*

*In 1.14, theater director, activist, and Quilombo editor **Abdias do Nascimento** surveyed the history of Black Brazilians' political representation since abolition and found it shamefully out of step with their demographic presence and historical contributions. For Nascimento, the true measure of Brazil's democracy was to be found not in "civil rights ... assured only in the letter of the Constitution," but in the effective empowerment of Brazil's Black citizens to elect and be elected. Nascimento offered a striking image of Black voters as an awakening giant whose "more than a million votes" would determine the outcome of the upcoming election of 1950. He called on his fellow Black citizens to wield this power wisely, choosing a candidate who would defend Black interests, including the "important and urgent ... task" of education. Indeed, in this majority Afrodescendant country, Nascimento's projected numbers of voters could have been much higher were it not for longstanding literacy requirements (upheld in the new 1946 constitution). With only about one-fifth of Black and brown Brazilians able to read at midcentury, much work lay ahead (including through the* **Teatro Experimental do Negro**'s *own literacy campaigns) before the "Black masses" could fulfill their collective electoral potential.*

*In 1.15, João Conceição, managing director of and frequent contributor to Quilombo, surveyed the variants of democratic regimes that took shape worldwide since the French Revolution – long a point of reference in Latin America's Black press – only to declare them little more than deformations of the radical republican promises of liberty, equality, and fraternity. He singled out the United States and England (and its empire) as democracies in name only because of their political and social exclusion of Black people. As for Brazil's own brand of democracy, Conceição cautioned that self-congratulatory assertions about the absence of discrimination, and selective celebrations of the public advancement of a few Afrodescendants, were distractions from and deterrents to genuine democratic progress, rather than evidence of it. He ended by spelling out what he saw as the rightful racial meanings of democracy in a world characterized by racial diversity and recovering from the legacies of racist atrocity.*

## 1.14 Abdias do Nascimento, "The Elections and Us," *Quilombo* (Rio de Janeiro, Brazil: June 1949)

After **May 13, 1888**, the Black man passed from the condition of slave to that of citizen, with the right to elect and to be elected to participate in the country's government. Let us ask today whether that man who fought, suffered, worked, and gave his life and his blood to build Brazil has [in fact] had an active voice on the nation's political stage since then, whether he has exerted influence in proportion to his strength in numbers. Unfortunately, history responds "no," and points to the melancholy fact of our having been the constant instrument of *caciques* and "colonels."[43] [History] reveals, too, that in most cases the Black man was not able to exert his prerogatives as a citizen due to ignorance or poverty, and, what is more, was deprived of his democratic rights by the shadowy heritage of slavery, which hindered [his adoption of] the conscious attitudes of a free man in the life of our society and in the civil government of the Nation.

It is true that one or another Black man has been able to attain political or administrative positions, but not as the representative of a [current of] thought, of an ideology that yearned to bring about the valorization of Black people within the ranks of our emergent ethnicity. The singular characteristics of Cuba's democracy, established since the **Constitution of 1940**, allow us to see eminent Black men attaining positions as ministers and senators – Ramón Vasconcelos, [José Manuel] Cortina, **[Salvador] García Agüero**, and others.[44] [They] belong to all parties, from the traditional, conservative [ones] to the liberal and the leftist, defending, as men of color and as Cubans, the particular interests of their ethnic group, which only then became integrated, in practice, into the civic life of the country. Physical liberation is not enough, according to the brilliant thought of **Luiz Gama**. There is a vital need to redeem the Black man as a person, a free and useful being capable of participating in all the responsibilities of state, from the smallest to the greatest.

[43] The terms refer to local-level party leaders who dispensed political favors in return for votes and loyalty, especially during the First Republic (1889–1930).

[44] José Manuel Cortina (1880–1970) was an Afro-Cuban lawyer, journalist, and politician who represented the Liberal Party in Cuba's House of Representatives and Senate, and twice served as the country's Foreign Minister. Ramón Vasconcelos (1890–1965) was a prominent Afro-Cuban journalist and Liberal Party politician who served as senator from 1936 to 1948, among other posts.

We are on the eve of the great [electoral] contest of 1950, [in which] the future President of the Republic, senators, congressmen, governors, and councilmen will be democratically elected. Those who aspire to be candidates are already in action, their eyes fixed upon power. The time has thus arrived to ask all of Brazil: should the Black man have a powerful and autonomous voice in this election?

Let it be known among parties and candidates that more than a million votes from the Black masses can and will determine victory. The population of color, as Brazilians and as Blacks, conscious of their role, will avoid bribery, the demagoguery of canvassers, the humiliation of being rounded up like sheep to vote for candidates that would only exploit their innocence and eternal good will. For the first time in the history of our institutions – this we affirm with the greatest emphasis – the Black man will raise his lucid voice as a man of the people, rooted in the flesh and spirit of our nationality, in order to demand, to cry out, that he too is a Brazilian citizen, that he too can legislate and administer, as is the right and the duty of those who were ever present in all stages of the building of our nation. With a seat in [legislative] assemblies and in the executive [branches], the Black man will continue to work for the good of Brazil, just as he did in the past in sugarcane fields, in mining, in coffee fields, in cattle ranching, in wars, and in *bandeiras*.[45]

We Blacks must remain alert and choose as our candidate he who, like [Harry S.] Truman, shall know how to courageously and patriotically confront repugnant discrimination in opportunities for well-being, and the humiliating discrimination to which we are subjected in many sectors of our country's administrative life.[46] Even more urgent and important, however, is the task of redeeming the Brazilian of color, dignifying him through education and economic advancement.

Our candidate must be aware of all the misery that besmirches and ruins us, in order to have the boldness to raise with us the banner of tangible, equal access to opportunities, since our civil rights are assured only in the letter of the Constitution that governs our destinies. Only thus will the Black masses, the long-suffering dark-skinned community with only sixty years of mutilated civic action and four centuries of dramatic

---

[45] In Brazil's colonial period, *bandeiras* were organized expeditions launched from coastal enclaves (especially in the South) to explore and claim inland territories and to enslave Indigenous people.

[46] During his presidency (1945–53), and despite fierce opposition even within his own party, Truman undertook important civil rights reforms, including executive orders in 1948 aimed at prohibiting race-based discrimination in the US armed forces and civil service.

Brazilian life, be able to pull from their midst enlightened Blacks who can enter the government and speak and defend the aspirations of those millions of Brazilians who have been systematically banished from the higher spheres [of power], as if the Republic wished to keep them away from becoming definitively integrated into our Nation.

We do not form cysts.[47] We do not plead minority rights. We do not aim to create a problem in the country. We argue, peacefully and sincerely, to those who wish to understand us, that the short period since slaves' emancipation created problems of assimilation and of [Blacks'] knowledge of their own rights. Solving [this problem] falls directly to us, the current Black generation, and with it comes the privilege to take the most decisive step since abolition to ensure that people of color can win the sacred good of a free personality, in a free community, within a prosperous and strong Brazil.

### 1.15 João Conceição, "The Democracy of the Blacks," *Quilombo* (Rio de Janeiro, Brazil: July 1949)

To the democracy of liberty, equality, and fraternity based on the French Revolution, powerful men, in their own interest, have added various qualifiers. From the democracy of the fall of the **Bastille** there emerged various satellites, malignant offshoots of a healthy body: socialist democracy, capitalist democracy, popular democracy, etc., in addition to countless "isms" that further contribute to complicating the story, with the exception of those used to name religions: Catholicism, Protestantism, **Spiritism**, etc.

Those variations on democracy were created by those on top to the detriment of those on the bottom, and there is no way to swap positions because the few on top weigh more than the many below. The scales are reversed.

There are nations that produced democracies of a genuinely national scope. We have the American [democracy], in which – of the original democracy of the French Revolution – only liberty remains, for equality and fraternity do not apply to its millions of Blacks. [There is] the Russian

---

[47] The accusation that some ethnic groups, specifically the Japanese and German immigrant colonies of Southern Brazil, were forming ethnic "cysts" in an otherwise homogeneous national organism was widespread in the 1930s and 1940s. By mid century, that same accusation was often turned against Black organizations and newspapers.

democracy, in which we know not what remains exactly, since the [political] horizon in that country is unfathomable. [There is] the English democracy, which has liberty and fraternity on the island, equality in some dominions, and the absolute absence of all three symbols of humanity [liberty, equality, fraternity] for the Blacks of the South African Union. In the Spanish democracy, they say there exists the shadow of an "ism."[48] Even in Brazil, the less sensible beat their chests and shout to the four winds that we too have our democracy "made in Brazil," where all are equal and enjoy the same rights before the law and to all things; [that] there is no racial discrimination or separatism. They say that the Black man does not become president of the republic [only] because he does not want to, and they hold up, as examples, the great men of the past, and some of the present, who were and are there for all to see, occupying [positions in] state governments or senatorial seats.

In the meantime, those present-day individuals held up as maximum exponents of the race in Brazil are completely divorced from it. They do not want to be Blacks, and do nothing to benefit those of their race.

Although what I write in this column of mine represents my opinions only (they say every leader is a bit of a demagogue), I feel that the only [democracy] in the Black man's interest is the democracy [emerging from] the fall of the Bastille: [the] *liberty* to be completely integrated in affairs, *equality* [that is] concrete and palpable, because in a world in which the majority of inhabitants are people of mixed race, there is no place for ridiculous and absurd restrictions toward the Black, [and] *fraternity* among Whites, Blacks, Indians, **mulatos** and any other peculiar pigmentations that may exist out there. Because, gentlemen, there was no point to all those wars and all that bloodshed if we are going to live under the empire of the democracies and pseudo-democracies that dominate the world today.

### 1.16 PEDRO PORTUONDO CALÁ, "THE RACKET OF THE BLACK PROBLEM," AMANECER (HAVANA, CUBA: MAR. 1953)

*In the 1930s, the journalist Pedro Portuondo Calá had worked with* **Gustavo Urrutia, Salvador García Agüero,** *and other leaders of the Federación Nacional de Sociedades Cubanas de la Raza de Color to formulate bold equal rights initiatives. During the drafting of the*

---

[48] This is a reference to the fascism of General Francisco Franco, who ruled Spain from 1939 to 1975.

**Constitution of 1940,** *they called for criminal penalties for racial and gender discrimination, labor protections for domestic workers, and (unsuccessfully) for a requirement that political parties nominate Black and White candidates in proportion to the racial composition of the party membership. In the 1940s, communist legislators proposed* **complementary laws** *(see 2.17) in order to implement a constitutional ban on discrimination. By the early 1950s, however, these proposals had stalled in the Cuban Senate. Meanwhile, government loyalists had gained control of the Federación, expelling communists from the Executive Board and muting criticism of the many failed promises to enact anti-racist legislation. Critics accused the Federación, increasingly dependent on government patronage in the form of political appointments and subsidies, of corruption. These complaints only grew louder when* **Fulgencio Batista** *took power in a coup in 1952, and many Black club leaders lent their support to the administration in exchange for government appointments. Without naming names, Portuondo Calá, a veteran of the civil rights struggle, expressed a deep disillusionment with this evolving "modus operandi" which he described as a "racket." Although expressed in a very different political context, this accusation resonates with the position taken by Brazilian Luiz Lobato above (1.13).*

The lack of scruples, which, when put into practice contribute to establishing the moral physiognomy of the social actor, degrades his sentiments and converts him into a negative factor in the great task of common dignity and betterment. In the same way, the lack of firm belief in the justice of the cause he defends devolves into defeatism and shameful capitulation.

This is poisonous to the process of building the common interest. Similarly harmful and frustrating is that other element, equally wretched, which, while lacking in experience or merit of any sort, sees itself as qualified and capable of intervening – unlicensed and unauthorized – in matters of indubitable public importance. These matters, because they may affect the moral and material interests of the collective, should be cause for careful and thoughtful planning.

Tolerance of these false priests of the common cause is to blame for promoting a "modus operandi" so well-developed that, alongside the so-called "Black problem," these individuals have created a "racket" or exploitation. Although with different techniques and tactics, Whites and Blacks participate equally in its benefits, each taking his turn. They have "intelligence" to spare but lack scruples and morality.

In the face of irritating racial discrimination and its harmful deriva-
tives, the ones who take a stand are those who – without stridency or
indiscretions – adopt an honest and loyal, cordial and considered attitude,
combating it [discrimination] without creating disagreeable implications
or dangerous reactions. They are truly inspired to promote the dignity of
our social group, its improvement, its well-being.

Those who align themselves with these projects are men and women
whose record of work for the common good is above any doubt and all
slander. They are romantic idealists, true to their own principles, accustomed to the costliest abnegation, in sacrifice to their concept of individual
and collective dignity. Nevertheless, they are not the ones who benefit
most from their own labor.

At the bend in the road, other apparent "defenders of the cause" crouch
in constant ambush, prospering on the sidelines of the distressing situation
that subordinates their own brothers. These are the unscrupulous ones,
veritable speculators in the pain and sadness of those who witness their
best talents run aground in a social climate of continual injustices.

This type is just as damaging as he who discriminates. The latter
threatens the unity among Cubans by attempting (and often succeeding)
to revive colonial vices arising from the system of slavery. The former, the
"racketeers" or false priests, iniquitously exploit the "Black problem,"
hoisting it up (not as a torch to purify the impure), but rather as an article
of merchandise, to be priced on a stock exchange of iniquities. They
obtain, with their posture of self-anointed social leaders (in reality they
are phonies and extortionists), positions and advantages and sinecures for
their personal benefit.

These merchants live off the collective indifference, bordering on cowardice, of those who could call them out and keep them in line, eliminating
in one stroke a disturbing and unworthy element. For there is no other
way of bringing to justice those who, instead of sincerely joining those
who truly fight against discrimination and its evils, dedicate themselves to
praising and flattering – lavishing with depressing and shameful flirtation;
those who, because they are true agents of discrimination, deserve to be
called out as enemies of the Cuban spirit and traitors to the democratic
ideas of **José Martí**.

They are Judases who cause great harm to their own. Because they give
false direction to the community, they weaken the spirit of struggle and
create confusion. As is natural, the sowers of division, of the bad seed
planted by **Cain**, take advantage of this. For this reason, it is the duty of
the people who struggle sincerely against these evils, to denounce them

and put them on the pillory, to mark them with the "I.N.R.I."[49] and expel them from the temple. In this manner, those who have been taken in by their falsehoods and self-serving praise will know that they are despicable fakers who do not have the backing of the [Black] community. The community also judges them, though for the time being, it does not have at its disposal the means to punish them.

It is the duty of honest men and women to denounce the "racket" of the Black problem and to unmask its false priests.

---

[49] From the New Testament (John 19:19), the initials for "Iesvs Nazarenvs Rex Ivdaeorvm" (Jesus Christ King of the Jews) that Pontius Pilate inscribed on the cross when Christ was crucified. Here the expression is used to signify a mark of dishonor (as originally intended by Pontius Pilate), not to suggest a similarity with Christ.

# CHAPTER 2

# Racism and Anti-Racism

Latin American politicians and intellectuals consistently argued that racism was mild or non-existent in their countries, especially in contrast with the United States. Often, White Latin American writers suggested that to speak about racism was itself racist, and would have the effect of dividing the national community. In response to such claims, manifestations and denunciations of racism were a constant topic of discussion in the Black newspapers. Authors in the Black press offered a wide range of perspectives on the prevalence and causes of racism and articulated varied strategies to combat racism in contexts where so many denied its existence.

Discrimination occurred in multiple forms and in multiple settings. The papers denounced color bars in public facilities, including theaters and dance halls (2.2), barbershops (2.6), and hotels (2.8, 2.12, 2.13). They called out racism in the justice system (2.5, 2.7; see also 1.8), in **scientific racist** academic writing that posited the inferiority of all Black people (2.3), in employment (2.17, 2.18), in public hostility toward cross-racial romances and courtship (2.4, 2.7), and among children (2.14).

Not infrequently discussions of racism were framed as comparisons with conditions in other countries, often prompted by public comments of or controversies over Black visitors from abroad.[1] African American journalist Robert Abbott's positive comments on **racial democracy** in Brazil provoked a deeply skeptical response from O *Kosmos* (2.8); conversely, African American anthropologist **Ellen Irene Diggs**'s indignation

---

[1] See also Chapter 7, "Diaspora and Black Internationalism."

at her exclusion from a Rio de Janeiro hotel drew support and affirmation from the Black papers (2.12, 2.13). Reflecting on the well-known color bars in the African colonies, in the United States, and even in Venezuela, *Revista Uruguay* asserted the complete absence of race prejudice in Uruguay (2.11) – a position sometimes taken in the region's Black press, especially when comparing Latin American countries to the United States.

The Black papers sought to identify and explain the causes of racism. Some found it in negative stereotypes of Africa (2.3), others in White guilt over the sins of slavery and the centuries-long mistreatment of Black people (2.1). The Brazilian paper *Getulino* found the original source of racism in the country's landowning elite, and its more recent (in the 1920s) source in European immigrants to the country (2.9; see also 2.2, 2.6, 2.10, 2.13).

Finally, how best to combat racism? All of the papers agreed that egregious incidents of racial exclusion needed to be publicly called out and confronted. The Cuban newspaper *La Igualdad* recognized that those confrontations could provoke White fears and antagonism, and sought to assure White readers that it was pursuing racial equality only in the public sphere and not in the more intimate settings of the home and the family (2.4). *A Voz da Raça* urged its readers to combat racism by, paradoxically, following the example of Nazi invocations of race pride, replacing Nazi Aryanism with the exaltation of Blackness and race mixture (2.10). *Quilombo* took the opposite approach, opposing Nazi-style racism and urging Black mothers and caregivers to inculcate anti-racist values in their own children and the children that they cared for (2.14). In 1950, *Quilombo* organized a Congresso do Negro Brasileiro to focus public attention on the problem of racism and racial inequality and to highlight Black voices in that debate (2.15, 2.16). In Cuba at the same time, the readers of *Atenas* wrote to the newspaper to demand federal legislation outlawing acts of discrimination (2.17). When the leaders of the Cuban Revolution announced a campaign against racism, in 1959, Cuban activists quickly adjusted their strategies (2.18).

## DISCUSSION QUESTIONS

- Where *does* racism come from? What do you think were its root causes in the Latin America of the 1870–1960 period?
- When different writers sought to demonstrate the illegitimacy of racism and the righteousness of equality, what principles, ideas, texts, or

thinkers did they invoke? Why do you think they chose to substantiate their arguments in that particular way?

- How did authors in the Black press respond to the idea of **racial democracy** and to claims that race and racism did not exist?
- What differences and similarities do you see in the ways the writers of these articles diagnosed the problem of racism and its consequences? How did different writers' understanding and framing of racism and its harmful effects shape the anti-racist strategies they endorsed (and enacted in their own writing)?
- Experiences of racism provoke complex emotional responses, including anger, shame, frustration, embarrassment, and self-doubt, to mention just a few. In these articles, what are the principal emotions that we see and hear, both from the writers and from the victims of discrimination?
- How did the writers, and the victims of discrimination, seem to view those who practiced discrimination? What were Black people's thoughts on, and attitudes toward, racists as people and toward racism as a phenomenon?

### 2.1 "WHITE FACES AND BLACK [GUILTY] CONSCIENCES," EL PROGRESISTA (MONTEVIDEO, URUGUAY: OCT. 2, 1873)

*In this article the anonymous author traced the causes of White hostility toward Blacks to White guilt and fear of someday being called to account for the crimes of the African slave trade. White people not only knew that they, or their ancestors, had committed atrocities, they also continued "enjoying with impunity the fruits" of those criminal acts. This led them to "scorn Black men and to throw them out of society," and to prevent Black people from seeking education, so as to keep Afro-Uruguayans "as far away from justice as possible."*

*The article opened with a reference to Black men actively pursuing university education and seeking to become philosophers. The balance between the costs and benefits of higher education was a recurrent topic in the Black press (see 3.5, 3.8, 3.11). Here, the reference served as a transition to the author's philosophical analysis of the causes of racism.*

### (COLLABORATION)[2]

Great is the surprise caused to certain White faces by [the fact] that the Blacks and *mulatos* seek to become university graduates. But surprise will

---

[2] This probably indicates that the author was not a member of *El Progresista*'s staff.

turn to astonishment when they learn that [Blacks and *mulatos*] not only seek to become university graduates but that some take their pretensions to the extreme of wanting to become philosophers.

And furthermore, through the medium of philosophy, they seek to know the true cause of the hatred that [Whites] have always shown toward their race.

. . . . . . . . . . . . . . . . . . . . . . . . . . . . . . . . . . . . . . . . . . . .

Philosophy, that science invented by men who are friends of humanity, to teach oppressed peoples to understand their strengths, and to teach the ignorant to develop their intelligence, is the best guide that men can have when they wish to understand the origins of their ills.

So it is not strange that men of color pursue the development of their intelligence through philosophy, to find the cause of their hardships.

I could never convince myself that enlightened men of recognized capacity, proven liberals and democrats, would disparage their fellows solely for their dark color.

I based my reasons on [the idea that] those men could in no way doubt that Blacks were human beings like they were, and therefore their brothers.

Therefore it had to be some other cause besides color that nourished their persecutions, but my limited intelligence could not find it.

Paging through philosophy, I found a paragraph that says: *to know the causes, it is necessary to investigate the law that governs the succession of facts*, which has suggested to me the following chain of reasoning.

When a criminal has been enjoying with impunity the fruits of his crimes, nothing causes him greater fright than to think that his victims might demand an accounting of his crimes in court. For this reason he will try by any means possible to finish them off, or at least to keep them as far away from justice as possible.

Today many *black* [guilty] *consciences* are afraid of our race's enlightenment, because they fear that one day we will be able to call them to account for their past cruelties.

One can't conceive of any other reasons for that rage they always show when it comes to our race.

Why that effort to abuse us? Why that contempt with which they treat us?

What right do they have to scorn Black men and to throw them out of society?

Who has told them that Blacks are not human beings like they are, and therefore their brothers?

If they had respected the laws of humanity, if they had observed the religious teachings that order them to love their neighbor, what were their duties when they found those ignorant men on the African coasts?

Their duty was to give them the enlightenment that they lacked, and to turn those ignorant men into a free and civilized people.

But the White men, the civilized men, the propagators of the faith, did not see that those innocents were human beings like them, and they cruelly ripped them from their homes to commit the greatest barbarism ever known, *the commerce in human flesh!*

Later they realized their transgression, but instead of remedying it, they tried to finish off the Blacks, so as to leave no trace of their abominable crime.

(To be continued)

## 2.2 "SOCIAL MOBILIZATION," LA BROMA (BUENOS AIRES, ARGENTINA: JAN. 24, 1880)

*Despite constitutional guarantees of equal rights and treatment for all Argentine citizens, in January of 1880 several public venues in Buenos Aires, including theaters and dance halls, barred Blacks and* **mulatos** *from their* **Carnival** *dances. Journalist, intellectual, and poet Froilán P. Bello*[3] *sounded the alarm through a series of front-page editorials in* La Broma, *calling upon the city's authorities and editors of mainstream newspapers to denounce these discriminatory acts and upon fellow Afro-***Porteños** *to mobilize in public protest.*

*Like his counterparts in other countries, Bello feared that such racial exclusions – notably, ones perpetrated by foreigners (see also 2.6, 2.8, 2.9) – would undermine the very foundations of Black citizenship and risk turning Black Argentines into foreigners in their own land. In response to these affronts, he underscored Afro-Argentines' status as natives: their hard-won rights and their willingness to exercise them (decorously, civilly) to demand redress. Finally, Bello denounced the racialized double standard for access to these establishments, and by extension, for the*

---

[3] Froilán P. Bello (1853–93) was a poet and journalist active in multiple community associations and publications (including his own illustrated arts magazine, *El Eco Artístico*). María de Lourdes Ghidoli, "Bello, Froilán Plácido," in Knight and Gates, *Dictionary*, vol. I, 291–92.

*enjoyment of full civil rights. Criminals, wastrels, and lowlifes were allowed to run these venues and were embraced as customers as long as they were White, whereas no amount of law-abiding behavior could grant Black or mulato Argentines unhindered access. Bello's indignant tone captures the frustrations, quotidian and existential, of living in a society where assurances of equality on paper coexisted with unpredictable discrimination in practice.*

The society of color has once again proven before the eyes of the world that it has feelings, and that it knows how to think for itself, displaying a precise understanding of the rights and guarantees stipulated in the constitution.

Just one attempted restriction thereof was enough to produce a unanimous mobilization of opinion, which will soon return things to their natural state.

Yes, we are sure that we will bring about the repeal of that ridiculous and shameful prohibition imposed by the management of these theaters against the entry of "people of color."

We have full confidence in the authorities. We believe they will know how to ensure that the law is respected with all due zeal, within the mechanisms of our republican system.

They [theater managers] want to prohibit our entry to a public establishment for the paltry reason that our faces are dark.

And that is, quite simply, the only reason for their actions.

If only the managers of these theaters nurtured the same sentiments as many "Blacks" and many *"mulatos"*![4]

We are certain that none of our brothers would trade the humble job of "servant" for the more lucrative one plied by those vile traffickers in human flesh!

In the light of day, it can be seen very clearly that we are not the degraded ones who do such lucrative business dealing in unhappy prostitutes.

Never, ever, would our terrible misfortune drag us to the extremes of performing the contemptible and filthy role of pimp, as they scandalously

---

[4] The quotation marks around these words indicate that these were the terms used by theater managers to issue their prohibitions. Bello, like others in Buenos Aires' nineteenth-century Afrodescendant press, found these terms offensive, and eschewed them except as reported speech. "People of color" or "society of color" were the preferred terms (themselves often in quotes) – when writers referred to race or color at all.

do, taking carriages to the doors of the brothels, buying "dresses and shoes" for poor women to ensnare them and drag them more easily to the dens of immorality.

And these are the people who forbid entry to "Blacks and *mulatos*"? God help us!

We are barred from entering the theaters because of the dark color of our faces, and yet a thief who has just committed a robbery enters freely to mingle and disappear into the bustle of the masked crowd.

He is White, and so the manager doffs his hat to him, shakes his hand, rubs elbows with him, and many times [even] helps him escape to free him from the clutches of the law.

A "*compadrito*," a shirtless man, one of those idlers by trade, enters the theater trying his tricks and wiles on his comrades or the women, and [when] the manager sees him, instead of showing him the door he shows him his approval with a smile – because, in the end, he is White!

Cardsharps who spend their lives in the backrooms and dive bars, on the filthy felt of the gaming table, and who never let the grimy card fall from their hands as they await the opportunity to clean out their fellow man's pocket – those men can indeed enter anywhere they like, because, in the end, they are White.

But it is not the sole fact of not being permitted to enter a masked ball that alarms us.

No. We would never be so frivolous.

What we foresee, which we are attempting to forestall by bringing to bear every method the Constitution allows, is something more serious.

Today, it is the theater that is closed to us. Tomorrow it will be another public establishment. And some other day, it will be the church, where all of us have the right to go worship God, the benevolent father of all human beings, without distinction of races or colors.

We must not, then, remain quiet in the face of such an iniquitous attack, lest we find that, when we least expect it, we will be completely deprived of the enjoyment of all of our rights, until we are excluded from the land where we were born under the sweet breeze of liberty – a liberty won with the life and the blood of our ancestors.

Let us protest publicly, petitioning the relevant authorities to repeal the attempts to seize from us that fundamental right.

Let us gather together at a demonstration and, for the first time, raise our voices to demand our due.

Let's go! Let us not permit a debased foreigner to come suppress our rights and trample so miserably on the laws that govern us.

Let's go! On your feet, society of "color"! Let us not permit a stranger to come insult us in our own home.

Let us go forth with circumspection, orderliness, and all proper moderation to show them that we follow the footsteps of progress in this civilizing era that mobilizes all nations of the earth.

Let us go forth, yes, in the certainty that we will be heeded by the authorities [in our desire] to teach a lesson to the retrogrades who applaud the measures taken by the traffickers in prostitutes.

On your feet, therefore, men of "color."

The time has come to put an end to the insults and ignominious humiliation of which our race has been victim these many centuries.

F. P. B. [Froilán P. Bello]

## 2.3 "HATEFUL INJUSTICE," LA FRATERNIDAD (HAVANA, CUBA: AUG. 21, 1888)

*Writers in Latin America's Black press were ever conscious of the harmful effects of racist stereotypes about Black sexuality that circulated widely in the region. Concern over these stereotypes led to many articles encouraging, or imploring, Black readers, especially Black women, to live within strict boundaries of propriety, domesticity, and respectability. The author of this article from the Cuban newspaper* La Fraternidad *took the less common approach of attacking the racist presumptions about Black sexuality.*

*The article was one of dozens of responses by Black writers to the best-selling book* Prostitution in the City of Havana, *published by physician Benjamín Céspedes in 1888. The book combined clinical case studies of advanced venereal disease with a historical and sociological account of prostitution in Europe and Cuba. Céspedes was unabashedly racist in his interpretation. According to him, the immorality of Black and mixed-race Cubans was responsible for the problem of prostitution and, more broadly, for the profound corruption of Cuban society.*

*The writer of this article responded with barely concealed fury. He insisted that Céspedes had failed to distinguish the "corruption" of some Afrodescendant Cubans from the honesty of the majority. He noted indignantly that Céspedes had willfully overlooked the enormous progress that Black Cubans were making on "the path of culture." Even those unfortunate members of the race who did participate in prostitution were victims of a perverse society, not the source of perversion. Céspedes' book was a case, he argued, of the victimizer blaming the victim.*

A book titled *Prostitution in Havana,* crudely written by *Dr.* Benjamín de Céspedes, has recently been released to the public. This book is one of many that are sprouting up, in these times of observation and analysis, with the presumptuous aim of improving existing conditions, and the columns of a *decenario*[5] like this one are not the most appropriate place to judge it or to assess its true merit.

But that is not our object, and indeed we would make no objection to its publication, nor challenge any of its harshest concepts, if one of its chapters did not pulsate with the most irrational animosity toward, the most tremendous injustice against, the race of color, which we have the duty to defend.

It is abundantly clear that the author of the aforementioned book belongs to the class of the prejudiced: this is the only way to understand why he engages in intentional inexactitudes, for no reason but the *patriotic* goal of putting down and insulting the race of color which has come to be, in these times, the cause of all the misfortunes, all of the disorders, of the ruin, of the decadence, both material and moral that are overwhelming the country. This is how it must be: the Black man in Cuba has never been anything but a beast of burden, and in the absence of any other, now they dress him in the *Sanbenito*[6] for a degradation of which he has been the first victim.

In this way it has become the fashion to declaim against *Africanism*: and in this way moral sense has been subverted in this degenerate land, where one can see, and see without surprise, the victimizer judging the victim, the seducer made judge over the seduced, the exalted and wicked spitting derisively on the honorable and hard-working multitude who have sweated, at the cost of their lives, to carve the pedestal on which his arrogance rests. Under the pretext of describing *the prostitution of the race of color,* the *doctor-author* unleashes all of his cruelty, exhibits all of his resentment toward *all of the race of color.* The footnote on the first page of the chapter in which he deals with this question is not sufficient to conceal his true beliefs, a note that, by the way, poorly papers over the problem and is in evident conflict with the general and slanderous claims of the text.[7]

---

[5] The Spanish equivalent of "weekly" or "monthly" used to denote a newspaper published every ten days, roughly three times a month. This was a common format for newspapers in the Black press.

[6] An article of clothing worn in public processions of penitence by individuals found to be heretics by the Spanish Inquisition.

[7] The footnote being referenced, on p. 170 of *Prostitution in Havana,* reads: "For the record, in revealing the vices that endure within the race of color, we do not refer to that numerous and honorable class of that race, which is as virtuous and estimable as the others who live in Cuba."

Consider whether this is not so: the author says at the beginning of the aforementioned chapter 6 – to be precise – "*But this impenitent race, after ten years of redemption,*[8] *today is more enslaved than ever, to its indolence, its vices, and its depredations.*

*If at least, like isolated manure, it would destroy itself, without contagion, in its own putrefaction – but no, its intimate contact infects everything it touches, the race that is the origin of all of our misfortunes, must serve also as a vehicle of our miseries . . ."*

The stupidly derogatory casualness of these quoted paragraphs releases us from any effort to prove that the damning accusation is directed at the whole Black race, since the whole of it, and not only the part that is corrupted – against whom he should have limited his charges – has been manumitted.

Furthermore, is it not a notable falsehood, unworthy of refutation, to argue that this *impenitent* race has moved backward in recent years?

Already no profound sociologist, the *doctor-author* is so deeply myopic that he is not able to see, in his wrathful and willful blindness, the giant steps that this race has taken along the path of culture and true progress. Or does he propose [to measure] the growth, development, and regeneration of a whole people by the regeneration, growth, etc., of the individual? With no less nonchalance and injustice, he claims that: "In the lymphatic organism of Cuban society, the suppurating abscess of prostitution lies in the customs of the race of color."

Once again, false. As irregular and censurable as the customs of *a part* of the race of color may be, can they justly be understood as the generative cause of this stain? Could we not, should we not, with a better and more valid basis, attribute the degradation of customs to, among others, the corrupting onslaught of single men, always renewed and always anxious to satisfy their carnal desires?

In all times the enslaved race has played a purely passive role, and if they have brought their savage practices to this land, nonetheless one cannot attribute to them the refined sybaritism[9] and the unbridled sensuality that rule today. This is patently shown by the austerity of the natives of Africa, who today are anathematized as the source of all evils, forgetting that they were also the origin of all [our] prosperities.

---

[8] Céspedes used "ten years of redemption" to mean emancipation from slavery, despite the fact that the gradual abolition of slavery in Cuba did not end until 1886, only two years before the publication of his book.

[9] Devotion to luxury and pleasure.

We do not have to follow the *doctor-author* in his long and unenviable work of denigrating the *whole* race of color, under the pretext of combatting a social ill; but we will not finish without noting the curious phenomenon occurring here. This is a case, as is commonly said, in which the butchered meat remains quiet while the butcher's knife complains.[10]

The slave, a being without free will, a non-entity, the principal and martyred victim, must, at the end of the day, be guilty of all evils, past and future.

Most uncharitable, to be sure, is this effort to lay one's own opprobrium and shame on the doorstep of another.

Here we place a final period; although we absolutely do not relinquish [our right to] refute other inexactitudes that our author commits, even at the risk of upsetting the bliss of the illustrious members of the Society of Mutual Praise.[11]

## 2.4 "A CLARIFICATION," LA IGUALDAD (HAVANA, CUBA: MAR. 18, 1893)

*The civil rights campaign led by the **Directorio Central de las Sociedades de la Raza de Color** and the editors of* La Igualdad *in the early 1890s faced criticism and opposition from many quarters (see 1.7). The newspaper* El Porvenir, *published by a prominent émigré journalist in New York – a major center of exile politics and publishing in the 1880s and 1890s – was particularly caustic in its attacks. When the Directorio asked Cuban political parties to announce their support for equal civil and political rights or risk the abstention of Black voters,* El Porvenir *wrote dismissively that the men of color were "putting their opinions up for auction to the highest bidder."*

*Setting aside that insulting accusation for a future issue, the writer of this essay responded only to a "question" that the editor of El Porvenir had posed about the call for "equality of social treatment." This was a page out of the playbook of White supremacists in the United States, who often accused Black civil rights activists of promoting "social equality," by which they meant social and sexual contact between Black men*

---

[10] The author means that it is a case of the victimizer blaming the victim and, on top of that, whining about how hard the job is.

[11] This is a reference to several prominent White intellectuals whom writers in the Black press had called out for their favorable reviews of *Prostitution in the City of Havana*.

*and White women. Whatever thoughts* La Igualdad*'s writers may have held privately about this racist canard, they were careful, in print, to clarify that they advocated only equality of treatment in public. They did not propose to regulate the racial discrimination that many White Cubans practiced in their homes and families.*

From New York, [the editor of] *El Porvenir* asks us what we mean by "equality of social treatment."

And he asks because he does not understand this demand "as it applies to that which political parties or laws may sanction."

Our esteemed colleague's query is based on his understanding that we ask for the promulgation of a law "stipulating that a millionaire be obliged to socialize with a poor artisan."

There lies our colleague's mistake, and that of those who, like him, are opposed to our demands. We do not ask that a millionaire be obliged to have dealings with anyone, *in his house*, with whom he does not wish to. But we live in a country where *public establishments* have functioned in the past and function in the present under regulations set by the government, and remain under its oversight and surveillance. And as it is not possible for the government to make racial or color distinctions in the supervision and surveillance of these *public places*, we ask that, within them, all citizens, White or Black, should receive the equal treatment to which their equal payment [as patrons of these establishments] gives them a right. Here the state, in times past, *prohibited* (the editor of *El Porvenir* should bear in mind) public establishments from serving Whites and [people] of color together. The state established segregation and, of course, the prejudices that grew up in its shadow. It is not too much to ask that the state work, likewise, to bring about the disappearance of the very practices that it established.

What does this have to do with an individual's intimate feelings? All [Cubans] will welcome whomever they like into their homes. They will unite with whomever they wish. But in public places they will have to tolerate the *public*, of which the Blacks also form part.

[The editor of] *El Porvenir* will already see, then, that if this is the uncertainty he harbors, we have quickly clarified it for him.

Because the hour is late, we cannot say more in answer to the article that we just received from this colleague. In our next issue we will take up the other insinuations contained therein.

## 2.5 "WHERE IS JUSTICE?", O BALUARTE (CAMPINAS, BRAZIL: JAN. 15, 1904)

*Despite assurances of legal equality for all Brazilian citizens during the First Republic (1889–1930), Black Brazilians faced systematic discrimination in employment, government posts, and public venues, and at the hands of the police and the judicial system. This was especially true in southeastern and southern Brazil, where substantial European immigration and a comparatively smaller Black population contributed to a harder color line and to regimes of segregation grounded in custom and local laws (2.8, 2.9, 2.13). Black Brazilians faced more severe punishments than Whites for comparable crimes, and Whites were more frequently absolved in incidents leading to the harm or death of a Black person than vice versa.*

*The Black press frequently denounced such instances of unequal treatment. This article exposes the impunity enjoyed by a wealthy, well-connected White young man after his "barbaric murder" of "a poor Black man named Brasilio" in a small rural town in São Paulo state. The author condemned as farcical the trial, and the broader judicial system, that allowed a White murderer to go free simply because his victim was Black. He called into question the very integrity and reputation of Brazil's Republic, where "the law is . . . a dead letter and our constitution is a heap of theoretical provisions with no practical application." He ended by foretelling a settling of scores, when "the people" would once again rise up to claim their rights – a likely reference to the mass movement that resulted in the abolition of slavery in 1888.*

Our readers surely recall the barbaric murder that took place in Santa Cruz do Rio Pardo, perpetrated against a poor Black man named Brasilio.

The young man identified as the author of this appalling act [is] the relative of some of the highest party authorities in that place, or to put it more clearly, of the political bosses of that unfortunate city, where cannibalism reigns proud and the cruel dagger of the triumphant murderer devastates and massacres at will, because the law is at present a dead letter and our constitution is a heap of theoretical provisions with no practical application.

To keep up appearances and obey the protocols of style, a *rigorous* inquest was opened, with all the formalities of a legal process.

But what kind of inquest was this, in which the prominent officials were themselves the relatives of the accused party? Why was a special commissioner not appointed to lend more seriousness to the trial under-way? Why should we not obey the stipulations of the laws in force under this Republic, [a Republic] rendered anarchic by the very authorities who should honor it for the salvation of our character and for the moral stability of our government itself?

No! Everything succumbs to despotism; the dagger is the law, the murderer is not a criminal, he is the law itself; the highway robber is also the law, the old sword of the miserable slanderers is not a venomous Hydra,[12] that too is the law. It would seem, after all, that in these early years of the twentieth century, the law is crime and crime is the law. Justice does not exist, until one day other nations will single us out as the most barbaric, most debased and servile people to inhabit this miserable little world, full of turmoil and horrors.

So go on, rest, you unfeeling mighty ones with no love for the glorious traditions of this unfortunate Brazil; rest now, because the people will not forever be a cardboard puppet. No. The people who today serve as automaton dummies for the perfidious and base machinations of the rural inquisitors will someday once again be the people of yesteryear when, in fighting to repossess their rights, they rehabilitate themselves before the world by reclaiming their blighted pride. History is the formid-able tribunal of the times, in which fulminating judgment awaits those who, with impunity, kill harmless individuals whose only fault is to have black skin.

Progress, civilization, and the dignity of free men will put an end to the regime of anarchy, where murder is nothing when he who kills is *something*.

## 2.6 AND 2.7 TWO ARTICLES ON RACIAL INJUSTICE IN CUBA

*Although Cuban civil rights activists celebrated a victory when the Constitution of 1901 established the legal equality of all Cubans, Black Cubans continued to experience systematic discrimination. The news-paper* Previsión, *affiliated with the **Partido Independiente de Color**, fre-quently reported on individual instances of racial injustice, often by way of comparison with the United States. The US had invaded and occupied Cuba for a second time between 1906 and 1909, and diplomats, business-people, and tourists from the US remained prominent, and*

---

[12] In Greek and Roman mythology, the Hydra is a serpent-shaped, many-headed sea monster with poisonous breath and blood.

*disproportionately powerful, fixtures of Cuban social life. Black writers expressed concerns about the imposition of Jim Crow[13] in Cuba and frequently sought to link their criticism of Cuban racism to widespread anti-imperialist sentiment on the island.*

*In "Pure Democracy" (2.6), a writer attributed the case of a barber shop in Camagüey that refused service to a Black man to the spread of "foreign customs" introduced by settlers from the United States. In "Moral Lynching" (2.7), a writer in* Previsión *used the term to describe two instances in which the court system wrongly convicted Black men who engaged in romantic relationships with White women. Although interracial relationships were not criminalized in Cuba as they were in many parts of the United States, these two White families were able to use false accusations of rape or theft to exact punishment. The author's claim that moral lynchings were worse than actual lynchings was probably not meant to be taken literally, but rather to highlight the need to document and publicize these instances of racial injustice, as African American activists had done with lynching. Sadly, there were several instances of literal lynching in Cuba in the years that followed.*

## 2.6 "Pure Democracy," *Previsión* (Havana, Cuba: Sept. 15, 1909)

We read in *El Camagüeyano* what happened three days ago in that capital between a citizen of the race of color and a barber who is not of Cuban nationality.

The **moreno** could not get anyone to cut his hair in that barbershop, where, so stated the employee, he is ordered not to do this kind of work because he does not know how.

The Correctional Judge, surely basing his argument on something, absolved the barber and did not understand, as the appellant did, that this was unconstitutional and prejudicial toward a citizen of a democratic republic.

But we are not going to debate, at present, whether the shop owner should have been absolved or convicted. We will only look at the matter from another angle, which changes it from a trivial affair into an issue of relative interest.

What just happened for the first time to a member of the Black race in Camagüey happens to his counterparts in the United States all the time.

---

[13] The name, in the US, for laws and practices designed to segregate, humiliate, and disenfranchise Black citizens.

Slowly but surely, some are trying to circumvent the narrow space that [Camagüey's] rare democracy has conceded to the race of color.

And this is our point. What has happened to our fellow citizen is nothing more than the result of the direct influence, too direct, that foreign customs are having on us.

This is a foreign barbershop, where they do not know how or do not want to cut Blacks' hair.

Tomorrow there will be an American Theater too, in which entry will be forbidden for the men of color. Later, if the American influence continues the way it is going – and it will continue and grow even stronger – perhaps our men of color, whom we consider as men who deserve consideration and respect for their decisive and valuable participation in our struggles for independence and for their work ethic and love of progress, one day not too distant will be mistreated and persecuted here, as they are in our neighboring nation.

## 2.7 "Moral Lynching," *Previsión* (Havana, Cuba: Dec. 15, 1909)

We take from an American newspaper, as a curious note that we make public, two statistics about the things that happen over there. If the Cuban Blacks were to compile a statistic, it is obvious that we would know for certain how many of us are put out of action by prejudice here each year, just as the American Blacks know how many are lynched each year over there.

Lynching around here is only moral and the worst thing about it is that a great number of Blacks do not know it, they hide it because speaking about these things would be *"to separate the Black race from the White race."* To prove that we are correct, we will point to two intense cases that would have put anyone other than the Cuban Blacks on notice. Anyone else would be informed about these events, which affect everyone in general, although some say and would like to make us believe otherwise.

All have already read in *Previsión* what happened to the citizen Melgares,[14] in the town of Colón, because he carried on amorous relations with a White woman. Prejudice, lying in wait like the wild beasts of the jungle, has made the unhappy lover its prey, furiously striking him with its claw. It removes him from society and locks him up – God knows if forever – in a gloomy dungeon of the [Castillo del] Príncipe.[15]

---

[14] Máximo Arango, "Injusticia humana," *Previsión* (Sept. 10, 1909).
[15] A fortress in Havana used to detain prisoners (see 1.8).

Only because a Black man, breaking with old practices, came together with a young peasant woman, who in proof of her love offered herself, giving him the fruit of her virginity, and because he could not be punished materially has the moral lynching solemnly been brought to effect. He has been convicted of rape. Where a feeling of hopefulness produced a spark, they have wanted to punish the boldness of a Black man and the weakness of a White woman, to the detriment of the moral interests of the entire Black race.

But as if this were not enough, we [now] find ourselves in the presence of another moral lynching, which was performed on the person of the beardless youth Pedro Crucet. Having gone to work as a mason in a house where robes have their place,[16] [Crucet] admired the beauty of one of the daughters of the owners of the house, as is natural in all young men. Finding sympathy and acceptance, he made his declaration in writing. This found its way into the hands of the relatives of the respondent in love and they, indignant at the audacity of the Black man, wanted to make sure that for the rest of his life he would never again commit this kind of offense. Their first act was to call the Master Builder and threaten the young man with a criminal case if he continued, which would have resulted in his going to prison. And unfortunately this prediction has come to pass, and the young man finds himself condemned to three years and eight months for robbery, the accusation made by the family of the girl, who allege that it took place in the same house in which he paid homage to love. And if God does not enlighten the magistrates of the Supreme [Tribunal], he will go to prison to serve his sentence, thus consummating a moral lynching greater than the ones carried out by the savage Americans of the South of the United States of North America. This is why, Cuban Blacks, "1844 is not a date, it is a man with gray skin and a cowardly soul," who is still fighting, living, and machinating for your extermination.[17]

\* \* \*

**Census of those lynched in the US over the last sixteen years.**

The figures that we include below represent the number of persons who have been lynched by mobs in the US, showing that the law is broken and,

---

[16] This phrase seems to be a way of connoting the home of a lawyer or judge without naming the individual.

[17] In 1844, as part of an investigation into a suspected rebellion, the Spanish colonial government unleashed a brutal wave of repression against enslaved and free people of color, including torture, imprisonment, execution, and exile. We are not able to identify the source of this particular quotation.

even worse, that the magistrates charged with enforcing it are the enablers of and sometimes accomplices in its violation.

1894, 190; 1895, 171; 1896, 131; 1897, 166; 1898, 127; 1899, 107; 1900, 116; 1901, 135; 1902, 96, 1903, 106; 1904, 90; 1905, 66; 1906, 68; 1907, 51; 1908, 65; 1909, (Oct. 30), 50.

## 2.8 ABÍLIO RODRIGUES, "BLACK AND WHITE," O KOSMOS (APR. 18, 1923)

*In 1923, Robert S. Abbott, founder and publisher of the African American newspaper, the* Chicago Defender, *traveled to Brazil to see first-hand the conditions in which Afro-Brazilians were living. The* Defender *had already published a number of articles encouraging African Americans to consider emigrating to Brazil, and after he returned to the United States, Abbott wrote additional articles praising Brazil's racial openness and egalitarianism.[18] While in Brazil, he expressed similarly optimistic views, provoking this stern reply from* O Kosmos. *The piece was itself partially a reprint of an earlier article, in Rio de Janeiro's* A Pátria, *by Black journalist José do Patrocínio, Jr.[19] Abbott's depiction of Brazil, Patrocínio's original article suggested, might "inspire obvious joy among the Blacks of North America," but it was nothing more than "fantasy" and "illusion." The fact was that "at every turn we see prejudice that excludes, that humiliates, that embitters the man of color." Abbott himself fell victim to that prejudice,* O Kosmos *added, when he was asked to leave the hotel where he was staying in São Paulo, at the request of other North American guests. The North American journalist's portrayal of Brazilian race relations might be "infinitely flattering," Patrocínio concluded, but in fact did tremendous damage. The false belief that "race struggle does not exist among us" contributed, in both writers' view, to apathy and quiescence among Black Brazilians.*

In his kindness, a friend who, like me and others, ardently desires the well-being of the Blacks in Brazil, offered me a copy of the March 14 [1923] issue of the Rio de Janeiro newspaper *A Pátria*. Had it not been for that kindness, I would not have had the pleasure of reading an article, with the

---

[18] For those articles, see Hellwig, *African-American Reflections*, pp. 55–81.

[19] José do Patrocínio, Jr. (1885–1929) was a writer and journalist, and the son of famed abolitionist leader **José do Patrocínio, Sr.**

above title, by José do Patrocínio, Jr., on the illustrious North American journalist Dr. Robert S. Abbott, "leader" of the Black race in Chicago, who a few days ago gave a lecture at the Trianon theater in Rio de Janeiro.

José do Patrocínio, Jr., begins the article by saying that naturally his absence at the lecture was noted, since it is well known that he is a Black person, whether by the color of his skin or by the traditions of his name.

He was surprised that *A Pátria* was the only paper that publicized the event and that praised the distinguished journalist [Abbott].

The theme of the lecture was: Brazilian democracy is the true democracy, because it rests on the principles established by human equality.

José do Patrocínio, Jr., comments: Dr. Abbott's intention was infinitely flattering, to establish a favorable contrast between his country and ours.

But the words that must be heard by the Blacks of Brazil are not those so eloquently offered by the "leader"; rather, they should be other, truer words. That equality applies to the Blacks here: fantasy, pure fantasy.

One sees that in every career, it costs Blacks triple the effort to achieve a better position. Mediocrity is not tolerated from them, and their worth is questioned at every step. In the desire to destroy them, abandonment and destitution have been their lot ever since, thirty-four years ago, they were given the charity of freedom!

Dr. Abbott believes in "the principles established by human equality," certainly because of the illusion of seeing first-hand the contact between Black and White in all public social events. But that is only the appearance, because here the Black person does not go beyond what he should be to [what he] could be. The information gathered by Dr. Abbott would inspire obvious joy among the Blacks of North America. But for the Blacks of Brazil, it would produce the true disappointment of sadness, keeping them under the illusion of equality in which they persist, disdained, and all their actions singled out as useless and barely tolerated.

What we should have heard from Dr. Abbott was an energetic lesson in how to dispel the apathy that defines the Black man of this land, who seems to completely accept that life is a dream that evaporates in the grave.

Abolitionist propaganda was not aimed at the Blacks. It was aimed at the Whites, to prove to them that they were committing an iniquity. The abolitionists did not teach the Blacks how to react against that iniquity.

That is the reason why, in one of his impassioned speeches, **José do Patrocínio, Sr.**, had a phrase that became the abolitionist motto: Slavery is theft! The victim of theft fights back against the thief, he doesn't beg the thief, or at most he convinces the thief to return what was violently seized.

That is what is human.

The Black race, which under the whip was the most fertile source of greatness and prosperity in this country, has become useless, if not harmful, to Brazil.

Resigned to the pious disdain of the White, who made them believe that race struggle does not exist among us, never again did [the Black race] produce a Viscount of Jequitinhonha, nor a Rebouças, nor a Cotegipe, nor a Tobias Barreto.[20]

Sadly there are those who hide their Black origins like a disgrace. Why?

There are corporate bodies in which Blacks are prevented from rising to positions of visibility and command. Why? If anyone refers to the mixing of blood that is the ethnic characteristic of Brazil – and it is through race mixture that we entered into civilization – a clamor arises against that outrage. Why? Mr. Eloy de Souza is a singular exception in the Congress.[21] Why? To Mr. Juliano Moreira, and Mr. **Evaristo de Moraes,** the doors of society only open reluctantly, forced open by their indomitable intellectual abilities.[22] Why?

Cruz e Sousa, head of the movement that renovated Brazilian poetry, was excluded from the founding of the Academy of Letters.[23] In the Metropolitan Football League, players of dark color are excluded from the important games.

At every turn we see prejudice that excludes, that humiliates, that embitters the man of color.

And we continue to be undermined by the illusion that "Brazilian democracy is the true democracy, because it rests on the principles established by human equality."

There you have, in brief, the article of José do Patrocínio, Jr., which thanks to the kindness of a friend I was able to read, because otherwise it

[20] Francisco Jê Acaiaba de Montezuma, Viscount of Jequitinhonha (1794–1870), was an important politician and public official (senator and minister of justice). André Rebouças (1838–98) was an engineer and leading abolitionist. João Maurício Vanderlei, Baron of Cotegipe (1815–89), was an important politician and public official (senator and several times a cabinet minister). Tobias Barreto (1839–89) was a poet and philosopher. All these men were of African descent.

[21] Eloy de Souza (1873–1959) was a journalist and politician from Rio Grande do Norte who served in Congress from 1897 to 1937, first in the Chamber of Deputies and then in the Senate.

[22] Juliano Moreira (1872–1933) was a pioneer in the introduction of psychiatry to Brazilian medicine.

[23] João da Cruz e Sousa (1861–98) was a journalist and poet, renowned for his introduction of Symbolism as a literary movement to Brazil. The Brazilian Academy of Letters was founded in 1897, a year before his death.

would have gone unseen, as was surely the case for most of the Blacks in Brazil.

What I truly regret [is that] after the illustrious lecturer arrived in São Paulo and took rooms in one of our hotels, the Palace Hotel, upon returning from a stroll, he was invited by the owner of the hotel not to continue as a guest, because his room had already been taken by someone else. Why? Because some White North Americans were staying in the same hotel and demanded that the owner dismiss the Black guest.

Even here, in a foreign land, they want to enforce the old prejudice that exists in North America. And yet, what was the attitude of the hotel proprietor, as a Brazilian? It was to respond to the request made by the North American guests. Is this the afore-mentioned equality characteristic of true Brazilian democracy?

Illusion, perfect illusion!

### 2.9 BENEDICTO FLORÊNCIO, "THE BLACKS IN SÃO PAULO," GETULINO (SÃO PAULO, BRAZIL: OCT. 5, 1924)

*Quoting from one of São Paulo's major newspapers, this article opened with the striking image of Afro-Brazilians being treated as "foreigners in the very land where they were born!" Its author,* **Benedicto Florêncio,** *located the origins of anti-Black prejudice in the landowning class, enraged at the loss of their absolute power over their former slaves and the resulting "unexpected equality that placed the Black on the same level as the White in the social scale." The former slave owners would never recover from that blow, Florêncio predicted, and would remain fiercely anti-Black; but as they died off and disappeared, their children and grandchildren would accept people of color as fellow Brazilian citizens, entitled to full racial equality. The more worrisome source of prejudice and discrimination, he said, were the European immigrants who flooded into São Paulo following the abolition of slavery. The immigrants discriminated against Afro-Brazilians relentlessly, and if Black people did not fight back, they would soon "not be able to enter the hotels, the bars, the cinemas, the shops, the theaters." Anti-immigrant sentiment surfaced regularly in the Afro-Brazilian press and played a major role in the founding of the* **Frente Negra Brasileira** *in 1931.*

We concluded our last article with this sad and painful truth: "even the foreigners want to transform us into undesirable guests?!"

And almost on that same day, a respected São Paulo evening paper, commenting on this momentous subject, also wrote that the Blacks "are becoming foreigners in the very land where they were born!"[24]

Here we can already see, in light brushstrokes, the "why" of our oft-proclaimed inferiority, that *sickness* that merited the wise, healthy criticism of Rui Barbosa in his famous lecture in Buenos Aires.[25]

But those are not the only reasons that serve as the basis for the injurious persecution of which we are becoming the victims.

Another hidden cause exists, a powerful cause that profoundly contributes to excite the hatreds of prejudice against our unfortunate but heroic race.

That cause is the unexpected equality that placed the Black on the same level as the White in the social scale.

That fact was undeniably a profound blow to the White slave-owning class, and in the soul of that business partnership of vast resources, it opened an almost incurable wound.

From one moment to the next, the power of the plantation owner disappeared, that centuries-long ancestral right that authorized him, whip in hand, to uproot lives, to rip apart souls, to martyr women and stain their honor, and to kill men, torturing flesh and cutting up bodies!

From the discontent of that class, today in full agony, comes the greatest ferocity of prejudice, of uncontained anger against the Brazilian Black man.

However, this aspect of the problem is less grave and almost does not constitute any threat to the stability of our sacred rights as free men.

Tomorrow, death, obeying its eternal mission, will have exterminated our last compatriot enemies, and their descendants will no longer have to continue the thankless mission of cultivating race hatred against us.

The son of the plantation owner, and his descendants, will see in the Black man not a piece of property that was lost or "illegally usurped," but rather a Brazilian citizen studying and training with them in the classroom; cultivating love of country with them in the same uniform and with the same symbol of greatness; in short, striving alongside them in the same field of struggle and action to live here with honor and die with dignity!

---

[24] This statement, from *A Gazeta* (Sept. 24, 1924), was reprinted in "A Theoria do Preconceito," *Getulino* (Oct. 5, 1924), 1.

[25] Rui Barbosa (1849–1923) was a Brazilian abolitionist, congressman, cabinet minister, and three-time presidential candidate. In 1916 he gave a series of lectures in Buenos Aires on international law and the role of neutral nations in the war; it is unclear to what part of those lectures Florêncio was referring. Barbosa, *Embaixada a Buenos Aires*.

There does exist, however, prejudice that is absolutely barbarous and intolerable because of its source, which is being carried out by certain foreign people against the poor Brazilian Black.

That the antiquated old plantation owner should be against us, that part of his generation should have antipathy toward us, is understandable and perhaps even acceptable. But that foreigners, mere guests here in our land, should have the criminal petulance to persecute us is truly barbarous, surpassing all the limits of stupidity, and needs to be repelled, if necessary even with iron and fire!

What have they to do with our situation and existence here?

The only thing left for them to do will be to search out other lands, to transport themselves to other countries where there are no examples of the stupid, backward, inferior Black people that here are found on such a large scale.

Leave us here happy and ignorant; move away to the great civilized centers. There is even a saying that gives that wise advice to those malcontents....[26]

We propose to fight against this *foreign* aspect of the problem, even to the courts.

We do not need to specify here exactly how certain foreigners persecute the Brazilian Black, since these ways are as varied as they are well known: it begins in certain barbershops and moves on to certain bars and taverns.

If we continue to retreat into the silence of cowardice, if we flee in fear from the mass of our offenders, tomorrow our fate will be that of true social outcasts.

We will have no barbers, no shoemakers, no tailors; we will not be able to enter the hotels, the bars, the cinemas, the shops, the theaters; in sum, we will be expelled from the tramways and thrown off the trains, left without the right to walk on the sidewalk!

"Silence is consent," which is why we must act with assurance and without conditions.

Even in the very churches we are being victimized. There are cities where a young girl of color cannot be a daughter of Mary, and where a Black boy cannot march in the processions dressed as an angel!!

Meanwhile Saint Benedict is not White![27]

We will get there on another occasion.

---

[26] This may refer to the saying, "Let those who are uncomfortable pick up and move" (6.3).

[27] Saint Benedict (1526–89) was born in Sicily of enslaved African parents and later freed. He is the patron saint of many Black churches in Latin America, including the one in

## 2.10  ARLINDO VEIGA DOS SANTOS, "AFFIRMING THE RACE," A VOZ DA RAÇA (SÃO PAULO: BRAZIL: JUNE 10, 1933)

*In this complex and troubling article, Arlindo Veiga dos Santos, president of the Frente Negra Brasileira, embraced Nazi racial ideology as a potential avenue for Black advancement in Brazil. Veiga dos Santos advocated monarchy as the "most perfect" form of government (3.11) and was a harsh critic of "liberal-democratic republicanism." He supported the overthrow of Brazil's First Republic (which in this article he compared, unfavorably, to an Afro-Brazilian street dance) in 1930, and then, in 1933, Hitler's seizure of power in Germany. Dos Santos expressed admiration both for the Nazis' authoritarianism and for their "affirmation of the German race," which he presented to readers as a possible model for Brazilian race pride. The irony, of course, is that the Nazis based their racial ideology on the same "Aryanizing" tendencies that Veiga dos Santos found so problematic in Brazil. Nor would the Nazis have viewed Brazilian race mixture in the same positive light that dos Santos did.*

*Like "The Blacks in São Paulo" (2.9), this article expressed strong anti-immigrant sentiment, closing with a plea to "shut the doors of Brazil [to immigration] for twenty years or more."*

Alarms are sounding in the encampments of incompetence, because the dictator Hitler, in an intense desire to restore Germany to its traditional path, began the campaign of active affirmation of the German race, the only one on which that nation can count to carry out the immense work of national rescue.

Absurd foolishness of those crystalline intelligences that do not understand (leaving aside the natural exaggeration of those who suffered so much from Jewish cosmopolitanism), that do not understand the deep reasons for the nationalist attitude toward all the miseries of the democracy that permitted all the forms of liberal stupidity that were leading Germany to ruin!

Hitler is right! So expressive is his affirmation, and so resonant in the German soul, that the world of those who are injured protests noisily … but only with noise! Because there is no one who does not see that the strong attitudes of the great Leader are rousing from lethargy a people

Campinas in which the earlier Black newspaper *O Baluarte* was based. He is also the namesake of this article's author.

desperate for salvation from the stupefying opium of fourteen years of a liberal-democratic republic.

\* \* \*

Those who are most scandalized by the severity of the German dictator are the liberal journalists of a celebrated American country that has suffered more than forty years of liberal-democratic *batuque* and that now wishes to continue democracy (as long as a small group of mental defectives and schoolchildren rule), under another name presented as new!!!²⁸

But what would have happened in Brazil if by some chance the people who for forty years led the official *batuque* had affirmed our Luso-Indian-Black Race instead of making the national Home a noisy international street party, in which every newly arrived foreigner handed down the law and gave advice leading to perdition? What would Brazil be today, if our Black People had not been always denied, marginalized in national life, ceding their place to all the newly arrived opportunists, while the immigrants were being served their banquet?

\* \* \*

We too have a Race! There is not, nor can there be, a single National Type. We are a Mixed Race, with our Blacks, **Cafusos**, **Caboclos**, Negroids, Whiteoids, and even the savage Indians who still live in the forest.

Our lives have been greatly complicated by the insane idea, held by numerous imbeciles, of wanting to turn the Brazilian Nation into an Aryan people, thus destroying the Mixed Race that the Brazilian is!

We were already more or less defined during the Dutch war, when we gave the European "Aryans" a good lesson!²⁹

And by 1889 we were a very serious matter in the eyes of the world.³⁰

So why do we not always affirm our Black-Indian-Luso Race, which was and continues to be something new and proud in the world?

Why don't we esteem it as we should!?

---

²⁸ *Batuque* refers to sessions of African and Afro-Brazilian drumming and dance, often represented in Brazilian culture as occasions of noisy disorder. The phrase "democracy [...] under another name" refers to **Getúlio Vargas'** provisional government, which ruled Brazil from 1930 to 1934.

²⁹ From 1630 to 1654 Dutch forces occupied northeastern Brazil, until they were driven out by Portuguese and Brazilian forces; see 1.2.

³⁰ In 1889 Brazilian army officers overthrew the monarchy of **Dom Pedro II** and declared the First Republic.

Let us affirm it, therefore, now that Brazil is undergoing great organic transformations, and is on the threshold of even greater ones.

Let's annihilate the internationals who seek to command in Our House, whether they be Brazilian (in name) internationals, or foreigners.

The German affirms the German race? A beautiful example, a glorious lesson!

Let us do the same, affirming the Brazilian Race!

And let's lock the doors to Brazil for twenty years or more, to get this rectified!

### 2.11 "THE RACIAL PROBLEM IN THE AFRICAN COLONIES IS ATTACKED BY THIRTEEN BLACK EDITORS," REVISTA URUGUAY (MONTEVIDEO, URUGUAY: JULY 1945)

*In the spring of 1945, delegates from the Allied and neutral nations met in San Francisco to write the charter for a new international organization, the United Nations. In preparation for that event, the Council on African Affairs, an organization composed of African American intellectuals, sent an open letter to President Roosevelt and US Secretary of State Edward Stettinius, protesting racial discrimination and inequality in France and England's African colonies and in the United States, and demanding that the Roosevelt administration take action against those ills.[31] Revista Uruguay used the Council's letter as a starting point for an extended discussion of racial conditions in Uruguay, where, it insisted, "racial prejudice does not exist." (For a contemporaneous criticism of this position, see 7.12.) Afro-Uruguayans were free to study and rise as high as their ambitions could take them; though it is noteworthy that, of the Afro-Uruguayan professionals that the magazine mentioned by name, half were deceased (8.9). In comparison with the African colonies, the United States, and even the Latin American country of Venezuela, Uruguay offered enviable conditions of equality and opportunity for people of color, the magazine argued.*

Reflecting world events, and in these moments in which men are working hard to find a solution to the social ills from which the community of nations suffers, *Revista Uruguay*, this publication edited by Black journalists, disagrees completely with all those who affirm that racial prejudice exists in our country. We express our point of view, precisely taking into

[31] Von Eschen, *Race against Empire*, pp. 73–74.

account that here in Uruguay, very little or nothing remains to be done to definitively eliminate that color line, the existence of which is so absurd and vile in countries that support and defend democracy.

For this reason we are going to take up a sensational event for the civilized world, which is the statement, containing twenty-one points, presented by thirteen Black editors to the late, great, United States President Franklin D. Roosevelt, expressing the situation of the Blacks in the French and English colonies of Africa, and also of the populations of color in the United States. In their letter, those editors state that "there is deliberate oppression of the Westernized Africans who desire to advance themselves, educationally and professionally, [who are] paid salaries that in many cases are no different from slavery." "That the administration of the colonies is based openly and shamelessly on favoritism toward White men, and that in various ways the color line is inexorably drawn." These points presented by those vigorous men of color are in the possession of the US State Department and have been discussed with great interest at the **San Francisco Conference**, where a detailed report has been presented, by order of the late President Roosevelt. We have no doubt that that report will be one of the powerful arguments for the reconsideration of matters related to mistreatment and to the definitive elimination of that hateful and detestable evil, racism.

In the face of such events, we, the editors and official collaborators of *Revista Uruguay*, rejoice and take comfort from such a significant gesture toward all those peoples who have not yet been able to divest themselves of the spirit of the old slave trader, which left behind that accursed belief that today is something rejected by human civilization, a cause for embarrassment that they seek to make disappear from their history. *We who live in a country where social life is respected and protected by the laws* – with the exception of the economic problem of the poor and the rich, which has nothing to do with public opinion and the rights granted equally to all citizens by our constitution – long for and hope that the twenty-one points presented by our racial brothers will be taken into account and adopted by the statesmen who are called on to create laws that will make disappear the barbarism and the slave trading spirit that still prevails in many countries.

*Consistent with its guiding principles*, Revista Uruguay *declares that in our country racial prejudice does not exist*, and to corroborate our opinion we say that, while in Europe, Central America, and North America, events and cases occur that seem incredible for the times in which we live, in our country it is just the opposite. For example, we will cite a recent case that occurred in the city of Caracas (Venezuela). Senator Cárdenas[32] has just presented in the Senate the case of the Black singer Todd Duncan, who was rejected by the managers of the three principal hotels [in the city]. The aforesaid senator, in an attitude worthy of praise for all its eloquence, asks, in this case and in the future, that all those who refuse to provide lodging to people of color be sanctioned.[33]

While in those places cases like that do occur, here – and we say it with satisfaction – when the eminent Black contralto Marian Anderson[34] visited our capital, she stayed in our principal hotel, the Gran Hotel Lanata; and looking back to more distant days, the lodgings of the formidable Black boxer Jack Johnson, world champion in all weight categories, were nothing less than the Parque Hotel, one of the most esteemed hotels at the time. Many of the Black personalities who have visited our country have stayed wherever they wished, with no problems.

Not long ago, a young Black man, the intelligent and studious Mr. Pedro Ocampo Pérez, left for Brazil with a scholarship from the Civil Aeronautics Administration. We can also comment on one of the most salient cases in Uruguay, which is that of Black teachers and professors working in state institutions of public education. We must first mention the late Patricio Méndez Pérez, professor of violin in the Instituto Musical La Lira; public school teachers **Margarita Ubarne Mansilla de Espinosa** and Celestina Martínez; physician: **Dr. José María Rodríguez Arraga;** lawyers: **Francisco Rondeau,** [Martín] Estevarena, and **Salvador Betervide,** all deceased; this last [Betervide] was one of the youngest lawyers in our country and held a scholarship from the city of Melo (Department of Cerro Largo).

As it would be a little lengthy to list here all the names of Black people of high intellectual standing, we will limit ourselves to this brief survey, which we will continue to publish in future issues. But even so, before concluding, we can put before the general opinion of our collectivity – which allows itself to be *intimidated* by the phantasm of racism, and which we continue to insist does not exist – as clear justification for our assertions, [the fact that] we have students in high schools, the law school,

---

[32] Manuel Rodríguez Cárdenas (1912–91), Afro-Venezuelan composer, musician, and politician. Michelle Leigh Farrell, "Rodríguez Cárdenas, Manuel," in Knight and Gates, *Dictionary*, vol. V, pp. 354–55.

[33] On this episode, in which African American singer Todd Duncan was denied accommodation in three Caracas hotels, see Wright, "The Todd Duncan Affair."

[34] The famous singer Marian Anderson (1897–1993) toured Argentina, Brazil, and Uruguay in 1936.

the Universidad del Trabajo,[35] the medical school, and in chemistry and pharmacy; artists, painters, poets, reciters, actors, violinists, pianists, guitarists, tenors, sopranos. In the area of sports we have great figures generally acknowledged as first-class talents. We have highly regarded specialized workers: photo-engravers, typographers, linotypists, jewelers, electricians, mechanics; and let the record show that none of these has encountered the least resistance to advancing in their professions.

What more can we say to prove that the position of the Black in national society is highly significant? Even more, going more deeply into the area of organized labor, many Black men make their voices heard in advising and guiding the laboring masses in their social demands. This is why we began this article by saying that in our country little or nothing remains to be done to completely eliminate whatever vestige of racism might exist among a few mercantilists [slave traders] who are still around. *Conrazáneo*, our duty is to make ourselves worthy, preparing our children through education, so that tomorrow *they do not find themselves in inferior conditions* to occupy meritorious places in society. We ourselves must embrace the responsibility that we have in life, and the satisfaction that comes from doing one's duty.

2.12 JOSÉ CORREIA LEITE, "PREJUDICE, THE BIG HOUSE, AND THE SLAVE QUARTERS," ALVORADA (SÃO PAULO, BRAZIL: MAR. 1947)

*After spending several months carrying out research in Uruguay and Argentina (7.12), in February 1947 the African American anthropologist **Ellen Irene Diggs** traveled to Rio de Janeiro. She immediately became embroiled in a national cause célèbre when she was refused admittance to the Hotel Serrador.[36] Diggs publicly denounced this act of discrimination, noting that while racism was on the decline in the United States, it appeared to be increasing in Brazil. **José Correia Leite** emphatically agreed with Diggs and attributed that increase to Afro-Brazilians' refusal to confront racism directly and to combat it. If racial discrimination was gradually fading away in the United States, that was because African Americans had banded together in a movement to confront it. The fact that Blacks in Brazil had not followed that path had left most of them in*

[35] The Universidad del Trabajo del Uruguay, created in 1942, offers advanced training in science and technology.
[36] "Corajosa afirmação," *Alvorada* (Feb. 1947), 1.

the "slave quarters," he suggested, with a few privileged Afro-Brazilians living in the "big house." This choice of words was an ironic jibe at **Gilberto Freyre's** book, Casa-grande e senzala (The Big House and the Slave Quarters), a principal source for "the sentimental lie that in Brazil there is no prejudice."

The question of color prejudice in Brazil – which we always affirm is race prejudice – was roiling again last month.

This time it merited attention even in big headlines in some of our newspapers. This interest gives a new flavor to the longstanding problem, mainly because of the source and the way in which the dubious question was raised.

It was the voice of an authority on the subject. A Black woman with great intellectual and moral resources and abilities on this question, a special envoy from her country on a specific mission, she needed to make contact with our so-called elite. But it happens: there, in the door of the hotel, we see the branding iron of racial restrictions bite the flesh of the honored American.

Questioned by journalists, she made astounding statements. They were hard and bitter words that Brazil heard. Those words should remain engraved and smoldering in our memory, because they are major warnings for Brazilian Blacks.

Naturally, we are not including here the Negroids who are ashamed of their origins. In this land of *mestiços*, only the Blacks have the courage to make these statements; the rest are the legion of those banished and condemned by their low living conditions.

Commenting on this fact, let's consider its repercussions, because we know this is a matter that is always being debated. We don't really care about its pros and cons. None of this resolves or even reduces the conception of a reality the effects of which have left the mark of their injuries.

Recently, in an article in *Jornal de Debates*, the Black poet Solano Trindade[37] spoke well [concerning] the question of prejudice, [saying that] it is not the cause [of prejudice] that is important, but its effects. And we objected: those effects are largely caused through our own fault! And who says that? The journalist and fighter José Bernardo, in *Jornal de Debates*, when he affirmed this hard truth, which we italicize here: "*the*

---

[37] Solano Trindade (1908–74) was a poet, playwright, activist, and founder of the Teatro Popular Brasileiro. Niyi Afolabi, "Trindade, Solano" in Knight and Gates, *Dictionary*, vol. VI, pp. 208–9.

*fault is that of the Blacks."* We agree. Yes, because we Brazilian Blacks all descended from the slave quarters and still have the stigmas of the scorn that, speaking in human terms, should bring more courage and fervor to the face of certain Blacks who adopt the snobbery and polish of fancy dress, behave ridiculously and stand in the way of the problem of Black evolution in Brazil.

The Black man in Brazil is the weakest being to push around. So true is that that we have no doubt in believing that the conclusion drawn by Mrs. **Irene Diggs**, scrupulous observer of these subjects, is the result of our own negligence. If she says that prejudice in the United States is tending to disappear, and here the tendency is for it to increase, then obviously the Blacks there [in the United States] are imposing themselves through progress, and here, we are being swallowed by the sentimental lie that in Brazil there is no prejudice, yet it continues to be a vast slave quarters, with a few Blacks in the big house.

### 2.13  RAUL JOVIANO DO AMARAL, "A MISTAKEN THESIS," ALVORADA (SÃO PAULO, BRAZIL: JUNE 1947)

*In this article, Raul Joviano do Amaral,[38] an editor of Alvorada and a veteran of Brazil's Black press and associations, forcefully dispensed with the "mistaken thesis" that prejudice in Brazil, to the extent that it existed, was based solely on class and not race. This was a common conception among many Brazilians, both Black and White – indeed, Amaral expressed his dismay that his fellow Afro-Brazilians would accept this premise to avoid facing the ugly realities of discrimination or to "conciliate" White racists and improve their own individual situations at the expense of the collective. The belief that discrimination in Brazil was due primarily to class rather than race was fundamental to the emerging ideology of Brazilian **racial democracy**, as articulated by government officials and by many local and international academic researchers. In the face of such rosy proclamations, Amaral invoked the lived experiences and first-hand knowledge of "any black Brazilian." These, he noted, offered plentiful examples of the ways in which no amount of education or class refinement could override the specifically color-based*

---

[38] Raul Joviano do Amaral (1914–88) was an Afro-Brazilian lawyer, sociologist, and journalist. He was a founder of the **Frente Negra Brasileira** and the director of its paper, *A Voz da Raça*. In the 1940s and 1950s, he helped found the Associação dos Negros Brasileiros and the Associação Cultural do Negro, in addition to serving as editor and contributor in several newspapers.

*prejudice faced by Afro-Brazilians, especially in the South, where the color line and regimes of discrimination were particularly entrenched. Amaral's evident care to distance himself from "organizations that seek exclusively to combat [racial] prejudice" was a response to the virulent accusations of "reverse racism" that the Black press and organizations began to face as they mobilized both to seize the benefits and expose the shortfalls of Brazil's restored democracy after 1945 (for a similar dynamic in Cuba, see 2.7, 2.17).*

Any Black Brazilian can refute, instantly and with incontrovertible [examples] numbering in the tens or hundreds, the profoundly mistaken thesis that in Brazil there exists no color prejudice properly speaking, but rather that it is displaced by a class prejudice that affects all tiers of the population who do not belong to the so-called elite, because their educational, social, or economic levels take precedence over their color.

It is possible for that to be partly true in one or another state of the Federation. [But] that would be the exception, and the exception should not be easily generalized or parroted about as certain renowned Black figures do – whether in good faith, because they lack knowledge, or pretend to lack knowledge, of the precise dimensions of the problem.

It disgusts our spirit to accept – and we do so only for the sake of argument – the pacifism of those illustrious friends who trust that, through those means, they can conciliate situations that are truly humiliating for our community, if not for those [individuals] themselves or for their closest interests.

From the center of Brazil southward, what exists – and let's have the courage to say it – is racism pure and simple, fascist discrimination, race prejudice. Any conscientious analyst who puts in the time will verify that our democracy, this Brazilian **racial democracy**, is a tremendous failure, a front put up "for the English to see." [39] The blame falls exclusively to bad Brazilians, the self-satisfied defenders of slavery descended from the former owners of enslaved Africans, who obstinately and slavishly copy foreign examples.

There, yet again, we see proof of the trait for which we are known abroad: [as a] land of imitators, of execrable imitators. Truly, we seek to imitate everything that does not harmonize with our traditions, even at the

---

[39] This expression refers to actions that are simply for show or for the benefit of international observers. It dates back to the middle 1800s, when some Brazilians sought to preserve the appearance of complying with a treaty with the English that legally ended the slave trade, while continuing, in practice, to smuggle African captives.

expense of the one thing whose originality we have an obligation to preserve and value: our people, still in formation. But we deliberately do violence to everything that is ours. Sometimes, this happens out of sadism; other times, out of ignorance of our realities.

\*

We have strayed somewhat from the point of this article – on purpose. But in the lands of the South, prejudice is clearly about color and race, and not class. Daily events in [the states of] São Paulo, Rio [de Janeiro], Paraná, Rio Grande do Sul, Santa Catarina, prove this point exhaustively. Sometimes, they do so sensationally, as in the case of **Irene Diggs** or that officer in the army.[40] Thousands of other times, however, [they do so] silently. We do not profess unqualified support for organizations that seek exclusively to combat [racial] prejudice. But in the course of the campaigns to reeducate the Black man, this [the racial nature of prejudice] is a matter that will always rise to the surface. Let us pause just long enough to make sure we understand the issue well, and we will be able to plot more viable courses and more confident itineraries.

Because knowing, as we do, that a poor man in a tie, if he is White, can break through class prejudice, while a wealthy dark-skinned Brazilian in a tie cannot break through the color prejudice of [establishments like] a Roop, a Quitandinha, a Rio Branco, and others – knowing this, we try to prove the problem from other angles that are more dignified and suited to humanity's fleeting existence.[41] To be continued.

### 2.14 MARIA NASCIMENTO, "A WOMAN'S TURN TO SPEAK: RACIST CHILDREN," QUILOMBO (RIO DE JANEIRO, BRAZIL: DEC. 1948)

Quilombo *featured several women writers and contributors, most prominently journalist and social worker* **Maria Nascimento**, *whose column*

---

[40] On Irene Diggs, see 2.12. We have not been able to identify the case involving an officer in the army.

[41] The Casino-Hotel Quitandinha, inaugurated in the mid 1940s, was a luxury hotel in Petrópolis, Rio de Janeiro. The Instituto Rio Branco, inaugurated in 1945 in Rio de Janeiro, is the institute of higher learning within Itamaraty (Brazil's Ministry of Foreign Relations), serving as the only entry point into the diplomatic career. The Instituto, and Itamaraty more generally, were notorious sites of racial exclusion, as were military academies; both were frequent targets of the Black press at midcentury. We have not been able to identify the establishment named "Roop."

*"Fala a Mulher"* spotlighted issues facing Black women and children (see also 5.16). In this inaugural installment, Nascimento introduced herself to fellow Black female readers and writers, portraying her column as a "democratic" conversational space in which women could speak frankly, without fear of condescension or ridicule. Yet she emphasized the need for respect and decorum, ever aware – like her male colleagues in the region's Black papers – that public writing was just one more area in which Black people were scrutinized and judged rational or irrational, worthy or unworthy citizens.

Nascimento then shifted to her main subject: the inter-generational reproduction of anti-Black racism within families (even those composed of Afrodescendants or people from other stigmatized groups). Along with the many social burdens that already fell to them, Nascimento argued, Black women should take up the task of teaching anti-racist principles to White children, particularly those in their care. Black women had a duty to act, in this way, as a "harmonizing element, clearing up the subtlest of disagreements between Blacks and Whites." This, however, was not the conciliatory, complacent "harmony" symbolized by the historic **Black Mother** (5.11), but a hard-fought harmony born of Black women's anti-racist work.

Through this column, I will converse with my countrywomen of color. We will discuss our problems, my fellow countrywomen, with the openness of true sisters and friends who love each other. And even when the discussion should by chance turn heated, we will never lose our serenity. Through our manner of speaking and acting we reveal our condition as human beings or our unconscious behavior as irrationals. Let us, then, converse and act like people who only for lack of opportunities are not more [fully] integrated in this century of civilization and progress. Opportunities that, from now on, we will fight to obtain.

I invite my friends to write to me. Do not worry about grammatical errors, because this here is no Academy of Letters, but a democratic platform for the discussion of our ideas and problems.

As a conversation starter, I will relay an episode that illustrates well the complexity of the problems that weigh upon the shoulders of Black women, and the duty that falls to them as a harmonizing element, [tasked with] clearing up the subtlest of disagreements between Blacks and Whites which, if allowed to compound, can turn into grounds for calamity, hatred, and wars.

The situation is as follows: I have a friend, of a spontaneous and lively intelligence, [who is] a domestic worker. She has a small daughter, whom she takes to a day nursery every morning and picks up when she finishes work in the evening. On one occasion her employer's son, a boy of ten years, decided to accompany her to the day nursery. When they had returned [to the employer's home], my friend asked the boy,

"So, Robertinho, did you like the nursery?"

Robertinho shrugged his shoulders, made a scornful face, and – petulant little "master" of **Copacabana** that he is – responded,

"No, I did not like it. Too much mixture. White and Black children, all in the same rooms ... "

Now for some additional details: this child racist is the son of a Jew[ish man] and a Bahian [woman].[42] There exist thousands of White children just like this one, whom we Black women must teach that skin color makes no one better or worse, just as this friend of mine did. Because, unfortunately, some mixed-race women disguised as Aryans, like this "Bahian White," or that Jew[ish man], possibly a refugee from Nazism, do not stop their children from nursing such stupid prejudices.[43]

## 2.15 ABDIAS DO NASCIMENTO, "THE FIRST CONGRESS OF THE BRAZILIAN BLACK," QUILOMBO (RIO DE JANEIRO, BRAZIL: JAN. 1950)

*This article looked ahead to the Primeiro Congresso do Negro Brasileiro, organized by* **Abdias do Nascimento** *and* **Alberto Guerreiro Ramos** *and held in Rio de Janeiro in August 1950. Echoing points made in "Where is Afrology Going?" (6.8), Nascimento contrasted this event with the two* **Congressos Afro-Brasileiros** *of the 1930s. While in those previous events Black people had served as "raw material for academics" to study, "distant beings, almost dead," the Congresso do Negro Brasileiro would cast Afro-Brazilians as "shapers of their own conduct, of their own destiny." And while the earlier congresses had focused on questions of African-based culture, this Congresso would take a more activist approach, examining present-day living conditions for Afro-Brazilians and pushing "to*

[42] A "Bahian" is a person from the northeastern Brazilian state of Bahia, which has a majority Afrodescendant population.

[43] "Bahian White" ("branco/a da Bahia") refers to individuals of partial African ancestry who are treated as White in Bahia, though not necessarily in other (Whiter) parts of the country.

*accelerate the process of integration of Blacks and Whites that was created by our own historical evolution."*[44]

The sociologist [**Alberto**] **Guerreiro Ramos** is very correct in saying that the Primeiro Congresso do Negro Brasileiro, which will take place at the end of August this year, promoted by the **Teatro Experimental do Negro**, is an unprecedented event in the history of the man of color in Brazil. For quite some time, **Arthur Ramos,** the master whose recent death opened one of those voids in our culture that are impossible to fill, used to speak about Black leaders' responsibility for adopting measures to achieve improved living conditions for the population of color. Blacks would pass from the condition of being raw material for academics to being the shapers of their own conduct, of their own destiny.

The Primeiro Congresso do Negro seeks especially to emphasize current practical problems in the lives of our people of color. Whenever Blacks have been studied, it was with the clear purpose or the poorly disguised intention of considering them to be distant beings, almost dead, or even stuffed and preserved, like a museum exhibit. For this reason the Congresso will give secondary importance to, for example, ethnography or less pressing questions, giving less attention to the cephalic index of the Black, or whether or not Zumbi really committed suicide, than to exploring the means that we can use to organize associations and institutions that can offer opportunities for people of color to elevate themselves in society.[45] I want the Congresso to find effective measures for increasing Black purchasing power, turning them into effective and active members of the national community.

Guerreiro Ramos goes further, stating that for elements of the masses of color to take this position is nothing more than Brazil's response to the world's call for minorities to participate in the great democratic interplay of culture. The future Congresso will confirm that there exists in our country an elite of color capable of instilling confidence among the dominant classes, because our movement is not a diversion, it is not seeking picturesque goals, nor is it characterized by that irresponsibility that unfortunately has damaged most of the initiatives of the Blacks of Brazil.

[44] The Congresso did in fact carry through on that program; see its collected papers and communications in Nascimento, *O negro revoltado.*
[45] "Cephalic index" refers to the **scientific racist** discipline of craniometry, the measurement of skulls. Zumbi was the last leader of the seventeenth-century *quilombo* (settlement of escaped slaves) of Palmares, which was captured and destroyed by Portuguese forces in 1695.

During the Congresso the Blacks will seek to study themselves, to decipher their personality and configure their collective problems, thinking and acting realistically, leaving the racial question aside to confront the underlying [human/societal] questions. Truly a sociological Congress, it proposes to discover mechanisms to accelerate the process of integration of Blacks and Whites that was created by our own historical evolution.

### 2.16 ALBERTO GUERREIRO RAMOS, "AN INTRODUCTION TO NEGRITUDE," QUILOMBO (RIO DE JANEIRO, BRAZIL: JUNE–JULY 1950)

*In this essay, sociologist* **Alberto Guerreiro Ramos** *leveraged the idea of Brazilian* **racial democracy** *in order to articulate an avant-garde cultural politics of Blackness, or "negritude." This was not a reference to the cultural and political movement of Black affirmation and revolt espoused by Aimé Césaire,* **Léopold Sédar Senghor,** *and other Francophone intellectuals.*[46] *Nor, Ramos was careful to point out, was negritude "aggressive or isolationist," a "ferment of hatred" that divided Brazilians along racial lines – an accusation many White Brazilians leveled at Black organizations at midcentury. Rather, it was an argument that Brazilian Blackness was a defining feature of Brazilian society and culture. Negritude softened the "classical categories of Brazilian society," he suggested, endowing that society with a basic humanity and openness to human diversity. Those qualities, and that historical and cultural experience, in turn would enable Brazil to play a role of "global leadership ... in the politics of racial democracy" that, Ramos believed, the international community would embrace in the second half of the 1900s.*

Brazil must assume a global leadership role in the politics of **racial democracy.** Because it is the only country on earth that offers a satisfactory solution to the racial problem. In relation to men of color, Brazilian society offers practically all freedoms, rights and privileges. And if there is a problem for men of color in our country, it consists primarily of training them, through culture and through education, to use those freedoms.

Among us, any Black movement of an aggressive or isolationist character is a frontal assault on our national tradition, and consequently, it becomes merely a matter for the police.

---

[46] Diagne, "Négritude."

The **Teatro Experimental do Negro** is a vanguard movement for the cultural and economic elevation of the men of color, in which members practice the conscious elaboration of Brazil's traditional ideology with regard to race relations. Thus is our country made ready, through [the work of] one part of its intelligentsia, to offer the world a generic methodology for the treatment of racial issues.

This is our profound conviction. At the moment that we launch the myth of negritude into the life of our nation, we make a point to proclaim it with total clarity.

Negritude is not a ferment of hatred. It is not a schism. It is a subjectivity. A lived experience. A passional element that runs deep in the classical categories of Brazilian society and that enriches them with human substance. Human, all too human, is Brazilian culture; this is why, without disintegrating, it absorbs spiritual idiosyncrasies of the most varied kinds. Indeed, out of them [Brazilian culture] composes its ecumenic vocation, its understanding and tolerant nature. Brazilian culture is, therefore, essentially catholic, in the sense that nothing that is human can be alien to it.[47]

The magical enchantment of negritude was always present in this culture, exuberant in its enthusiasm, candor, passion, sensuality, mystery, even though only today, through the effects of universal pressures, is it awakening to a lucid awareness of its features. It is a badge of honor and pride for Brazil to have been raised in the cradle of negritude, the sweet and strange bride to all of us Whites and **trigueiros** . . .

## 2.17 "OUR READERS WEIGH IN," ATENAS (HAVANA, CUBA: AUG. 1951)

*Black activists and the multiracial Communist Party successfully advocated for an article in the* **Constitution of 1940** *making racial and gender discrimination criminal offenses. In the decade that followed, the same coalition engaged in a campaign to get the legislature to establish exact penalties and mechanisms of enforcement, without which the constitutional language was merely symbolic. In 1948, presidential candidate Carlos Prío Socarrás visited the* **Club Atenas** *and promised support for "complementary laws." But as president he failed to live up to this promise. Prío Socarrás also largely neutralized the movement for complementary laws by placing individuals loyal to his party in the leadership of*

---

[47] Ramos appears to have been referencing the oft-quoted statement by the Roman playwright Terence: "I am human, I consider nothing human alien to me."

*labor unions, formerly dominated by communists, and in the leadership of*
*many Black clubs.*

The "Our Readers Weigh In" section of Atenas, *a magazine produced*
*by the Club Atenas, reflected some lingering optimism that the comple-*
*mentary legislation would be forthcoming, as well as profound disap-*
*pointment with the long delay. As a letters-to-the-editor section, this*
*feature was somewhat idiosyncratic, paraphrasing and affirming letters*
*from readers rather than simply publishing them. On that model, editors*
*agreed with a reader who wrote that too many Black Cubans "of stand-*
*ing" were silent on matters of racial justice because they "fear that they*
*will be called racists" (see also 1.7, 1.14, 2.7, 2.13, 2.16). Yet these letters*
*also show how actively Black Cubans discussed racial discrimination and*
*mobilized to combat it. The editors warned that, in the absence of con-*
*crete action, Black voters would punish the ruling party in the next*
*elections. As it turned out, the elections were forestalled by a military*
*coup in 1952 and the seizure of power by* **Fulgencio Batista.**

The Sad and Lonely Poet. Versalles Street. Matanzas.

Although we had planned not to give space here to any letter lacking
a responsible signature, we will make an exception for yours, written
anonymously and signed with a pseudonym.

The topic that you raise is of paramount interest and great importance.
In effect, the long-awaited "Law for education and sanctions against
discrimination based on race and color" has not been approved with the
speed it deserves. This is why every day we see the proliferation of
establishments and public places that, under the title of "Social Club,"
find shelter behind the **Law of Association,** under which they register as
private social institutions with the provincial governments, artfully and
deceitfully protecting their personal exclusions and their racism.

These malicious businessmen, instructed by talented individuals who
write up their bylaws, attempt to circumvent the Constitution and the
statutes. They are destroying the equality and the mutual coexistence of all
the elements that make up our country and preserving, at all costs,
a situation of mistreatment for the ethnic group of color, which is
a component of Cuban society.

And worse still, foreseeing that any law that is passed in the near future
might affect them, they are already trying to shield themselves by creating
these private clubs. They are rehearsing now the selective and exclusion-
ary politics that they will later try to impose by right of customary law and
by the priority [of the law] that currently protects them.

But this effort will be worthless. We are forewarned. When our representatives and the other friends we have in the House and the Senate consider the anti-discrimination law, they can include a section that prevents and punishes any attempt by the racists to undermine what should be the solid guarantee that our Republic is required to offer to the true brotherhood of Cubans.

And as to what happens if the "Law against discrimination" should be approved "without sanctions," we do not believe it possible that anyone, with good sense, would accept such a monster. This would be the equivalent of accepting chicken and rice without the chicken. And much less do we believe that any Judas of color will arise to support such an absurd initiative.

The long-awaited "Law against discrimination of race or color," the complement to the egalitarian precepts of the **Constitution of 1940**, is the hot potato which the government, with its majority in Congress, must grasp fully and honestly. It must make good on its promises or run the risk of suffering the well-deserved consequences, in the next general elections, of its failure to keep them.

\* \* \*

Pedro Bárcena. 54 Rosa la Bayamesa Street. Camagüey.

You are more than correct, my friend. Discrimination against people of color in employment is among the worst that we suffer.

Ignoring what the Constitution and the current labor laws say, and the [ideal of] equality of opportunity for all – despite all of this, the doors are closed to our element. Our livelihoods and our means of production are taken from us, in order to better annihilate our ethnic group.

Without a means of earning a living, the economy of the people of color is reduced to the inconceivable. Then, almost without any economic pressure, with little effort, they can be erased as a representative symbol of the nation.

We know full well that man does not live by bread alone, but it is no less true that without bread he cannot live. The worker organizations, among other factors, are to blame for this grip on our throats, for the elimination of the element of color in employment. The guilds, unions, and federations only deal with the problem theoretically, contributing nothing more than empirical solutions.[48] And we ourselves are principally to blame because we do not defend our rights, or we do not know how to defend them.

---

[48] We do not know whether this contradictory statement was intentional, highlighting the intractability of the problem, or whether by "empirical" the author means "practical but limited; perfunctory."

Among the many complex forms that racial discrimination takes among us, as you say so well, Bárcena my friend, is the closing of the door to our group in the skilled trades and all types of occupations, so that we die of hunger or are overcome by our lack of resources. All the better to eliminate us from Cuba, with respect to areas of possible competition, or to present us as symbols of social inferiority, incapable of any progress.

Against all of this, and against many other things, the **Club Atenas** is studying the way to contribute practical and effective solutions. We are thinking of organizing, as a first attempt, as a preliminary matter, a Juridical Committee, composed of lawyers of solid prestige, of high reputation, and proven honesty, to practice the defense of the rights that we are due, individually and collectively. Within the current limits, this committee will promote broader measures and thereby prevent us from being cheated out of that which is ours. It is necessary to begin somewhere, and we believe that this is a good way to do so. Racial discrimination and its pretexts for denying livelihoods to our element is one of the greatest concerns of our people. On this topic we receive the largest number of inquiries, suggestions, and opinions, the better to put in practice measures against it. And this is why we take a stand against racism, calling on those of our kind, and friends of both races, to imitate us, to cooperate with us, without considering personal interests or partisan matters.

* * *

Genaro Morejón. 458 Lamparilla St. Havana.

Your opinion is very important. Many men of color, as you say very well, live beneath the tyranny of a word, "racist." As Armando Plá[49] once noted in a magazine that he edited in Camagüey, some of our men of standing and influence do not work in favor of us as individuals or a collective, demanding our inherent rights, because they fear that they will be called "racists." Thus they leave a great part of our class bereft of protection. And the other element, the one that has everything and also usurps that which belongs to us, knows this. As soon as one of us takes steps to demand something, or establishes some protest against any injustice, supposing he must have this complex, they always bring up the hackneyed term "racist," and thereby squash the best of intentions and neutralize the best of attempts.

Against this we must set ourselves. The racist is not the one who sees the harm and the scorn, and who demands what is his and tries to enforce the respect and consideration he deserves, but rather the one who unlawfully

---

[49] Afro-Cuban editor of the newspaper *El Noticiero* in the city of Camagüey.

takes that which belongs to another, putting forward the question of race or skin color. Our people should learn this well and take it into account and should always act accordingly.

## 2.18 "DISCRIMINATION: CUÉLLAR'S REPORT," NUEVOS RUMBOS (HAVANA, CUBA: APR. 25, 1959)

*In March of 1959, Cuba's newly installed revolutionary government, led by Fidel Castro, launched a campaign against racial discrimination in public spaces and employment. The government quickly began to take over and desegregate private beaches and to reconstruct and desegregate public parks. With support from the state, an integrationist movement began challenging racial segregation in private schools, clubs, and associations. These months marked a major symbolic shift as well, as officials pronounced that racism was anti-revolutionary, imperialist, and unpatriotic. Meanwhile, Afro-Cubans within the revolutionary coalition took part in conferences and panels on the problem of racism and the policies that should be adopted to combat it, including a forum on racial discrimination, held at the University of Havana and described in this report in* Nuevos Rumbos.

*The article reproduced a speech to the forum by communist journalist and ethnographer* **Manuel Cuéllar Vizcaíno**, *a veteran of the struggle against racial discrimination in the 1940s and 1950s. Reflecting the enthusiasm that many Afro-Cubans felt for the revolution in these early months, Cuéllar argued that the revolutionary campaign against racism provided an unexpected opportunity to combine a gradual approach to cultural change with swift revolutionary action against segregated associations and job discrimination. Cuéllar's analysis touched on many themes: the need for anti-racist education, issues of representation in the arts and media, inaccurate representations of African religions, the beauty industry (on which he deferred to Black feminist intellectuals), and crime reporting. Notably, he took the position that the government should no longer provide subsidies to Black societies. Unlike other writers who criticized such subsidies because of the ways they coopted and corrupted Black leaders (1.15), Cuéllar asserted that the problem was that these clubs practiced racial discrimination.*

*Membership in Black social clubs declined in the early 1960s and, gradually, the government closed them down, along with almost all independent social groups in Cuba, to be replaced by officially sponsored mass organizations. The Black press also disappeared, as did the Black-themed sections that had been regular features of the mainstream Cuban newspapers. By early 1962, the Cuban government declared, without basis, that racism had been eliminated on the island, putting an end to the campaign against discrimination. Although projects to expand public education, improve housing and sanitation, and provide healthcare provided important improvements in the lives of many Black Cubans, Black writers once again faced pervasive official propaganda that declared racism to be obsolete and denied the need for Black institutions or activism.[50]*

Old **Manuel Cuéllar Vizcaíno** slid his broad hand across his bald dome like a man trying to pull out his hair.

He was on his feet, ready to begin reading his report to the forum on Racist Discrimination, which took place last Wednesday in the Hall of the Martyrs, at the University of Havana.

Cuéllar took out his handkerchief, while at the head table, Dr. Carlos Olivares,[51] the president of the Commission, leaned back to listen to the veteran journalist. Sitting with the man in charge, among others, were Mr. Luis Bonne and the battle-hardened José Moré, President of the Asociación Nacional de Capataces y Auxiliares del Ramo de la Construcción (National Association of Foremen and Assistants in the Construction Sector).[52]

Finally, the journalist, raising his voice just as he did in the days when he read newspapers, books, and magazines aloud to the workers in the cigar factories,[53] presented the following document, which a reporter from *Nuevos Rumbos* took down in shorthand.

## TOWARDS AN INTEGRATIONIST PLAN

To Doctor Carlos Olivares, the official of the Revolutionary Government in charge of the work against harmful discrimination,[54] sent through the channel of our mutual friend Bonne.

---

[50] Benson, *Antiracism in Cuba*; de la Fuente, *A Nation for All*.

[51] Carlos Olivares Sánchez (1929–?), Afro-Cuban writer, activist, and diplomat, ambassador to the Soviet Union from 1962 to 1968.

[52] Luis Bonne Ramírez, Afro-Cuban student leader and revolutionary who later became a mid-level official in the Communist Party in the Province of Guantánamo. We do not have any information on José Moré.

[53] Beginning in the late nineteenth century, Cuban cigar workers commonly pooled resources to pay professional readers to read aloud to them during working hours. See Tinajero, *El Lector*.

[54] "Harmful" (*lesiva*) is a legal term, referencing Article 20 of the Cuban **Constitution of 1940**: "All discrimination for reasons of sex, race, color or class, or any other that is harmful to human dignity is declared illegal and punishable."

EVOLUTION

REVOLUTION

CONSTITUTION

EVOLUTION is natural progress.

REVOLUTION is rapid progress.

The CONSTITUTION is the guarantee of progress that has been achieved.

In EVOLUTION one plants a seed. One plants a seed and waits.

In REVOLUTION one acts, deducing or observing that the fruit is ripe.

The CONSTITUTION must be enforced. There is no other alternative.

Therefore, with an eye to an administrative or integrationist plan, it becomes necessary to discuss each of these three points, which are precisely the ones that the masses do not understand. Misunderstandings abound and reactionaries take advantage of them, criminally.

## EVOLUTION

Doctor Olivares was quite right in suggesting during the Round Table the seeds that are necessary to plant to achieve progress, with particular efforts devoted to childhood and to the popular subconscious. We must urgently undertake reeducation through all methods. Schools. The Fine Arts. Language. Journalistic reporting. The make-up worn by our women, etc.

I point him to the fact that in England they have prohibited the creation of new private schools. Those that already exist will remain open until the end of their course of study. But they will not permit the opening of one more. The [United] Kingdom wants *a level education, without inequalities in English citizenship.*[55]

[Our] artistic representations require rethinking. Above all, we must take care with theater, cinema, and television, providing *integrated* works that reflect Cuba's cordial [social] life, but without trying too hard, that is without inopportune mention of conflict – that is, without calling attention. Because sometimes an author of a work that aspires to be anti-discriminatory falls into exaggerated dramatization. And if not exaggerated, then imprudent. Because there are many real issues, undeniable, which should not be presented to the public in a negative way.

---

[55] Although some Labor politicians did call, unsuccessfully, for banning the aristocratic "public schools," private, fee-based education survived these efforts and continues to thrive in Britain. Kynaston and Green, *Engines of Privilege.*

There is an old tendency in journalism to exaggerate reporting on the Black delinquent, just as there is [a tendency] to hide the good qualities of persons with dark skin. I know what I am talking about. Just as they also confuse the real African religions with unrelated witchcraft, which comes from all over. There is much work to be done with the comrades who write true crime stories, whose greatest enterprise is sensationalism, without considering the harm that they do to the well-being of the nation. I know what I am talking about.

The make-up, the self-presentation, the personal appearance of our women, is colossal and is improving each day. Every day they appear more beautiful. But capriciousness is the rule, and the manufacturers of cosmetics and other beauty products prefer factories for blonde women or *trigueñas*, with capriciousness winning the day again. Because, in all things feminine capriciousness predominates, universally.

That said, it is necessary to re-examine this aspect according to the judgment of Doctor Ana Echegoyen[56] and others of our great ladies, such as Doctor Sántula Ribalta, of the University of Las Villas, with whom I have spoken.

Three or four years ago, Doctor Echegoyen, Professor of Education at our university, presented sixteen shades of the Antillean color scale at an event at the **Club Atenas**. Our girls, from dark Black [*negra prieta*] to the almost White, put on a show of dresses, hairstyles, and make-up. The fashion designers who triumphed were the ones who knew how to choose dresses according to the color and type of each [model]. It was a general triumph for our designers. In any event, the doctors I have mentioned [Echegoyen and Ribalta] will, themselves, provide you with the most accurate answers. I will stop here, convinced that you, simply by glancing over [my letter], know more than I do about EVOLUTION and how to plant its seeds, without the need for more details.

**REVOLUTION**

It is necessary to place Blacks deliberately in positions other than the customary ones. This is the revolutionary [approach], as is nurturing those areas in which they [Blacks] are scarce, where only a few tokens succeed. The state should set the example and then private enterprises should immediately follow suit, in a revolutionary way. The establishment of a legal system for appointments, without consideration

[56] Ana Echegoyen de Cañizares (1901–70), Afro-Cuban feminist, university professor, writer, and education activist.

[of race], will come later. First, [we must] establish the principles to smash harmful discrimination;[57] then, whoever does not rise to the occasion can stay behind. Very strict [enforcement] at the employment offices, which would be ideal in a well-functioning system. To be sure, convincing and providing arguments is also revolutionary labor. The leaders of this Revolution can achieve much by presenting arguments and convincing.

Providing support for those institutions that are already integrated is healthy and revolutionary. White and Black journalists who belong to our professional association have access to our beach resorts.[58] Similarly, doctors and dentists have theirs in Santa María del Mar. In the professions there has been much progress, and patriotism reigns.

When this [attitude] reaches the clubs of the labor unions it will be a great step forward. Union clubs everywhere, with their fabulous assembly-halls, their libraries, and their swimming pools. In all parts [of the island]. It would be best to accomplish this through the industrial federations. And be careful not to offer support to racist societies, whether they be for Blacks or Whites! Not one cent from the government to any of those associations that group men together by the color of their skin! None should be encouraged by funds from the state, by lotteries, or other benefits, because that would be encouraging discrimination! They are all anti-Cuban, and support will be provided only to those that fall in line [by] integrating. It should become established practice to criticize those revolutionaries who attend racist societies.

And enough on this point.

## CONSTITUTION

The Constitution must be enforced.

There is no other alternative.

There is no need, whatsoever, for **complementary laws,** because the Code of Social Defense and other laws establish the punishments. Also, any attorney or any judge knows perfectly well [which acts] are violations against human dignity.

---

[57] See n54 above.

[58] Prior to the revolution, beaches near Havana and other Cuban cities were almost all owned privately by social clubs, professional associations, and labor unions, and were for Whites only. According to Cuéllar Vizcaíno, the journalist and medical associations had, at this point, already desegregated their beach clubs.

The false club that takes strength from the *criollo*'s [Cuban's] shameful adulation of the Yankee cheats the [national] treasury and discriminates harmfully. So do some hotels.

With respect to the regional societies, I interpret them in this way. They are regional.[59] And to be a member, for example, of the Centro Gallego (Galician Center), you must be, or appear to be, Galician. But to be a doctor or laboratory technician [there] you need only the corresponding degrees and certification by the corresponding professional organizations.[60] Because in Cuba one may not deny a job to anyone, nor can the Black doctor be denied [work] at the Centro Gallego because of the color of his skin, just as the White doctor can see Black patients at the clinic of the Unión Fraternal (Fraternal Union),[61] which remains a racist society.

I would not like more legislation, because there are more than enough legal texts and everyone knows which ones to obey. Everyone knows when an act of discrimination is harmful. Against the false club, the law. Against the society protected by the Law of Associations, criticism and the withdrawal of the revolutionary element.[62]

---

[59] "Regional" here refers to the regions of Spain, such as Galicia, from which migrants had arrived in Cuba.

[60] The "regional" societies often offered medical and dental services to their members.

[61] A prominent Black social club in Havana, founded in the nineteenth century.

[62] The original version of this article continued onto the next page of the magazine. Unfortunately, the copy that we were able to consult was incomplete, ending here.

# CHAPTER 3

# Family, Education, and Uplift

## INTRODUCTION

Most contributors to the Black press shared their larger societies' conviction that the family was the basic building block of national life. Families were the cell-level structures through which nations were constituted. And if orderly, disciplined families were foundational to orderly, disciplined nations, they were even more essential for the Black population, who because of the vicissitudes of slavery and poverty found it especially difficult to constitute family units that fit the national ideal. Yet, these writers worried, the failure to do so both confirmed racist stereotypes and fatally impeded Black efforts to advance socially and economically. As a result, the Black periodicals returned again and again to what contributors saw as the need to create stable families and the consequences of not doing so.

In this view, families began with marriage, or at the very least with community-sanctioned unions. Black men and women, the papers charged, were far too reluctant to contract such unions. "We dare not put forth the percentage of us who are married," reported the Cuban paper *Labor Nueva*. "The statistics are painful and embarrassing" (3.9). Too many men (according to the papers) preferred the freedom and indulgences of the single life, and too many women fell into the trap of single motherhood. "Bachelorhood defiles and debases women," the Argentine paper *La Juventud* argued in 1878 (3.4; see also 3.5), a position echoed by the Brazilian paper *O Clarim da Alvorada* half a century later (3.11). Other writers reasoned that men and women complemented each other and were not meant to live apart (3.4, 3.10, 3.12). The Black papers thus played an important role in disseminating and enforcing a particular set of ideas about proper manhood and womanhood, and the centrality of sanctioned heterosexual unions, in communities with diverse opinions and practices.

Just as challenging as creating stable unions, writers argued, was the care and nurturing of the children produced both within and outside those unions. The poverty that afflicted most Black families forced many of them to send their children to work (3.5) or, even worse, to seek their livings unsupervised in the street (3.1). Some parents abandoned their children completely (3.7); others handed them over to White families, who all too often exploited their unpaid domestic labor (3.12). The papers urged all Black parents, whether single or married, to retain their children within the family unit and to inculcate them with morality, discipline, and a serious work ethic (3.1, 3.2, 3.5, 3.8, 3.10, 3.11, 3.12).

All the papers agreed on the need to educate Black children and on the kind of education those children should receive. *La Juventud* in Argentina, *La Verdad* in Uruguay, *Labor Nueva* in Cuba, and O *Clarim da Alvorada* in Brazil all concurred on the desirability of vocational education in the skilled trades over university-level professional preparation (3.5, 3.8, 3.9, 3.11). Racial barriers to Black entry into the professions, and the great investments of time and effort required for university studies, argued strongly for technical education over the liberal arts.

Meanwhile, what about those families who invested everything in bringing up their children and then suffered the unspeakable calamity of a child's (or more than one child's) death? This was a fate that befell all too many Black (and White, and Indigenous) families in the region; in the pages of *El Unionista*, bereaved parent Santiago Elejalde left a moving reflection on the loss of his two young sons: "Let us cry, then, all who have lost loved ones, be they small or grown" (3.3).

### DISCUSSION QUESTIONS

- Some of these articles explicitly blame parents and other Black adults for the problems facing Black communities. To quote Argentine writer and musician **Zenón Rolón**, "if the White man scorns you, the fault is yours for not making yourselves worthy" (3.5). Yet several articles offer hints of some disagreement over where blame lay and where Black writers should place their efforts. One writer argued that women who became pregnant outside of wedlock should not be "condemned to derision and shame" (3.7). Another revealed that he had heard critics argue that it would be better to speak "to the Whites, among whom [these prejudices] live" (3.9). Another suggested that the snobbery of elite Black people was more damaging to the community than the misbehavior of a few (3.6). What do you think of these different positions? Which, if any, of these perspectives seem justified by the facts presented in the articles?

- Why do you think that the Black papers so frequently advocated for vocational education, instead of domestic service on the one hand or university degrees on the other, as the approach most likely to pay dividends to the Black community? Which of the reasons they offered seem convincing to you? What flaws or problems do you see in their approach?

- *O Clarim da Alvorada* proposed that "the family is the mother-cell of all civil society. The family is the union of the man and the wife with their children, under the government of the man" (3.11). But this is not the only way to organize families. How did writers' acceptance of a narrow ideal of what constituted a moral family shape their view of the many Black people who could not or chose not to conform to that ideal? Do you think that the fact that most writers were men influenced the ways that they thought and wrote about these topics? How might different definitions or different personal experiences have led to different conclusions about the state of Black families?

- Based on what you read in these articles, what do you think it would have been like to be a Black child in one of these cities? Who would be likely to be living in your household? What kinds of work would you be expected to do? Would you go to school? If so, would your classmates be White or Black? How would expectations around your behavior be different if you were a boy or a girl? How different might your experience have been if you were a child in the 1870s, the 1910s, or the 1930s?

## 3.1 "EDUCATION, AND SOME PARENTS OF OUR SOCIETY," EL PROGRESISTA (MONTEVIDEO, URUGUAY: SEPT. 4, 1873)

*A constant theme in the Black press, in every country, was the pressing need for Afrodescendant children to be educated. Often this message was directed at Black parents in the harshly moralizing tone adopted by this writer in El Progresista. Like its neighbor Argentina, Uruguay was a pioneer in Latin America for its early establishment of obligatory public education. But that initiative did not begin until the late 1870s, after this*

*article had appeared. In the meantime, in surveying the Black commu-
nity's educational challenges,* El Progresista *blamed not national policy
but rather the failures of Black parents. The paper described gangs of
children roaming the city in search of cast-off items to salvage and sell (a
topic addressed in Montevideo's mainstream newspapers as well) and
charged Black parents with dereliction of their parental duties. The writer
urged parents to remove their children from the dangers of the street and
place them in public schools (which did exist at that time but not in
numbers sufficient to serve the total population).*

Now that we once again have the opportunity to take up the journalist's
pen and freely and spontaneously state our aspirations, or better said, our
ideas, we will begin with a few words on the scant discipline, and abundant freedom, that some parents give their children.

One sees that while on the one hand our race progresses, on the other
we have to lament the greatest of calamities, which is, as we said previously, *the little education that some parents give their children.*

If you think not, let's fix our gaze on those moving scenes that we can
contemplate daily without going very far, some with one's heart pierced
by pain, others with a smile on one's lips, a smile of triumph that some
people only display when they contemplate a nearby scene of misery.

But let's continue with the subject of education.

We will begin by painting one of those sad pictures that one sees with
frequency with these unfortunate creatures.

Let us direct our steps, if we wish to witness one of these heartrending
scenes, to the outskirts of our city, and we will see there a gang of urchins
in search of bones, iron, etc. But they busy themselves not only with that
sad task; most of the time they spend in foolishness of different sorts,
insulting with outrageous comments those who do not follow their corrupt and degrading doctrines, or throwing stones at peaceful passers-by,
or abusing each other over all kinds of trifles.

Most of those unhappy beings belong to our society [of color].

Now for those parents who send their children in search of bones,
iron, and other articles, wouldn't it be better to send them to school,
where they could polish their understanding and be shown the road to
civilization?

Wouldn't it be better for those idle parents, instead of showing their
children the road to vice, to set them on the path of virtue?

Isn't it the greater glory of parents to see their children defend the rights
of their forebears?

We think that the hearts of those who consider themselves true parents cannot experience a greater joy.

But these [parents] are not like that. Those who steer their children toward the road of depravity are not parents; they cannot be considered worthy to hold that sacred name.

Those parents who give their children all the free will that they desire, without considering that later on this will be their perdition, do not realize that they are their children's guide, that they steer them not just on the road of degradation but to the fetid cells of prison.

Not long ago we were among the onlookers who had to lament one of these heartrending, terrible scenes.

A mother, full of suffering and her eyes flooded with tears, asked one of the most important people in our city, almost on her knees, to intervene in the matter of her child who was behind bars.

But this mother didn't understand that the blame for the misfortune in which her child found himself fell to no one other than to her.

Poor child, who had fallen from the lush and pleasure-loving field of liberty to the corrupting and contagious prison of the guilty.

And why?

Because his parents, instead of having shown him the road of virtue, showed him the road of ignominy; they didn't know to place him under the orders of a teacher who would tirelessly and indefatigably cultivate his meager talents, to send him on the path by which men enjoy their rights and freedoms, in all their plenitude.

But that man, one of many who reprimand these mothers for the excessive liberty of their children, gave as his only reply to the afflicted mother:

Evil mother, you still have the effrontery to come before me, after I have given you the greatest advice on how to raise your child? You didn't know how to follow that advice, and now you suffer your remorse and the disgrace of your child.

*You are to blame for your misfortune; if instead of sending your child in search of bones and other trifles, you had sent him to school, none of this would have happened.*

There it is, heartless parents, who send your children in search of vile objects: see this example, which is enough to make your faces burn and your hearts tighten.

Give your children education, because God proclaims it from his heavenly throne, teach your children and you will see, crowning your faces, the pure halo with which the Creator rewards those who keep his holy commandments.

But do not teach evil to your children, because then divine justice will fall on your heads.

Set your children on the path of virtue, and keep them away, with all the vigilance that it takes, from the road of *reproach* and *ignominy*.

That is enough for today.

### 3.2 "LUXURY," LA JUVENTUD (BUENOS AIRES, ARGENTINA: JULY 2 AND 9, 1876)

*Clothing, and the question of luxury, was hotly debated in the Afro-Argentine press (for similar debates in Cuba, see 5.6). In the late nineteenth century, the residents of Buenos Aires focused heavily on appearances. The city's burgeoning print culture depicted dressing elegantly after the latest fashions as a statement of belonging in the modern city. This presented a particular challenge for Afro-Argentines, who had long been depicted in visual and textual representations of slavery as ill-dressed, and who generally had limited means. Their efforts to dress fashionably were sometimes met with stereotypes that cast Black people in finery as comically overdressed. Such efforts also sometimes incited the disapproval of fellow Afro-Argentines, who saw expensive clothes as a betrayal of the community's working-class origins and solidarities. This article by a rare female contributor to the Afro-Argentine press highlighted the gendered and domestic dimensions of this critique. The author warned that "exorbitant" sartorial tastes in young girls threatened their modesty, generosity toward others, and future happiness as wives and mothers.*

When I see girls as young as five years old in exorbitantly priced dresses, fully embroidered and with ribbons at the waist that cost a hundred pesos per yard; hats made of the most exquisite velvet, adorned with fine, and extremely expensive, feathers; velvet boots, long gloves, and English lace at the neck and sleeves – when I see girls dressed this way, I feel pain in my soul.

How will these children become accustomed to the simplicity, the modesty that are so becoming in an adult woman? How will mothers be able to steer them away from the desire for luxury, when they themselves have induced it? How will these young girls become good wives and above all good mothers if their own mothers, accustoming them to luxury, set them up for unhappiness? The first ill they inflict [upon their daughters] is the boredom arising from having all their desires met – they become capricious. Nonetheless, society considers them fortunate, and they end up believing themselves entitled to be scornful toward other [girls and women]. And yet the woman of worldliness and experience looks at them with a smile on her lips and oppression in her soul.

In sum, it is undeniable that luxury chills the soul and leaves it numb to all generous sentiments, because little by little, and irreversibly, those poor women become accustomed to feeling love – but not for the sublime, for the beautiful and the great. They feel love, yes, but for appearances, for things that are eye-catching, and for *gold*, always gold, though it offers little progress.

Catalina

### 3.3 "GIVE WAY TO NOBLE SENTIMENTS," EL UNIONISTA (BUENOS AIRES, ARGENTINA: JAN. 20, 1878)

*Reports of the deaths of young children were, sadly, quite common in Buenos Aires' Black press in the 1870s and 1880s. Infant and childhood mortality rates were exceedingly high across the city in the years before running water, sewage, and widespread sanitation campaigns. But rates were highest among the city's poor and working-class sectors, to which most Afro-Argentines belonged. In this article, Santiago Elejalde[1] shared his grief at the loss, in quick succession, of his two young sons (Joaquín, 3 months, and Santiago, 2 years and 4 months). Strikingly, Elejalde defied contemporary conventions of masculinity that prized stoicism, self-restraint, and silent suffering, instead baring his pain as a bereaved father and counseling others to do the same. Only through such unburdening of "noble sentiments," he suggested, could one find resignation and peace.*

There are difficult moments in a man's life, when it is impossible to contradict the impulses of the heart and to transmit to the page anything but its sensations, be they happy or sad, sweet or bitter.

This life that appears so pleasant to us has its sorrows and unavoidable sufferings, which can rip apart the soul of the most indifferent [man]. Happy is he who escapes life's sufferings – something exceedingly difficult to do.

There are depraved beings, corrupted hearts, which look upon everything with indifference. But there comes a day when, touched by regret,

---

[1] Santiago Elejalde (1853–?) was an Argentine journalist, congressional orderly, and entrepreneur. María de Lourdes Ghidoli, "Elejalde, Santiago and Mateo," in Knight and Gates, *Dictionary*, vol. II, pp. 444–45.

they are moved, they cry, and they suffer. For we are all subject to that harsh but inexorable law of nature, which can be summarized in these brief words: live, suffer, die.

And in effect, happiness is a flattering illusion that preoccupies our imagination in vain, and that almost always abandons us when we begin to become lulled, fascinated by the pleasures it offers us.

A bitter truth: just yesterday, my humble dwelling was a divine mansion that afforded happiness. In it were three angels who contributed to its luster. Many times, fatigued by the tasks of the day and weighed down by the heavy burden that the obligation of fatherhood imposes upon men of the [working] poor, I returned to my home to rest from my labors.

How great was my joy when I saw two of my children running hurriedly to greet me, extending their little hands! "Papa, what did you bring us?" was the first thing they said, and both began to cover me in kisses.

Who would fail to enjoy this or to count himself fortunate? The greatest happiness to which one could aspire in this world is to have someone to sweeten one's hours of exhaustion by affording such pleasures.

Yet fate has wished that two of those children, who only yesterday exuded health and made my poor existence sweeter, should disappear from the world just as they began to live. But they had already kindled in their parents' hearts a deep love, and even awakened the curiosity of strangers for their vivaciousness.

A child who speaks, who replies like a mature person, who even in his last moments recognizes his own [family], who looks with loving eyes upon his father and mother and who embraces them and holds them tight, such was my Santiago. My Joaquín did not [yet] speak, but this did not prevent him from attracting his mother's attention and mine through his tender glances and the movements of his little hands, which seemed to want to say something.

When children disappear from life in such a way, the spirit is disturbed and the soul is shaken. This is why my heart is overwhelmed by pain in this moment and cannot write anything other than its sensations.

I understand everything, and I know there is no longer any remedy. I am prepared to let myself be ruled by resignation. If I cry, it is in my role as a father, and who can deny me this only consolation?

These noble sentiments cannot be smothered in the depths of our soul, for they would spell our end. They need room to expand so as to give way to resignation, without which no calm or tranquility is possible. Let us cry, then, all who have lost loved ones, be they small or grown, for the

suffering is no different, and the heart needs to unburden itself to give way
to resignation, the only balm that heals the wound of souls in pain.

S[antiago] Elejalde

### 3.4 "MARRIAGE AND ITS BENEFITS TO SOCIETY," LA JUVENTUD (BUENOS AIRES, ARGENTINA: JAN. 13, 1878)

*Through this editorial, Arístides Oliveira – a Brazilian-born man who rose
to prominence in the Afro-***Porteño*** community as an orator, writer, and
active member of several associations – offered a fervent argument in
favor of matrimony. Legitimate marriage was essential to curtailing the
licentious and unproductive impulses of single men (who, Oliveira suggested, preferred a life of reckless freedom, perversion, and dissipation)
and harnessing their energies toward the project of productive manhood
and virtuous fatherhood. Marriage also brought benefits to women,
ensuring they would be respected and supported by devoted husbands,
and to children, who would be spared the stain and vulnerability of
illegitimacy (3.7). The patriarchal family created by marriage was also
the cornerstone of social order, comprising a "small state within the
State." For Oliveira, as for other Afrodescendant writers in and beyond
Argentina in these years, it therefore seemed urgent that Afrodescendant
men in particular submit to their obligations within heterosexual families
in order to prove their moral probity and worth to the broader society.*

In all eras and in all countries, marriage has been honored and bachelorhood censured. The Hebrews excluded bachelors from their assemblies.
The Spartans forbade them from entering their theaters, and they had
instituted festivals in which women were flogged in public squares.[2] The
Romans did not accept [bachelors'] testimony in legal affairs, and they
solemnly honored the virtuous citizens who had contracted many succes-
sive matrimonies.

In early Christian times, bachelorhood was considered grounds for
disqualification from public office. For long periods in Germany and in
Switzerland, the riches of bachelors devolved to the state after their death.

In other countries, [the state] imposed taxes on them.

Why was marriage awarded such respect? Why was bachelorhood held
in such dishonor?

---

[2] This appears to be a reference to the annual ceremony of *diamastigosis*, in which boys and
young men (not women) received public whippings as a religious rite of passage.

Because always, and in all eras, it has been understood that marriage was the cornerstone of the social edifice, and that bachelorhood was one of the oldest agents of its destruction.

Indeed, with marriage populations grow, [whereas] bachelorhood tends to make them decrease. And it is unquestionable that a state whose population decreases declines visibly.

With marriage there is order and harmony in society. Women are considered man's best companion, the family forms a homogeneous whole, an association that binds members who differ in ideas, sex, strength, and tendencies, subjecting them all to a single authority: that of the father.

This small state within the state is immensely useful to the social order.

Bachelorhood defiles and debases women, subjecting them to an odious burden and making them the toy of [men's] passions; it engenders only disorder, disturbances, divisions and even crimes. With marriage there is morality in society. Men fulfill the duty that nature has imposed upon them, and they preserve, amid the gentle pleasures of family, the treasure of good habits, dedicating themselves with eagerness to the labors and hardships of educating their children.

In bachelorhood, men – abusing a liberty that exonerates them from all responsibility – feed the flames of their perverse instincts. In satisfying [these instincts], they unscrupulously desecrate the domestic hearth and the sanctity of marriage, working ceaselessly to corrupt [society's] customs and abandoning to public charity the fruits of their rakish escapades.

So important is marriage to society, that experience demonstrates that over the same number of years, proportionately more bachelors die than married men, and that the latter live longer than the former. **Buffon** has held this opinion, and later demonstrated it (and many other things) to be true. It is easy to notice this advantage inherent to the married state; husband and wife, despite the hardships and cares particular to this condition, come together according to natural laws, reciprocally completing each other's faculties. They help each other, they come to each other's aid, they mutually console and care for one another. They are compelled to devote themselves to greater activity, [and] exercise and work are the firm pillars of health and virtue.

The bachelor, always distracted by new goals, hounded by pleasures, frequently straining his nature, and even seeking to preserve through his excesses a fleeting and clandestine love, exhausts his nervous system, debilitates his strength, [and] wastes his body in the excessive repetition of sensual pleasures.

It is known that a man alone and without a fixed course easily falls prey to boredom and hypochondria; he becomes sad, ill-humored, and sometimes develops a horror of life. The cause that often keeps many men in bachelorhood is the corruption of their habits. The man who lives in dissipation no longer finds in his heart those strong and virile virtues that would make him prefer the austerity of duty to the charms of misleading pleasures. He believes himself free – why place himself under a yoke?

If he can alight, like a butterfly, on this or that love, why chain himself with indissoluble bonds? He has no responsibility for his actions – why overwhelm himself with the heavy burden of family? And besides, with his crude pleasures, would he know how to understand the gentleness of pure love and the sweet pleasures of fatherhood?

We have heard it said many times that the luxury of our era dissuades [men] from marriage, because it is very expensive to maintain a wife and children.

One could perhaps accept this reasoning, but only in very few occasions. Examine the life of the bachelor: you will see that it is more expensive, and that keeping sweethearts drains more gold, than an orderly marriage.

Recall [Benjamin] Franklin's famous phrase: "feeding a vice costs more than raising three children."[3]

Marriage is the common, natural calling of the prudent, orderly, chaste man.

Let him therefore fulfill his destiny.

A[rístides] Oliveira

### 3.5 AND 3.6 A DEBATE OVER PROPER BEHAVIOR (BUENOS AIRES, ARGENTINA: 1878)

*From his temporary residence in Florence, Italy, Afro-Argentine musician* **Zenón Rolón** *took stock of the situation of his fellow Afro-Argentines, especially those in Buenos Aires, and declared it lamentable. In "A Few Words to My Brothers by Race"[4] (3.5), Rolón spoke directly to members of a community that, in his view, had failed to take full advantage of the*

---

[3] Franklin's original quotation is, "What maintains one vice would bring up two children."

[4] The pamphlet was also referred to as "A Few Words to My Brothers by Caste." On the distinction between "caste" and "race" in this context, see Geler, *Andares negros*, pp. 187–91.

freedoms afforded by independence and abolition. Though legally and civically free, Afro-Argentines remained in bondage to the "vile passions" of idleness, ignorance, immorality (alcoholism, violence, prostitution, obscenity), servility, disunity, and luxury (3.2). Rolón was aware that, in thus airing the community's internal problems, he risked alienating some of his "brothers by race" and providing grist for anti-Black stereotypes (hence his warning to Whites who were "not progressive" to "burn this book"). Yet in his view, the greater risk was that some Afro-Argentines, in their public misbehavior, confirmed those shameful stereotypes in ways that irreparably damaged the community's dignity and its members' collective standing as citizens. Rolón's pamphlet is an unusually stark example of the "respectability politics"[5] of a relatively privileged sector of Afrodescendants who, in Buenos Aires as in other parts of Latin America, sought to bring the rest of their community into line with bourgeois social expectations (see also 3.4, 3.9, 3.10, 3.11).

Rolón's pamphlet generated great controversy in the Afro-**Porteño** community and press, as the irate response by La Perla collaborator Julio Cabot (3.6) illustrates. The exchange reveals the variety of experiences within the community, primarily related to class, as articulated around touchstone issues: education, child-rearing, and work (training children in the arts and trades versus placing them in service [see also 3.8, 3.11]), as well as proper comportment for women and men. Cabot defended the worth, honor, and progress of "our society" on all of those dimensions. He did so by insisting that Afro-Porteños' humble backgrounds and occupations were nothing to be ashamed of. And whereas Rolón grouped all Afro-Porteños into the same category, Cabot made internal distinctions, emphasizing that any individuals who acted dishonorably were, by definition, not part of "our society." The subtext of Cabot's response, as of many of his contemporaries, was that Rolón was elitist, jaundiced, and hopelessly out of touch with his own community.

---

[5] Historian Evelyn Brooks Higginbotham defines the "politics of respectability," in relation to the African American experience, as follows: "Respectability demanded that every individual in the Black community assume responsibility for behavioral self-regulation and self-improvement along moral, educational, and economic lines: the goal was to distance oneself as far as possible from images perpetuated by racist stereotypes." *Righteous Discontent*, p. 196.

## 3.5 "Zenón Rolón's Pamphlet," *La Juventud* (Buenos Aires, Argentina: June 30, 1878)[6]

### Preface

As I took up my pen to address these lines to you, I doubted – as I still doubt – the reception and welcome you may give them. But encouraged by the honest intentions of my thoughts, I have pushed aside all manner of fear, and the proof of this lies in these *few words* that, however poorly, I have the honor to present to you.

Since I believe you, dear readers, to be my brothers by race, I hope you will find in them, if not a consolation, then at least evidence that one of our own takes an interest in the common cause. But if, on the contrary, you are White and not progressive – then burn this book, I beg you, [for] it could harm you.

To whom better than you [my brothers by race] could I dedicate this tract? To no one, assuming you are the ones destined to value its aims.

I have no illusions, nor am I capable, of offering you a literary essay, but rather, and humbly, a badly organized treatise. If it has any merit at all, it is my good intention and patience in composing it. And if it were to achieve my purposes, that would be the greatest reward imaginable for your young friend,

**Zenón Rolón** (Florence, June 16, 1877)

### A Few Words to My Brothers by Race

> The world belongs to the brave.
>
> (German proverb)

When I contemplate the map of the world and see, drawn upon it, these extensive continents inhabited by many and diverse men; when I observe their capricious configuration, and when I reflect upon the immense past of our globe and the chaos in which it once lay, my eyes instinctively seek those two pieces that so resemble each other – Africa and South America!

In one I see the origin of the sons of **Cain**, and in the other, their vicissitudes and moral progress.

---

[6] Editors' note: we have omitted the prefatory remarks by the editors of *La Juventud*, and we include only the first (larger) installment of Rolón's tract. The second installment appeared in *La Juventud* on July 10, 1878.

Our race was divided between two continents and two religions. But if we compare our progress to those inert Africans, we can see that at least they preserve the attribute of independence. For if they be slaves, they are slaves to their own kind, whereas we, to our shame – despite the great steps that **England** took to free us from the slave-trading pirates; despite the sympathy that all great men have had for our cause and the interest they have taken therein – have remained in the same position and in the same condition in which we were left by those who, republicans by principle and avengers of humanity, cut our chains.

May of 1810 and January of 1855 are two memorable dates for the history of our political revolutions, and for our race.(1)[7]

The South American revolution resulted in the expulsion of the Iberians, our oppressors. Blessed be this revolution that brings so much glory to all South Americans. It is also one of the greatest pages of History, [for] it brought not just the freedom and progress of an entire continent, but also avenged this part of humanity [Africans and their descendants] that had long been unjustly trampled.

Half a century has elapsed, and still we see our brothers oppressed in plain sight.(2)[8] Today, this crusade no longer concerns England nor others as it once did – it falls to us by the laws of nature.

I do not understand, nor do I want to stir up in [others'] spirits, the revolution of hatred – no. I speak of a moral revolution, the daughter of education and law, perfected through work and duty, which are the inexhaustible sources of the wealth of nations.

Having thus hastily sketched our history, let me now examine what steps we have taken. Let me examine our current state and see what progress has been made. I will demonstrate this in just a few words: Our race, having lost the purity of its heart and the dignity of the individual, moves through life idle, dissolute and depraved. The cry of freedom that resounded in its ear was not understood for what it was, nor was it received with the honest joy of those who aspire, through [freedom], to work and education. And so [our race], not understanding that it was thereby freed from the control of others, ended up becoming a slave to its

---

[7] Footnote in the original; see below. Rolón refers to May 25, 1810, when Buenos Aires declared self-government from Spain, and to January 5, 1855, the decisive last battle of a Liberal insurrection in Peru that deposed the reigning Conservative government and resulted in the abolition of Indigenous tribute (a tax imposed exclusively on Indigenous people) and of slavery.

[8] Footnote in the original; see below. The reference is to Brazil, which did not abolish slavery until 1888.

own vile passions. Chains gave way to vice, and vice gave way to ignorance – a degradation all the greater for being self-imposed.

And what of [our race's] progress? *It consists of the short trousers, the bare feet, and the hemp shirt of our forebears having given way to the frock coat, the gloves, and the [walking] cane.*

Are we to call it progress that, while you dress with the same luxury and care as those who can afford to, you are ignorant, and servants? As greatly as I esteem you, so do I wish to see you [dressed] in all possible luxury, but educated, knowing your responsibilities and your rights, so as not to be consigned to servitude.

Do not object to this. Much less should you ask whether this be my advice, this the defense I seek to make for our cause. For in pointing out your faults, my spirit is not haunted by fears of the curses with which you might seek to brand me. I harbor no hopes based on interest, except that of speaking the truth. I reserve that right, for we are joined by the love [that binds] brothers and compatriots.

I recall that, while strolling through the outskirts of the beautiful city [Buenos Aires], I saw you with knife in hand, or speaking obscene words, or with whores. I saw you unhinged by wine, scorned by *all* – [saw you] be your children's shame and your own ruin. I heard you being branded as **compadritos**, with that ever-so-expressive phrase, *he is acting like a black!*[9]

Do you not yet feel ashamed? Well, the time has come. And the day must need come when that spell of stultification in which you are submerged will break, [and you will] remember that you are men and will behave as such.

I do not mean to say with this that I expect you all to become doctors and university graduates. It would be impossible. It is enough to be craftsmen, for in them we find the most honest, the truest citizen. The greatest and most powerful nations are precisely those built on manufacturing, and consequently, their wealth lies in the worker.

At present, you are nothing. It does not even occur to you that in the Argentine Republic – where, incidentally, our numbers exceed eight to ten thousand men of color – there are many families [of color] who live as servants in the homes of Whites, and these go unseen, along with so many of our [families] that become concealed, so to speak, by our own doing.[10]

---

[9] "*Ha hecho cosa de negro,*" or the shorter "*cosa de negro,*" was and remains a common phrase in Argentine Spanish, meaning something reprehensible, shameful, or bungled.

[10] The author seems to refer here to the processes by which Afro-Argentines became officially invisible toward the end of the nineteenth century, as national censuses and other state records suppressed a race or color variable (Andrews, *The Afro-Argentines of Buenos Aires*). Rolón suggests that Afro-Argentines are undercounted, partly because of the

Do not dismiss these as fables. And if to excuse yourselves you should tell me that you have no means or fortune, that the White man still scorns you, that you were not educated, that no one has taught you anything, I will respond that you have minds, that you should think. For if the White man scorns you, the fault is yours for not making yourselves worthy even of yourselves.

In terms of education, I tell you that schools exist, and that if you valued your children a bit more, they would have learned. No examples are necessary to convince you of this. And yet, what happens? You have a child who has barely reached puberty, and instead of giving him a trade, you look to place him as – what? – a servant, a coachman, a cook, a cart driver, etc., etc. Such is the education he receives, and therefore, that is what he knows.

But if instead of taking him to Mister N. to place him among his servants, out of an interest in the lucrative salary that debases your child, you were to lead him to a craftsman, would this not be better for him? At least he would be free in his own right, and a true citizen.

The craftsman, like the farmer, can hold his head up without blushing.

The most famous and greatest men have been sons of the common people – Giotto, Ghiberti, Michelangelo, Galileo, Canova, Verdi, Garibaldi, Moltke[11] and so many others were born in conditions like yours. That has not prevented them from bringing honor and glory to the countries of their birth.

America itself offers us plentiful examples, such as [George] Washington, [Benjamin] Franklin, [Andrew] Jackson, [Thomas] Jefferson, [Abraham] Lincoln, Perry, [William] Penn, [Andrew] Johnson, and Wellington.[12]

---

situation of many families who lived with employers (rather than in independent house-holds) and partly because many families concealed their own African origin.

[11] These were all European men who achieved fame across different fields: Giotto di Bondone (d. 1337), Lorenzo Ghiberti (1378–1455), Michelangelo di Lodovico Buonarroti Simoni (1475–1564), and Antonio Canova (1757–1822) were Italian artists; Galileo Galilei (1564–1642) was an Italian astronomer, physicist, and engineer; Giuseppe Verdi (1813–1901) was an Italian opera composer; Giuseppe Garibaldi (1807–82) and Helmuth Karl Bernhard von Moltke (1800–91) were military leaders in Italy and Prussia respectively.

[12] We are not able to identify which Perry or Wellington Rolón meant to include here, possibly Admiral Matthew C. Perry and Arthur Wellesley, Duke of Wellington. Wellesley was not American, and neither man would typically be identified as a "son of the common people," but then neither would Penn, Washington, or Jefferson.

And having already examined our own insignificant progress, I must conclude with its cause, that [which] exhausts our strengths and impedes our progress, and which lies within us: that, *jealous each of the other, we live divided even in the bosom of our own families.*

The degree of unity among our race in the other South American republics is unknown to me, but it is possible to deduce what it might be. For example, among us, the spirit of associationism does not exist. If we get as far as forming an association, it is because of the speculative self-interest we suppose to find in it in that moment – and if I say "speculative," it is because [our interest] is not born of fraternal feeling, nor of honest and philanthropic aims. But we will, no doubt, find [the spirit of associationism] for throwing parties and disguising ourselves for **Carnival** – buffooneries fit for those who, having nothing better to do, waste time and resources.

[*La Juventud*'s] NOTE – The other part of the Pamphlet will appear in our next issue.

———————

(1) I say "our political revolutions," because since the African race is widespread also in South America, we must consider it as American. May of 1810 and January of 1855 are two great moments of the revolution. The first had its origins on the shores of the [Río de la] Plata – in Argentina, and two years later, the cry of liberty was transported across the **Andes** Mountains by that genius of war, General [**José de**] **San Martín**. The second, in 1855, saw Iberian power at last defeated in Peru, for although these were not the same Spaniards who fought in the revolutionary wars, it was their party.

Argentina, Chile, and Peru are the three cardinal points of our independence, and where freedom from slavery was preciously born through the influence of various great South American men, while England kept up the attack on the slaving ships.

On this subject, it is for me a duty and a need to devote a few words to the great philosopher of South America, the great republican, the heir of Mazzini,[13] the great defender of humanity – Francisco Bilbao.[14]

His image should live *in the heart of the men of color*, he, the great socialist, who like a new Jesus Christ, predicating equality, achieved *the resurrection of the Blacks* – he is and must always be for us a great book of revelations and advice, to which we must immediately refer whenever we have need of great thoughts.

(2) It is true; [more than] half a century has elapsed from 1810 until the present, and we still see them [our brothers] oppressed in Brazil.

———————

[13] Giuseppe Mazzini (1805–72), Italian politician, revolutionary, and proponent of social-democratic republicanism.

[14] Francisco Bilbao Barquín (1823–65) was a Chilean writer, philosopher, and politician inspired by the more radical messages of the 1848 revolutionaries in France, where he spent several years. He joined the popular Liberal uprising in Peru in 1854–55 but broke with the new government for not being radical enough.

### 3.6 "Rolón's Pamphlet," *La Perla* (Buenos Aires, Argentina: Aug. 1, 1878)

[Special contribution]

> There is no error that can be useful,
> nor truth that can cause harm.
>
> [Joseph] de Maistre, *St. Petersburg Dialogues*, vol. I, p. 491

We mentioned in an earlier article that there are charitable people who might sometimes play the role of parents, and it is in fact true: the proof is **[Zenón] Rolón**. All he had for a parent was a charitable lady who gave him his education.[15]

Rolón says: "You are servants, and ignorant." I ask: who was he? He was not a servant. Or has he forgotten what he once was, because he has gone to study in Europe?

In his country, those servants, coachmen, etc. are, for the most part, educated people. Some [may be] more learned than others, but they have an education – and so much so, that anyone who did not know any better might, when speaking to one of them, take them for a Rolón or another sage of the sort.

We arrive at this: "Whores."

We do not understand how a doctor of laws (as many claim Rolón to be) could commit such errors.[16] Whom is he calling whores? The young women of our society? We refuse to believe him, because that would be an insolent insult, since the young women of our society are the same ones Rolón has courted. If he refers to the [young women] who frequent the dance halls called *peringundes*,[17] those [young women] are not of our society – neither they nor the young men who also attend, for a great distance separates them [from us].

It might happen that some of our color frequent [such halls], but this does not amount to saying that they belong to our society. So detached are they that if one ever tries to speak to them (out of mere courtesy) about any useful thing, they refuse, and nothing can force them to draw nearer to us.

---

[15] This appears to be a sarcastic reference to the scholarship Rolón received from the government to study music in Florence (the "charitable lady" is the Argentine Republic).

[16] To our knowledge, Rolón never received a law degree.

[17] *Peringundes* (or *peringundines*) was another name for dance venues of questionable repute, also known as **academias**.

To say that our society has not progressed amounts to a simple lie or to ignorance of our social life.

Rolón, who makes a show of being so well versed in national history, and who has cited Deán Funes[18] for us, must not be ignorant of the fact that since the year 1820, the Argentine Republic has not had ten years of peace.[19] For those who, in moments of calm, dedicated themselves to doing something useful, there soon came the call to the barracks and everything went to the Devil. The only ones left behind were those who went abroad or hid under their beds to escape the carnage.

It is for that reason, along with others that shall remain unmentioned,[20] that our society has not progressed.

Our society has had great mutual aid associations. If they have perished, it was because of the causes I outlined above.[21] Even today there exists an association with that objective, which in practiced hands might yield good results.[22] So much has our community progressed that there has been an act of great moral significance for us, and that has been the creation of political clubs, so that we may ride the coattails of the *caudillos* of the neighborhood-level party committees.[23]

If dissent exists within any given association, [it is because] that is the end result of all associations, whichever they may be. What is more: if in order to say what Rolón says in his pamphlet he had to cite resounding names like Galileo, Verdi, and Lincoln, he could just as well have cited Catriel or Namuncurá[24] for all the difference it would have made.

---

[18] Gregorio Funes (1749–1829), known as Deán (Dean) Funes, was a clergyman, politician, writer, and the rector of the university of his native province of Córdoba, Argentina. The citation of Funes appears in the second installment (*La Juventud,* July 10, 1878), not included in this volume.

[19] The author refers to the decades of civil wars and other internecine political conflicts that followed on the heels of independence in 1816.

[20] In a subsequent article, Cabot chastised Rolón and others for belonging to "aristocratic" social clubs that differentiated by status as well as color, admitting brown men (*"pardos"*) but not Blacks.

[21] The author refers to La Fraternal (founded in the 1850s), dissolved in the 1870s due partly to internal conflicts.

[22] La Protectora, a mutual aid association founded by Eugenio Sar in 1877, remained in existence at least through the 1940s, although with an increasingly White membership.

[23] The *caudillo electoral* was the leader of the *comités*, neighborhood-level party organizations that secured loyalty by distributing low-level jobs, favors, and other kinds of patronage to potential voters (see 1.1, 1.4).

[24] Catriel was the dynastic name of several chiefs of the Pampa Indigenous peoples of Argentina. The author probably refers to his contemporary, Juan José Catriel (d. 1879). Manuel Namuncurá (c. 1811–1908) was a chief of the Mapuche Indigenous people. On some Afro-Argentine writers' dismissive attitudes toward Indigenous people, see 6.1.

He could have kept silent, and it would have been much better, for our community has never needed Rolón to come and give us lessons.

Julio Cabot

### 3.7 "CHILDREN ORPHANED THOUGH THEIR PARENTS LIVE," LA BROMA (BUENOS AIRES, ARGENTINA: AUG. 19, 1881)

*It was not uncommon in Latin American cities, in the nineteenth and early twentieth centuries, for infants to be abandoned anonymously on the steps of orphanages or churches (some even had doorways designed especially for that purpose), or in out-of-the-way places. Usually, these were children born out of wedlock, whose parent or parents could not afford to raise them or whose existence would be seen to stain the reputation of an unmarried woman. Although this was a broad social phenomenon, by no means specific to people of African descent, this writer implied that it was of particular concern for them. In Buenos Aires, as in other parts of Latin America, Black men and women had long borne the brunt of stereotypes of hypersexuality and of a propensity to concubinage and illegitimacy. The social pressures concerning honor to which this article referred were brought to bear with particular force upon Afro-**Porteñas** by male (and occasionally female) writers in the community press, who sought both to defend the honor of Black women and to discipline them to embody traditional ideals of respectable womanhood and legitimate motherhood (see 3.2, 3.4, 3.9, 3.10).*

*The author of this open letter, as an expression of friendship or love toward an unnamed woman, took a rather radical position, rejecting conventions of honor and dishonor as harmful to children, women, and families. He portrayed the obligation of mothers to care for their offspring, illegitimate as well as legitimate, as a matter of divine law. Yet despite his sympathy for Black women, his directive that they take it upon themselves to flout the social and legal conventions of gender and race placed responsibility for the problem on the group made most vulnerable by those very conventions.*

(Dedicated to my kind [female] friend X)

I intend to write briefly about the topic that serves as the heading for these lines, which, in my eager desire to show you my affection at any opportune moment, I dedicate to you.

I am certain you will accept them with indulgence, and that you will, with your learnedness, make up for the inadequacies from which they undoubtedly suffer. For you know my ideas, and through these hastily composed lines, you will easily be able to penetrate my thoughts and give them the form that I was not able to imprint upon them.

My title already indicates the path I will follow in the course of this article.

Indeed, my friend, many times have I felt my soul rent apart by those living tableaux that human societies witness so frequently, composed of children who are orphaned though their parents live.

Unhappy creatures whom charitable hands gather up and nurse – when they [the children] manage to escape death, the harsh sentence to which most are condemned. [And this] by the very people who gave them life, for whom not even the maternal instincts harbored by the wildest animals are enough to hold them back from their evil intentions.

It is very common to invoke reasons of tact or decency when throwing a child out on the street as soon as he comes into the world, exposing him to near-certain death unless some charitable soul happens by and takes him in. And anyone might accept these customs as good, even lending a hand to bring them to fruition when the situation arises, because they erase the traces of what is believed to be a fault and they cover up [a breach in] what heartless people call honor.

We do not accept these ideas, even if this means clashing with the majority that thinks the opposite. We would therefore never advise a young woman who may have compromised her honor, as those who believe in such things would say, to salvage it by condemning the fruit of her love affairs to death, or by failing to recognize him and denying him her affection.

We believe in the justness of the rules that govern society, because they contribute to containing passions and moralizing customs. But we do not by any means think that, when a [woman] who comprises part of that [society], obeying a law higher than the ones established by men – the law of nature – strays from the [rules], she should be condemned to derision and shame. Nor should she be forced, in order to atone, to commit a despicable and inhumane act like that of casting out the fruit of her womb.

To us, the child born from a furtive union is just as deserving of his parents' affection as those [children] whom society deems more fortunate, because they were born to unions that were legalized by man. Both are the children of God and have come into the world to fulfill immutable laws.

If most of the mothers who cast off their children reflected for a moment upon the principles that, by divine right, govern the human family, they would accept the ridicule that society heaps upon them. They would raise their children without feeling thereby dishonored, in the certainty that God would reward them in heaven.

My dear friend: I fear I have imposed on you long enough with my dull lecture, and so I draw it to a close, hoping that in due course you will offer me your important opinion on this subject, and that you will accept, without reservations, the affection professed by your loyal friend,

Diego

### 3.8 "AN INTERESTING TOPIC," LA VERDAD (MONTEVIDEO, URUGUAY: DEC. 15, 1912)

*Beginning in the 1890s, and even more so during the presidential adminis-trations of José Batlle y Ordóñez (1903–7, 1911–15) and Claudio Williman (1907–11), Uruguay's Universidad de la República underwent a process of expansion and modernization. University education was now free, accessible and of high quality, which raised the question: to what lengths should Black families go in pursuing higher education for their children? In this article, the editors of* La Verdad *argued that the benefits of an advanced degree did not compensate for the sacrifices of time, effort, and lost earnings demanded by university study. They suggested that, despite the supposed absence of racism and racial barriers in Uruguay, for reasons of "racial difference" Black graduates of the university simply did not have access to the same career opportunities as White graduates and would not experience the same levels of success. The paper therefore advised Black youths to pursue vocational education and apprentice themselves in the skilled trades – the same approach that* **Booker T. Washington** *was advocating in the United States, though the paper did not mention Washington directly.*

We feel it necessary, for the moment, to call a truce to the sermons we have been giving on community organization, since the movement currently under way allows us to presume that the impulse received in that direction will not stop there but rather will continue its triumphal march.

We are going to take up other topics that call the attention of the journalist who proposes to be useful to society, identifying those social and economic problems of greatest importance in our social setting.

One of these topics is in our judgment the most interesting, and one that must attract the gaze of those who look ahead and try to discover, on the basis of what the present teaches us, what the future holds for us. We refer to the guidance that we should provide our young people, so that their many efforts, once realized, do not go to waste, so that they do not end up disoriented, unable to apply themselves to their activities owing, perhaps, to causes that we will demonstrate below.

As a general rule, there is a great tendency among our young people, and among heads of families, toward the liberal professions. Without doubt it is very nice, very honorable, to have a family member with a university degree, earned through high intelligence and robust talent. One can imagine, therefore, without much effort, that as families talk about this, they lean toward this or that degree program. But experience has shown us that, save for one or two exceptions, the reality does not correspond to the sacrifices demanded by a long and costly course of study.

Even though in our beloved country, up until the present, race antagonism does not exist as in other countries (at least in any visible way), despite this, we see that the men of our **class**, once having completed their degrees, even in the most brilliant way that one could ask, do not find propitious means to develop their activities and apply with profit the lessons gathered in the classroom.

Since this is well known, and easily proven to those who care to look, we have decided to advise our young people and heads of families to seek their futures by acquiring a trade in the workshops of their choice. This will free them from dependence on a boss and make possible a life of leisure, supported by a lucrative job.

In future articles we will continue to discuss this important topic and will conclude by saying that, in our judgment, the causes that prevent the advancement of our men of letters without doubt must be sought in racial difference. If only we were wrong!

## 3.9 LINO D'OU, "SURGE ET AMBULA,"[25] *LABOR NUEVA* (HAVANA, CUBA: JULY 1916)

*In this essay, **Lino D'ou**, a retired military officer and former member of the House of Representatives, explained the need for a Black press in Cuba. Apart from the limited space granted to Black writers in the "White press," he argued that Black Cubans should worry less about changing the minds of White racists and more about taking control of their own*

---

[25] The title refers to a story from the Book of John (5:8) in the New Testament. Encountering a man who had been unable to walk for thirty years, Jesus directed him to "Rise, take up thy bed, and walk," and the man was healed.

*destiny. The role of the Black press, he suggested, was to speak difficult
"truths" to Black readers in order to help them "rise up and walk."*

*Much of the article reflected longstanding arguments that, in order to
expect equal public treatment, Black people needed to behave better in
their private lives. But D'ou also reframed these questions in response to
contemporary social scientific debates. First, he called for "selection,"
a nod towards North American and European eugenics movements.
Then he cited anthropological works that disproved the idea of innate
differences among the races. His idea of eugenics was, then, more in step
with Cuban social scientists who espoused "homiculture," racial
improvement through interventions in maternal and infant hygiene, nutrition, and care rather than selection.[26] Both legal marriage and the Black
press, he concluded, could be tools for Black people to take charge of
improving and cultivating their race, even to the point of surpassing
Whites.*

Some have wished to see a mistaken procedure in our conduct within the
columns of *Labor Nueva*. "That is not the way," we are told. "You want
to do away with racial prejudice but instead of speaking to the Whites,
among whom [these prejudices] live and breathe, you have created a *Black
magazine*, for the Blacks."

We are not impressed by this argument. In the first place, we have no
scope within the White press to express our thoughts. There, when we are
admitted, we are granted very limited space for maneuver. These limits are
natural, if one takes into account that our fight is for restitution and it is
the dominating race that keeps for itself the share of the pie that belongs to
us. But in any case, the fact is that we are more interested in making the
Blacks conscious of their destiny as a race than in doing away with
a prejudice that is in our hands to destroy, and not in the hands of those
who practice it – most of the time, peripherally – as a useful tool for their
own comfort.

We need the Cuban Black to realize that whatever his situation of
political equality with respect to the White – because of what our laws
prescribe and because they are, for the most part, applied by those in
charge – as long as we do not attain an adequate social position, we will
not be able to interact on equal footing. We need the moral concept of the
family to take root among us. The statistics are painful and embarrassing.
We dare not state the percentage of us who are married. The registrations

---

[26] Bronfman, *Measures of Equality*.

of our illegitimate births are cause for profound shame. We need a powerful stimulus to put an end to the pitiful state in which we find ourselves, from a moral point of view.

The efforts that some are making to become educated will help greatly to make possible our forward progress. But so that these implacable young people do not have, as a pretext, that they could not dispense, all at once, with those of us older Black folks who remain among the living, we who will always be an insurmountable obstacle, let's seek through our actions, not our words, to bring about the renewal.

Let us give a legal basis to our unions. Let us have a thorough concept of the responsibility of the home, which is the basis of society. And toward that end, let us establish our own social ranking, which cannot be like the White one, based on aristocratic illusions and professional interests, but which can be based on social responsibility. On one side, [we shall place] those who accept that marriage as an institution, with the efforts required for its full maintenance, is the legal status, and consequently, that its mode of gathering resources for life is the appropriate one for a free and educated person, whether a professional, an artisan, an industrialist. And on the other side, concubinage [and] cohabitation in all of its forms.

Our social condition is confused and chaotic. We face the task of selection. And for this we will not achieve our goal by smashing White racial prejudice but rather by making ourselves suitable for the aspirations of a race. For this reason, then, we who are involved must have a *Black press* that says to the Cuban Black, frankly, openly, which are the defects that prevent him from fully enjoying all of the rights that are intrinsic to him as a free and conscious human being.

We do not forget that, if the current Black generation was born free, they live alongside us, a great legion of freedmen weighed down, to our immense grief, by the terrible, ignominious load of slavery. Fortunately for the Cuban Black, our history shows, clear as day, how attainable are all the conquests of civilization even for this same Black man who suffered all the horrors of that accursed condition. And [our history] bears out the as yet unrefuted affirmation of current anthropology that denies the existence of cerebral conditions that would render any race incapable of speculative thought.

Let us tell the Black man the truth, clearly and constantly. Let us make him understand that self-interested politicians are singing him a false, deceitful tune. That his happiness consists in refining his spirit, in being moral and able to consciously practice altruism. And that when he comes to be in possession of these qualities, which he must acquire for himself, not only will he reach equality with the White man, but he can surpass him if [the White man], made drowsy by the comforts of life, enervated by concupiscence, annihilates his soul and his body in Lupercalia and Saturnalia or living in Baudelaire's "artificial paradises."[27]

### 3.10 CÉZAR JÚNIOR, "NORMS OF CONDUCT," O CLARIM DA ALVORADA (SÃO PAULO, BRAZIL: JUNE 22, 1924)

*A frequent topic in the Black papers was the need to conform to middle-class standards of correct behavior. Men and women alike needed to maintain social decorum and respectability. While this obligation weighed on all members of society, it lay especially heavily on Afrodescendants. Because of racial stereotyping, the failings of any member of the community could be, and often were, attributed to every member of the community (see also 3.4, 3.5, 3.9).*

*Following this line of thought, Cézar Júnior called on Black men to treat all Black women with respect and affection, "protecting them and honoring them." Any man who "stains" a woman's honor should be expelled from society; in this way the Black community would demonstrate that "honor is not the exclusive property of one race but rather of all races in which there are religion and good sentiments."*

The Black man generally doesn't know how to evaluate what something is worth, he doesn't know to value himself, the result being the scorn heaped on our race, and the disregard felt by many toward the laws of society. People pay little attention to how they behave in public or even the places they go, not remembering that we Black men or men of dark color are observed at every step and in all of our actions, so that the behavior of many determines how all of us are judged.

It is necessary, therefore, that we behave with the required composure in public places and that we always follow a straight line of conduct in our lives, making our actions conform to the healthy rules of morality. We must especially devote to our female compatriots of color all due respect, affection, and friendship, protecting them and honoring them. We must highlight their pure and noble character and not, as we have observed, try to throw them into the mud, staining their honor and shaming the aged gray

---

[27] Lupercalia and Saturnalia are ancient Roman festivals, here intended to connote public revelry and indecency.

hair of poor mothers who see in their daughters the only support for them in their lives and therefore wish for them an honest position in society.

The man who tries to stain the honor of a home, later abandoning his victim and leaving her wretched and disgraced, should be banned from human society and set aside as a useless good-for-nothing. He deserves scorn and, if necessary, death.

It is urgent, therefore, that our fellows no longer commit these infamous acts that so devalue our race, and that they seek to repair the damage that perhaps they have done, so that we can proclaim, with heads held high, that honor is not the exclusive property of one race but rather of all races in which there are religion and good sentiments.

A good rule of conduct is the road to happiness.

We must achieve it.

### 3.11 ARLINDO J. VEIGA DOS SANTOS, "SOME WORDS FOR BLACK PARENTS," O CLARIM DA ALVORADA (SÃO PAULO, BRAZIL: MAY 13, 1927)

*Here **Arlindo Veiga dos Santos**, later one of the founders of the **Frente Negra Brasileira**, set out a very traditional vision of the Black family. A proper family included a husband, wife, and children, all "under the government of the man" and reflecting "the most perfect state, which is – monarchy." Parents were responsible for teaching their children discipline and morality and for ensuring their education. Like* La Verdad *in Montevideo (3.8), Veiga dos Santos opposed the idea of university education for young Afro-Brazilians, steering them instead toward industrial and vocational education. (Given the prevalence of racial discrimination in white-collar and professional employment in São Paulo, this was not unreasonable advice.) He concluded by urging readers to join and support the recently founded **Centro Cívico Palmares**, of which dos Santos was an active member.*

To begin, we need to explain what we understand by *"negro"*: NEGRO is all people of color, Black, **mulato**, **moreno**, etc., descended from African and Indigenous people. This is not the place to explain the premises of that conclusion to which we have arrived.

The great work of Black Action in Brazil must, without doubt, begin with the family, because the family is the mother-cell of all civil society. The family is the union of the man and the wife with their children, under the government of the man. The family is the prototype of political society or the most perfect state, which is – monarchy.

However, within that society what it is now most important to under-line are relationships: they are a mutual giving and receiving of love and fidelity; they are the duties and the obligations that are met through the reciprocal flow of gifts.

Man and woman, incomplete beings in the social order, mutually depend on each other for the conservation and propagation of the species; consequently, for the bringing up and education of children, they cannot abandon that work to random chance.

It is necessary that their work not be limited to the animality of reproduction, but they must seek to carry it through to the end.

Moreover, it is principally the remit of parents, as the heads of this unique [social] body, to perfect, care for, and polish their work to a high gloss. Certainly, the education of the good mother must make her solici-tous and affectionate with her offspring; but not everything should fall on her shoulders in this respect. It is incumbent on the father to make every effort to secure an adequate upbringing for his children, in both the physical realm and the spiritual. Just as they gave children their being, so must the parents (and above all the father) provide their children with the conditions to conserve and perfect that being, which is to say – nourishment and discipline, along with other external conditions of life in modern societies.

As the strong race that, thanks be to God, we are, the miserable social and physical conditions in which we Brazilian Blacks live cannot break down our physical integrity. Therefore the crusade for the education of the body is less attractive or, better put, less urgent than the uplifting of our intellectual and moral level.

To you, Black Parents, is entrusted the natural and, in our case, nation-alistic and patriotic duty of educating and preparing your offspring to conquer the present and the future: first, by teaching them the *discipline* appropriate to your own possibilities and those of your children; [second,] by *correcting* them seriously to save them from the wave of immorality that touches everyone, and especially our People. This will be done with the common sense that is innate to parents and, more than anything else, through a religious intent.

It is incumbent on you to save your children from the illiteracy of reading, and even more, the moral illiteracy that causes the horrifying crisis of our national character.

In order to avoid great suffering and disillusion, and unless they have conditions of exceptional intelligence, we do not want the children of the People to earn university degrees and involve themselves in advanced studies that demand great wealth. Those leaps are not always worth their pain. What we need are able artisans and professionals, [drawn from] the common people who can understand for themselves the social and political moment and the meaning and necessity of intense social action.

What is important to us is that every Black person read and have firm moral principles. They can dance, sing, and have fun, but these principles they must never forget. Otherwise, to dance, to sing, and to have fun is to dig gaping abysses.

Meanwhile, it is clear that not all parents are able to do that educating, that teaching, that disciplining: nobody gives what they are not able to, or don't have.

But everyone can provide the material conditions for the acquisition of that education, teaching, and discipline, by saving, for the good of their children and of a bigger and better Brazil for all of us, a few *milréis*[28] every month, which often are heedlessly spent on wasteful sprees or binges. Why not apply a few little crumbs to the work of perfecting the Brazilian Black!?

That work of perfecting our People is the entire purpose of the

### Centro Cívico Palmares

It invites all of you, Black Countrymen and Women, to join in its work.

Our time has come.

Come help us, oh Black Parents who have not forsaken your descendants and who take pride in the glorious blood of our Ancestors.

Do not let posterity later say that in Brazil a strong people withered away because its children denied, because of lack of education, the blood of their parents, and that, through their egoism and cowardice, those accursed parents went to their graves full of depravity and degradation.

### 3.12 THE MAN IN THE SUIT [SALVADOR BETERVIDE], "AGAINST A CUSTOM," LA VANGUARDIA (MONTEVIDEO, URUGUAY: MAY 30, 1928)

*Throughout Afro-Latin America, the informal adoption of impoverished Black children by middle-class and well-to-do families was a widespread practice with deep historical roots. Often presented by the adoptive family as a generous act of charity, the practice hid a darker side, in which*

---

[28] The *milréis*, Brazil's currency at that time, was worth US$ 0.12 in 1929. United States, *Treasury Decisions*, p. 205.

*children were pressed into years of unpaid or poorly paid domestic ser-
vice. They could also lose contact with their birth families and relatives.*[29]

**Salvador Betervide**, *editor of* La Vanguardia, *here revealed that he
himself had been adopted in this way. Although that adoption opened
opportunities for him to pursue higher education in Montevideo and to
become a leading figure in the city's Black community, he strenuously
opposed the practice. "Children should not be given away, they are not
objects." He was equally critical of the White women who sought out such
children and the Black women who handed them over, depicting these
transactions as if men had no part in them. Well aware of the pressures
that led Black mothers to give their children to others, Betervide focused
in particular on longstanding ties between former slave-owning families
and the descendants of those families' former slaves. Poverty also played
a role in a choice that, in the end, Betervide could not accept. Only the
death of the mother, he concluded, could justify sending the child away;
and in that case, better to send the child to a state-run orphanage than to
expose them to the dangers and degradations of semi-servitude in
Montevideo.*

Black mothers give away their children easily, tranquilly. It makes one
angry to hear this assertion, repeated by many mouths and which I have
just heard from the lips of a White woman (a cultivated lady). Arriving
from the interior [of Uruguay], she brings for her service (she says to raise)
a handsome Black son of a poor mother who, young and full of life, gave
him away with an ease and lack of affection that the gracious lady
scornfully describes: "the Black women of the countryside give away
their children as easily as handing over a piece of meat."

It's angering but not surprising, because we know very well that this
custom of giving up one's children is an old practice followed by our
grandparents, who gave children to godparents or to the people they
served, to whom they were connected. Those ties were not just of friendship, which in our stage of evolution is a lie, but still a strong one. They
were also ties created by many years of living together as a family, the
pains that were suffered, the same hopes in common. I knew many such
cases, hundreds, including my own. I was given away to be raised (almost
in good hands) by a family in which the mother and her siblings had had
my grandmother as their nursemaid. She was a slave, and the daughter of
slaves, of the ancestors of that family; although that strong connection

---

[29] On informal adoption, see Hordge-Freeman, *Second-Class Daughters*.

softened the custom, it did not sufficiently justify the mothers' detachment.

But this was from another time that is now past ... [illegible]. Today most of the ladies who ask for children to raise are those who, obeying a stupid imposition of the times, renounce the most noble aspiration of the woman of earlier times, that of being a mother. How can she seek to raise as her own another woman's child? Who does not know the pain, who, in going against her own natural instinct, is not aware of that human feeling?

This practice is bad for various reasons, so let's work to make it disappear. In this sense we have the same rights and the same responsibilities, he [*sic*] who asks and he [*sic*] who gives. Children should not be given away, they are not objects.

To the mothers of the countryside who find themselves in such a bad way that they think they are merely trustees of their children, and to whom I now write: ladies, do not be deceived, the promises made by those seeking to become the mothers of your children are a lie. Your children, here in this lovely city [Montevideo], will pay with their lives for your ignorance or ambition.

The separation of little ones can only be justified by the death of the mother. The state maintains well-organized institutions, true homes to substitute for [the children's] own, in which they are raised and prepared for tomorrow's struggles. In my judgment, poverty never justifies such a fatal separation. A mother's sacrifice for her child is the most noble action by the woman who believes herself to be such. The pain and suffering, even the poverty experienced by the children at the side of their mother, are the greatest of lessons, preparing and ennobling the spirit.

# CHAPTER 4

# Community Life

## INTRODUCTION

The activities of Black community organizations and important celebrations or events in the lives of community members were almost never reported in the mainstream press. One of the principal functions of the Black periodicals, many of which began as newsletters for particular social clubs or organizations, was therefore to report on, and otherwise engage with, that social world. "Society" pages and local gossip columns provide an invaluable window into experiences of community life – including activities organized to support and sustain the papers themselves – that were, otherwise, rarely written into the historical record.

In this reporting, the term "society of color" was the name frequently given to the rich world of clubs and community organizations that Afro-Argentines, -Brazilians, -Cubans, and -Uruguayans created, partly in response to exclusion from White clubs and organizations. The term often also served as a polite way to refer to all people of African descent in a particular city or country, or more narrowly to designate those members of the Black community who strove for social respectability and upward economic mobility.

On the eve of abolition in Cuba, **Martín Morúa Delgado** offered a particularly prescriptive vision of what a Black "society" should be (4.4). Members needed to model politeness and correct social behavior at all times and to refrain from vices, especially that of gambling. In Morúa's view, the clubs' primary objectives should be to promote education and moral uplift; dances and other entertainments should be strictly secondary (see also 3.5). By following these rules, he predicted, Black Cubans might someday aspire to their own aristocracy.

Probably the closest approximation to that vision of a Black elite anywhere in Latin America was Havana's famed **Club Atenas**. Minutes from a 1930 meeting of the club's Board of Directors evidence the broad spectrum of activities that it sponsored, as well as its close ties to political power, with members who included Congressmen and Havana's chief of police (4.12).

Most Black clubs, however, lacked the prestige and the resources of the Club Atenas and found Morúa's restrictive vision of club life unattractive or difficult to realize. Most sponsored regular social dances for members and guests, both as sources of entertainment and as sources of income. Many of the most famous Black popular musicians in the region regularly played such venues, helping to develop dance styles that became wildly popular among White people as well (4.6). Music and dancing were therefore frequent topics and sources of controversy in the Black press. The papers reported extensively on social dances, praising those venues that maintained a high level of decorum (4.10, 4.15) and condemning those that did not (4.3, 4.10).

Annual festivities surrounding **Carnival** were of particular significance as moments when Black musicians and dancers performed in public spaces, in view of non-Black audiences. The Uruguayan newspaper *La Verdad* was thrilled to announce in 1911 that the Montevideo city government would provide state subsidies for public dances open to the "society of color" (4.8). Papers in Buenos Aires and Havana were less sanguine, critiquing the "vulgarity" and commercialization of the Black Carnival groups (*comparsas*) and their offensive, reductive, or overly cheerful portrayals of Black people and cultures (4.5, 4.14). Writing in 1937, Cuban author María Luisa Sánchez bitterly denounced the use of Carnival to sell Afro-Cuban culture to tourists and to distract Afro-Cubans from recognizing and combating the exploitative conditions in which they lived.

In reporting on the clubs and dances, the papers occasionally commented on their racial dynamics. The Brazilian newspaper *A Liberdade* condemned clubs that admitted lighter-skinned Afrodescendants while rejecting those of darker skin (4.9). The Uruguayan newspaper *La Vanguardia* questioned whether White men should be allowed at Black dances, proposing that they be admitted only if they were married to Black women or had "some other similar connection to us" (4.11).

Much community life took place outside the confines of the social clubs, in private homes and family parties. The papers reported on those events as well, covering weddings, birthdays, dances, travel, etc. (4.7,

4.13). Readers found their own names and those of their friends and relatives in the pages of the Black press, even if they were not always willing to pay the costs of maintaining those papers (4.1, 4.2).

## DISCUSSION QUESTIONS

- How did different authors implicitly or explicitly define the "society of color"? Who was in and who was out? What might it have meant to individuals to see their names, organizations, or photographs in print? How might this kind of reporting have helped to create and promote a sense of unity among readers? Can you find examples where the press may have revealed or exacerbated divisions within or among Black communities?
- These texts reveal a wide diversity of experience within Afrodescendant communities in these cities and countries. How did different writers (or the individuals about whom they wrote) respond to this diversity and the tensions it sometimes generated?
- Writers in the Black press mostly directed their words toward a Black readership. But they were keenly aware of how the wider society judged Black people based on their social events and activities. What do these texts reveal about writers' sense of the effects, positive or negative, of placing Black associational and cultural life in the public eye?
- How did writers in the Black press regard the popularity of Afro-Latin American musical and dance forms inside Black institutions and outside them, particularly among White co-nationals? Was the commercial success of Black bandleaders or government recognition of Black participation in Carnival helpful to the cause of racial advancement, as writers defined it? What risks emerged if White audiences and officials began to give attention to Black popular music, but not to other forms of Black talent and creativity, or political demands?

## 4.1 AND 4.2 TWO ARTICLES ON THE FINANCIAL DIFFICULTIES OF THE BLACK PRESS (BUENOS AIRES: 1876, 1879)

*In Buenos Aires as elsewhere, the Black papers were perpetually short of funds. This reflected the modest economic situation of the target readership, who frequently struggled to keep up with subscription costs. In response, as "To the Public" (4.1) demonstrates, editors (who often poured modest earnings from regular jobs into these papers) sometimes*

*threatened to use their positions to publicly shame those who failed to*
*make timely payments (see also 4.7). The author of "An Initiative" (4.2)*
*took a less punitive approach, appealing (as the Black papers often did) to*
*the generosity of "friends" and "collaborators," and proposing*
*a fundraising campaign. This author identified the lack of an in-house*
*printing press, or at least typesetting equipment, as the main obstacle to*
*sustainable publication.*

### 4.1 "To the Public," *La Juventud* (Buenos Aires, Argentina: July 2–9, 1876)

It is not the first time that we find ourselves in the unavoidable position of having to address our subscribers through a public notice in one of our standing front-page sections, with the goal of informing them of the critical situation we are undergoing. Yet many of them, we think, will turn a deaf ear, in light of the fact that up until the current notice, they have not been able to cover the *debt* they owe the Administration of this weekly paper.

These are the kinds of reasons that contribute powerfully to putting us in a tight spot when it comes to overcoming the many obstacles that rise up in our path.

For this and other reasons that we shall avoid making public, we have resolved that any *subscriber* who has had two monthly payments come due without paying them will have his or her name made public, without distinction of *sex*.

We bring this to our subscribers' attention in hopes of reaching a better understanding.

The Administration

### 4.2 "An Initiative," *La Perla* (Buenos Aires, Argentina: May 24, 1879)

For some time now, we have wished for, and have attempted to obtain, a small printing press that would belong to us, so that we could more regularly fulfill our duty by founding a newspaper that would be useful to our community.

We have made all possible efforts to obtain it, but in vain. All work in favor of that idea has yielded negative results.

Without resources, what can we do?

Well, those of us who aspire toward that goal, much attached to the cause and progress of our community, wish only to be able to count on the cooperation of all of our friends to reactivate efforts on behalf of this initiative.

Various papers have been founded with the laudable desire to serve our social interests, and all have succumbed – for lack of what? For want of two type cases that would belong to us, and would be useful for many other jobs.

Well then; we count on the assistance of our friends, and we hope to carry out this initiative by means of a public subscription, whose auspicious success we predict by virtue of the state of progress to which we aspire.

We will return to this topic in more detail. For now, we limit ourselves to affirming that this great idea will soon become a reality.

Z. Z.

### 4.3 "HOW LONG?", LA JUVENTUD (BUENOS AIRES, ARGENTINA: JUNE 30, 1878)

*Many writers in the Black papers saw social dances as an important part of community life. Even (or especially) then, they sought to draw crucial distinctions between what they saw as acceptable and scandalous. In this piece, an unnamed writer in Buenos Aires'* La Juventud *(which, like its peers, covered countless community dances) expressed outrage at a subset of gatherings that, he argued, posed particular risk to the honor, respectability, and sensibilities of the women "of good families," young and old, who attended. These were the "immoral" rifas – public, for-pay parties hosted in a range of venues (in this case, someone's "rooms" in a group home or tenement). The author equated these rifas with the disreputable* **academias,** *and he urged "those who are called on" to be mothers and wives in his community always to choose instead a decorous tertulia – an invitation-only gathering hosted in a private home. This piece nonetheless reveals that these genres overlapped – and that the rifas had wide appeal.*

Scandalous acts, recently committed, leave us duty-bound to object loudly and publicly. Recent disturbances, occurring with countless daughters of good families looking on, induce us to ask their parents or guardians: How long will they continue to allow their daughters to witness so many immoralities, which discredit them and perhaps even drag them along a ruinous road?

How long? Or do their parents feign ignorance of what so often happens? Was it not indecorous, that which took place the evening of last Saturday the twenty-second, at a *rifa* hosted by a Mister Simonet? In his rooms, in the very space where people danced, enormous knives were brandished, resulting in a racket of mythical proportions.

Could the harm caused by this unpleasant experience ever be repaired, given that mothers and daughters alike feared for their lives?

I have long insisted that, in my view, a *rifa* is nothing more than one of those dance halls called **academias,** in which anyone who pays his way believes himself entitled to insult and yell, to act in an uncouth way. This, when carried out in the presence and sight of those who are called upon to be virtuous wives and tender mothers, always in some ways tarnishes them.

Always choose a private *tertulia* over a *rifa* – this advice is backed by sound reason, good sense, and self-respect. It pains us to say it, but soon we will return to this topic with greater attention.

## 4.4 MARTÍN MORÚA DELGADO, "SOCIETIES," EL PUEBLO (MATANZAS, CUBA: JULY 18, 1880)

*New freedoms of the press and association enacted in 1878 created the conditions for a rapid expansion of Black associations and for the publication of the first Black newspapers in Cuba. In the city of Matanzas,* **Martín Morúa Delgado** *and* **Rafael Serra** *edited* El Pueblo *at the headquarters of the Sociedad La Unión in early 1880. Morúa was also the secretary of the society and had a paid post as a teacher in the society's school.*

*In two essays on "Societies" (the second of which is included here), Morúa expressed a common view that the new Black societies were responsible for the civilization and uplift of the Black race, preparing formerly enslaved Cubans for full and equal political rights. The final, gradual abolition of slavery began in 1880 and ended in 1886. Morúa argued that the leaders of many clubs had abandoned their educational mission by organizing too many dances and by permitting gambling at club gatherings.*

*The immediate context for this article, and for the hurt feelings he referenced in its first lines, was a disagreement about whether it was proper for Morúa to hold two posts in La Unión simultaneously, his resignation from both, and his public falling out with the remaining club leadership. The article thus reflected a second very common theme in the Cuban Black press in the 1880s: accusations of self-interested behavior and what Morúa called "petty quarrels and dishonorable reprisals" among the leaders of the Black societies.*

We continue upon our previous article here, deeply regretting that some people might feel resentful or singled out by it. But this very fact obliges us to continue with more determination, for if it is painful to someone it must be because we have touched him with the tip of our whip.

We want to see our societies marching in step with the ideas of our century and for this reason we indicate the good path that, according to our limited perspective, our Directors ought to follow.

An educational Center should lack nothing in order to carry out the mission to which it has been entrusted.

It should be equipped with a good teacher and supported with all the supplies of a school. The man who devotes himself to guiding souls, whether they be innocent or sinful, should want for nothing.

The schoolteacher is the one who deserves the most consideration from the Directors of a Center. Do these gentlemen treat them as they should ... ?

The main thing in these cases is the school for children during the day and the one for their parents at night.

If the gentleman Directors take care with these, which we believe are the most important precepts, they will do well, without a doubt, in the positions that have been conferred upon them.

Before they give orders, these men need dignity and integrity, maturity of thought. They should seek the common good and not allow themselves to be dragged into petty quarrels and dishonorable reprisals that diminish the soul and degrade the body.

When the societies change teachers frequently, it is not possible for the pupils to advance in their studies since, as great as the knowledge and determination of the teacher may be, his seedling will fall on infertile ground; because he will need several months to get to know the disposition of the students (an indispensable measure for every good teacher), and if once he knows the intellects he must cultivate he is removed, all benefit is lost, time is wasted, and the teacher, the school, and its Directors suffer discredit.

Recreation ... it is a duty to provide it to the members, like the other [activities] I have enumerated [mutual aid and education], but we do not believe that it should dominate, as usually happens, the spirit of our Presidents.

Recreation should be dispensed in a very small dosage. If it is necessary for the expansion and repose of the mind, it is also harmful when overused, and more gravely so for those of us who ought to be tired after providing ourselves with *so much recreation.*

The good just the same as the bad, everything has its limits. We should never permit ourselves to reach them, since beyond lies suffering.

In the societies, the recreation we employ should be mixed with education.

A literary and musical evening should be the choice of our directors in order to supply recreation and education to the members.

We do not believe that it is necessary that the gentlemen who take part be consummate artists nor admired men of letters, for it is only by taking a first step that we can hope to finish.

In addition to entertaining us, these gatherings teach us the good manners of society, the treatment we owe to the ladies, and what we gentlemen may gain from friendly and agreeable conversation. In sum, they remedy our comportment and moderate our manners to the same degree that they supply the economy and subsistence of the institution.

Dancing should be much more infrequent, since it only produces expenses and immoral habits.

What conduct our youth adopts in these dances!

We see the ladies seated during intermissions, ornamenting the main hall, and the young men in small groups in the lobby, in the courtyard, or even in the street.

What delicacy can one observe in the conversations that four or six lively youths carry on? . . .

The [musical and literary] evenings condemn this abandonment of and insult to the ladies.

The [musical and literary] evenings oblige us to honor them and to show them the respect deserved by their sex. They oblige us to be responsible for the rules of politeness of which we are so lacking. They oblige us, in sum, to respect [women] more, in this way making ourselves worthy of respect and deserving of the consideration owed to free men.

The [musical and literary] evening is an exercise for a people that wishes to be enlightened and the greatest and most magnificent ornament for those who already are.

Never, not even under the cover of recreation, should any kind of gambling be introduced into the institutions of our race.

We should banish this thought entirely.

From the instant our Directors accept a gaming table in their educational centers, they imitate the modern atheist who believes in God but denies his existence. From that moment, it ceases to be a Center for moral education, to become one for spreading a greater or lesser degree of vice.

Gambling is the perversion of the masses, the dishonor of a people, the negation of progress, the contradiction of liberty.

An immoral people, a perverted people can never be a free people.

The duty of our societies is to purify men and not to pervert them.

I condemn gambling with all the energy I can call upon, not only in the societies but wherever it leaves its poisonous footprint.

What title befits those Directors who introduce gaming in order to [financially] support their societies?

Oh, respectable sirs! Take great care on this slippery terrain. Work hard to support your institutions but do not degrade them, do not prostitute the people you want to regenerate, do not destroy the building you want to reconstruct, do not annul all of your accomplishments with a single thoughtless act.

The men who imagine this kind of *salvation* cease to be the friends of the race of color.

Their dedication to improvement makes them destroy.

This usually happens only when the directors lack the necessary knowledge to occupy their posts and we are of the opinion that those who do not know how to lead should follow, as the poet (1) says:

> . . . . . . . . . . . . . . . . . .Better
> To give a man to each post
> Than to give a post to each man.

For those who do not know how to be directors, that title is superfluous, they have it only in order to have it. They [these directors] are nothing but a nuisance until they do serious harm.

I have already said it on another occasion, we should not look for genealogies in our race, since we already know, generally, from where it came and how, whether [its representatives be] sons of our soil or citizens of another nation.

Our duty and also that of the Directors of our societies is to purify those whom we believe to be bad, not choose from among the good and bring them down to the level of the others.

Far be it from me to indulge in vanity, or in the ridiculousness of self-aggrandizement – another, even more dangerous [vanity] – for I defy those who wish to prove that they are superior to the ones that they cast aside and who are their brothers in race and misfortune.

Here is a promise for those who aspire [to leadership]: after twenty-five years, we will be able to claim *some* aristocracy, for by then there will be a group that is enlightened while the rest have preferred to live in darkness.

Then we will be able to consider ourselves superior, given that we will live in a different world from the one they inhabit.

Let us be more humanitarian by ceasing to be so selfish.

Let us love progress more and let us accept responsibility for the current situation, taking full measure of the future that awaits us.

Let us see more clearly than we have until now, and let us not confuse dignity with superstitious preoccupations that are unworthy of our love of freedom. Above all, let us know our place and let us keep each in his place since we understand too well that we need more knowledge to command than to obey.

Have I said all that was necessary?

Morúa

(1) From the play by D. Fernando Zárate, "Mudarse para mejorarse."

## 4.5 "OUR CARNIVAL ASSOCIATIONS," LA BROMA (BUENOS AIRES, ARGENTINA: MAR. 3, 1882)

*During* **Carnival** *season,* La Broma *and other papers typically ran front-page editorials celebrating the Afro-***Porteño*** community's many musical troupes (***comparsas***). Editors warmly praised these groups as pillars of the community's associational life and as beacons of progress and refined modernity, spaces where the community's young people could hone and display their musical talents.*

*By Carnival of 1882, however, a new fad concerned* La Broma's *editors: those respectable musical comparsas were losing ground to troupes of young Black Argentines in blackface, who performed stylized, mocking versions of the community's traditional* **candombes**. *The editors were not ashamed of candombe, despite its increasing portrayal by White (and some Black) Argentines as a marker of African "barbarism" (see 6.1). But they bristled at the idea that it would be shamelessly exposed and ridiculed before critical or ignorant audiences by young people who shirked the duty of perpetuating that custom "in its own place," in the privacy of the community.*

*Yet the article allows a glimpse into what blackface (and related performances of African exoticism) might have meant for these young Afro-Porteños: if Blackness was a mask that could be easily put on for Carnival, it might be possible to take off afterward. This younger generation of Afro-Porteños*

*may have seen, in these blackface candombe troupes, a way of "unmarking"*
*themselves as Black and asserting their shared Argentineness with White*
*Carnival revelers who had long used blackface. At the same time, their*
*actions contributed to cementing "el negro" as a laughable stock character*
*confined to Carnival, thus fueling the dominant myth that "real" Black*
*people belonged to Argentina's past.*[1]

It would appear that the spirit of our brothers by race is impervious to any
good influences where the **Carnival** associations are concerned.

The committees that are specially constituted to award prizes to the
assembled **comparsas**, whether for their instruments, their numbers [of
members], their costumes, or their songs, fail to motivate them.

[They go] always for what is easiest, always for what is most vulgar,
always for what is exceedingly coarse. [They aim] always, moreover, to
mock the ways of our late grandparents, or more accurately, the ways of
a certain portion of our [present-day] community.

"We expose ourselves gladly to the criticisms made of us," [they
think] – [they] are mistaken! They expose themselves to the laughter of
sensible people because there can be no more unworthy farce than the one
currently taking root and spreading among our youth.

What a pity!

The venerable association "[The] Southern Star," [or] the new association "The Unfortunate Ones," composed of members of other [associ-
ations] that, like these, have struggled for our moral uplift, make little
progress.

Why?

It shames us to say it: because a large portion of our youth, who could
well dedicate themselves to studying and learning musical instruments –
which would always be more beneficial – entertain themselves [instead]
beating the old and shabby [drum] skin, which today is only used as the
sole reminder of the longstanding (though concealed) customs of
yesteryear.

Today any child of four or five years of age takes an empty olive barrel,
puts a skin on it, and plays it with *vigor* and *skill*, on a par with the oldest
**candombe** player.

And so, what novelty is to be found in the attempt by a certain number
of young men to *suffocate* us with an *instrument* we know so well? We
appreciate and respect [the drum] in its own place, but we must reject [it]

---

[1] Geler, *Andares negros*, chapter 5.

during Carnival days, because we find it ridiculous that one should don a mask to play a role that one is duty-bound to play unmasked.

There are countless such young men who, if one of *our aunties* earnestly asks them to play the *drum* or the *masacalla*[2] at one of the few remaining centers [founded by] our grandparents – which stand as a reminder that they had more skill and ability to bring us together than many of [these youths] – refuse to do so. They walk out, making a show of being ashamed and turning up their collars to show off for the chicks. And yet they shamelessly paint their faces with blackened cork and expose themselves to public hilarity in the middle of Calle Florida or in front of the Confitería del Gas,[3] as we had the misfortune to witness this year.

We know that in our effort to change opinions – to correct this harm that, through inattention, might take root even among our children – we will do everything possible to demonstrate patiently the ill outcomes that result (and, worse, will continue to result) from carelessly allowing our youth to spurn musical associations for their socializing and even for their education. These include "The Southern Star" and "The Unfortunate Ones," as well as "The Republican Society," "The Oriental Navy,"[4] "The Suitors," "The Suitors of the [Río de la] Plata," "New Creation," and even "Bright Star of the South," "6 January," "Republican Symbol," and so many others which, with little sacrifice and great reward, have shone on the streets of this capital, earning the applause of Blacks and Whites, nationals and foreigners, and even of the *gurunguses* or *second-rate* people – who, as is known, are the most critical, because they cannot tell ignorance from education.

Our youth should reflect upon all this with some good judgment, and present themselves for the next Carnival in the manner of, or if possible within, associations like "[The] Southern Star" and "The Unfortunate Ones," which are the only comparsas of our community to have won a prize that we do not consider undeserved.

Come now, young men! The doors to those associations are wide open.

The example was set long ago by those who, today, observe this retrogression with sorrow.

Let us nip this in the bud.

---

[2] A kind of shaker used as part of **candombe**, usually made of metal and affixed onto a wooden pole.

[3] Calle Florida was one of the most elegant streets in downtown Buenos Aires, studded with restaurants, private clubs, bars, and cafés. The Confitería del Gas, on the corner of Esmeralda and Rivadavia, was a café patronized mainly by the city's elite.

[4] "Oriental" in this context referred to someone or something from Uruguay.

Let us move forward, not backward! The powerful echo of those who desire the moral and material progress of our society demands it.

Onward! Though selfishness may, unfortunately, conspire to keep us alone on this zealous march, and [though our opponents] may go so far as to place barriers along such a beneficial path, onward!

Long live the musical comparsas!

## 4.6 MIGUEL FAÍLDE AND RAIMUNDO VALENZUELA, "GRATIFIED," LA FRATERNIDAD (HAVANA, CUBA: JULY 31, 1888)

*Gatherings that centered on **danzón**, a partner dance developed by Afrodescendant musicians and dancers, were among the primary recreational activities organized by Black societies in Cuba in the 1880s. As the danzón became popular among White Cubans as well, many White journalists and critics denounced the style as scandalously sensual and voluptuous. In this context, some writers in the Black press expressed dismay at what they saw as an excessive enthusiasm for social dancing among Afrodescendant Cubans (4.4). Others expressed anxiety about White men attending dances at societies of color (see also 4.11).*

*In this letter, the two most famous stars of the emerging danzón scene, Miguel Faílde from Matanzas and Raimundo Valenzuela from Havana, offered a contrasting account of danzón's popularity. They described a successful tour to Santa Clara province, in which the danzón was an uncontroversial element of dignified and wholesome Black associational life and of civic culture more broadly. In their account, the racial and class segregation of Cuban clubs and societies was obvious and unremarkable. But they presented the reception offered the orchestras by "almost the entire population" at the port of Cienfuegos, by a working-class club "for White people," and by an elite "Liceo," as triumphs for the musicians themselves and for the constituency served by the newspaper* La Fraternidad, *the "men of color."*

Distinguished friend:

We request hospitality for our few poor lines in the columns of the newspaper that you edit to the applause of all men of color: our mouthpiece. Never have we had more cause for this request, for in them we wish to express our gratitude, as intense as it is sincere, toward two communities on this island, recently visited by ourselves and by the worthy comrades who make up the orchestras to which we belong.

The two communities to which we refer are Cienfuegos and Villaclara, in which we received a thousand expressions of affection, from all social classes, over the short period of what we will call our *Sanjuanera*[5] tour. Anything we say about these expressions will be but a pallid sketch, and our quickly strung-together sentences will be a poor indication of the depths of our thanks.

You may judge from the facts.

We made our arrival at the first of these towns (Cienfuegos) on the 20th [of June], at nine in the evening. Shortly before reaching the point called Cayo Carena, we were met by the orchestra directed by our friends Señores Vicente and Sánchez, who awaited our arrival on a tugboat. When they could make out our steamer arriving, the orchestra greeted us with a beautiful **danzón**, while countless flying flares, rockets, and other fireworks alerted the inhabitants of Fernandina de Jagua[6] of our happy arrival to this most welcoming city.

To such a gallant and extraordinary welcome, our own orchestra (although incomplete) could not but respond with another danzón. When we reached the dock, we could see a proud and imposing spectacle: almost the entire population of Cienfuegos waited there to welcome us. Right away we were attended by a Committee from the Sociedad "El Progreso" which led us, to the sound of the aforementioned orchestra and accompanied by a numerous public, to the headquarters of that Society.

There the reception was beyond description. The room was laid out as if for a great holiday. Many ladies, young women, and gentlemen, the most distinguished members of the Society, were gathered in the courtyard.

Sweets, beer, ice cream and other refreshments were served in profusion. It was around half past eleven when this regal reception concluded and we retired to our beds.

The deferential treatment we received was not limited to the "El Progreso" Society; we were also the objects of innumerable acts of kindness at the dances held on the 23rd, 24th, 28th, and 29th in the "Centro de Artesanos (Artisans' Center)," which is for White people.

We omit from this brief sketch some of the attentions of which we were the objects, on the part of individuals, because otherwise we would never finish.

[5] The Fiestas Sanjuaneras (Feast of Saint John) are a midsummer carnival lasting from June 24 to June 29.
[6] The name given, before 1829, to what is now the city of Cienfuegos.

Then Villaclara had its turn.

Our voyage to this town took place on the 3rd day of the current month. As in Cienfuegos, the reception in Villaclara was splendid. We received the most brotherly of welcomes from a numerous public, with the notable presence of the White youth who belong to the "Liceo"[7] in that city.

In the evening, at a dance at that Society [the Liceo], we were approached by a committee from the Sociedad de Color "El Trabajo" who, after presenting themselves to us, begged us to put off our return to Cienfuegos for another day, as they wished to have the pleasure of hosting a meal and a gathering in our honor at their Center.

Could we possibly fail to respond to such an honor? Of course not! So it was that, at five in the afternoon the following day ([July] 4) we found ourselves at the Sociedad "El Trabajo" before a splendid dinner, fit for the most demanding gourmet. The members competed amongst themselves to shower us with every kind of attention.

At nine o'clock at night a very lively dance party began, attended by the most select members of our race from the city of Villaclara. Two orchestras played: the local one, directed by the intelligent maestro Sr. D. Luis Martínez and the one directed by Señores Vicente and Sánchez.

On the fifth [of July] we returned to Cienfuegos, carrying in our hearts the indelible and very pleasant memory of our short stay in such a hospitable city.

In Cienfuegos, more honors, some from societies, some from individuals, up until the moment of our return to Havana.

This poorly stitched-together sketch of our tour this year to the towns of Cienfuegos and Villaclara bears little resemblance to reality. It would be hard, even for a more expert pen than ours, to describe all the honors bestowed on us with the thoroughness that they deserve. Our own lack of skill in the first place, and the brevity with which we lay out these lines, together with the fact that we do not want to hurt any feelings, prevent us from going into the details that would bring this description more faithfully to life.

Our object is nothing more, as we said at the start, than to make known our gratitude toward each and every one of those to whom we are indebted.

We have the satisfaction to report that, in the two towns which we have mentioned, everyone, without distinction, wished to be the most attentive.

---

[7] An elite literary and cultural society.

For this reason we extend our thanks to all, which we send from the column of this newspaper, in the firm conviction in the certainty that we will never be up to the task. We will strive to express our gratitude, which we extend to you as well, Mr. Director, for the favor, mentioned above, that you do us by inserting these lines.

Havana, July 1888. On behalf of the orchestra, Miguel Faílde, Raimundo Valenzuela

## 4.7 "MOSAICS," LA FRATERNIDAD (HAVANA, CUBA: 1888–89)

*Most Black periodicals in Cuba included sections called "Mosaics" or "Local Gossip," which included multiple short notices of community activities. Though brief, these notices offer significant insight into the relationships and communal ties that operated in and around the newspapers. They highlight some of the ways that newspapers helped to generate feelings of community among people who understood themselves to be linked together, even at long distances, as a reading public. A selection of Mosaic entries from* La Fraternidad *in 1888 and 1889, for instance, sheds light on the role of a newspaper publisher in the Black community, the use that readers made of widely circulated newspapers to locate relatives separated by enslavement or migration, and the "harmony and good conduct" that reigned during a hard-fought baseball matchup between two Black social clubs.*

**Aug. 31, 1888**
As had been agreed, on the 26th of the month that is now ending, the "Simpson" and "Universo" clubs spent their strength on the picturesque [baseball] diamond belonging to the [Club] "Almenares," with the victory going to the latter.

We would not be concerned with Sunday's match if it were just a matter of sizing up the greater or lesser merit of the players of the two clubs. It would matter little to us, being impartial, that victory belonged to one or the other; but what we do find it important to set down in these brief lines is the harmony and good conduct that was observed by both clubs during the game.

The large public which, despite the [illegible] of the situation, attended the function of which we write, left us more than satisfied; and it is worth noting the unity that reigned between the public and the *Umpire* during the course of play; with no need to lament, as on other occasions, the countless quarrels brought on by dubious calls.

Several families from the neighboring city of Matanzas visited us on the occasion of the party.

At the end of the match, the players headed to the Sociedad "Bella Unión Habanera," where a splendid banquet awaited them, which the "Universo" and "Niágara" Clubs held in honor of battle-hardened "Simpson."

The moments we spent in the company of such lively youths seemed too short.

At ten the dancing began, lasting until dawn.

Here are the runs scored by innings in Sunday's match.

"Universo" –2–4–0–4–2–1–0–0–3 – 16
"Simpson" –1–0–4–1–3–0–0–0–0 – 9

\*\*\*

Mr. Gualba, the Publisher of this newspaper, has changed his residence from 39 Obrapía [Street] to 6 Compostela [Street]. Now his friends, in particular, and those who have matters pending with him, know where to direct [their communications], especially the agents who are behind on their payments, of whom there are a few, and whom it will be necessary to [publicly] name to see if in this way they will pay what they owe. Nonetheless, our Publisher, who faithfully fulfills the obligations required by courtesy, offers his new abode to all.

Important warning: *he does not give lodging to the wanderer*, because the room is too small.

### Sept. 20, 1888

Mrs. María Soledad Freire, who lives at number 96 La Lealtad Street, desires to know the whereabouts of her son Ruperto Cosido, who was the slave of don Serapio Arteaga. She has not known his whereabouts since 1868.

The *morena* Rosalía Hernández desires to know the whereabouts of her daughter Lorenza Ortal, who was sold many years ago to don José Setién, in Vuelta Abajo. Please send any information to number 125 Compostela Street.

### Jan. 22, 1889

Mr. Fernando Antonio Vázquez has come to our editorial offices to ask that we make known to his son living in New York that he lives (in the sense of existing) and where he lives (in the sense of residing) at number 128 Estrella Street, at the corner of Escobar [Street].

We copy this message to our active New York correspondent so that he may, in turn, do the same for Mr. Fernando of the same surname [the son in New York], who by this channel wished to have news of his dear father. Our respectable friend is satisfied.

## 4.8 "THE FESTIVAL COMMISSION AND THE SOCIETY OF COLOR," LA VERDAD (MONTEVIDEO, URUGUAY: FEB. 5, 1912)

*Throughout Latin America,* **Carnival** *is a highlight of the annual social calendar. Beginning in the late 1800s, the Montevideo city government took an increasingly active role in regulating and shaping the celebrations, including the many dances held in social clubs, theaters, and other public venues. In 1912 the city took the unprecedented step of providing a state subsidy for two Carnival dances to be held at the Teatro Cibils, exclusively for "the society of color." This was an instance of state-mandated racial segregation. But it also reflected the longstanding practice in the city of separate Carnival dances for Black and White audiences. In light of that history,* La Verdad *was delighted with the city's decision to underwrite the dances, which the paper interpreted as the formal recognition of Black people's "place" in Uruguayan society and in the Carnival festivities. The paper urged its readers to observe proper standards of conduct at the dances, so as to make themselves worthy of the "great honor" that the city had accorded them.*

The Festival Commission deserves sincere and enthusiastic applause for its sympathetic attitude in including the collectivity of color in its program, assigning it a place in the festivities and the means to occupy that place.

This action is very praiseworthy and meritorious, especially when one considers that in past times our **class** was never taken into account in matters of this nature. It was left to its own scarce resources, which had to be very limited because its component elements have no greater benefits than the scarce earnings provided by their daily labor, which in this current period of painful want barely suffice for the most pressing necessities.

There is another aspect of the topic under discussion, which reflects great honor on our class.

The worthy Festival Commission has notably interpreted the views of the high authorities of the State, who wish to clearly demonstrate that in our country there are no pariahs, regardless of one's position in society. For them we are citizens, fellow countrymen, with the same rights as everyone, given that in the hours of trial, when all must come together in the common defense of the nation, our participation, as citizens, has been and always will be spontaneous and determined, as befits men with noble hearts.

Let's recognize, then, that the hour of vindication has come. Our poor race, which has provided so many worthy services in all aspects of community life; our race, which has always been the prototype of loyalty and valor, whenever it has been necessary; our race, in short, which not long ago was considered something undefined, with no one greatly concerned about it, [now] begins to harvest the fruits of its perseverance and loyalty from the high authorities of the State, who, in distributing their generosity to the social clubs in general, did not want their fellow citizens, the men of color, to suffer the slightest injury to their self-esteem as Uruguayans.

It is a most beautiful action, which we must take into account so as to seek by all the means at our disposal that our conduct on this solemn occasion accord perfectly with the most fundamental principles of culture and sociability.

## 4.9 MATUTO, "MUSINGS," A LIBERDADE (SÃO PAULO, BRAZIL: DEC. 28, 1919)

*The problem of color prejudice among Afrodescendant people, especially within social clubs that restricted membership to persons with lighter complexions, was a common theme across the Latin American Black press. In this article the pseudonymous writer Matuto[8] took up the "delicate" question of color lines within Afro-Brazilian social clubs, to which Matuto was very much opposed. As he explained, excluding dark-skinned people from club functions could have the terrible effect of dividing family members from each other. It also, of course, defied the ideas, so vigorously promoted in the Black press, of racial fraternity and equality. This led Matuto sadly (and controversially) to conclude, it was not Whites who were imposing racial barriers on Brazil, but rather Black people themselves.*

---

[8] "Matuto," meaning "peasant" or "backwoodsman," was a nom de plume used by one of *A Liberdade*'s regular contributors (or possibly one of the editors).

"Beware the friend who harbors dangers."

I don't know why, but there are times when the smallest thing is a big thing, and then the big and extraordinary things are a flood. Probably my readers are saying, "how tiresome this Matuto is being, making a huge preamble before saying little or nothing." And those readers are right. But there are matters and things that sometimes resemble each other, and we can't always say that they are identical unless we reflect a bit. What I am doing is to explain one of the delicate cases, which I almost lack the courage to discuss. In spite of hearing it from a third party, I have my suspicions; nevertheless, as one who dots his i's, it is necessary to inform my friends of what is happening.

The case and the thing here is nothing more than a prejudice ... of color. Imagine, my readers, among them the *mulatos* and *mulatas*, that you belong to a [recreational] society or group. One or both of your parents have jet-black skin. In a moment of enthusiasm, a member who is a little Whiter, without thinking of the harm that it could do, proposes that, at a given party, only *mulatos* and *mulatas* be admitted. Once that proposal is approved, it has to be put into practice.

On the day of the party, [what if] our parents or a Black relative wants to accompany us? Grave disappointment! Because they are Black, they cannot attend a party for which their child paid the necessary admission, because of color prejudice! But does this society or group actually exist? This is what we're going to find out, and I am obliged to say that ... with all the evasiveness of a man of color, and under the conditions, etc., I almost believe it. Matuto was always one of those who deny [the existence of] prejudice in Brazil, and I am forced to continue to deny it, as far as the Whites are concerned. Because we see the truth: there is only one dangerous prejudice, and it is imposed by the descendants themselves. In the United States of North America, the struggle is the White against the Black; in the United States of Brazil it is the Black against the Black! What a contrast! Unfortunately, he who can do nothing for or against this situation is the reader's humble friend, and very much your servant,

MATUTO

## 4.10 "NEWS," A LIBERDADE (SÃO PAULO, BRAZIL: DEC. 28, 1919)

*This social note in* A Liberdade *presented contrasting examples of what the writer saw as successful and unsuccessful club management. The Centro Recreativo Paulistano maintained "rigorous" discipline at a recent dance, enforcing rules respected equally by the women and by*

*the men, "who often are not so attentive." The Brinco de Princeza club, by
contrast, apparently experienced occasional disruptions and outbursts of
violence. The paper described the club's members as women who "live
from their labor," most likely as domestic servants, and who looked to the
club for respite from their "many, many hours of work." At its most
recent dance a fight broke out that the members were able to defuse
without police intervention. But* A Liberdade *predicted more such epi-
sodes in the future, provoked by board members who had only been
suspended when they should have been permanently expelled. While the
Centro Recreativo Paulistano provided a positive example to the other
Black social clubs of "discipline" and "composure" (qualities highly
valued in the Black press), according to this report, the Brinco da
Princeza provided the opposite.*

### Centro Recreativo Paulistano

Having moved its headquarters to Largo Riachuelo, no. 56, and holding
its dances on Sundays from 9:00 pm to midnight, I had the pleasure and
the honor to attend, like all those present, and to see the correctness and
hard work of the distinguished Board of Directors. It has been some time
since I have seen such order and respect as I saw that Sunday.

The ladies seated in their chairs respected all the signals given by the
masters of ceremonies, they obeyed the stern orders of the [male] officers,
and when the auctioneer announced the prizes, they listened with full attention. The gentlemen, who often are not so attentive, this time did not have the
courage to leave their chairs to visit the buffet, even to smoke a cigar.

In short, the Paulistano's Board of Directors did not cease for one
moment to maintain a rigorous control that will serve as an example to
other recreational societies.

I give my sincere congratulations to the distinguished Board of the
Centro Recreativo Paulistano.

### Centro Recreativo Brinco de Princeza (Princess's Earring Recreational Center)

The aforementioned society is a society of ladies, each of whom lives from
her labor. It chose Monday as the day for its dances, for a moment of
happiness and satisfaction, to forget the many, many hours of work. After
a long period of peace and harmony, the Board of Directors was obliged to
suspend two ladies who are well known in our social milieu and to throw
a little rascal into the street once and for all.

The Board of Directors, who thought they had calmed the disorder so common in their dance hall, faced another occurrence on Dec. 8th, when they decided to prolong the dance until a later hour. This did not happen[,] because of the disorder that broke out.

After midnight, when everything was chic and beautiful, Roberto Cardoso became inflamed with jealousy over a little *mulata* named Floripes, who lives in Maria Thereza Street, and who was dancing with Octávio Cardoso de Mello. It wasn't long before Roberto, armed with a cane and looking to avenge his betrayal, gave Octávio two blows with the cane, leaving him stunned. Happily there were no injuries that made it necessary to call the police; in the end those present seized [Roberto] to prevent graver consequences.

At its meeting, the Board of the Brinco de Princeza ordered the suspension for a certain period of two [male] directors, when it should have eliminated them to give a good example to the other societies. These suspensions can only do damage; after these will come others, because one of the suspended directors does not have the necessary composure.

There the matter rests.

### 4.11 CARLOS ZODOCAR [CARLOS CARDOZO FERREYRA], "CULTURAL CHITCHAT," LA VANGUARDIA (MONTEVIDEO, URUGUAY: APR. 15, 1928)

*In this article, Carlos Cardozo Ferreyra, one of the editors of* La Vanguardia, *addressed the question of whether to admit White men to dances held by Black clubs or families. In principle Cardozo was not opposed to their admission. But in practice, he noted two objections: first, in deciding on their dance partners, Black women were "completely enchanted" with the White guests and showed a "veiled disdain" for the Black men in attendance. Second, White men sometimes admitted Black men to their own dances but all too often excluded them. On both these grounds, Cardozo proposed that White men should only be admitted to Black dances if they were married to Black women or "have some other similar connection to us."*

*One would like to have access to female writers' perspectives on this issue; we did not find such articles in* La Vanguardia *or any other of the Black papers.*

The author of these chitchats will always remember the conversation that he had one time with the gentlemen [Isabelino José] Gares and Jorge

Maciel Brown, on the theme of the subtitle.[9] Mr. Maciel Brown, with gallantry of expression and profound understanding, said certain things to us that day, and made suggestions that give rise to this column.

The topic is difficult and extremely complicated. But we hope to escape from the mire.

I still don't know what the idea of *race prejudice* means to my collectivity.

For me, it is White people's disregard of the worthiness of Black people. That hostility and rejection of which they make us the object, all because of the color of our skin.

Nor do I know which idea predominates concerning the weapons to be used in fighting for our rights: hatred without quarter toward White people, the same way that they do [to us], something that is old, broken, and unedifying, which would give us no practical result other than to worsen our situation; or to fight to bring together both races – the supreme ideal – a work of deep human solidarity and mutual acknowledgment.

Here we have the two formulas, one of which we have to choose. And in the interest of explaining my reasoning, I say plainly and directly that the more reasonable, the more logical, the better and more beneficial, is the latter.

Now we will speak of something that is implicitly at the heart of this topic and that, furthermore, serves to illustrate my idea.

Once at a certain dance, purely and exclusively for Black people, some White men arrived. They were well-behaved, polite, and good, but to the great dismay of our young men, we saw that our young women were dancing and were completely enchanted with them. Some of the young men of our race, seeking to invite the young women to dance, felt a veiled disdain! What do we say to these demonstrable facts? If we ourselves allow them [the White men] the privilege of feeling superior?

Well, sir, if the dance is purely and exclusively for Blacks, Whites should not have been allowed to enter, unless, as a prestigious gentleman of our race said, the White person had the formidable credential of being married to a member of our race, or some other similar connection to us. Then, yes!

Furthermore, in order to allow Whites to enter one of our dances, it is necessary (as I have pointed out elsewhere) that when they give their parties, to which one must buy a ticket, they not impose improper restrictions.

---

[9] The column did not have a subtitle.

That way, we would not look askance at this question.

To the contrary, it would be the supreme ideal.

But for that to apply, it is necessary that our [White] brothers not be elastic in their decisions.[10]

Another major point concerns our behavior, which one could describe as servile, toward the White man. He is the preferred one. And his [golden] locks are frequently the downfall of gullible women dazzled by the fictitious fantasy of that fool's gold.

As we are treated, so should we treat others. Doing so, we will achieve our rights.

For lack of space, in the next issue I will continue this chitchat, which I have just barely sketched out.[11]

## 4.12 "ORDINARY SESSION OF OCTOBER 15, 1930," BOLETÍN OFICIAL DEL 'CLUB ATENAS' (HAVANA, CUBA: OCT. 20, 1930)

*The **Club Atenas** (Athens Club), founded in Havana in 1917 and comprised mainly of professionals and government employees, quickly became one of the most prestigious Black associations in Cuba. The club organized concerts, artistic gatherings, and literary contests and hosted international visitors. This report of a regular meeting of the club's Board of Directors reveals many interesting details about the everyday workings of the club. Finances were an important topic: members late in paying their dues were admonished, and arrangements were made to manage the fees charged to members for the use of the Club gymnasium. The Board also discussed an upcoming dinner in honor of Estanislao Mansip, a member of the club who was the Chief of Police of Havana at the time and an important figure in the Liberal Party. Finally, the Directors organized a committee, including Félix Ayón, a member of the Cuban House of Representatives, to request payment of a subsidy approved by the Havana municipal government. These last two items reflected the prominence some members of the elite Black clubs achieved within Cuban politics, especially in comparison with Black clubs in other parts of Latin America. Another Board member present at this meeting, Manuel Capestany, was later elected to the Cuban Senate. Yet success within the political party system did not necessarily translate into the power to effect political change. And government ties could be*

---

[10] That is, that they be consistent.
[11] Cardozo did not return to this topic in subsequent columns.

*compromising, given the authoritarian and clientelist dynamics of the political system in Cuba (1.16).*

*Ordinary Session of October 15, 1930*

**Attendees:**
President: Cornelio Elizalde Lima
Secretary: Ramón María Valdés
Conrado P. Thorndike
Belisario Heureaux
Moisés Sariol Lamarque
Félix Ayón Suárez
Federico Matienzo Valdés
José González Benítez

Section Presidents
Juan Jerez Villarreal, Literature.
José A. Rojas, Fine Arts.
Manuel Capestany, Economic Interests.
Ángel Suárez Rocabruna, Recreation and Sports.

### APPROVAL OF THE MINUTES
To approve the minutes from the session held on the first of October, 1930.

### RETURN OF SOCIAL LIFE
To terminate the suspension of social events.

### CHESS SET
To accept, and to give the most expressive thanks to members Mr. Félix O'Farrill, Mr. Ignacio Corzo, and others for the donation of a chess set of large proportions.

### "CUMBRE" MAGAZINE
To return the tickets sent for the benefit to collect resources for the support of that publication, because the Club lacks available funds for this purpose.

### HOMAGE TO MEMBER ESTANISLAO MANSIP
To accept and assign to gentlemen members four tickets for the dinner being organized in this city to honor our member Mr. Estanislao Mansip.

## MEMBERSHIP REQUESTS
To pass along for investigation by the Moral Interests Committee the membership requests made by these gentlemen:

From ÁNGEL GÓMEZ DUQESNE, 47 years old, lawyer, resident at 160 Colón St., Sagua la Grande, married to Mrs. Tranquilina Duquesne, a certified midwife, at the same address.

From JOSÉ MARÍA MONTALVAN, 26 years old, lawyer, resident at 5 Marta Abreu St., Sagua la Grande, married to Mrs. ANA PINO PÉREZ, who attends to the tasks of her household, at the same address.

## CALL FOR AN EXTRAORDINARY MEETING OF THE PLENARY COUNCIL
To issue a call for an Extraordinary Meeting of the Plenary Council to hear the presentation of the reforms to the bylaws agreed to by the same Council in the session of July 5, 1929.

## THE MOVEMENT OF FUNDS
To approve the movement of funds presented by the Treasurer, corresponding to the months of July and August.

## RESIGNATIONS OF MEMBERS
To approve the resignations of the members Mr. Agapito Rodríguez Pozo, Mr. **Salvador García Agüero**, Mr. Justo de Lara Mena, and Mr. José C. Fuentes.

## MEMBERS IN ARREARS
A kind note is to be sent by the President of the Institution to the members who are in arrears, advising them of the penalties set out in the bylaws for failure to pay.

## A PRIVATE COLLECTION OF FUNDS
An account is made of the collection of funds undertaken by the Delegate, Mr. Joaquín López, for the bronze plaque that will be mounted on the house where Mrs. LEONOR PÉREZ (Mother of the Apostle, **José Martí**) passed away, in order to preserve her memory, in preparation for their transmittal to the "Club Tenerife" of this city, which has taken the initiative in this proposal.

## MUNICIPAL SUBSIDY

To commission Mr. Cornelio Elizalde, President of the Club, and the representative, Mr. Félix Ayón, to take the proper measures to obtain the payment of the subsidy approved by the municipal government of Havana and sanctioned by a final ruling of the Supreme Tribunal of the Republic, January 5, 1928.

## THE PAYMENT OF FEES

The treasurer will take over the collection of fees for the Gymnasium from the Recreation and Sports Section. He will issue statements for each trimester in advance, informing the Executive Council of cases in which payment of these charges is not made within thirty days.

### 4.13 [SELVA ESCALADA,] "SOCIAL NOTES, BY SELVA," NUESTRA RAZA (MONTEVIDEO, URUGUAY: JAN. 26, 1935)

*A principal function of the Black press was to report on social life in the Black community. The newspapers provided coverage on significant happenings – baptisms, weddings, dances, parties, the arrival of visitors, deaths of community members – that were unlikely to appear in mainstream newspapers. Coverage of events tended to describe them in uniformly positive terms, as "select," "elegant," "beautiful," etc. Social reporting also made visible a large and cohesive community of readers and subscribers who were eager to see their own names in print, or those of friends and neighbors.*

*The social pages were the only section of the papers in which there were often more female names than male. In this sample page, eighty-one women and girls were mentioned by name, and forty-nine men and boys. This reflected the fact that, while the clubs and community organizations chronicled in other parts of the paper were directed almost entirely by men, family-oriented social events and daily social life were organized primarily by women. In its early years,* Nuestra Raza *delegated coverage of social events to female reporters Selva Escalada and Iris María Cabral. After Escalada left the paper in September 1935, and Cabral died in May 1936, the paper's social notes shrank noticeably, covering fewer events and individuals.*

### Tabares–Miranda Wedding

As we had previously announced, the wedding of the distinguished young woman, Miss Aurora Esther Tabares, to Mr. Adolfo Martiniano

Miranda, took place on December 29. The religious ceremony was held in the Crypt of María Auxiliadora; Mrs. Julia Aguilar de Miranda and Mr. Casimiro Gutiérrez served as godparents, and in the civil ceremony, Dr. Luis Aparicio and Mr. Ceferino Gutiérrez served as witnesses for the bride and Mr. José Pedro Aguilar and Mr. Miguel Cuneo López for the groom. The large number of people who came to be present for the ceremony greatly honored both members of the couple.

## Tea Dance

Inaugurating the series of events that the Comité de Damas Melenses (Committee of Ladies from Melo)[12] – on whose activities we report elsewhere – plans to organize, on the afternoon of January 20 [the group] held a Tea Dance that was invested with unusual resonance.

The ladies who organized the party, jointly with Mr. J. Carlos Nieres, spared no effort to ensure that no desires were left unmet, elegantly welcoming the select group that attended.

As an aside, in brief and well-chosen words, Mr. Nieres spoke to those present about the motives that have guided the Ladies' Committee, ending with a vibrant exhortation to the Black race.

The event was enhanced by an excellent orchestra comprised of the young men Valentín Pereyra, José Saia, Alejandro Macedo, and Claro Maciel.

Among those in attendance, we were able to take note of the following:

Ladies: Virginia de los Santos, Felicia M. Silva, Dominga Acuña, Delia Núñez, María Julia Rosas, Juanita Silva, Juana L. de Meisos, Enilda Núñez, María L. de Sosa, Aurelia Morales, Nieves Lopes de Silva, María Nicodemi, Albertina A. de Arrillaga, María B. de Palomeque, María N. de los Santos, María C. Moras, M. Santos de Sosa, Delia Santos Gallego, I. Santos Gallego, M. A. Silva, Antonia Tele, María F. Núñez, Aleja B. de Alcántara, Manuela R. de Chávez, María C. de Macedo, Josefina B. de Loriente, Pola Acosta, Delia Acosta, María V. de los Santos, Amanda de Luz, Esther López, Pura López, Nieves López de Rodríguez, Floriana López, Saturnia López, Juana Pereira, Elvira Miquelini, Josefa Gamboa, Petrona Espina.

---

[12] The Comité de Damas Melenses was an organization of Afro-Uruguayan women who had moved to Montevideo from the small Uruguayan city of Melo, many of them to work in domestic service. The committee's goal was to raise money to build a headquarters for the Centro Uruguay, a Black social club in Melo; that goal was eventually achieved in the 1950s. Chagas and Stalla, *Recuperando la memoria*, pp. 101–6.

Gentlemen: Ricardo Palomeque, Juan Sosa, Luis Alberto Carballo, Julio Rodríguez, Abesúe Pérez, Julián Miguel Alamo, Jr., José Leandro Andrade, Ezequiel Asunsión, Julián Alamo, Mario Martínez, Juan Silva, Carlos María Sosa, José Salas, Dionisio Alvares, Ramón Suárez, Alaric Robinson, Valentín Manuel Pereyra[,] José Rodríguez, **Pilar** and Ventura **Barrios, Elemo Cabral, I.** José Gares, Vito Pereyra, Juan Carlos Nieres, **Mario Méndez,** etc.[13]

## Baptism

In the house of Mr. Marcilio Rivero and his wife Doña Margarita Castro, there was a splendid party to baptize their little son, José Miguel, and to celebrate New Year's Eve.

Those present danced to the strains of an excellent orchestra and at midnight did justice to an exquisite dinner, amidst much praise of the hosts for their good taste and the attention lavished on their guests. After dinner, dancing resumed and continued until dawn, when the attendees retired, pleasantly impressed. The following persons were present: Señoras [married women]: Leonor V. de Olivera, Jorgela B. de Martínez, Juana N. de Larrosa, Adela S. de Caetano, Esther S. de Martínez, Nora S. de Rodríguez, Mrs. de Bartabúru, Carmen S. Carnocebich, and Mrs. de Silva; Señoritas [unmarried women]: Olema Martínez, Agustina and María E. Castro, Hortensia, Amelia and Lucía Rivero, Olga and Elida Bottaro, Juanita and Irene Olivera, Ofelia and Dominga Delgado, Trinidad Birriel; and a group of gentlemen.

## Birthdays

To celebrate the birthday of Don Floricio Silva, a lovely party was held on January 10, consisting of a dinner offered by his friend, Mr. Wenceslao Barboza, and [Barboza's] wife, lasting until 1:00 am.

Those present at the well-stocked table were: Señoras [married women]: Juana D. de Silva, Petrona M. de Barboza, Isabel de Dacuna; Señoritas [unmarried women]: Amada Dacuna, Elsa Barboza, Julita Silva; Señores: Wenceslao Barboza, Juan P. Dacuna, Fermín Gadea, Leoncio Gadea, Ramón Morales, Juancito Dacuna, Ramón Espiñeira and others.

---

[13] In this list of male attendees, José Leandro Andrade was a star Afro-Uruguayan football player, a member of the country's Olympic team in 1924 and 1928 and its World Cup team in 1930. **Pilar** and Ventura **Barrios, Elemo Cabral,** I[sabelino]. José Gares, and **Mario [Rufino] Méndez** were editors of or contributors to *Nuestra Raza.*

The event was graced with some compositions performed on the guitar by Mr. Ramón Morales.

- Simple and interesting was the party held a few days ago in the home of Mr. and Mrs. Lima Rocha, celebrating the birthday of their young daughter Inés. The very large group that surrounded Miss Lima on her birthday, which lack of space prevents us from listing, made quite clear the high esteem in which she is held by her friends and relations.
- The little children Eva and Anastasio Souza celebrated their 2nd and 4th birthdays on the 19th and 22nd of this month.
- The respectable Mr. Laureliano Ocampo celebrated his birthday on the 19th.
- On January 3 the very nice young woman Aidee Araújo celebrated her birthday in San Carlos. Many friends came to greet her and were very well attended to by the gracious honoree.
- Mr. Joaquín Barboza celebrated his birthday on January 12 in Rocha, warmly congratulated by his friends and relatives.

## Ill

Mr. Julián García Rondeau is much improved from the serious illness that had attacked him, requiring his internment in one of our hospitals. We send best wishes for his rapid recovery.

## Travelers

– To Buenos Aires, Mrs. Asunción Silvera.
– From Minas, Mrs. Luisa Duarte de Santos.

## New residence

Mrs. Bernarda A. de Silva invites her friends to her new residence in 4403 Iglesias Street.

## Grateful thanks

Eduviges Izeta de Piñeiro and her children gratefully acknowledge the condolences they received during their recent period of mourning.

## [Deaths]

### ARQUIMEDES AMARAL

The young man Arquimedes Amaral passed away in the Pasteur Hospital, where he was being treated for a serious illness.

This lamentable death, which occurred on January 11, puts many families in Rocha and the capital [Montevideo] in mourning. To his relatives we send our condolences.

### MANUELA BENAVIDEZ
The passing of Miss Manuelita Benavidez, on January 5, has been much lamented.

For quite some time Miss Benavidez had lived apart from society; she was one of the most cultivated women in our milieu. May there be peace in her tomb.

### MIGUEL ANGEL CLAVIJO
As the result of a blow received in an incident involving two friends and companions from work, our particular friend Don Miguel Angel Clavijo passed away on January 11.

Clavijo was an honest and hardworking laborer, head of a humble home that his death leaves in a desperate situation. May there be peace in his tomb.

### AMBROSIA E. DE DUARTE
Mrs. Ambrosia Enríquez de Duarte has just died in the Pasteur Hospital. A model mother, Mrs. Duarte's death leaves a very large absence.

### 4.14 MARÍA LUISA SÁNCHEZ, "THE SUGAR HARVEST AND THE COMPARSAS," ADELANTE (HAVANA, CUBA: APR. 1937)

*In 1937, the Havana city government invited Afro-Cuban* **comparsas** *to participate in public* **Carnival** *celebrations for the first time in nearly twenty-five years. The comparsas had been banned in 1913 because officials found them "uncivilized" and thought that they tarnished the image of the city. By the middle of the 1930s, the emerging academic field of folklore studies had recast Afro-Cuban music and dance as important and even heroic elements of the national patrimony. Influenced by this view, the city government now saw the resurrection of comparsas as a way to attract tourists from the United States and to improve Havana's reputation as a haven for gambling and prostitution.*

*Writers in* Adelante *were deeply divided over the issue. Several regular contributors were members of the* **Sociedad de Estudios Afrocubanos** *and the* **Club Atenas**, *organizations that supported the return of the comparsas. Other writers argued that the newly inaugurated street parades were*

*not authentic folklore, but rather sexualized and "anti-artistic" perform-*
*ances that demeaned Black culture. One of the most powerful arguments*
*in this debate came from María Luísa Sánchez, a female writer about*
*whom historians know little. Her account was inflected with the radical-*
*ism of the Communist Party, which emerged in the 1930s as a key site of*
*Black mobilization and anti-racist politics. Sánchez used the city's choice*
*of the sugar harvest as a theme for the comparsa presentations to draw*
*comparisons among slavery, labor in sugar production in the 1930s, and*
*the tourist economy. The result was a devastating critique of politicians'*
*deployment – and tourists' consumption – of Black culture and Black*
*bodies for their own purposes.*

The President of the **Sociedad de Estudios Afrocubanos**, Fernando
Ortiz,[14] respected and beloved by all those who take an interest in folkloric and eminently Cuban research on our Black population, recently
published a magnificent appreciation of the **comparsas**, as an element that
promotes the development of a specifically national culture, full of local
color, a source of diversion for the popular soul.

The comparsas of 1937 have paraded noisily and cheerfully, still somewhat timid, but brimming over with enthusiasm and local character ...
like an anesthetic ... like a sedative.

The comparsas in the time of slavery were a way to forget, to not think,
at least once a year – in the midst of the harvest, the fierce whippings, the
hard tasks of the season, the festivals of the masters – about the miserable
existence, the brutal oppression, the savage commerce in their own selves,
by those same masters who laughed at their foolery, at their happy
comparsas, their "garish colors," with uncomprehending smiles, with
banal commentary, with vulgar discrimination, showing off their own
"refinement" through the cruelty of their grotesque mockery, full of the
contagious sensuality of the voluptuousness that the energetic dances
awaken ... The masters' desires caught flame to the rhythm of the
comparsas! ... There is no liquor more thrilling!

The Carnival troupes of 1937 pass by, agile, noisy ...

The tourists laugh, the tourists smile uncomprehendingly, with banal
commentary, with vulgar discrimination, showing off their own
refinement ... The tourists drink the liquor of their arousal ... they pass

---

[14] Fernando Ortiz (1881–1969) was a White anthropologist who, after an early career
denouncing Afro-Cuban culture as criminal, became a leading folklorist. He founded
the Sociedad de Estudios Afrocubanos and edited the journal *Estudios Afrocubanos*.

through streets full of people... People who do not realize that their own hunger is the reason for the noise! ... who forget their new masters ... who forget that they have masters, that they are slaves, that once a year, and only for a few months, there is a sugar harvest, there is scrip to spend in the company store ... Who forget that their children suffer, that their children die of whooping cough, of malaria, of typhoid, and tuberculosis ... because they are hungry, because there is no money ...

Everyone forgets the profound tragedy! ... All the Black comparsas forget their sad hovels, their damp hovels, their Black hovels ... And they forget the "Cueva del Humo" and the "Llega del Pon", "Isla de Pinos" and the terrible "slaughterhouse" of "Las [Y]aguas."[15] So many Blacks in slave barracks! ... And the ever-present threat of returning [to sleep out] under the archways of the city, with a doorjamb as their only pillow... All this for tourism and the Carnival troupes and ... to forget!

Promises of houses for the unemployed! – Forcible evictions from the shack by the sugar company – Everything for tourism, for the beautification of the city! – Work from sunup to sundown, the scrip, the dead time[16], [homelessness] under the archways! ...

Promises of land distribution for the peasants! – a plan for concentration camps,[17] like forced labor prisons – But there is something "providential" that comes from "above": the Carnival parades! They have the Carnival parades! Now nobody remembers the filthy shacks, the long days of rough, poorly paid labor ... the violation of social legislation! Now nobody remembers the harvest of hunger and blood! Now nobody remembers the prisoners and the epidemics! Now nobody remembers the masters!

The struggle seems far away... the street is rich with lights, tourism, Carnival ... Now they have the Carnival parades ... now the people ask for nothing! ... The people do not roar, or even remember ... or think about the way out ... they do not confront the problem!

---

[15] Names of famous slum neighborhoods around Havana.

[16] During the summer months, relatively little labor is required in cane cultivation, especially compared with the very high demand for labor during planting and harvest seasons. Under the labor system that operated in the Caribbean in the early twentieth century, agricultural workers suffered mass seasonal unemployment and starvation during what they called the *tiempo muerto*, dead time.

[17] During the independence war of 1895–98, Spain carried out a policy of "reconcentration," under which peasant families were uprooted from their homes and forced to move into fortified encampments; the goal was to prevent them from providing support to the independence forces. Of an estimated 400,000 civilians confined in the camps, 200,000 died. Ferrer, *Insurgent Cuba*, p. 152.

Noise, lights, excitement stronger than liquor. . . stronger than the pain! The Carnival parade is a drug, it is the opium of the masses rediscovered![18]

## 4.15 "A PLEASANT INTERVIEW WITH DOÑA MELCHORA M. DE MORALES," REVISTA URUGUAY (MONTEVIDEO, URUGUAY: MAY 1945)

Revista Uruguay *was the organ of the Asociación Cultural y Social Uruguay (ACSU), an Afro-Uruguayan social club founded in 1941 that exists to this day (now under the name of Asociación Cultural y Social Uruguay Negro [ACSUN]). A major part of ACSU's program was the organization of social dances that provided entertainment for the club's members while simultaneously raising money for the club. In this article, the reporter interviewed one of the community's matrons, Doña Melchora Morales, to get her opinion of those dances, which she compared very favorably to those she had attended in the early 1900s, when she was a teenager and a newly arrived rural migrant to Montevideo.*

*One of the primary themes of the article was that of respect for community traditions and for the community's elders, including Doña Melchora herself and her houseful of "furniture and objects from yesteryear," which the interviewer identified as an invaluable cultural patrimony. Doña Melchora's enthusiastic account of dances attended forty to fifty years earlier expressed a vision of a bygone golden age of social cohesion. She particularly praised the gentility and respectfulness with which the younger dancers treated the older women in attendance. Throughout, the reporter was quite deferential, observing elaborately respectful conversational protocols. Doña Melchora seemed inclined to extend her reminiscences, but when she was called to the small laundry that she ran in her home (and from which she was preparing to retire, with a government-guaranteed pension), the reporter seized the opportunity to slip away, citing the need to write up the interview for* Revista Uruguay's *female readers.*

Complying with a request from our [the magazine's] director, we went to the home of the distinguished matron, Melchora M. de Morales. At the exact moment that we arrived, our kind collaborator was a bit concerned

---

[18] A reference to Karl Marx's famous claim that religion is "the opium of the people."

about an illness that, while not serious, was afflicting one of her agreeable daughters.

As soon as we arrived, the kind lady received us with her characteristic affability, ushering us into "a very comfortable little room, by the way," in the words of the lady of the house, adorned with furniture and objects from yesteryear from which she would not part for all the gold in the world. They represent mementos of her elders, relics of great value to the lady of the house and that the reporter knows to value, because there are [similar objects] in his house as well!

Informed of our mission, Mrs. Morales explained the reasons for her absence. First, because she was away from the capital [Montevideo], taking advantage of Tourism Week to visit her relatives in their neck of the woods in a coastal department,[19] and second, a few difficulties related to her activities. (Doña Melchora has a small laundry from which, after more than twenty years, she plans to retire under the shelter of her pension. A well-deserved rest indeed. The reporter makes this point at the request of the lady herself.)

Coming to the main reason for our interview, which had no goal other than to hear her impressions of social life, in particular of the recent dances of the Centro Uruguay,[20] which she attended with her daughters and other relatives, [Doña Melchora] lacked the words to describe those events. Having attended other meetings of the centers [social clubs] that also host dances, none of them – the lady says – are like those of the Centro Uruguay. In my opinion, she adds, those dances have made me remember those of past times, and what times [they were], my reporter friend! To tell those stories would require many pages of your interesting *Revista Uruguay* (a compliment to us, to which the lady added: it is only just!).

"As I was saying, with no disrespect to the present, those were golden times! Yes sir, golden, pure gold."

"Can you tell us something of those times that you remember with such enthusiasm? Logically those have to be very pleasant memories, since of course they are of your youth."

"Yes, my friend, I was eight years old when my parents decided to sell their little farm and move to this city. In those early years we did not take part

---

[19] Tourism Week was established in Uruguay in 1919 as a secular alternative to Holy Week (the week before Easter Sunday), with the supplementary purpose of promoting domestic tourism within Uruguay. The country is divided into nineteen departments, the equivalent of states or provinces in other countries.

[20] "Centro Uruguay" is shorthand for the Centro Cultural y Social Uruguay. The Centro later changed its name to the Asociación Cultural y Social Uruguay.

much in social life, since we were from the countryside, but little by little my parents started entering the "rodeo" of social life. Please pardon the comparison. And I remember that it was on the eve of the **Carnival** of 1900 that, at the invitation of friends, we attended a dance in a hall on what used to be called Daimán Street. What a party, my reporter friend! I will never forget it. It was my first appearance in society, and I say society because, in addition to the nature of the dance, with masks and costumes, I can assure you that it was an excellent social occasion. How thorough and conscientious were the gentlemen of the committee! And the matrons and young women who comprised the arrangements committee, the same![21] Everything was beauty and distinction, the hall tastefully decorated with colored lights, an orchestra, and what an orchestra, my friend! And girls and young women wearing splendid dresses and costumes – fantasies, as they were called in those days. A buffet that, well, lacked for nothing, and everything served with delicacy and correctness. At the end of each part of the dance program, the young couples would invite the mothers to join them at tables overflowing with happiness [and] indescribable moments. I have noted with pleasure that [same] attentiveness at the dances of your Center. How they remind me of those happy times of my childhood!"

Doña Melchora falls silent, which the reporter respects. Her thoughts are ranging possibly even beyond her own imagination.

"Well, my friend, if you're not pressed for time, shall I continue with my memories?"

"Not pressed for time at all, Doña Melchora, unless you need to attend to your work."

"No, for now it is a great pleasure to continue this agreeable chat, with the most pleasant reporter of *Revista Uruguay*."

"Thank you, madam, for such a gracious compliment."

"Not at all," she responds.

"As I was saying" – but at that very moment they need her in the laundry. Despite the lady's kindness, and her desire to continue sharing with us a pleasant page of her memories, we leave, making our excuses and promising to return very soon. Doña Melchora was insisting that we stay. With a "See you soon!" we set off for the office to oversee "the memories of Doña Melchora" and offer them to the female readers of our magazine.

Assistant

---

[21] Dances at Afro-Uruguayan social clubs were often organized by gender-segregated committees of men and women.

# CHAPTER 5

# Women

## INTRODUCTION

The Black newspapers and magazines were produced almost exclusively by male writers and editors. Female contributors to the publications were rare, and the perspectives, and even the language, of the papers' articles and features were relentlessly and unselfconsciously masculine.

Nevertheless, female readers and supporters were absolutely crucial to the Black press's survival, both as subscribers and by organizing benefits to raise money for the papers (5.3). As a result, the papers made occasional direct appeals to female readers (5.9) and included special features – social columns, poems and short stories, advice columns – intended to speak to them. Some of those features were written by women (1.5, 2.14, 4.13, 4.14, 5.3, 5.5, 5.6, 5.8, 5.13, 5.16, 8.5); others claimed to be written by women but contained hints of male authorship (5.7).

While the papers often invoked an ideal of Black women leading fulfilled lives in the home, caring for their husbands and children, they also acknowledged that for most Afrodescendants, that ideal was simply unattainable. Poverty and the need to support their families forced Black women into the labor market, in most cases as domestic workers. An 1881 piece in *La Broma* saluted Buenos Aires' Black laundresses as women who simultaneously brought cleanliness and sanitation to the city's upper- and middle-class households while resisting the temptation and dishonor of sex work (5.1). The Uruguayan newspaper *La Verdad* called on Black families to educate their daughters to enter the world of work (5.7; see also 8.10); *Nuestra Raza* profiled **Margarita Ubarne de Espinosa**, who had faced down racial barriers to pursue a successful career as an educator (5.12). In the 1940s, Uruguayan and Brazilian publications reported on the efforts of Black (and White) domestic workers to organize and achieve the workplace protections enjoyed by industrial and commercial workers (5.14, 5.16).

The papers offer occasional evidence of Black women's political participation, and the limits of that participation. In Cuba, female readers wrote to the pro-independence newspaper *La Doctrina de Martí*, and to the **Partido Independiente de Color**'s newspaper *Previsión*, to express their support of the papers' causes (5.3, 5.5). After female suffrage was enacted in Cuba in 1934, Calixta Hernández de Cervantes called for the inclusion of Black women in party lists for election to public office (5.13).

As we saw in Chapter 3, motherhood was a fraught and frequent topic in the Black press. The papers worried about high rates of illegitimacy and single motherhood in their communities, and enjoined mothers to prepare their children to lead honorable and productive lives (3.1, 3.4, 3.7, 3.9, 3.10). In 1889 the Cuban newspaper *La Fraternidad* published a harrowing account of a traumatic labor and delivery that the mother barely survived, and that the child did not (5.2). In 1928 the Brazilian paper *Progresso* joined the public campaign underway at that time to erect a statue in honor of the **Black Mother**, the symbolic figure representing the many enslaved and free Black women who were forced to care for their enslavers' or employers' children, to the detriment of their own (5.11).

Finally, female beauty was a regular topic in the Black papers, which offered advice on how to achieve it without violating norms of proper behavior (3.2, 5.6, 5.7), and public contests to determine who best embodied it (5.10, 5.15).

## DISCUSSION QUESTIONS

- Several of these articles offer eloquent and heartfelt portrayals of Black women in specific situations: as poorly paid laundresses (5.1), in childbirth (5.2), and caring for other women's children (5.11). In each case, how might those portrayals have been different had they been written by women who had actually experienced those situations?
- Beauty contests limited to Black women were a regular feature of the Black press (5.10, 5.15). In what ways, if any, might such contests have benefited or harmed contestants? What about Black women in general? In what ways might those contests have benefited or harmed the editors of the papers? What about Black men in general?

- Domestic work is perhaps the most difficult, and also the most poorly paid, vocational category in modern economies. Yet in almost every country in the Americas, it was the occupation that Black women in the 1800s and 1900s were most likely to enter. Why do you think that was the case? And what do the articles in this chapter (5.1, 5.11, 5.14, 5.16) reveal about the multiple challenges of domestic work?
- To judge from these articles, what were the roles of Black women in local and national politics? How did those roles change over time? What were the institutional vehicles through which women participated in politics? What were the goals of that participation?

### 5.1 "THE LAUNDRESS," LA BROMA (BUENOS AIRES, ARGENTINA: OCT. 27, 1881)

*Through the late nineteenth century, laundresses washing clothing on the wide, shallow banks of the Río de la Plata were a common sight in Buenos Aires. Many of these were Black women, for whom laundering, along with ironing, sewing, cooking, cleaning, and other domestic services, constituted a main source of employment. Indeed, the Black laundress became an iconic figure in representations of nineteenth-century Buenos Aires, a romanticized emblem, for many White writers and artists, of a bygone time.*

*Yet the work of washerwomen was thankless, harsh, and dangerously unhealthy, as this article made clear. Moreover, any job that brought women out of their homes and onto the streets cast doubt on their honor. This risk was especially acute for Black women, who in Argentina as elsewhere were often depicted as morally loose and sexually available. In this article, the pseudonymous Prometeo turned this logic on its head to issue an impassioned defense of Black laundresses. A beautiful young woman who could have traded her charms for material comforts, but persisted in the grueling job of laundress, irrefutably proved her virtue – something that, he implied, could not be said of many high-society ladies.*

It strains belief that no writer, not even in a moment of levity, should yet have dedicated a few short lines to this subject, which I – a mere literary amateur – nonetheless intend to develop, as my limited faculties permit and from a social perspective.

What is a laundress?

"She is a poor woman, a wretch, who must be looked upon with scorn because of the dishonorable trade she plies and because it is generally women of ill repute who do that work."

Such is the answer that, to my mind, a question of this sort would provoke, when directed to one of those frivolous and pretentious people who cannot perceive decency unless it is covered in silk and stones, obtained by means only God knows.

The laundress is, to me, a heroic woman, worthy of all praise.

Her calloused hands attest to the endless labor to which she is dedicated.

In summer, harassed by a feverish sun, her face flushed, her brow dripping sweat drop by drop, treading with her torn soles upon fiery sands, she does not yield to fatigue and works with fervor and perseverance to earn the bread with which she will alleviate her children's hunger!

One must admire her on one of those cold winter mornings! While the ladies of the comfortable classes, following a long evening of pleasure, rest upon their soft and springy beds, she abandons hers, counting herself fortunate to find enough strength to brave the hardships of the day.

Behold her! With what cheerfulness she takes her little pail and places her washtub upon her head, without fear of sullying her hair with the water that pours from the fabrics entrusted to her for cleaning.

Observe her! She fears not the cold, she gracefully raises [the hem of] her dress to her waist and kneels comfortably to begin her task.

The waters are thick with frost, her feet and hands are stiff with cold, her lips and cheeks covered in crimson spots from the gusts of air that graze them.

Contemplate her on one of those hot days, as she carries upon her head a bundle of clothes that makes her flexible figure bend beneath its weight, and reflect for a moment – you, daughters of fortune, who pass the days of your existence without knowledge of the hazards of fate – reflect, for a moment, I say, [upon] the life of this martyr, who, from the moment dawn appears in the East to the time the sun hides at dusk, courageously withstands a hard and unyielding job that would exhaust the health of the most robust man; and tell me whether that woman deserves admiration or contempt!

But this is not all. There comes a moment in life, of the sort that leaves an everlasting memory – a moment of mourning, of grief, of terror, when even the bereaved dare not touch the articles of clothing that had belonged to a family member who has ceased to exist because of a contagious illness.

Everyone refuses to take them for fear of contagion – the laundress is the only one who, with her own hands, washes those clothes to strip away the miasmas they contain – without noticing, poor soul! that she exposes herself to contracting the same illness that led the last owner of those garments to his grave!

And yet, what reward does that poor woman receive in exchange for so much suffering, so much abnegation?

One day she falls ill upon her hard bed, without enough resources to meet the demands of her needs.

Not one of those people who had received her services, and who have particular reason to treat her with consideration – because families have secrets that the laundress must certainly know, which would cause more than one person to blush should she fail to keep them – none of those people, I say, *has a spare moment* to go console her as she lies prostrate on her sick bed. And in the end, the [pauper's] hospital is the only institution to which, due to her lack of resources, she can turn for treatment .... and from there, one is unlikely ever to leave, unless it be to the grave!

Many young women of graceful features, flexible figure, and charming gaze have I seen dedicated to these arduous tasks, and I have become convinced of their honor.

For who can tell me that a laundress, being young and beautiful, is safe from the temptations that a thousand libertines, of those who swarm around in cities that, like Buenos Aires, possess a thousand beauties – who can assure me, I say, that more than one of these [men] has not made them propositions that would dazzle a poor young woman, in exchange for her honor?

That love which the laundress shows toward her work gives clear and evident proof of the virtue of her heart.

For what woman, having lost all modesty and shame, would resign herself to the sad and hazardous life of the laundress, instead of [enjoying] the lively and indulgent life that is offered to her?

No! We must admire those women because, even when many of them have committed some misstep, they give unequivocal proof that they have not entirely lost their virtue when they know how to earn their bread with the sweat of their brow!

Prometeo

## 5.2 "FROM CIENFUEGOS," LA FRATERNIDAD (HAVANA, CUBA: JAN. 31, 1889)

*This account of a difficult labor and delivery was one of very few articles in the Cuban Black press that described intimate or private events within individual Black households. The woman giving birth,* **Úrsula Coimbra** *de Valverde (see* Figure 0.3), *was a musician and piano teacher, and one of the most important Black women writers in Cuba from the 1890s through the 1910s. Childbirth was not only an extremely harrowing and dangerous experience for many women in Black communities, it was also a social event that could include older female relatives and extended family and friends. The midwives who managed these events were frequently Afrodescendant women and community leaders; in this case, after three days of labor the midwife, Amelia Gostly, called in physicians who were able to save the mother but not the child.*

January 26, 1889

Señor Director of *La Fraternidad*, Havana

My good sir and esteemed friend: with deep sadness I recount the following episode: *Spare her, blessed God! Lord, please do not make her suffer!*

I heard these phrases, these exclamations, among other lamentations, last Monday, at the home of my special and esteemed friend, Coimbra.[1] Compelled by the true friendship which all of his family professes toward me, I rushed over, wishing to know the causes for the sad sighs and painful laments that had reached my ears. I arrived and found my cherished friends Valverde[2] and the Coimbras (father and son), full of confusion, with anguished faces, and hearts full of sorrow, along with a great many people who, like myself, are honored by their friendship. I inquired as to what made them so sad, and they told me the story that follows.

Oh, friend Director [of *La Fraternidad*], it still saddens me to retell it!! Since the previous Friday [January] 18, my kindhearted and loyal friend Ursulita had felt ill. Supposing (correctly) that her discomfort was the result of her impending motherhood, her solicitous husband sent for the midwife, Madame Amelia Gostly, who, fulfilling the responsibilities demanded by her profession, installed herself, together with Mrs. Pérez de Coimbra,[3] at the head of Ursulita's bed. But, oh evil fate! … they waited through *Friday, Saturday, and Sunday* without the desired result. And sadder still, Valverde saw his loving wife, the Coimbras saw their affectionate daughter, and the elder Coimbra saw his much beloved

---

[1] Musician and composer Marino Coimbra.

[2] Nicolás Valverde, Úrsula Coimbra's husband, was a tailor by trade. He edited several newspapers in Cienfuegos and, later, in Veracruz, Mexico.

[3] Úrsula's mother.

granddaughter suffering cruel agony and, according to the predictions of Señora Gostly, nearing death's door.

On Monday at midday, Mr. Coimbra (grandfather) begged the midwife to speak with frankness, and the lady asked him to send for Doctors Frías and Peña. After a dangerous and difficult two-hour operation, which the patient endured with heroic bravery, they were able to remove the stillborn fetus. Señores Frías and Peña have performed an operation that once again does them honor, and proves how well-deserved are the high reputations that they enjoy in this city. They combine talent, ability, and skill with their excellent demeanor toward their patients, without a doubt the product of their brilliant education. Persons as learned as these two doctors deserve widespread applause and esteem. Ursulita is saved! And I, her most loyal and faithful friend, together with her family, through these columns, offer a prayer of thanks for Doctors Frías and Peña and I cry out:

Thank you, Almighty God! Thank you for this kindness!

## 5.3 "FROM OUR HEROINES IN EXILE," LA DOCTRINA DE MARTÍ (NEW YORK: MAY 6, 1898)

*La Doctrina de Martí was established by a group of Black Cuban and Puerto Rican writers and activists in New York, along with a few White allies, during the final war of independence against Spain (1895–98).[4] In this letter to the editor, a group of women living in Key West, Florida, explained why they had chosen to create a committee to collect funds to help support the newspaper. They summarized the editorial stance of the newspaper: "decorous" unity in the independence movement was only possible if workers and Afrodescendant people received equal and respectful treatment; and independence should be accompanied by profound social transformation. Most writers in this newspaper emphasized the role of men of color in this struggle, as soldiers, workers, and political organizers, but this letter offered a different view: "we women are struggling for our rights and guarantees." The writers expressed the conviction, unusual in the context of the Black press, that despotism should be eliminated from the family as part of a "radical" project for the "abolition of all privileges."*

Committee to Aid
"La Doctrina de Martí"

---

[4] Mirabal, *Suspect Freedoms*, pp. 97–138.

Key West, Fla.
Key West, March 16, 1898
Señor **Rafael Serra**,
         Director of *La Doctrina de Martí*, New York
Distinguished Compatriot,

We are hopeful for the triumph of our longed-for national independence and convinced of the necessity of the existence of *La Doctrina de Martí*, because the battle to create, through nobility of spirit and character, happiness for all in a country bequeathed to us by sickly despotism will be no small matter. Convinced of this urgent need, we, your sisters and admirers, have gathered together to contribute, modestly but constantly, to the maintenance of your newspaper, which we love for its tendency toward decorous unity among the elements [of the nation] that have been segregated by the inhumanity of despotism, and for your tenacity in persuading those who, despite their talent and education, do not know the virtue of true sacrifice for the creation of a successful and happy fatherland. And none of this will be possible as long as [people] refuse to understand that the abolition of all privileges must be radical.

For we [women] understand that if women are struggling for our rights and [constitutional] guarantees, we ought not, once we attain them, become vain, and exercise despotism over our children because they are weaker, instead of consecrating ourselves to educating them for freedom. For this reason, though independence is the most certain means towards our glorious aim, we believe and we hope that the struggle to redeem Cuba cannot end with the mere fact of independence.

You will forgive us that, in order to send you five little pesos for *La Doctrina*, we should have chatted so long, but we must have some opportunity [to do so], your countrywomen, who will not abandon you in your noble labors.

Yours in P[eace] and F[reedom],

Inocencia Araujo, President, Antonia Fernández, Treasurer, Julia Guerra, Secretary

## 5.4–5.5 TWO ARTICLES ABOUT WOMEN IN PREVISIÓN (HAVANA, CUBA: MAR. 1910)

*The newspaper* Previsión *is mostly remembered as part of a dramatic project to create an independent political organization for Black men, the* **Partido Independiente de Color**. *Two articles provide evidence of the*

*role that the newspaper's editors and writers imagined for Black women. "At a Trot" (5.4) was the regular political column in the newspaper. In this installment, editor* **Evaristo Estenoz** *deployed the recurring fictional character José Rosario, a Black Cuban everyman, to complain of the number of government jobs held by women. Estenoz, whose most consistent political goal was the equitable distribution of government jobs to Black men, expressed a view of female domesticity and vulnerability that did not reflect the actual lives of most Black women, who had no option but to work for wages.*

*"To the Men of Color" (5.5), a letter from a female reader, was a rare instance of a Black woman expressing herself within the pages of* Previsión. *Carmen Piedra adopted the same masculinist logic expressed by male writers in the newspaper: anti-racism was the duty of men, like any defense of family or community honor. But Piedra turned this idea on its head, shaming men of color in order to encourage them to take action. "If I possessed the so-beautiful title of man," she wrote, "I assure you that I would be one of the most fervent in the struggle to conquer the rights of our race."*

### 5.4 "At a Trot," *Previsión* (Havana, Cuba: Mar. 15, 1910)

The politicians, the legislators, the moralists, the writers, and all those who one way or another take up the question of the common good, channeling humanity's steps toward clear and open paths, have a duty to be very frank and sincere in the exposition of their ideas.

We, who fight for the political and moral exaltation of our race, without concern for the difficulties we encounter, feel each day stronger in the pursuit of our work.

We ask for morality, much morality, in order to cleanse our political environment.

There is an occurrence that until today has gone unnoticed by our legislators and writers, and it is the large number of ladies and young ladies who earn their livings in government offices.

We believe that [the] woman should be exalted to the greatest possible degree of comfort, granting her the means to fulfill in every way her elevated mission as daughter, wife, and mother simultaneously; and preparing her so that she may influence, with her wise suggestions, the best path of national development, from which she, like us, derives her happiness and sorrows.

But between this belief and having an extremely large number of women in our public offices, torn from their homes and put before the gaze of the anonymous [crowd], lies an unfathomable abyss.

We see with sadness that because of the unfortunate choice to take this route, thanks to a spirit of imitation that comes to us from North America, morality is losing out among us. The family is collapsing, slowly but surely, and no one dares to alert the public authorities that along this path lies total dissolution.

We treat this topic superficially today, not wanting to show the public the evil-smelling sores that characterize the state of things, because we have full confidence that those who are responsible for these *pranks* will try, with all the means at their disposal, to prevent the enthronement of an era of true immorality, comparable only to the one about which the Bible speaks.

Cuba must be neither a Babylon nor a New York, but rather a Switzerland, a Holland, or at the very least a Belgium, a small nation that, because of its morality, its honesty, and the work ethic of its sons, would be worthy of the respect of the strong and powerful nations.

José Rosario is morality itself, he practices it and he proclaims it to the four winds, certain that his voice will reach every corner and is already taken into account when it comes to matters of great importance for the well-being of Cuba.

Many times we have seen that he who has the desire to act does more than he who has the ability to act. It is proven; we are the ones who have to work for morality. That is why we did not find it strange when, walking along a narrow path in a very dense forest, we stumbled upon José Rosario, half-melancholy and half-smiling, saying to his bay pony, "My little Pastorcita, you who mean so much to me, why do you choose to follow the bad advice of those who tell you it is necessary to start off at a gallop? Don't you understand that everything is sinking around you, and that this way, softly at a trot, with the two-by-two of your creole gait, we will arrive safe and sound at the destination to which we aspire?"

### 5.5 Carmen Piedra, "To the Men of Color," *Previsión* (Havana, Cuba: Mar. 5, 1910)

Men of Color, you who have the high honor of being Black; who, when the Fatherland has needed you, have known how to answer the call of duty with pleasure, wherever it may take you, willing to abandon your homes and spill your blood; why do you tarry on the beautiful path that will lead our race to greatness and free it from the moral slavery in which it lives submerged?

Why, if God in heaven has given you the beautiful title of men, do you not all contribute to the redemption of our race, making the White man see that you have more than enough civic responsibility and worth to defend what is truly yours[?]

If I possessed the so-beautiful title of man, I assure you that I would be one of the most fervent in the struggle to conquer the rights of our race.

Have you by chance not observed the degree to which the Black man is the object of exclusion? It is past time, then, for you to draw back the veil that has you blindfolded.

Carmen Piedra

### 5.6 "ENQUÊTE: WHAT DO YOU THINK ABOUT THE JUPE-CULOTTE?"[5] MINERVA (HAVANA, CUBA: APR. 15, 1911)

*In the early 1910s,* Minerva *combined many common features of the Black press – political, cultural, and historical writing, as well as sports reporting, by male authors – with design and content more typical of a ladies' magazine. Perhaps the most striking feature of the magazine was the extensive attention given to women's clothing and physical appearance in posed photographs of young women (see Figures 0.8 and 0.12), extensive social reporting, advertisements for beauty products and hair stylists, and several regular columns dedicated to fashion reporting. These topics sometimes appeared in short notices in other Black newspapers. But the publishers of* Minerva *directed themselves toward female readers whom they understood to be consumers of fashion, responsible for keeping abreast of and understanding contemporary styles. The technical sophistication displayed in the fashion reporting, along with frequent advertisements for wholesale fabric and sewing machines, suggests that some readers were also fashion professionals: dressmakers and stylists (see 2.18).*

*In this "survey," the editors of* Minerva *sought readers' opinions on a running controversy over whether women should wear a style of wide-legged trousers known as split skirts. Over several previous issues, the magazine's regular fashion reporter (writing under the name María Antonieta, possibly a pseudonym) had introduced readers to the style and to the controversies*

---

[5] Fashion reporting in *Minerva* focused almost entirely on new styles coming from Paris and London, and was therefore frequently laced with French terms such as *enquête,* survey, and *jupe-culotte,* split skirt.

*raging in Paris and London. She summarized: "The partisans of the manly style will be those women of talent and the anti-trouser contingent will be women of elegance and beauty." Then she made some technical observations about various models (framed, as usual, around the mistakes so many Cuban women purportedly made in their understanding of fashion) and, finally, identified herself as firmly in the anti-trouser camp.[6] In response, Carmela López de V. Cañizares and Dolores S. de Echemendía each revealed some hesitancy about claiming expertise and putting their opinions into print. Yet their answers were anything but tentative, suggesting the degree to which, for Black women readers and writers, the question of fashion, though always printed in the non-political sections of the magazine, could in fact be deeply political. López de V. Cañizares explained that she was willing to engage in the debate, even at the risk of public disagreement, because she was a feminist. Echemendía asked why men, who never gave much thought to fashions that injured or debilitated women (such as corsets and high heels), were so alarmed by the prospect of women putting on trousers. Perhaps, she teased, they were afraid of "feminist currents" in the field of fashion when, in fact, feminists were too busy distinguishing themselves in intellectual and artistic pursuits to pay much attention to such things.*

### A Word about the Split Skirt

Let us dedicate our attention for a brief instant to something that is, for us, not just a problem of the moment, but a matter of vital and very great importance, equally of interest to all [women].

I refer to the fashion of the Split Skirt, which has had and still has so many detractors (justified or unjustified), but which in our world is the topic of the moment.

Of course, I do not think myself able or qualified to offer you my opinion on this matter. But spurred on by a desire to oblige persons who are, I think, worthy of consideration, I cannot dodge this request. For this reason, and perhaps committing a very grave error, I will give you my opinion about the aforementioned fashion.

Needless to say, I have great sympathy for this fashion not only because it will relieve us somewhat of the tiresome need, imposed by [traditional] dresses, to gather up our skirts when it rains, even when this means showing our legs, but also because I think that our morality and our decency suffer no loss when we wear them [split skirts].

[6] María Antonieta, "Correo de modas," *Minerva* (Mar. 15, 1911); María Antonieta, "Correo de modas," *Minerva* (July 1911).

There are styles that have a great acceptance among us which, though they put our charms more fully on display, do not, for this reason, cause the slightest damage to our honesty.

Why then, is such a resolute war being waged against the Split Skirt? ... Does it undermine, in some way, our morality? To my mind, it does not; but if my opinion is completely wrong, if I do not hold the opinion of the majority, I pray that you will pardon my indiscretion in this case, as I have done no more than set out my ideas, faithfully and freely.

And before closing, I should first make clear that whatever verdict is handed down in this matter, I will gladly accept it since before and above all, I am a feminist.

Carmela López de V. Cañizares

### "For Minerva"

We cannot say much about the split skirt.

Because women worship that Sovereign known as "Fashion," it will be the case that some will desire to follow the commandment to wear them [split skirts], others will not wear them, and others will criticize those who do wear them.

This style will hold its bloom only a little longer than a rose ...

But why has the stronger sex become so alarmed by this innovation? Why do [men] give more importance to the split skirt than to the corset, the hoop skirt, and the Louis XV heel,[7] styles that are anti-hygienic and pose a threat to the health of their *compañeras*?[8] Why this panic? Do they fear, perhaps, that feminist currents will be more formidable in the field of clothing than in the intellectual arena? Have no fear! The woman who triumphs in the academies and the museums will always value the degree she receives from an educational institution more than the anti-aesthetic fashion of the split skirt.

Dolores S. de Echemendía

### 5.7 MARGOT, "IN FAVOR OF FEMALE EDUCATION," *LA VERDAD* (MONTEVIDEO, URUGUAY: OCT. 15, 1911)

*In debating the most appropriate education for the community's children, the Black papers occasionally focused specifically on the needs of girls and young women (see also 3.2). In this article, the pseudonymous writer Margot observed that young women were traditionally educated to be*

---

[7] A shoe with a heel higher than 2 inches.

[8] The use of this term, meaning "female comrade," signifies a partnership among equals.

*wives and mothers. But if those conditions didn't materialize for them, they needed to be prepared to make their way independently of men, to earn their own livings, and to be "active members of society." After this rather progressive beginning, however, Margot swung back to the idea that women's principal duties were to please the men in their lives by being attractive, cheerful, and hardworking, rather than ugly, bilious, and sour. Education should cultivate their spirits, making them lively and appealing even after their physical beauty had faded (by age 40!) to "no more than a ruin of what it was." "Work," Margot declared, "is the source of happiness and the most powerful antidote against wrinkles."*

*All of the credited writers for* La Verdad *were male, and Margot may very well have been so as well. The only woman known to have written for the paper was* **Margarita Ubarne**, *later* **Ubarne de Espinosa** (5.12), *writing under the pseudonym Lirio del Valle (Lily of the Valley).*

Until today, women have been educated exclusively for matrimony. From their most tender years, they have been taught the duties of a wife and mother, and those who did not become one or the other, found themselves condemned to suffer the bitterness and disappointments of a mistaken existence, completely opposed to the one for which they had been prepared.

Whence the figure of the ugly and bilious old maid, for whom life never held roses, because only through love did she seek them, and love always closed its doors to her. The only remedy that the unhappy one knew to apply to her misfortune was a profound hatred toward her peers. She hated women because she supposed them to be happy; [she hated] men because they didn't love her. Don't educate girls for marriage: educate them for life.

Rich or poor, place in their hands or in their spirits the means to make do without a brother or a husband, and should fortune ever turn against them, by this means you will help them avoid suffering and humiliation in the future. Teach them that work is the source of happiness and the most powerful antidote against wrinkles.

Study girls' aptitudes and cultivate those seeds from which they will gain the greatest benefit. Don't ever force tastes uselessly, as the only result will be to waste time and make their characters sour.

Beyond instructions, give your daughters a solid education, attending simultaneously to the soul and the spirit. Teach them to obey, without making them automatons bereft of will. The great merit of female teachers is principally to teach at the same time obedience and fortitude. Allow girls to express their little opinions, as this is the only way to know those opinions and to correct their defects. To prepare girls well for their future struggle, they need to be taught to know how to suffer in silence. Make them see the ridiculousness of a complaining woman; how disagreeable she makes her own life and the life of others. Let them understand that being soft and delicate is not the way to please a man, and that for a father, brother, or husband, coming home tired from the tasks of the day, finding a happy woman, full of life, is much more attractive than the spectacle of a beautiful woman reclining on her couch, unable to move or smile because of her headache.

England and Germany have understood the great benefit that would result from reforming female education, and now they are seeing the happy outcomes of their efforts.

In those two countries, women's activeness rivals that of men. Rich or poor, they consider themselves to be the active members of society, bringing their share of labor to the work of progress. There, the husband finds in his wife a companion capable of understanding and even helping him in his tasks; the children, a mother who takes interest in their studies and helps solve the difficulties that they encounter.

And don't believe that, by being reasonably learned, women cease to be feminine and enchanting, because that somewhat manly education will increase her graces rather than diminish them. Youth and beauty are as fragile and ephemeral as the flower to which they are often compared. But the flower has perfume, and when the petals fall, dried out and discolored, the sweet smell remains, that soul of the flower that just days before bloomed from the bud. So it is with woman: by forty, her young, beautiful body will be no more than a ruin of what it was; but the spirit does not age. And I will say more: cultivation of the spirit slows for many years the physical ravages of time. And if you think not, compare the physique of those women who lead an active life to those who live in continual idleness. While the former arrive at thirty with an agile body and a soul full of life, the latter at the same age are old and spent. For Sarah Bernhardt, for Melba, for Carmen Sivia, fifty never arrived and those stars ceased to shine without passing through decadent phases.[9]

Oh, if women understood the thousand advantages that intellectual light provides, there would be fewer sad little heads in the balconies, little heads empty of ideas and whose horizons extend no further than the romanticism embodied in the longing for a sweetheart, who for so many will never arrive.

Physical beauty is at the mercy of any physiological setback and can be extinguished like a burning meteor that has blazed ephemerally in the

---

[9] Sarah Bernhardt (1844–1923) was a famous French actress; Nellie Melba was the stage name of Helen Porter Mitchell (1861–1931), a famous Australian soprano. We have not been able to identify Carmen Sivia.

heavens of life. Spiritual beauty persists; the select souls come into being bearing the scent of the realm of ideas; the superior spirits are like gardens in an eternal springtime.

A woman of robust mentality always provokes universal and sincere admiration, much deeper than the wake left by physical beauty among the sensuality of men, as fleeting as all the passions of the flesh.

Mothers: guard the future of our daughters! They don't always have to be at your side, receiving cooing affection and sweet maternal caresses. Look to the future, which appears too hazy and misty, impossible to scrutinize through its darkness ...

## 5.8–5.10 THREE ARTICLES ABOUT WOMEN IN O MENELIK (SÃO PAULO, BRAZIL: 1915–16)

*The three articles that follow illustrate the complex, diverse, and consequential roles that women played in the Black newspapers and their accompanying associational life. Especially in the nineteenth and early twentieth centuries, it was rare to see female writers in these papers; when women appeared as writers, it was usually through one-time special contributions, as in "A Life Lesson" (5.8). More frequently, male writers wrote about women or addressed them as readers. In "To Our Female Readers" (5.9), the editors of* O Menelik *used the language of romance, commitment, and courtship to describe the idyllic relationship between a newspaper and its readership. Behind that rosy sentimentality (which recapitulated dominant gender norms, with women as "charming" and "delicate" recipients of passionate male attention), we can perceive the centrality of women to the papers and their social networks as loyal readers, supporters, and subscribers.*

*"Beauty Contest" (5.10) offers one of the earliest instances, in Brazil's Black press, of what would become a mainstay of the Black papers and associations (see also 5.15). While beauty contests assigned women to idealized roles as objects of male pleasure, organizers conceived of them as rejoinders to White standards of beauty and expressions of pride in their community. Yet for all the efforts of male writers to encourage women to be docile, dainty, and demure, women had their own ideas, as the author of "A Life Lesson" (5.8) made clear. This young woman, an educated, avid reader of romances, wrote beautifully and frankly on sensitive topics like Black male beauty and her own love affair. She then deployed her talents against her inconstant fiancé, getting the last word in the very public space of the Black press.*

### 5.8  "A Life Lesson," *O Menelik* (São Paulo, Brazil: Oct. 17, 1915)

One fine afternoon, after my lessons, the sky was a deep, pure blue – unbroken but for a few white spots. The breeze was pleasant and refreshing, and I, taking advantage of the coolness, went for a stroll along the beach. To distract myself, I brought along a little novel.

In the distance, the sky appeared to meet the land. The sea was wild … as if blanketed in white foam!

As I resolved to break away from the marine madness in which I had too long lost myself, I was interrupted by a young Black man, of good stature and with a magnetic pair of eyes. After greeting me, he said: "Are you still in school, miss?" "Yes," I responded, "ever since I was seven years old."

"How old are you now?"

"I will be fifteen in May."

"Ah, well … perhaps … if I could have the honor of accompanying you on this lovely walk … if only I could be worthy of such a thing … "

"More than worthy," I responded.

And so we ambled along the ocean's sandy coast!

At every step, from his lips there fell a declaration of love.

Dusk descended ever so slowly!

And when it did, we bid farewell amid impassioned pledges.

Fifteen days later, I was happily by his side, considering him my betrothed. But that happiness lasted only a few months.

Despicable intrigue conspired to separate our futures.

What torments did I endure, my God! But I made peace with my fate, unleashing upon him an intense hatred that will not end so soon.

Leopoldina Dias. Santos, January 1913

### 5.9  "To Our Female Readers," *O Menelik* (São Paulo, Brazil: Jan. 1, 1916)[10]

After spending forty days far from the fond affections of your delicate hands – the sweet cradle of your soul – "O Menelik" began to pine for you.[11] And so, returning once again, nestling beside [your] generosity – my female beauties, behold it here.

---

[10] This anonymous piece was likely authored by Deocleciano Nascimento, accountant and published poet, and founder and editor of *O Menelik*.

[11] *O Menelik* first appeared in October 1915, aspiring to be a monthly paper. But the reference to a forty-day gap suggests that the editors missed their deadline: instead of

Behold it here, vowing that from now on it will appear the first Sunday of every month to bring you news from the stars, hoping to be received with the usual charming smiles from your rosy lips! And all the while, its humble editor casts a thousand kisses of gratitude at your dainty feet.

### 5.10 "Beauty Contest," *O Menelik* (São Paulo, Brazil: Jan. 1, 1916)

With this issue, we launch a women's beauty contest. The contest will take place across two issues, organized as follows: in the first issue (beginning with our very next one), we will publish a general list of all those [women] who received votes, and in the second, the final results of the contest.

A portrait of the winning contestant will grace the front page of our newspaper, should she consent to let us so proceed.

N.B. The contest is, of course, among "the **class [of color]**" and votes must be cast by men who are our subscribers. To that end, they must fill out the following form:

| DEAR READER |
| --- |
| Who is the most beautiful young woman, in your estimation? |
| It is:. . . . . . . . . . . . . . . . . . . . . . . . . . . . . . . . . . . . . . . . . . . . . . . . . . . . . . . . |
| Street:. . . . . . . . . . . . . . . . . . . . . . . . . . . . . . . . . . . . . . . . . . . . . . . . . . . . . . |
| *Signed* . . . . . . . . . . . . . . . . . . . . . . . . . . . . . . . . . . . . . . . . . . . . . . . . . . . . . . . |

### 5.11 DAVID RODOLPHO DE CASTRO, "BLACK MOTHER," PROGRESSO (SÃO PAULO, BRAZIL: AUG. 19, 1928)

*In the 1920s, White and Black Brazilian journalists and public figures mobilized to create a statue to the **Black Mother** in Rio de Janeiro, as well as a holiday in her honor on September 28. The date was chosen to commemorate the passage of the **Free Womb Law** in 1871, after which all children born of enslaved mothers in Brazil were legally free at birth (although they could not enjoy this freedom until the age of majority). In*

appearing in December 1915, issue number 3 appeared in January 1916. On the material and financial difficulties of the Black press in Brazil and elsewhere, see 4.1 and 4.2.

*portrayals by White Brazilians, the Black Mother evoked nostalgia for a bygone era or for slavery itself, presented as a rosy and benevolent arrangement in which the love between Black nursemaids and their White charges bequeathed Brazil a legacy of racial harmony.*

*Black writers took different approaches to the Black Mother. Some echoed White writers' nostalgia as a way of rendering homage to Black women and their descendants. Others deployed the Black Mother as a symbol of the bonds of fraternity that ought to exist between Black and White Brazilians, but too frequently did not. In this article, a contributor to* Progresso *sounded some of those common themes, calling on Black Brazilians to "keep the flame of love for the Black Mother alight in the hearts of the Whites." But he also offered a rare, searing critique of the suffering of historical Black nursemaids, who were forced to set aside the needs of their own children and families to care for the children of the White "masters." Those Black Mothers, and their abandoned sons, were owed a debt of gratitude, the author argued, that should no longer go unrecognized or unpaid.*

When we turn our eyes toward the ashes of the past, toward the arrogant muteness that enfolds those hearts cast, perhaps, in the molds of truth (yet unconscious of their debts of gratitude), [we see that] the abnegation of the Black Mother has passed unnoticed. We uncover what happens to spirits deprived of the beneficent light of instruction, and of the maternal education that is the principal factor of all human progress. We cannot allow a sacred duty, long forgotten, to remain silenced. We must never allow ourselves to disremember the dark torpor of ignorance as we educate our progeny.

Let us not forget, however, that the cornerstone and pedestal of this monumental task, uncommonly worthy of honor and praise, is maternal education: those drops of morning dew on flowers that slowly wither. Any individuals who seek social stability while denying or fleeing domestic duties are not worthy of the air they breathe.

The bedrock of our demand is maternal love, the divine substance that emanates from the Being of Beings into the depths of our hearts, the innermost recesses of our souls.

The cradle provides the foundation for our progress in all fields of human knowledge. We do not wish to see our children lost in the desert of doubt, or worse, in the black ocean of faithlessness.

As descendants of Blacks, we endeavor, as much as our strength allows, to keep the flame of love for the Black Mother alight in the hearts of the

Whites, who are her true children. We can say, with our nation's history as our witness, that the Whites are Blacker even than our ancestors, and that the White masters are more properly the sons of Black women than even our elders ...

We believe that those fortunate ones have more of a right to be considered [the Black Mother's] sons. Our grandmothers were never able to nurse, let alone raise, their children because they were forced (under threat of the whip) to deny their rotund breasts to the fruits of their love, so that they could, with extreme solicitude, raise the children of "their Lordships."

The outcome of this prohibition was sorrowful: mothers abandoning their children for the masters' [children] who, as adults, repaid such dedication with the lash. Wretched victims of inhuman slavery!

Their children grew up, most of the time, without the pleasure of feeling a maternal caress, the tenderness of a mother. In almost every case they did not even have the chance to meet her ... because they were sold away at the age of three or four.

When our ancestors' mothers, who nursed the children of the "Masters," were able to raise their own, they did so on bean broth, mush, and water. The heart of the Black Mother was nothing more and nothing less than a vast desert of hopes, or an interminable night of disbelief. Resistance always fails in the face of force ... The [enslaved] offspring of captivity who were raised deprived of caresses were more despised than unreasoning creatures. A horrifying and barbaric sight!

Among the historical paintings of scenes of slavery we find the works of renowned painters. One of them [is] of a Black woman of slender or medium build, wearing a white cotton shirt of the sort no longer seen in public, exposing her engorged bosom, and for a dress something resembling a nun's habit, as befits her suffering. In her dark arms she holds a plump, White infant, who avidly sucks from her rotund breasts the most precious and pure nectar of her indescribable nature.[12] A mother of another's children, in perpetual abandonment of her own, is worse than a flower without perfume. Yet even without its scent, [the flower's] elaborate and refined texture still draws the gaze and curiosity of observers. From the sarcophagus of necessity there emerges, occasionally, something unanticipated that astonishes the civilized world.

---

[12] The author likely refers to the famous 1912 canvas by Brazilian painter Lucílio de Albuquerque (1877–1939), "Mãe Preta," in which the Black nursemaid's own baby lies on the floor at her feet while she nurses her White charge.

It must be said: education molds the character, and instruction illumin-ates the spirit. We want to make it patently clear in these lines that the Black Mother is the true and legitimate mother of Brazilians. It is not our aim to offend anyone's sensibilities. We have as our only and exclusive goal the fusion of Whites and Blacks for the glorification of the Black Mother. This anomaly of sentiments [by which the Black Mother is deprived of her due], this irregularity of principles, must be extirpated for the order and progress of Brazil.[13]

São Paulo, 11–7-1928. David Rodolpho de Castro

## 5.12 AGUEDO SUÁREZ PEÑA, "A GREAT WOMAN: MARGARITA U. DE ESPINOSA," NUESTRA RAZA (MONTEVIDEO, URUGUAY: MAY 30, 1934)

*As a counter to images of Black exclusion and failure, the Black papers frequently profiled Afrodescendants who had achieved undeni-able success in the professions, the arts, or sports. In this article,* Nuestra Raza *focused on* **Margarita Ubarne de Espinosa**, *a schoolteacher who, earlier in the century, had been an occasional contributor to* La Verdad. *Teaching was a profession that was notoriously resistant to entry by Afro-Uruguayans.* **Aguedo Suárez Peña** *explained how, through-out her career, Ubarne de Espinosa "opposed race prejudice with her iron will and her privileged intelligence." To leave no doubt about her profes-sional success, he mentioned her close ties to some of Uruguay's most prominent families, who relied on her to tutor their children for high school and college. In short, she was "a great woman, a great spirit, a unique intellectual of our race, who does not fear the famous ghost of racial prejudice."*

*Eleven years later, Ubarne de Espinosa's professional success was cited, along with that of other Black professionals, as evidence of the absence of racial barriers in Uruguay (2.11). That article appeared in* Revista Uruguay, *edited (and perhaps written) by Aguedo Suárez Peña, whose views had apparently evolved in the interim.*

---

[13] The motto "Order and Progress" first appeared on the Brazilian flag at the start of the First Republic (1889–1930). The author's invocation of that phrase is one example of Black writers' frequent recourse to the tenets of republicanism, in those years and beyond (see 1.1, 1.6, 1.15, 2.5, 2.8).

When I read in these columns, this last March, the interesting story on **Dr. [Francisco] Rondeau**,[14] and what the distinguished lawyer said about the injustices of which he has been victim, committed by the men of his time, injustices that resulted in his never occupying the position that his intelligence and knowledge deserved – I decided to present **Mrs. Margarita Ubarne de Espinosa**, as a unique example in our race of perseverance, of imposing her personality and her great intellectual capacity [in areas] where racial prejudice is the most hermetically sealed. When she began to teach in the schools of the capital [Montevideo], she found, here and there, among men and women, attitudes and gestures that showed their antipathy toward her presence as a Black woman. They knew that she had the virtues of great talent and maximum knowledge; but it didn't matter; she was Black and they had to remove her from the national body of teachers.

But this superior woman, dismissing the attitudes in the environment in which she developed her teaching activities, opposed race prejudice with her iron will and her privileged intelligence. And now we see her in her position as an educator, honoring our race and showing to the country a teacher equal to any challenge.

Very few members of our collectivity know the strong character and tenacity of Mrs. Ubarne de Espinosa. What a shame that we do not have our Social House.[15] I am sure that [if we did,] she would give interesting lectures there on how our members should present themselves when, with indescribable sacrifices, they obtain their academic degrees.

Mrs. Ubarne de Espinosa is always studying. Her manner of teaching is so interesting that, at the request of her disciples and their parents, she is obliged to give them private lessons until they enter the university or high school. This detail gives a clear sense of her connections with extremely distinguished families. Those families receive this great woman, who, well before that moment, had helped make ideas shine through and make race prejudice disappear.

I feel a great admiration for the members of my race who distinguish themselves in any aspect of life. I give them my encouragement, urging them to continue and to go further and further. When **Dr. Salvador**

---

[14] "Hablando con el Dr. Francisco Rondeau," *Nuestra Raza* (Mar. 1934), 4–5.

[15] At this time, *Nuestra Raza* was promoting the idea of a Casa de la Raza, which would serve as both a social club and a civic organization to represent the city's Black population. See "Casa de la Raza" and "Necesidad de la fundación de un Club," *Nuestra Raza* (Apr. 1934), 5, 10–12.

**Betervide** obtained his law degree, I had high hopes for him, knowing his great talent and that he was a very worthy representative of our collectivity. But time has passed, and though he has not failed in his career, his name does not have the prestige that Mrs. Ubarne de Espinosa has in the national teaching profession.

For me, Mrs. Margarita U. de Espinosa is a great woman, a great spirit, a unique intellectual of our race, who does not fear the famous ghost of racial prejudice. Multifaceted, dynamic, and intelligent, we find her dominating her milieu, with stupendous authority. She is also a gifted devotee of the arts. Two years ago I saw her taking education courses, exclusively for teachers, where they showed their work in painting, embossing in wood and bronze, and other forms. It was a singular exposition of art, in which the distinguished educator showed sensitivity and culture.

I admire the beautiful spirit of this great woman who, knowing her extraordinary features, I sincerely believe lends honor to the collectivity. I present her not as an unknown in our milieu but rather as a voice of encouragement for those university graduates who do not know how to present themselves in such a way as to represent us with dignity, wherever that may be.

## 5.13  CALIXTA HERNÁNDEZ DE CERVANTES, "HORIZONS," ADELANTE (HAVANA, CUBA: JULY 1936)

*After the mass uprising against President* **Gerardo Machado** *in 1933, the magazine* Adelante *emerged as a space for Black writers of diverse political affiliations to debate which strategies to adopt with respect to the largely discredited Cuban political system. Calixta Hernández de Cervantes was one of a handful of Black women writers who contributed regularly to these conversations.[16] Her articles were part of a broader tendency in* Adelante *to represent the Cuban people as a coalition of Black people, women, and workers rather than a single homogeneous constituency. Hernández, a teacher, combined an emphasis on gender equality in the workplace with a particular focus on creating more opportunities for Black women in caretaker professions. According to her view, Black women with degrees in pedagogy and social welfare were uniquely qualified to educate less fortunate Black women and to formulate social policy to protect them.*

[16] Brunson, *Black Women, Citizenship.*

*In this essay, she turned to the question of Black women's political participation and representation. Black men were guaranteed the vote in Cuba in 1902, but suffrage was extended to women much later, in 1934. Hernández de Cervantes celebrated the subsequent election of women to political office but noted the absence of Black women among them. She offered a critical assessment of the rapid incorporation of Black women voters into the Cuban party system and urged working-class Black women to use their political power to help elect elite Black women to public office.*

The Cuban panorama offers a new horizon for women's struggle. With the elevation of several ladies to important elective offices in the government machinery, a new cycle has opened for female conquests, every day more positive and beneficial in their lineaments, which point toward a new social structure.

The House of Representatives, the Provincial Assembly, and not a few municipalities of the Republic have offered the beautiful spectacle of courteously seating estimable and intelligent ladies, who, in representation of our sex, have gone to cooperate with the men in the arduous and honorable work of national reconstruction.

All of this is very good, and we congratulate ourselves for it since, from any point of view, these events represent a significant step forward in the sphere of human conquests, which is our country's due in light of its specific conditions of progress and civility. Yet, it occurs to us to ask, why did no woman of color obtain the votes necessary to secure an office in the last elections? Is it possible that female voters of color were unaware that the names of the non-White women appearing on several candidate lists were the greatest and most estimable among our female contingent, and that the triumph of these energetic fighters would have translated into a positive and humane aid for them [Black women] in their abandonment, which is as real as it is unjust and tragic? Who will raise their voices in Congress to ask for justice for the little Black women workers who are displaced from decent jobs and must resort to the broom, the stove, or the ironing board? Why did the Black women who went to cast their votes by the hundreds not stop to consider this aspect of their problem and act consequently, in accordance with their needs and following the dictates of their instinct for survival?

To all these questions and a few others that could be posed, one can only answer that there was a lack of consciousness of the responsibilities of citizenship that were acquired along with the right to vote. *Muñidores*[17] with no conscience and no decency led the Black woman (blind, ignorant, and trusting) – I refer to the majority – where they wished to lead them. And though it is painful to admit it, we have given a palpable demonstration that we do not have the necessary ability to act in accordance with the requirements of reason, justice, and consciousness of our own responsibility.

During the last elections, many automobiles circulated around the city filled with Black women who went happily to fulfill the sacred obligation of every voter; along with the "chauffeur" in each vehicle there was always a "shepherd" responsible for bringing that flock to the polls where they had to make their cross-marks in the place [on the ballot] that suited the unscrupulous vote-gatherer. With the electoral struggle carried out in this way, the results were those that one might logically expect: few women elected, and none of color.

Female comrades; open your eyes and be more cautious the next time; do not allow yourselves to be guided by those who only seek their personal profit; choose, weigh, study the candidate lists and select from among the many names that appear on them those of our own female fighters, who will help us and will achieve for us a goal that we ought, by now, to have attained: absolute equality in all aspects of the lives of citizens, beginning with the right to work, which is the cornerstone of human dignity.

## 5.14 "OUR WOMEN WORKERS ARE MOBILIZING," NUESTRA RAZA (MONTEVIDEO, URUGUAY: AUG. 1940)

*In every Latin American country, domestic service remains a very large occupational category that is majority female and closely tied to non-White racial status. Since domestic workers work, and often live, in their employers' homes, it has proven very difficult for them to organize unions or other collective mobilizations.*

*This article reported on an effort to create such an organization in Uruguay, based on an interview with one of the organization's directors. The anonymous interviewee stated that the group was not a union but rather an association that sought to lobby the government for pensions and other protective legislation and to provide educational and mutual aid services to its members. The reporter did not specify the racial*

---

[17] Party operatives responsible for rounding up voters and getting them to the polls, often through the distribution of favors.

*composition of the group, and the director (also of unspecified race) stated that the members were not interested in addressing issues of race or Blackness, which "stir up social or psychological arguments that we don't want to discuss. Here we are all comrades [compañeras], and it is enough that we live the reality of being poor and being workers." This was a position that was very common in Latin American labor movements, which feared that employers might exploit race as a source of division and conflict among workers, thus undermining their efforts to organize.*

Women today collaborate with men in social activities and participate with them in public life, their civil and political rights proclaimed and assured. But not, as would be just, on the same plane of economic equality as concerns salaries and work regimen. In this respect the exploitation of the feminine worker is unspeakable.

If we consider the insufficiencies in State services to poor women: assistance in old age and infirmity; assistance to working women and their children; to single mothers; efficient assistance, protection, and education to workers' homes; and if we consider the living conditions of women in various sectors of work, and above all of female workers in domestic service, the picture is desolate; and even more so if we take into account, beyond the workers' own subsistence, the demands of their families, who have the same rights as others to nutrition, education, instruction, and to persevere.

Dr. Victor Zerbino,[18] explaining certain social problems concerning infant mortality, underlined that "the protection of the child is the protection of the mother; it is the protection and organization of the family, which is a function of the State: labor legislation, distribution of wealth, assistance to the family, investigations of paternity and [paternal] responsibility ... And we know that state protective services have few resources, and their action does not arrive directly to the home."

\* \* \*

There is now a bill to provide retirement pensions to female workers in domestic service, who have gathered to struggle for that just protection, perhaps the first of the many that they hope for every day.

We entered the headquarters of the Agrupación Pro-Jubilación [Association in Favor of Pensions] and interviewed one of its directors.

---

[18] Victor Zerbino (1886–1943), a leading Uruguayan pediatrician.

"Is this a union?"

"Not really. For now, it is a simple workers' association that works in favor of the right to a pension, which we named after Dr. Solís Vila, the author of the bill under consideration in Parliament. But with the enthusiastic blessing of numerous meetings, presided over by the energetic director Miss Dominga Ríos, and the secretary María L. R. Correa, we are considering the possibility of a broad mutual-defense organization of female workers, with impartial leaders and no distinctions of religion or politics."

"?" [*sic*]

"We will study the rules and procedures and will request our legal incorporation, so as to transform the current Agrupación into a vast feminine center of education, culture, social assistance, and recreation. We will seek in that way to cooperate in raising the cultural level of the woman worker, through adequate instruction, classes, lectures, concerts, art exhibits, etc. We also need to establish classes in sewing and dressmaking, and culinary courses, for the technical perfecting of our members, preparing them to cook in the great hotels, which for a long time have been monopolized by a dozen foreign 'maestros' of moderate competence."

"Speaking of cooking, *Nuestra Raza* recently published an interesting historical piece by the Northern [Brazilian] professor **Dr. Gilberto Freyre**, which highlighted in Brazil, since colonial times, the extraordinary genius of women of color in everything having to do with haute cuisine, which even today is still their purview."

"True, we read it. Furthermore," our informant continues, "in our future center there is no interest in reviving color prejudice or reaffirming racial exclusivism. How dark-skinned people feel in society; how they are situated; how they are viewed culturally – this stirs up social or psychological arguments that we don't want to discuss. Here we are all comrades, and it is enough that we live the reality of being poor and being workers."

"Very good. Also, there are so many specific instances of moral affinity between Whites and Blacks, who esteem and appreciate each other."

"Exactly. And that affinity will continue to exist in our institution, for the most useful and efficient ends. And if we find the support that we expect and the resources that we will pursue through various festive initiatives such as raffles and bazaars, benefit shows, dances, etc., we will add to the services already mentioned all forms of assistance to working women, including medical, dental, legal, and financial services.

"It would be an extraordinary organization in the country, if it were extended to all female workers."

"That's possible. But what we call domestic service includes a considerable legion of workers, who come here and will come here to unite to struggle for just improvements, above all the enforcement of the labor laws, which will imply equal rights and consequent economic relief, a factor in [creating] that 'vital space' that, in the end, can be limited to the home – a home no less worthy for being modest, but with its daily bread assured."

\* \* \*

So you see that our women workers are organizing! Our mothers, sisters, and spouses! At the first smile of hope – the promise of goodness and justice – they move, the irresistible waves surrounding the immovable rock of men's egotism and indifference! These women, perhaps the hardest working of all the workers, are agitating for the just rest that repays their long, bitter period of … [illegible]

### 5.15 "CONTESTS FOR 'THE QUEEN OF THE MULATAS' AND 'THE PITCH DOLL'," QUILOMBO (RIO DE JANEIRO, BRAZIL: JUNE 1949)

*Following on earlier traditions (see 5.10), Rio de Janeiro's **Teatro Experimental do Negro (TEN)** imagined beauty pageants as instruments of anti-racism, correctives to the exclusion of Black women from Brazil's beauty contests and standards of beauty. Contests for the "Queen of the **Mulatas**" (for lighter-skinned women of mixed African and European ancestry) were separate from those for the "Pitch Doll" (for darker-skinned women of predominantly African ancestry). Writers in the Black press typically deplored social distinctions based on color, but here the separate contests guaranteed that women with darker complexions would also be able to "show off their gifts of beauty, elegance, charm, and social distinction." Well-versed in performance and pageantry, the directors of the TEN made these events a highlight of Rio's social calendar, where people of different races and classes could "fraternize" while displaying an "elevated social level." Quilombo featured photographs of the winning contestants, thus disseminating images of Black women from Brazil and elsewhere (see Figures 5.1 and 5.2). The magazine's writers did not ask whether events focusing on attractiveness and bodily appearance might contribute to the oppression of Black women. Instead, they presented affirmations of Black female beauty as directly linked to*

FIGURE 5.1 Photograph accompanying "Contests for 'The Queen of the *Mulatas*' and 'The Pitch Doll'," *Quilombo* (June 1949). Original caption: "Terezinha de Jesus and Dalva, extremely strong contestants for the throne of the *mulatas* last year, photographed in the sunroom of the former woman's home."

FIGURE 5.2 Cover from *Quilombo* (May 1950) featuring Caty Silva, winner of the recent "Pitch Doll" competition.

*longstanding political battles: the valorization of Black men and women in Brazil's past and present (as in the reference to the **Black Mother**) and of Brazil's deeply "mixed" civilization.*

Twenty thousand *cruzeiros* in awards for the winners – A night of art and elegance during the coronation party.[19]

The customary contests for "The Queen of the *Mulatas*" and "The Pitch Doll" will take place this year on one and the same date. The celebrations will increase their liveliness and splendor, surpassing the spectacular artistic and social successes of previous dances. And the

---

[19] 20,000 cruzeiros was worth approximately US$1,080 in 1949. International Monetary Fund, *Annual Report … 1949*, p. 96.

pretty young women, [their skins] the color of cinnamon or ripe *jaboticaba*,[20] will thus have a unique opportunity to show off their gifts of beauty, elegance, charm, and social distinction.

Effective immediately, the director of the **Teatro Experimental do Negro** is accepting registrations from contestants for this sensational competition, which year after year rocks the very foundations of the city, and which in 1949 promises to take on an unprecedented degree of extraordinariness. Our next cover will feature the photograph of the first registered contestant.

The contest will end in September, in honor of the "Day of the **Black Mother**,"[21] with a soirée so entertaining and elegant that it will make history, and a show featuring the most beloved artists of the radio, theater, and cinema. Valuable prizes will be offered to the winners, along with bronze trophies representing an Ebony Venus, designed by the famous national sculptor Bruno Giorgi and valued at 10,000.00 cruzeiros, as well as more than ten thousand cruzeiros in cash.[22]

Despite its elevated social level, the ball for the closing ceremonies of the "Pitch Doll" and "Queen of the *Mulatas*" contests of 1949 is a democratic festivity – [one] of fraternization among races and various social strata, in which formal dress is not required. Black people should not miss this gala soirée for their "Queens'" pageant, since, by attending, they will be lending prestige to one more initiative in favor of the aesthetic and social valorization of the racially mixed qualities of our civilization.

### 5.16 MARIA NASCIMENTO, "A WOMAN'S TURN TO SPEAK: THE NATIONAL WOMEN'S CONGRESS AND THE REGULATION OF DOMESTIC LABOR," QUILOMBO (RIO DE JANEIRO, BRAZIL: JULY 1949)

*In Brazil as elsewhere in Afro-Latin America, Black women have been disproportionately represented in domestic work. An unregulated part of the labor market, with rules set entirely by private employers and no social safety net, domestic service has historically been a site of extreme precariousness (see 5.1, 5.14), exploitation, and abuse – a space particularly redolent of the labor arrangements of slavery. Maria Nascimento, along*

---

[20] A tropical fruit that is purplish-black in color.
[21] A holiday honoring the Black Mother on September 28 (see 5.11).
[22] Bruno Giorgi (1905–93) was a well-known Brazilian sculptor; on the exchange rate for cruzeiros, see n19 above.

*with other Black women activists, intellectuals, and contributors to* Quilombo, *was at the forefront of efforts to regulate domestic labor in Brazil at midcentury, understanding that improving conditions in that sector would make a crucial difference in the lives of many working Black women. As an activist in the* **Teatro Experimental do Negro***, Nascimento founded a women's department within that organization, the Conselho Nacional de Mulheres Negras, to advocate for the specific needs of that group.*

*In this article, Nascimento applauded the call by an emerging national women's movement to regulate domestic labor, highlighting the particular stakes of such legislation for Black women and children. She ended by hailing the emergence of a new "Black woman" who, regardless of her line of work, rejected the logics bequeathed by slavery and was "learning to walk with her head held high."*

The resolutions passed this past May by the women of all of Brazil, gathered here [Rio de Janeiro] in a national conference, deserve full attention.[23] [So do] all of the articles in favor of the life, happiness, and progress of women and, by extension, of the Brazilian people, of whom they are the dedicated and suffering mothers. The initiative to hold this meeting can thus only be worthy of praise, and its conclusions [worthy of] support. God willing, these [conclusions] will soon become reality.

Among the important resolutions reached, I would like to refer to the one that deals with the regulation of domestic labor. The Conference, taking into consideration that no legislation currently exists to protect the rights of domestic workers and professional laundresses, saw fit to include in its resolutions the securement of legal norms that will establish the obligations and benefits pertaining to that enormous class [of workers].

It is unbelievable that, in a time in which so much is said about social justice, there should exist many thousands of [female] laborers like domestic workers, who have no [daily] timetable for beginning and ending their service, no support during illness and old age, no protection during pregnancy and post-partum, no maternity hospitals, no day nurseries to shelter their children during working hours. For domestic workers, the [labor] regime is that same servile regime of centuries past, [or indeed] even worse than in times of slavery.

---

[23] The Conferência Nacional Feminina (National Women's Conference), organized by various women's organizations, including members of the Communist Party, with the aim of creating a unified, national women's movement.

Beyond that purely economic aspect [of the problem], there is another that is even more painful: the moral violence of which domestic workers are frequent victims. The lack of prestige [of domestic work] among official bodies tasked with protecting labor has consigned domestics to ignominious police control. Many people do not know that instead of [being issued] a work permit, domestics are registered with the police. Thus, under the guise of [providing] a system for identifying domestic workers, what the police actually do is to pre-judge all domestics as thieves or criminals. And even so, our Constitution speaks of the dignity of work!

I know that the "naïve ones of Leblon"[24] might retort that there are many day nurseries, many maternity hospitals out there. But, my "little angels," those institutions are destined entirely for commercial employees, industrial employees, bank employees, and other classes protected by labor legislation, and there is never even the smallest opening for poor Black women who toil at oven and stove. The existing day nurseries are not sufficient for even a third of the children who need them. When these [children] are also of color – God's poor little ones, who some racists affirm are children of the devil – the situation becomes even worse.

It so happens, however, that the Black woman is opening her eyes. During slavery and even now during the Republic, she led a passive existence, nursing the "little masters" and the children of "Doctor so-and-so." Subjugated, diminished, she took refuge in her natural sweetness and gentleness, without weapons to fight and resist the vilest assaults on her personal honor and dignity. Happily, that time is now passing. [Whether as a] domestic worker, public servant, commercial worker, industrial worker, medical doctor, lawyer, or mother and homemaker, the Black woman is learning to walk with her head held high and assert her personality.

There are many problems, many situations to resolve. The regulation of domestic labor, however, is of an urgency that permits no further delays. All of us who are true friends of our people of color must put forth every effort to obtain protective measures for that class [of workers], so hardworking, humble, suffering, and indispensable.

[24] Leblon is a wealthy, overwhelmingly White beachside neighborhood of Rio de Janeiro.

# CHAPTER 6

# Africa and African Culture

## INTRODUCTION

Views of Africa in the Black press evolved dramatically in the ninety years covered by this volume. The first generation of Afro-Latin American journalists had grown up with African parents and grandparents, and were often sympathetic to their social and cultural practices (6.1). By the turn of the century, however, doctrines of **scientific racism**, with their visions of Africans and their descendants as the bearers of genetic and cultural inferiority, led to much more negative views of Latin America's African heritage, even within the Black press (6.2, 6.3). Emerging critiques of scientific racism in the 1930s and 1940s produced a rehabilitation of that heritage (6.5, 6.7, 6.9), though some doubts persisted (6.8). Ethiopia's tenacious resistance against Italian invasions in the 1890s and 1930s (6.6), the region's role in World War II (6.4), and decolonization in the 1950s and 1960s (6.10; see also 2.11) further raised Africa's profile and image in the Black papers.

The chapter begins with a spirited defense of the African national associations that functioned in Buenos Aires (and other Latin American cities) during the 1800s (6.1). An earlier article in the same paper, *La Perla*, had described the associations' cultural and religious observances as "semi-barbaric practices" that had no place in a city that prided itself on its Belle Époque modernity. The author of this reply conceded that the associations' activities were indeed "out of step with the century's progress ... But between that and being semi-barbaric, there is a gap as great as the one between day and night." The African associations pursued the same goals of mutual aid and solidarity found in all civilized societies, he argued, and their African founders, "who gave rise to [our] own generation," deserved respect and acknowledgment, not contemptuous dismissal.

Later articles in the Cuban newspaper *Previsión* and the Brazilian newspaper *Getulino* took the opposite approach, viewing African-based culture as a direct threat to twentieth-century modernity. *Previsión* criticized Cuban civil and religious authorities for permitting "African celebrations" of music and dance in the streets (6.2); *Getulino* rejected **Marcus Garvey**'s calls for Afrodescendants to return to Africa (6.3). If Black people did so, the paper argued, they would "revert, after a short time, to the sad condition of savages."

More positive views of Africa appeared in the 1930s. Foreseeing the war that would erupt in Europe at the end of the decade, the Uruguayan paper *Nuestra Raza* predicted that France's African troops would prove crucial to the outcome of that conflict (6.4). Transcribing an African folktale, the Cuban newspaper *Adelante* implicitly accepted African religious beliefs and worldviews as part of Cuban popular culture (6.5). And looking back at Brazil's nineteenth-century history, *A Voz da Raça* highlighted the role of Islamic African merchants in urban retail commerce and urged Afro-Brazilians to retake their place in the commercial sector (6.7).

Two articles on **Candomblé** took opposing views of this African-based religion from Brazil. *O Clarim da Alvorada* regarded it as "fetishism, and fetishism is still the African mentality, unable to develop its own culture and impermeable to any kind of culture" (6.8). According to this view, fascination with Candomblé also distracted the community of "Afrologists" (scholars who studied Africa and its diaspora) from what should be its true objects of study: racial discrimination, prejudice, and inequality. Writing in *Quilombo*, anthropologist **Édison Carneiro** took a much more positive approach to Candomblé, arguing that, like every other religion in Brazil, it was entitled to respect by the authorities and to the full protections of religious freedom (6.9).

Finally, writing in 1960, Brazilian activist **José Correia Leite** surveyed the movements of national independence sweeping through Africa, which "excite our spirits as Afro-Brazilians" (6.10). Across Afro-Latin America, Africa would increasingly enter writers' and activists' imaginaries as a site of shared struggle and a model of political and cultural liberation.

Africa and African culture were important topics within several articles that we have included in the chapters on Community Life (4.5, 4.14) and Arts and Culture (8.1, 8.4, 8.6, 8.7, 8.11). Readers may find it fruitful to consider those texts in comparison with the ones included here.

## DISCUSSION QUESTIONS

- For twenty-first-century readers, it can be startling to see Black newspapers expressing negative views of Africa and African culture (6.2, 6.3, 6.8). Reviewing the articles that expressed such views, what seems to be the reasoning behind Black journalists' rejection of Latin America's African heritage?
- Conversely, for many writers at different times, Africa was a source of pride and inspiration (in addition to examples in this chapter, see 8.1). What elements of Africa, its history and culture, did writers celebrate? How do you see them marshaling those elements toward arguments for fuller belonging as citizens of their respective nations?
- Though culture can be and is practiced by individuals, it is most effectively constituted and reproduced by collective groups of people, often organized into formal associations. What examples of such groups and organizations can you find in these articles? How do those organizations compare, in their goals and practices, to those that you read about in Chapter 4?
- In his 1940 article, "Where Is Afrology Going?" (6.8), Brazilian author Luiz Bastos suggested that the field of "Afrology" – what today is called Black Studies, or African Diaspora Studies, or Africana Studies – had embarked on a fruitless and erroneous mission by concentrating on the study of **Candomblé** and other African-based cultural forms. What is your own sense of the appropriate mission for African Diaspora Studies today? How does that sense compare (or not) to Bastos' critique?

## 6.1 "SEMI-BARBARIC TRADITIONS," LA PERLA (BUENOS AIRES, ARGENTINA: JAN. 15, 1879)

*In the second half of the nineteenth century, as they sought to justify brutal wars against Indigenous communities, White Argentine elites successfully presented the project of nation-building as a choice between "civilization" or "barbarism."*[1] *Afro-Argentine writers placed themselves fervently on the side of "civilization," but they often disagreed about what constituted "barbarism," especially when African traditions were involved. This article was part of an argument, played out over several issues of* La Perla, *over the proper form the community's associations*

---

[1] The foundational text was Domingo F. Sarmiento, *Civilización y barbarie: Vida de Juan Facundo Quiroga* (1845).

*should take – in this case, the extent to which they should reflect African traditions. In an earlier piece,* **Casildo Gervasio Thompson** *had argued that Afro-Argentines should organize in mutual aid societies, like La Fraternal or La Protectora, modeled on those established by Buenos Aires' many European immigrants.[2] Thompson presented these as the civilized alternative to the African religious brotherhoods and "nations" that had functioned in the city since at least the early 1800s. Those, in his view, were at once outdated – "the traditional associations of our grandparents," "sad relics of the past" – and "semi-barbaric" in their unrestrained performance of African ritual music and dance.*

*As a rebuttal, the author of this piece, Maximiano,[3] defended those organizations and their cultural practices, arguing that African traditions like Days of Kings processions, drumming, and funeral rites served the same laudable purposes of community-building and mutual aid that Thompson idealized. To Maximiano, African traditions, though perhaps out of step with modern progress, should be treated with respect and distinguished from barbarism, a condition that he and several other Afro-Argentine writers, like many White Argentines, attributed to the Native peoples of the Americas.*

In the issue of *La Perla* of the fifth of this month, in an article titled, "How Naïve, Sir!", written by the young C. G. T. [**Casildo Gervasio Thompson**], one reads the following paragraph:

"We have said that 'La Fraternal' was 'the first beacon placed in the desert of ignorance' because before it, there existed only the traditional associations of our grandparents, in which young people and old grew dull from the stultification to which they were driven by their semi-barbaric practices. Of these, all that remains as a sad relic of the past is the occasional out-of-tune *marimba*[4] and a drum or two, whose lugubrious sound is drowned out by the deafening sound of progress."

The beauty of the phrase does not prevent [the reader] from noticing the scope of its meaning. Worthy as the authoritative word of this article's

---

[2] Casildo G. Thompson, "¡Qué inocente señor!", *La Perla* (Jan. 5, 1879), 1–2.
[3] This could be Maximiano Vieytes; if so, political rivalries may have played into these cultural polemics. Vieytes appeared as a member of the Club Unión Autonomista (*La Perla* [July 27, 1879], 3) in support of the Partido Autonomista Nacional, the main political rival of the Partido Nacionalista, which Thompson supported.
[4] The marimba, a percussion instrument similar to a xylophone but with wooden slats, was sometimes used in **candombe** (along with drums).

learned young author may be, we cannot permit him to hurl such an insult at our parents.

What is it that the writer calls "semi-barbaric traditions"? Could it perhaps be the old brotherhoods in which Africans gathered and still gather to celebrate their holidays and to offer each other protection?

Have they not always lived in families, in a community? Has mutual respect not reigned among them just as it has in the most civilized society on earth? If so, then what could have earned this characterization?

[Could it be] the drums, the processions headed by the King and Queen, or the syncopated sound of [the brothers'] instruments accompanied by their sad song, through which they bid goodbye to the brother who departs, never to return? Outside of these, we are not aware of other customs, and we can affirm that Africans have brought no other traditions to America.

This being the case, we fail to see what could have given rise to such a harsh characterization. To say that these are old customs, that they are out of step with the century's progress – that we might concede. But between that and being semi-barbaric, there is a gap as great as the one between day and night.

Our young writer, in his zeal to write the history of our past, distorts the facts, and reprehensibly so. For he does not respect what he should respect, and he portrays as barbarians those who gave rise to his own generation. While it is true that they were not learned, they were very far from resembling the first inhabitants of the Americas.

We could expand upon many more facts to prove that none of the aforementioned customs could be characterized as semi-barbaric, but we do not wish to abuse the good will of the gentlemen editors of *La Perla*.

Maximiano

## 6.2 JONATÁS [EMILIO PLANAS], "WELCOME," PREVISIÓN (HAVANA, CUBA: OCT. 20, 1909)

*Emilio Planas y Hernández emigrated from Cuba to Key West as a child. He attended the Cookman Institute, a teacher-training institute for Black students, graduating in 1888. For the next decade, he lived in the Cuban settlement in Tampa, contributing to various Black publications, teaching at the Black educational society La Liga, and participating in the exile nationalist movement. After the first United States occupation of Cuba, he returned to the island as a Protestant missionary, becoming a pastor in* *a local church and the director of an industrial school for Black students, modeled on the **Tuskegee Institute**.*

*In this article, under his customary pen name, Planas congratulated the editors of* Previsión *on their new publication before shifting gears to what he saw as a major obstacle to Black progress: Afro-Cuban spirituality, drumming, and dance. His objections were based on the moral judgments of a Protestant missionary and educator. But, at the same time, he amplified a view common among White Cuban statesmen that African culture was inconsistent with modern citizenship.*

*Historians have argued that, by criminalizing Afro-Cuban culture, the Cuban government undermined the promise of equal citizenship under the law. Planas argued the reverse. It was, he wrote, the permissiveness of White authorities toward Black "immorality" that undermined the moral uplift of the race and the full enjoyment of equal rights. It should be the work of Black writers and politicians to raise a cry of protest against "grotesque contortions" and the "clumsy drum."*

From my corner, with my heart bursting with joy, I say welcome to *Previsión*. The iron will of **Evaristo Estenoz** once again presents in the arena of the press a newspaper that is genuinely Black. That is to say, from this day forward the Black race has its own mouthpiece, within which there will be space for all of the complaints, all of the laments of those who, with hatred for none, but with a passion for their rights, demand more freedom, more respect, more consideration.

At first glance and for a great number of our Afro-Cuban[5] brothers, with the guarantee of the Constitution, with fourteen or fifteen Representatives of color, and with several dozen placed [in government jobs] ranging from file clerk to street sweeper, the Black Cuban is wholly satisfied, even though the project of his moral abasement continues in systematic fashion, as if obeying an underhanded and wicked directive.

We say this, because not a single day goes by without the press telling us of an African celebration; sometimes the Roman [Catholic] Church acts as an enabler, as was the case in Regla or in Matanzas. Other times, the mayor of the town and the judge attend the festivities and applaud the grotesque contortions, to the sound of the clumsy *drum*, as happened in Corral Falso. In others, finally, like Sabanilla del Encomendador, every day drums are heard wherever you go. In a nutshell, here in the

---

[5] This was an unusual usage at the time, but had already emerged among a handful of writers in exile in the United States, in conversation with proponents of the term "Afro-American."

province of Matanzas, where there are still many who dream with pleas-ure of the times when the Black man made sugar for free; here, I can say with total confidence, the campaign to discredit the Black masses is scandalous. The political bosses, in order to win votes, offer to let the *bembés*[6] go out, and the *ñáñigos*. In Matanzas there have been Sundays when, with the acquiescence of the authorities and with permission from the mayor, there have been as many as eight *diablitos*[7]in the street.

Tell me if it is [right] for patriots, lovers of the ideal symbolized by the equilateral triangle on our flag, the ideal of equality and fraternity, to allow one part of our population to fester in bestial African atavisms; if patriots who are conscious of their duty to past and future generations can and should tolerate such a shameful spectacle; adulating the illiterate masses so as to have them always willing to deify those who, based on merit or culture, do not deserve it.

To be able to say this, to be able to continue to make our case before the Government, to be able to say to our Representatives in the Congress that it is time that they see this, since it is shameful to all of us who have dark skin; to raise continuous protests for this and other things that are permit-ted to our poor brothers who are submerged in the shadows of ignorance in order, then, to undermine all of us; for all of this I give welcome to *Previsión*. Although I know it will not reap great harvests of *pesetas* [coins], what it will [reap] is the consideration and respect of all the Whites and all the Blacks who are honorable and patriotic.

### 6.3 CLÁUDIO GUERRA, "BLACK LETTERS," GETULINO (CAMPINAS, BRAZIL: DEC. 20, 1924)

*This piece, composed as an open letter to **Benedicto Florêncio** (2.9), scoffed at the idea that Black Brazilians had anything to gain from **Marcus Garvey**'s calls for a return of the African diaspora to Africa. For author Cláudio Guerra (on whom we have no biographical information), it was entirely understandable that African Americans, "rejected from society by a terrible and reciprocal racial hatred," would respond enthu-siastically to Garvey's program. But that program made no sense at all for Afro-Brazilians, who had been instrumental in creating the country that now "embraces you like an affectionate mother." And what could Black*

---

[6] A ritual complex within the Afro-Cuban spiritual practice known as **Regla de Ocha**. At a *bembé*, participants drum, dance, and sing in order to venerate deities known as *orishas*.
[7] The *diablito* is a masked figure who plays a central role in **Abakuá** dance practices.

*Brazilians hope to accomplish in Africa, Guerra asked, describing the
continent and its people in satirically negative terms that borrowed heavily from the racist tropes of the day. By presenting the United States,
Africa, and the Garvey program of return migration all in such a harsh
light, Guerra sought to persuade readers to re-affirm their allegiances both
to Brazil and to Blackness. "Brazil is for the Brazilians, which means it is
for the Blacks." Interestingly, during the nineteenth century, many formerly enslaved people did, in fact, emigrate from Brazil to various parts of
West Africa.*[8]

To my very esteemed friend, Mr. **Benedi[c]to Florêncio.**

I'm feeling an irresistible itch to put in my two cents about a certain idea
invented by North Americans and imported among us under the label
"Black Convention."[9]

I fear, however, that my esteemed friend may not agree with me, but . . .
be patient, Mr. Florêncio, sir. Let me say my piece before I burst.

It's fair enough for Black North Americans to say, through those high-
sounding bards of theirs, that Africa is for the Africans.[10] It's even tolerable for Black North Americans to want to emigrate to the region that was
the cradle of their grandparents. One could go so far as to say it's a matter
of justice for folks over there, given that, as we know, they are rejected
from society by a terrible and reciprocal racial hatred. Yet if you can wash
your feet in a basin in your own house, it's just plain stupid to go down to
the river.

According to the beliefs of any plain old Yankee,[11] "America is for the
Americans."

But the Black did not figure into that equation, nor did the Chinese or
the Japanese, even when they were born there. Of these [groups], moreover, the Black is the one considered most undesirable. So it's completely
natural that people who are officially repudiated in that way would try to
hightail it out of the evil-stepmother country in which they had the good

---

[8]  See Matory, "The English Professors of Brazil"; Law, "The Evolution of the Brazilian
     Community."

[9]  The author refers to the 1924 international conference of the **Universal Negro
     Improvement Association** (UNIA), headed by **Marcus Garvey** and held in New York
     City (see 7.7).

[10] This is a reference to Marcus Garvey's promotion of the idea of a Black homeland in
     Africa, glossed as "Africa for the Africans."

[11] A term commonly used in Latin America to refer to citizens of the United States.

fortune to be born.[12] Let them go to Africa, kick out the place's owners, if they can; [let them] play the wild animal tamer, learn the local language, or impose their own; [let them] wear a loincloth or make the local Black men wear coats and the local Black women use rice powder and carmine,[13] or let those [women] who go there put on loincloths ... in sum, let them do whatever they can or want to do. All of that is well and good. But for a Black Brazilian to embrace that idea is, in my view, the maximum absurdity, deserving the least tolerance possible.

Africa is for the Africans, my Black brother. It was for your great-grandfather whose bones have by now turned to dust and returned to the earth. Africa is for anyone who did not do the work of cultivating and giving life to an immense country such as this.

Because look, my brother, they devoured our flesh, and now they want to gnaw at our bones.

Africa is for anyone who wants it, except for us, that is, the Blacks of Brazil who in Brazil were born and raised, and in Brazil multiplied. It's impossible to think that the Black Brazilian could do anything useful in Africa – not a chance. At worst, they'd revert, after a short time, to the sad condition of savages. What would that literate minority do in Africa, in the middle of such a huge number of uneducated people? What would those people do in Africa without any money? What on earth would those folks, who spend their entire lives shaking their hips to the sound of raucous hurdy-gurdies or to an off-key jazz band, do in Africa?[14]

Oh my dear Mister Florêncio, help me, for God's sake, to offer advice to the inexperienced innovator: Wouldn't it be better, my dear brother, for you to refashion your manners, to oversee your child's education with the greatest of care rather than throwing him to the lions without spiritual comfort, without paternal guidance or anything at all? Wouldn't it be better if you, my dear *cafuso*, bought yourself a civic catechism,[15] and by studying it, came to know the greatness of your country's institutions? Wouldn't it be better if you were more Brazilian, that is, if you were more patriotic toward this blessed land that witnessed your birth, that embraces you like an

---

[12] "Good fortune" is intended sarcastically.

[13] Rice powder was commonly used in cosmetics designed to lighten the complexion. Carmine was used to give red color to lipstick and blush.

[14] Guerra appears to refer here to African Americans who might be contemplating a return to Africa.

[15] Civic catechisms were educational manuals that combined teachings, prayers, and principles of Catholic doctrine with patriotic vignettes about great people and events in Brazilian history.

affectionate mother, this land that is ours – listen up, my brother – it's ours, you hear? Ours, because it was we who first built it up, we who gave everything, even our blood, to defend its integrity when foreigners invaded.[16]

Brazil is for the Brazilians, which means it is for the Blacks, you hear?

Let the Americans go get themselves in hot water. It's cooler here where we are. We're not budging.

"Let those who are uncomfortable pick up and move." We are in our home.

Yes, Mr. Florêncio, sir, I feel like I've taken a huge load off, like the washerwoman who just got done talking behind her neighbor's back.

I am grateful and much obliged to you for having endured me so patiently.

I will sleep peacefully tonight.

Farewell, until the next letter.

Cláudio Guerra

São Paulo 22/11/1924

P.S. Please be so kind as to nag your in-house editor to look this over, because my Portuguese, which is already basic, tends to revert to the Latin from which it came. [CG]

### 6.4 NAGEL [ISABELINO JOSÉ GARES], "DEMOCRACY AND THE BLACK RACE," NUESTRA RAZA (MONTEVIDEO, URUGUAY: MAY 1934)

*As part of its Popular Front orientation and its implacable opposition to fascism,* Nuestra Raza *regularly published articles on the Spanish Civil War, Italy's invasion of Ethiopia (see 6.6), and other aspects of European politics. Writing the year after Hitler's seizure of power,* **Isabelino José Gares** *(see 8.9) correctly predicted eventual war between France and Germany, and foresaw the major role that France's African troops would play in that conflict.[17] Gares compared those African soldiers to the Black troops who helped win "American independence," by which he meant Latin American independence. Gares did not address whether African military contributions to the impending fight against fascism would justify future claims for full French citizenship (or self-determination). But*

---

[16] This is most likely a reference to the role of Black soldiers and officers in fighting off the Dutch occupation of Northeastern Brazil (1630–54); see 1.2.

[17] When Germany invaded in 1940, about 63,000 African troops took part in the unsuccessful defense of France. After the Armistice of June 1940, African soldiers fought for both the Nazi-allied Vichy government and the Free French resistance. Lunn, "Tirailleurs Sénégalais."

*discussions in the Afro-Latin American press of Black service in the region's independence wars nearly always made that point, and Gares made certain to remind his readers of France's "enormous historical responsibility" as a beacon of "liberty and democracy."*

In the post-war period, not only were old Europe's fields and cities in ruins, its national treasuries empty, but the continent was also wrapped in a dense cloud of painful uncertainty. In these chaotic circumstances, there arose, one soon after the other, two governmental regimes ideologically antagonistic in their economic and social goals and principles.[18] But this antagonism did not prevent their coinciding in their methods of diffusing themselves across all regions of the globe, as if they had found the magical secret of a governmental panacea. What is certain is that, either the [two] systems are spurious, or their propagandists were very bad, because they have only had the diabolical virtue of confusing and disturbing the world's tranquility. Capital is in hiding, impassively watching the millions of unemployed men, women and children without bread or home who are multiplying endlessly.[19]

It is clear that Hitler is a circumstance of this chaotic situation. Emboldened by nationalist sentiment, he is dragging his country down with ignominious oppression, awakening ancestral animosities and infamous hatreds against races and peoples. Who knows what dark ideas this modern Attila[20] holds, threatening peace in Europe with the overpowering will of his perfidious interests?

All eyes turn toward France, whose government many see as fearful and vacillating in its ceaseless search for diplomatic formulas and clauses, in the face of the sterility of the Versailles treaties or the byzantine discussions in Geneva.[21]

One should not judge the self-denying French spirit by the concerns of the chancelleries. This I believe, in spite of the contrary opinion of Oscar [Oswald] Spengler,[22] in his latest book, *The Hour of Decision*, and of

---

[18] Soviet communism and Italian fascism.

[19] Gares was writing during one of the lowest points of the Great Depression.

[20] Attila, also known as Attila the Hun (c. AD 406–53), was the ruler of a coalition of Central and Eastern European tribal groups that warred against (and, after Attila's death, ultimately defeated) the Roman Empire. In the 1800s and 1900s, he was often invoked as a symbol of bloodthirsty savagery.

[21] The Treaty of Versailles (1919) concluded World War I; "discussions in Geneva" refers to the League of Nations, headquartered in that city.

[22] Oswald Spengler (1880–1936), German historian and philosopher, author of *Decline of the West* (1918).

other writers who – they say – glimpse the decadence of that great peace-loving people.

The hour is difficult. Facing the imminent danger of the coming to power of foreign elements in its internal politics, and a civil or international war that could bring as fatal consequences the overturning of liberty and democracy, France knows its enormous historic responsibility; doubtless that accounts for its extreme prudence.

France still feels the gnashing of the broken chains of the **Bastille**, still hears the frantic cries, it seems, in the streets of Paris of its heroic people in [17]92, and it serenely prepares to resist any possible aggression.

From the immense possessions that the French rule in West Africa, 100,000 Black men have already been transferred to military encampments.

So it is that large contingents of the Black race are preparing to cooperate with their generous blood and their intrepid valor, as in the great achievement of American independence, in this dark hour in the great country that has liberty as its standard and democracy as its bulwark.

Surely the Black armies are aware of their historic responsibility in this transcendental moment that faces each one of them; on the fertile fields of France, they must raise their sharp swords and advance courageously toward victory or death.

### 6.5 MANUEL CUÉLLAR VIZCAÍNO, "THE LEGEND OF SENSEMAYÁ," ADELANTE (HAVANA, CUBA: NOV. 1935)

*By the end of the 1920s, the field of folklore had begun to formulate and broadcast a new set of ideas about African culture in Cuba. Folklorists, the most famous of whom were White, began collecting artifacts, stories, and songs from Afro-Cuban informants. These White intellectuals no longer saw African culture as atavistic or criminal. It was a harmless, distinctive, and – they thought – rapidly disappearing element of the national patrimony (see 4.14 and, for comparison, 6.8).*

*But not all of those who built the field of folklore studies in Cuba were White. **Manuel Cuéllar Vizcaíno** was one of several Black intellectuals who participated in the creation of the **Sociedad de Estudios Afrocubanos**. By the mid 1930s, his radio program featuring "classical" Afro-Cuban drumming, singing, and folktales aired three times a week. Cuéllar was born on a rural sugar plantation and had worked in the cane fields as a young man, which may have helped his ethnographic collecting among sugar workers.*

*As the editors of* Adelante *noted, Cuéllar presented "The Legend of Sensemayá" in a way that highlighted the "innocent, natural way that these African legends are told." It is notable that Cuéllar told a tale of* **Yoruba**-*speaking Cubans engaging with supernatural powers without any hint of the disapprobation that writers of an earlier era had heaped on Black "witchcraft." Cuéllar's friend and collaborator,* **Nicolás Guillén**, *published a poem titled "Sensemayá" several years before this publication, punctuated by the repeated chant "Mayombe-bombe mayombé." Whether or not Cuéllar was Guillén's ethnographic source, it is clear that the two intellectual projects, Afro-Cuban poetry and Afro-Cuban folklore, were deeply intertwined.*

There were two siblings, still just children. One was a boy. The first, who was a boy, was called Didún. Didún, in the **Yoruba** language, means sweet. The girl was named Itana, which is also Yoruba. It means flower.

Didún did not love Itana like the other children in the village loved one another. And Itana did not love Didún, because she wanted to know everything before he did. Without making noise, almost without breathing, Itana followed Didún each morning when the sky began to spill its brilliance over the wet leaves, or each afternoon, when the sun, very red, fell in pieces behind the black trees. And always, when Didún returned, Itana was already at home making noise and breathing heavily.

One day when Itana followed Didún into the deepest part of the jungle, she saw that a very beautiful woman, more beautiful than any woman they knew, spoke to Didún. And the woman said to Didún that she would help him to be a nimble and strong man, stronger than any man he knew. But Didún had to care for Itana like the other children in that land did. And the apparition said more to Didún. She told him that whenever he might find himself in danger, he should call her with his thoughts, and he would emerge victorious. She would come to his aid beneath the sun or in the shadows. But Didún said to the apparition that he, being a boy, did not know how to call with his thoughts, that she should tell him her name so he would be able to call her. Yet the apparition said that he, having seen so few moons, could not know her name, because her name had a meaning that Didún could not yet understand. In place of her name she would give him a word that he could use as if it were her name, and she said: "Sensemayá." Having spoken, she departed. And when Didún returned home, Itana, who knew enough, was already there, making noise and breathing heavily.

Over many moons, Itana did not follow Didún, because Didún took care of her and because Itana already knew plenty, enough to be frightened by what she knew. But one morning, when the brilliance of the sky was not yet on the wet leaves, Didún went out into the jungle leaving Itana rubbing her eyes with her fists. But Itana, without making any noise, almost without breathing, followed Didún. Once in the jungle, before the astonished eyes of Itana, a very large and long animal, like none that they had ever seen, attacked Didún. Didún fought off the monster, because Didún was already very strong. But the monster, being very big and very long, was defeating Didún. Didún wanted to call the apparition, but he had forgotten the name she had given him. Itana did remember, but she was afraid of the monster and of Didún. The battle was very fierce, breaking up branches and sending clumps of earth and handfuls of roots flying. Didún, trapped, was about to be swallowed by the monster when Itana, now unafraid of Didún, shouted: "Sensemayá," "Sensemayá."

Sensemayá did not come. But it started to rain heavily, in torrents, a downfall from the heavens like none they had ever seen. And the monster, who feared water more than anything, let go of Didún. And retreating into the deepest part of the jungle, its legs swallowed by the rising mud, it left for good, leaving only this chant behind as it vanished into the abyss:

Mayombe-bombe mayombé
Mayombe-bombe mayombé

---

[Footnote in the original] The LEGEND OF SENSEMAYÁ is by our comrade Manuel Cuéllar, the founder and Director of the radio program that bears the same name [Sensemayá]. The tale was collected by our comrade from the lips of Lucumíes [Yoruba-speaking people], during his wanderings in the sugar fields. So faithful has he remained [to the original], that he offers it to our readers in the same innocent, natural way that these African legends are told.

## 6.6 MARIO RUFINO MÉNDEZ, "THE WORK OF FASCISM," NUESTRA RAZA (MONTEVIDEO, URUGUAY: NOV. 24, 1935)

*As one of only two independent nations in early twentieth-century Africa, Ethiopia was a particular focus of interest for the Black press. The Afro-Brazilian newspaper* O Menelik *(5.8–10) was named in honor of Menelik II, the monarch who had led the defeat of Italy's invasion of Ethiopia in 1895–96. When Italy, now under Fascist rule, attacked the African nation a second time, in October 1935, Black papers called for international sanctions and ran frequent articles on the Italo-Ethiopian war. In the first month of the conflict,* Nuestra Raza *published this powerful image by its staff illustrator,* **Mario Rufino Méndez** *(see Figure 6.1).*[23] *The cover showed Il Duce (the Leader), the title accorded to Benito Mussolini*[24] *by the Fascist party, wearing a Fascist cap and jackboots, and massacring the Ethiopian people with a bloody axe. A distraught world (prominently featuring South America) looked on in horror, waving its arms in protest and demanding to know, "What are you doing, Duce?" To which Mussolini replied, "Civilizing … ". The cartoon vividly expressed the brutality of the Italian invasion, the global threat posed by fascism (a frequent theme in* Nuestra Raza*), the cynicism of Mussolini's justifications for the invasion, and the paper's hopes for an effective international response to Italian aggression. That response did not come until the outbreak of World War II, when British troops (mainly African recruits from British colonies on the continent) invaded Ethiopia from neighboring Somaliland and, in alliance with local forces, overturned Italian rule.*

## 6.7 ARLINDO VEIGA DOS SANTOS, "BLACKS AND COMMERCE," A VOZ DA RAÇA (SÃO PAULO, BRAZIL: AUG. 1936)

*This article recounted the role of free Africans in retail commerce and the skilled trades in nineteenth-century Brazil and encouraged twentieth-century Afro-Brazilians to re-enter those areas of the economy. Muslim traders and craftsmen from West Africa,* **Arlindo Veiga dos Santos** *recalled, brought their skills with them to Brazil and competed successfully against Portuguese immigrants and their descendants. They were then pushed out of those areas of the economy by the European, Middle Eastern, and Japanese immigrants of the late 1800s and early 1900s. Veiga dos Santos reported, somewhat optimistically, that Afro-Brazilians were now, in the 1930s, returning to retail commerce and the skilled trades. He urged his readers to pursue opportunities in those callings and to become customers of Black businesses.*

*The article presented the argument, made often in the São Paulo Black press, that turn-of-the-century immigrants had received unfair and unjustified preferences in Brazilian life, from which Afro-Brazilians suffered materially. It also suggested that the African merchants and craftsmen*

---

[23] Burgueño, *Mario Rufino Méndez.*
[24] Benito Mussolini (1883–1945) was the founder and leader (Il Duce) of Italy's Fascist Party and, from 1922 to 1943, Prime Minister and dictator of Italy.

FIGURE 6.1 Mario Rufino Méndez, "The Work of Fascism," *Nuestra Raza* (Nov. 24, 1935). Original caption: " – The World: What are you doing, Duce? – The Duce: Civilizing... "

*came to Brazil not as slaves but as "free men from Africa." While there were occasional isolated individuals who migrated voluntarily from Africa to Brazil, historians are not aware of any significant migration of free Africans to Brazil in the 1800s (or earlier).*

In the old days, before the great immigrations that, through the initiative of the illustrious statesmen of stupidity, came to Aryanize Brazil, the country's commerce was in the hands either of naturalized Portuguese or their sons, and of free Blacks, who had either come as free men from Africa or were freed slaves.

These free Blacks could be from many of the African races but, we have good reason to believe, were principally from races that were Mohammedan [Muslim] or culturally Mohammedanized: the Sudanese, the Hausa, or the fearsome **Yoruba**, who left in the unwritten history of Brazil the violent stamp of resistance to the process of enslavement or to the miserable proletarianization that followed freedom.[25]

In Bahia and in other provinces where these groups predominated, along with Yoruba or Hausa pride, so did the Moorish or Semitic instinct for commerce, so that even into this current century we saw the commercial shops of those African people on proud display, sometimes with signs in Yoruba or other languages of their last surviving speakers.

But that is over. Recently, and perhaps even now, the façades of commercial establishments provocatively display signs in German, Italian, other languages, and recently, loudly calling out in the Northwest [of São Paulo state], Japanese inscriptions. And the Black, every day more proletarianized, losing his property through robbery or through more or less legal processes, is almost completely removed from the work of Mercury,[26] ceding his place to everyone and being rejected as well by the prejudice of buyers who, we think, thought it wrong to leave the Italians, Syrians, and other businessmen to go give profits to their Black countryman.

To the Black was left the heavy work of farmer or laborer, earning a pittance, with even his work as a skilled tradesman disappearing. Gone are the old tailor shops, the shoemakers, the goldsmiths, and even that [trade] in which the African People were masters in Brazil: ironworking, from blacksmiths to tinsmiths to foundries!

---

[25] Dos Santos was referring to the wave of slave rebellions that took place in Bahia during the early 1800s, culminating in the Malê Revolt of 1835. See Reis, *Slave Rebellion in Brazil*.
[26] Mercury was the Roman god of commerce and financial gain.

***

Still, it is with immense joy that I begin to see Blacks losing the fear of returning to commercial tasks. Black small businessmen are appearing, of all shades of color, including greengrocers, sometimes provoking great resentment from others, as we have observed. Until quite recently, newspaper vendors were exclusively White. The same was true of shoeshine boys and other lighter jobs.

This isn't much, but it is something. Blacks need to lose their love for dependent positions, in which they are eternally subjected to bosses who scorn and frequently belittle them, including in their salary.

It's not that we want all Blacks to be businesspeople. That's neither our character nor our advantage. The Black should be everything that the others are ... and also businesspeople. And Black buyers should not flee from buying from Black businesses. Very much the contrary.

So lose your fear, my countrymen. Be shopkeepers, grocers, peddlers, just like the others. Compete with the foreigners. Call out and hawk your wares courageously, and we will have taken one more step toward the redemption of our People.

6.8 LUIZ BASTOS, "WHERE IS AFROLOGY GOING?" O CLARIM DA ALVORADA (SÃO PAULO, BRAZIL: SEPT. 28, 1940)

*This article addressed a recurring question in the Black press: Who should be studying and writing about Black history and culture, and how should they be writing about it? Luiz Bastos wrote, specifically, in reaction to the* **Congressos Afro-Brasileiros** *of 1934 and 1937, organized by* **Gilberto Freyre** *and* **Édison Carneiro**, *respectively, at which students and practitioners of African-based cultural forms in religion, music, and the plastic arts had presented numerous papers and "communications" on those cultural practices. Bastos argued that this approach was fruitless and wrongheaded.* **Candomblé** *and other African-based cultural expressions reflected "the African mentality, unable to develop its own culture and impermeable to any kind of culture." The subject of Afro-Brazilian studies, he suggested, should not be African-based culture but rather the "Black question" in Brazil: the systematic exclusion of Black people from economic and social opportunity. The mission of "Afrology" should be to analyze and combat the "racial and economic oppression" affecting*

*Black people, not to study African-based cultural forms that Bastos saw as*
*a major impediment to Afro-Brazilian advancement.*

*For very different approaches to Candomblé and other African-derived*
*religions, see 6.5 and 6.9.*

1  Decidedly, Afro-Brazilian studies are taking the wrong road, which
will not lead us anywhere.

A few years ago, some learned, or almost learned, young men set
themselves to giving lectures and publishing works and studies,
some of them undeniably interesting, on Afro-Brazilian subjects.
Very good. But if future such studies do not change direction, we
will be stuck in endless small talk, which teaches nothing and
resolves nothing.

Let's remember that two **Congressos Afro-Brasileiros** were held,
which had as their sole result the dissemination everywhere of
**Candomblé**. Besides that, they introduced to Brazil a group of would-
be Afrologists, who formed a cartel that currently holds monopoly
control over the market.

2  The first problem, in our judgment, is that up until now, with just a few
exceptions, the study of Afro-Brazilian topics has been purely descrip-
tive and superficial.

Religion, or better said, the different forms of religious beliefs and
rites, the anatomy and physiology of the Brazilian Black, have
been studied in all their minute details, undeniably so. And some
Afrologists know more about Candomblé and African [subjects]
than many of the most celebrated *pais de santo*[27] of Bahia and its
surroundings.

But for now, their work does not go beyond that. Meanwhile, it
would be interesting to go more deeply into the subject and ask for
example why, almost one hundred years after the abolition of the
[Atlantic slave] trade, do the multi-colored descendants of the former
slaves still retain the same beliefs and fetishistic rites, in spite of
mixture and Christian indoctrination?

It is not enough to transcribe the seemingly unconnected words of
the Candomblé songs; to the contrary, one has to investigate their

---

[27] *Pais de santo* (fathers of the saint) are male leaders of Candomblé congregations; *mães de*
*santo* (mothers of the saint) are female leaders.

social meaning, which is clearly based on a combination of racial and economic oppression.

Without doubt it is important to know the various Black gods and their powers for good and evil, as well as to study the hysterical crises of their female worshippers, and the different forms of religious syncretism. But it is also necessary to understand them and explain them, and it is impossible to do that without setting the Black within society, within the social and economic milieu within which he develops, and within the economic and social forces that act on him.

In effect, the Black has always been studied as a function of the White. Black influences on the language and customs of the White have been researched, but not the influence of the White on the Black, as though the latter were not a living being, capable of having emotions and of reacting to the influence of the White and their civilization.

3 It is just this point that is the second important problem that we note in Afro-Brazilian studies. Behind this superficiality, which sees the Black as a "thing" and not as a living being, lies strong racial prejudice.

None of our illustrious and enlightened Afrologists refers to that prejudice, which still persists so strongly in the White mentality, nor perceives or understands the depressing influence that it exercises on the mentality and soul of the Black. Fifty-two years after their legal emancipation, the Black still feels the weight of three hundred years of slavery, of economic, social, and moral oppression. Fifty-two years after his emancipation the Black has not gone beyond [being] the miserable inhabitant of the **favelas**, the unskilled laborer, the common soldier, or fetishism.

Why? Because the prejudice of the White against the Black still exists, deeply impregnating all the layers of Brazilian society, regardless of pigmentation. Among the Whites, simply because they are White and because from their earliest lessons they learn that "the Blacks are not people" but rather an inferior race. Among the *mulatos*, to please the Whites and to pretend that they are not Black. And finally, among the Blacks, because from their birth, it is driven into their heads that they were born to serve the Whites and are inferior to them.

Tourists cannot take photographs of Blacks because "it would be depressing for Brazil if we were considered to be a nation of Blacks." We are, without doubt, a nation of Aryan Latins.

Who spreads and feeds this prejudice? To find out, just take note of its principal consequences: first, the creation of an army of men rejected for the lighter jobs and obliged to look for jobs that are heavy, unappealing, and poorly paid; second, the dividing of the proletarian classes.

It is not unusual to find the Black worker, doing the same work as a White worker, earning less. While the White worker can rise through the ranks, becoming a manager or some similar position, the Black can never be stimulated by that hope, no matter how intelligent he may be.

4   It is clear that that prejudice can't disappear from one day to the next, with a simple decree, in the same way that one would appoint a [cabinet] minister or break up an **Integralist** cell. But this would be possible through serious work among Whites and among the Blacks themselves, making them see that "Blacks are people, too."

And this is the third problem we see. It's not enough to go to the Candomblé congregation, to attend ritual drumming sessions and *capoeira*[28] circles, and then run to the library to write a great article "about the Blacks," with footnotes in English, German, and Latin, footnotes that in general have nothing to do with the topic, which in this case is the Brazilian Black.

Our Afrologists, who are so well intentioned, owe it to themselves to take on a more concrete and perhaps more fruitful task: fighting to socially and morally uplift the Black, helping him to realize his own worth and personality, unveiling the forces that he holds within himself, and finally, incorporating him into the Brazilian Nation. Because in truth, if we pay close attention to the facts, we will see that the Black not only has not absorbed White civilization but has stayed at the margins of our nationality.

5   Nor was he even able to form his own culture. Let's not confuse Candomblé with Black culture. In spite of its close connection with Catholicism, Candomblé is still fetishism, and fetishism is still the African mentality, unable to develop its own culture and impermeable to any kind of culture. A few days ago, someone asked [me], "Where is the Black poet of Brazil?"

---

[28] *Capoeira* is a martial art developed among enslaved Africans in Brazil in the 1700s and 1800s, and performed in circles or "rings" (*rodas*). Today it is widely practiced around the world as a form of physical training and conditioning.

There is none, he doesn't exist. Blacks in Brazil not only did not succeed in soaking up White culture, they did not succeed in developing their own culture. With rare exceptions, the few who become intellectuals immediately consider themselves to be Latin and think like Whites, or if they wish, don't think at all.

As yet in Brazil there is no **Paul Robeson** or **Langston Hughes**, who know that they are Black, recognize the qualities and defects of their race – which every race has – and feel no shame or inferiority, nor aspire to be White.

6  Here we arrive at the heart of the matter: to alter the path that they have been following, the first task of the Afrologist is to recognize the existence of a "Black question" in Brazil. Having done this, it will be possible to remedy some of the many current problems, some of which we have mentioned.

But to achieve this, it is not enough to write articles, but instead to address a concrete task: to combat race prejudice, to educate and elevate the Black socially and morally, to pull them away from the fetishism and the Candomblé that only makes their spirit more and more brutish, and to help them to create their own culture.

7  But, some of the Afrologists will say, understandably indignant, why don't you do all that yourself?

Because, I will say, I do not have the honor of being an Afrologist.

But if I can get some student of these questions to pay me some attention, even if it's for the purpose of fighting with me, then without doubt I will have accomplished something.


## 6.9 ÉDISON CARNEIRO, "FREEDOM OF RELIGION," QUILOMBO (RIO DE JANEIRO, BRAZIL: JAN. 1950)

*Édison Carneiro was an Afro-Brazilian anthropologist and ethnographer whose numerous books and articles helped pioneer the study of Black history and culture in Brazil. In 1937 he convened the second **Congresso Afro-Brasileiro**, in Bahia (one of those subjected to criticism in 6.8), and the following year helped found the União das Seitas Afro-Brasileiras da Bahia (Bahian Union of Afro-Brazilian Sects) as a means for the city's African-based religious congregations to band together to resist police persecution.*

*This article proposed the extension of that local model to the nation as a whole, in the interests of protecting not just the African-based religions but other non-Christian religions such as Islam, Buddhism, and **Spiritism**.*

In Brazil, no civil liberty has been violated with such impunity as freedom of religion. Though the democratic principle on which it rests is as clear as the light of day, the constitutional text is not clear, and any policeman thinks that he has the right to intervene in a religious ceremony, to sow terror among the worshippers. This violence has become a habit, with no one raising a single voice in protest, even when the house of worship, in accord with the Constitution, is legally incorporated.

This disrespect of such a basic freedom applies only to the so-called inferior religions. And the more "inferior" they are, the more harassed. One does not see the Catholic Church disturbed by the police, even when its slow-moving processions block traffic in a city without streets like Rio de Janeiro. Nor are the Protestant sects. Other more discreet religions with fewer members, like the Buddhists or the Muslims, escape only because their prudence protects them. The more popular religions, with greater appeal to the masses – **Spiritism** and **Macumba** – are almost daily victims of the "moralizing" influence – the depredations, the beatings, the blows – of the police.[29] All week long, the daily newspapers, criminally oblivious of the dangers to which they expose all Brazilians, incite the police to invade this or that house of worship, heaping ridicule on the ceremonies that take place there. And nobody speaks out in defense of the fundamental right, enjoyed by the leaders and members of these houses, to express their religious sentiments as they see fit.

The law assists the persecutors of these religions; after affirming the absolute freedom of conscience and of religion, the Constitution (art. 141, § 7.°) authorizes state intervention whenever a religion "disturbs public order or good customs." In the absence of an implementing law to regulate the matter, the interpretation of each case falls to the police – and we know what can happen, in terms of irregular and arbitrary treatment, when any human right is handed over to our heroic, native-born Javerts.[30] As far as public order and good customs are concerned, is it the police who should decide these questions?

It is exactly these so-called constitutional reasons – just read the daily news reports – that the police invoke to interfere with the freedom of

---

[29] For another reference to state repression of Spiritism and Macumba, see 7.11.

[30] A character in Victor Hugo's *Les Misérables*, Javert was the relentless police inspector who pursued the protagonist, Jean Valjean.

religion. The practitioner of Macumba who smokes the cigar of Velho Lourenço, who swallows hot coals, who walks barefoot on shards of broken glass, is not violating "good customs." But this does not prevent his being beaten, thrown in the dungeon, reviled and slandered by the hacks of the tabloid press. Nor does the Spiritist medium who serves as a vehicle for the dead, guiding to the hearts of the living the brothers and sisters from space, pose a danger to "public order." Really, what "public order," what "good customs" are these? We all know that what subverts [public] order is police interference in these religions. And as for customs, is it possible that "good" customs are limited to playing cards, to horse racing at the Jockey Club, to lounging on the beaches of **Copacabana** and Guarujá, to speculating on the stock market? To the contrary, one can argue that these religions continue the traditional habits of the White, the Black, and the Indian. And even more so when, as in fact happens, "good" customs are so penetrated by magical, pre-logical survivals from the ancient religions of those three human groups.

Bahian Candomblé, despite its international fame and the respect that it deserves from men of standing, still pays a fee to the police to put on its festivals. The other day, a court decision prevented the Brazilian Catholic Apostolic Church[31] of the ex-Bishop of Maura from functioning. Macumba in Rio, Pará in Porto Alegre, Xangô in Maceió and Recife, Pagelança and Catimbó, Tambor-de-Minas, Spiritism[32] – all religious (or apparently religious, like Freemasonry) institutions existing in the country have suffered, at times more, at times less, for this or that reason, restrictions on their religious freedom, if not suppression of that basic, fundamental right, a logical corollary of the rise of the bourgeoisie. What to do, in the face of this police interference, other than to resist, peacefully but firmly, in defense of this right?

Enjoying the declared support of tens of thousands of people, in every Brazilian city, the persecuted religions need to come together, they need to organize themselves to achieve collectively – above the divergences and differences in their conceptions of the world – a right that serves everyone's interest. Experience has shown that it is not the

---

[31] The Brazilian Catholic Apostolic church was founded in 1945 by Carlos Duarte Costa, an excommunicated Catholic bishop who favored a more socially progressive role for the church.
[32] On these various religious practices, see Bastide, *African Religions of Brazil*.

police who ensure the exercise of the rights of man but rather the organization, vigilance, and combativeness of the citizenry. Fighting together for freedom of religion, the small religions will win their place in the sun.

### 6.10 JOSÉ CORREIA LEITE, "THE AFRICAN RENAISSANCE," NIGER (SÃO PAULO, BRAZIL: JULY 1960)

*The midcentury African independence movements sparked enormous interest and excitement among Black writers, intellectuals, and citizens throughout the Americas. In this article, long-time Afro-Brazilian journalist and activist* **José Correia Leite** *surveyed those movements, which he collectively characterized as an "African renaissance." He also noted their connection to the First Congress of Black Writers, held in Paris in 1956, in which many of Africa's most prominent writers and intellectuals took part. In so doing he subtly underlined the relationship between print culture and political movements, reaffirming the political significance of the Black press in Brazil and other countries.*

Although Africa may be an old continent, we have the sense these days of confronting the discovery of a new world. The wave of nationalism that, since the end of the Second World War, began to undermine and excavate the foundations of the great colonial empires, came from India, continued through Pakistan, Ceylon, Burma, and swept through Asia to arrive at the Black Continent.

Today, Africa is finding the path of its own destiny, with its spirit turned toward the generous nations, as we see in the verses of the poet [Léopold Sédar] Senghor of Senegal: "Make it so that we reply, 'Present' to the rebirth of the world, like the black yeast necessary to the white flour." "Who will teach rhythm to the dead world of machines and cannons?"

That sensibility will certainly not prevent the peoples of the African nations from confronting the struggles and problems that exist in the north and the south of the continent and, above all, the struggle in the Portuguese possessions. The pages of independence were written in blood. From the Mau Mau terror that tormented Kenya, to the blood that transformed Congo and Nyasaland, sooner or later this will lead the Portuguese government to acknowledge the signs of the times and to give Angola and Mozambique their independence.[33]

The prospects for these current developments in Africa were still dim when Alioune Diop, editor of the magazine *Présence africaine*, organized the First Congress of Black Writers, held in Paris at the Sorbonne.[34] That event took advantage of the moment to debate the subjects relevant to the bases of a cultural unity that the African populations believe to be theirs.

In a vanguard of Black intelligence, male thinkers gathered from Africa, America, and Europe. The world received news of the themes, affirmations, and contours of an awakening to the responsibilities of Black values in the current context of the modern world.

Among the men participating in that memorable conclave were Sékou Touré, today president of the Republic of Guinea, [Philibert] Tsirinana, president of the Republic of Madagascar, and so many others who, like Jean-Paul Sartre – the paladin of existentialism – brought concepts from the university to the aspirations of that event, which the author of "Black Orpheus" classified as [representing] a new aesthetic of Négritude.[35]

We cannot remain confined within the limitations of distancing ourselves from these events that excite our spirits as Afro-Brazilians.

---

[33] The Mau Mau Uprising (1952–60) was a guerrilla insurgency fought against British rule in Kenya. Kenya became independent in 1964, the Republic of the Congo in 1960, and Nyasaland (today the Republic of Malawi) in 1964. Angola and Mozambique won independence from Portugal in 1975.

[34] Alioune Diop (1910–80) was a Senegalese writer and intellectual, and the principal organizer of the First Congress of Black Writers and Artists, held in Paris in 1956.

[35] Ahmed Sékou Touré (1922–84) was a labor leader, politician, and first president of the Republic of Guinea following its independence in 1958. Philibert Tsirinana (1912–78) served as the first president of the Malagasy Republic. Jean-Paul Sartre's (1905–80) essay "Orphée noir" was published in Léopold Sédar Senghor's *Anthologie de la nouvelle poésie nègre et malgache de langue française* (1948). A Portuguese translation, "Orpheu negro," was published in *Quilombo* (Jan. 1950), 6–7. On Négritude, see Diagne, "Négritude."

# CHAPTER 7

# Diaspora and Black Internationalism

## INTRODUCTION

In addition to reporting on politics and culture in the cities and national contexts in which they were published, Afro-Latin American newspapers included extensive coverage of Black populations in other countries. Articles on Black people and racial conditions in Latin America, the United States, Europe, and Africa provide important evidence for what scholars call "practices of diaspora," international communication and engagement among Black peoples that grew out of, and helped to forge, feelings of connectedness and racial solidarity.[1] The Black press also reported or offered commentary on more formal political movements promoting Black internationalism, such as Garveyism (6.3, 7.7).

Black papers in Argentina and Uruguay reported regularly on their northern neighbor, Brazil, "the South American country in which the African race and its descendants have the greatest presence" (7.1). In 1879, the Argentine paper *La Juventud* led a fundraising effort to send money to the province of Ceará, where the Great Drought of 1877–78 had left widespread hunger and disease in its wake. Sixty years later, in 1938, the Uruguayan paper *Nuestra Raza* described the repression unleashed by the recently installed dictatorship of **Getúlio Vargas**. "The Brazilian people are suffering all the tortures and persecutions of a Nazi regime," to which opposition is "a moral obligation of racial solidarity for all Blacks" (7.11).

In 1894 the Cuban paper *La Igualdad* published a long article on Puerto Rican journalist Tomás Carrión Maduro's visit to Haiti (7.3).

---

[1] Edwards, *The Practice of Diaspora*; Guridy, *Forging Diaspora*.

255

Carrión Maduro took pains to refute racist images of Haiti as a land of barbarism, "where there [allegedly] are people who eat people." If anything, he reported, the island was noteworthy for its high degree of civility and, he asserted, its lack of political corruption, a striking implicit contrast to Cuba and Puerto Rico.

Throughout Latin America, writers and intellectuals of all races observed with mixed horror and fascination the workings of racial segregation and anti-Blackness in the United States. Afro-Cubans suffered those barbarities at first hand when they traveled to the United States, making it imperative that they be aware of hotels willing to accept Black guests (7.2). During the independence wars of the late 1800s, Afro-Cubans living in the United States took part in fundraisers and other events organized by local exile communities, in which African Americans also participated (7.4).

Black newspapers in Brazil devoted many pages to coverage of the racial situation in the United States. *O Bandeirante* used the United States as a foil to demonstrate the high degree of racial egalitarianism and fraternity that, it asserted, prevailed in Brazil (7.5; see also 6.3). In the same vein, *Getulino* argued that if African Americans were to emigrate to Brazil, they would soon drop the racial hostility and resentments that were a logical reaction to White racism in the United States, and would happily adopt Brazil's more relaxed racial mores (7.6). In 1928, *O Clarim da Alvorada* reported on the small colony of African Americans who had taken up residence in São Paulo city, finding them arrogant, standoffish, and "judging themselves superior to the Blacks of South America" (7.8). Quite different in tone was a 1953 article in the Cuban paper *Amanecer*, which presented statistical evidence of African Americans' social and economic progress in recent years and suggested that Afro-Cubans would do well to "imitate our neighbors to the North" (7.15).

Diasporic ties were further thickened by personal connections and friendships among African American and Afro-Latin American writers and intellectuals. In 1935, Cuban politician and activist **Salvador García Agüero** published a poem paying homage to African American author **Langston Hughes** (7.10). In the mid 1940s, North American anthropologist **Ellen Irene Diggs** and Cuban poet **Nicolás Guillén** both spent several (non-overlapping) months in Montevideo, Uruguay (7.12, 7.13). Each was warmly received by the local Black community, but Diggs provoked some discomfort at the end of her visit by giving an interview to an Argentine news magazine in which she made negative comments about her Afro-Uruguayan hosts (7.12).

Finally, we note a genre of article in the Black press in which writers adopted a broad global perspective to make some large point about their own countries. In 1928, Uruguayan lawyer **Francisco Rondeau** rebutted **scientific racism** by listing a "brilliant group of men of color" from Europe, the Americas, and Africa, thus demonstrating high Black intellectual achievement (7.9). Following World War II, Brazilian activist **Abdias do Nascimento** surveyed global patterns of racial oppression to show that racial discrimination and inequality were far from being exclusively Brazilian, or North American, or South African problems, but rather affected the world as a whole (7.14).

### DISCUSSION QUESTIONS

- In this chapter we see several examples of writers using other countries as lenses through which to comment on racial conditions in their own countries. How accurate do they seem to have been in describing conditions in those other countries? What do you make, for example, of Tomás Carrión Maduro's assertions of government transparency in Haiti (7.3), or *Amanecer*'s analysis of African American progress in the United States (7.15)? Why might writers in the Black press have chosen to represent conditions in Haiti or the United States in these ways?
- For most contributors to the Black newspapers, the United States represented the epitome of racial inequality and oppression. How did writers view African Americans' responses to that oppression? Which aspects of those responses did they think might be applicable to their own situations of inequality? Which aspects of the North American experience, if any, did they portray as too different from their own to draw any lessons from?
- The word "diaspora" – meaning a community of common origins dispersed among many national communities – does not appear in any of these articles; despite that omission, what evidence can you find in these texts that writers saw themselves as part of a Black diaspora or hoped to convince others to participate in such a community?
- In what ways did authors express or describe resistance to diasporic community building or Black internationalism? What was to be gained, for some authors, in expressing their national belonging first and foremost, and asserting difference rather than similarity with Afrodescendants in other parts of the world?

- How did the disproportionate power that the United States wielded in the region, and anti-imperialist movements that grew up in response, influence diasporic conversations among African Americans and Afro-Latin Americans?

### 7.1 "BRAZIL," LA JUVENTUD (BUENOS AIRES, ARGENTINA: JAN. [SIC: FEB.] 7, 1879)

*In this article, the editors of* La Juventud *called upon their fellow Afro-Porteños to come to the aid of the population of Ceará, a province in northern Brazil, during a historic drought (1877–78) that caused mass death from famine and disease. The duty to contribute to* La Juventud's *fundraising campaign stemmed in part, the author noted, from a history of friendship and mutual aid between Argentina and Brazil. But more importantly, he argued, the composition of Brazil's population – its status as "the South American country in which the African race and its descendants have the greatest presence" – incurred a particular obligation among Afro-Porteños to assist their Brazilian "brothers": "[f]ulfilling this duty falls, in great part, to us." The author did not mention it, but quite a few members of Buenos Aires' Black community had emigrated from Brazil.*

*This was a clear call for diasporic solidarity. It was also an opportunity to decry the "scandal[ous]" fact that slavery persisted in Brazil (see also 3.5). This sad portrait of Ceará's suffering – under the entwined scourges of slavery, poverty, famine, drought, and disease – triggered one of the few explicit reflections, in Buenos Aires' Black press, on Afro-Argentines' own history of slavery. That same sad portrait of Brazil simultaneously allowed the author to consider Afro-Argentines' own comparative privilege as citizens of a country in which Afrodescendants were free, could speak their minds, and had modest resources to spare for others in need.*

> Oh, cruel night!
> Like the vultures of an ill omen
> Your shadows will remain
> Etched in the minds of the men
> Swept up in your violent hurricane.
>               [Tiburcio] Puentes Gallardo[2]

---

[2] Tiburcio Puentes Gallardo was one of the editors of *La Juventud*, and likely the author of this piece.

Our readers may find themselves surprised upon reading the title of this article and the verse that precedes it. They may ask themselves, What does it mean?, thinking perhaps that what lies in store is some kind of literary exercise or historical episode.

Not so. That verse is nothing more than a righteous cry, ripped from the depths of our heart, upon remembering our sad history of enslavement and dishonor.

There arise in the life of nations certain painful events that, much as we may wish to evade them, cannot but bring to mind indelible memories. They cause our chests to exhale [the] resonant sighs, songs of redemption and love, [and] cries of pain and grief with which so many writers have crowned the great tragic epics, [and] which capture their pens while they weep like latter-day Jeremiahs at the gates of a destroyed Jerusalem! . . . . .

Brazil experiences today the suffering provoked by a period of dismay and sorrow. The news transmitted to us just two days ago by the submarine cable is harrowing in the extreme, capable of touching the fibers of the hardest and most unfeeling heart.

Pestilence continues to decimate the Province of Ceará, producing between one thousand and fifteen hundred victims per day. They are, besides, emaciated by the destitution that afflicts those unfortunate settlements.

Brazil has been and is our friend and our ally. In liberty's long battle against tyranny, it was Brazil that contributed mightily, placing 10,000 men under the command of General Urquiza. [It was those troops], in the battlefields of Caseros, who helped bring down the barbaric and bloody authority with which Rosas had lorded over our nation's soil for twenty years.[3]

In the **Paraguayan War**, there too we find [Brazil] fighting with ardent enthusiasm side by side with our victorious troops, winning triumphs and laurels. These everlasting marks of honor have adorned the brows of the Argentine officers who led them to victory, contributing as well to increasing the well-earned fame and the unimpeachable worth of those allied armies.

When a terrible scourge descended with cruel viciousness over the horizons of this city, and when death, waving its scythe over the heads

[3] The Battle of Caseros (February 1852) ended Argentina's midcentury civil wars. The forces of Juan Manuel de Rosas (governor of Buenos Aires and de facto ruler of the Argentine Confederation for twenty years) were defeated by those of General Justo José de Urquiza, which included troops from neighboring Uruguay and Brazil.

of an entire people, brought sadness, mourning, desperation, and horror to the bosoms of our anguished families, Brazil was one of the first countries in the world that hastened to alleviate our ill fate, sending us a generous contribution.[4]

Our society, the population of this entire Republic, is bound by the essential duty to extend a liberal hand toward that friendly and generous country as a just reward for the abovementioned favors that, not so long ago, it granted us. Fulfilling this duty falls, in great part, to us.

The neighboring Empire is the South American country in which the African race and its descendants have the greatest presence. How, then, can we remain deaf and indifferent upon hearing the pitiful cries of our brothers, many of whom still groan under the master's lash, subject to the harshest deprivations, much as it may scandalize the rest of humanity?

Who fails to be moved by the mere contemplation of the sad and dismal scene presented by misery, hunger, and death, which spread violently, dragging thousands of precious lives in the wake of their devastating maelstrom?

Pestilence and hunger!

As if the humble condition to which those unhappy [people] find themselves reduced were not harsh enough, now – heaping upon their ill fate – hunger and pestilence afflict them, snatching away their lives in the midst of the most atrocious suffering.

What must it feel like, to fight for life between the horrors of hunger and pestilence?

The mere thought of it causes dread.

We here, one way or another, possess the freedom even to speak up to the government when something is not to our liking. We are not lacking in five pesos with which to contribute to this support effort, alleviating and making more bearable the suffering of our fellow man.

Who among us will refuse to contribute at least one peso to come to the aid of the unfortunate of Brazil?

No one.

A subscription list to this end has been made available at this newspaper's offices, although we wish to make it known that we will not accept any contributions in excess of five pesos.

---

[4] The author was referring to the yellow fever epidemic of 1871 in the city of Buenos Aires, which led to an estimated 14,000 deaths (out of a population of approximately 200,000). At the time, the Brazilian government (which had ample experience with similar outbreaks at home) sent money, doctors, and emergency medical provisions to Buenos Aires.

A human duty to show gratitude, on one hand, forces us to take the former step; a sense of consideration toward our society and the [humble] condition of the majority of people who comprise it, on the other hand, force us to take the latter.

The goal is not to accumulate enormous sums, but to contribute with a small amount that will help mitigate the hunger that afflicts our brothers of Ceará.

### 7.2–7.3 TWO NOTES IN THE AFRO-CUBAN PRESS ABOUT NEW YORK (HAVANA AND NEW YORK: 1893–96)

*Writers and readers of the Cuban Black press frequently traveled to or settled in the United States. This mobility was visible in the papers in notices as simple as "Central Hotel" (7.2), alerting readers of* La Igualdad *to a hotel offering accommodations to Black travelers. Writers who lived for longer periods in the United States frequently contributed articles as correspondents for newspapers in Havana while agents and supporters collected funds in the United States to send to the editors of those papers. Migrants used the circulation of newspapers to maintain their ties to community and family, as when they published notices in the Black newspapers to help locate missing relatives (4.7).*

*Exiled journalists also sometimes published Black newspapers inside the United States. These were read locally and distributed through the mails to various émigré communities and to Cuba. "A Grand Summer Evening" (7.3), appearing in* La Doctrina de Martí, *a newspaper published by* **Rafael Serra** *in the late 1890s, announced a Cuban-American Festival in New York. The event raised money for the victims of the independence war that had begun a year earlier, and it featured independence leader and future Cuban President Tomás Estrada Palma. Like many other reports in the newspaper, it reflected the unusual diasporic context in which* La Doctrina de Martí *was produced. Travel and settlement in the United States offered not only first-hand knowledge of US-style racial discrimination and violence, but also close contact and conversation with African American journalists, musicians, and activists.*

### 7.2 "Central Hotel," *La Igualdad* (Havana, Cuba: Apr. 14, 1893)

In the neighboring city of New York, according to a helpful press release in our possession, Sr. D[on] Gervasio Pérez has established a great central hotel at 154 and 156 W. 14$^{th}$ Street, which offers the traveler every sort of amenity appropriate to the occasion.

The hotel is set up with all the latest advances and is on a par with the best in the city.

We pass along this notice to the innumerable families that travel to New York each summer and to those who are preparing to attend the imminent opening of the Chicago Exposition.

### 7.3 "A Grand Summer Evening," *La Doctrina de Martí* (New York: Sept. 16, 1896)

A GRAND SUMMER EVENING
Cuban-American Festival
*to benefit the wounded and orphaned of Cuba*
*organized by*
THE FRIENDS OF **ANTONIO MACEO**
Selzer Harlem River Park & Casino
Second Avenue between 126 and 127 Streets
*The evening of Wednesday, September 30, 1896.*
Music by the famous Standard New York Orchestra.[5]
Entrance, 25 cents.

Speakers will include eminent orators, including the Honorable Tomás Estrada Palma, Plenipotentiary Minister of the Cuban Republic, Bishop [Alexander] Walters, Reverend Ernest Lyon, Reverend H. Creamer, and T. Thomas Fortune, Editor of the *New York Age*.[6]

The whole [Cuban] colony is invited to this noisy party which, judging from the excitement, promises the greatest benefits to the cause of the Redemption of Cuba.

*President,* G[ermán] Sandoval.[7]

---

[5] A dance band led by the African American composer and musician Albert Mando.

[6] Alexander Walters (1858–1917), bishop of the African Methodist Episcopal (AME) Church, was a central figure in the creation of the civil rights organization called the Afro-American League. T. Thomas Fortune (1856–1928) was also a primary organizer of the Afro-American League. His *New York Age* was the most important Black newspaper in the United States at the time. Reverend Lyon was the pastor at St. Marks AME Church, a civil rights leader, and an important figure in the "Colored Annex" of the New York Republican Party. Reverend Creamer was the pastor at the Ebenezer Baptist Church, another Black congregation, and the father of Henry S. Creamer, who was a dancer, vaudeville performer, lyricist, and one of the founders of the Clef Club, an early organization for Black musicians and composers in New York.

[7] Germán Sandoval (1847–?) was an early Afro-Cuban settler, and a founder and leader of many Black Cuban organizations in New York, including the Logia San Manuel, Cuban Republican Association, and La Liga. Hoffnung-Garskof, *Racial Migrations*.

## 7.4 TOMÁS CARRIÓN MADURO, "HAITI," LA IGUALDAD (HAVANA, CUBA: SEPT. 5, 1894)

*The independent Republic of Haiti, founded by formerly enslaved people who successfully defeated French and English attempts at recolonization, held a prominent place in the imaginations of Black writers in Cuba, as in the rest of the Americas. The Spanish colonial government and many White Cubans used the specter of a second Haiti – by which they meant Black supremacy, remorseless revenge against Whites, misrule, and general savagery – in efforts to discredit the Cuban civil rights movement and the independence movement. Writers in the Black press, most famously* **Juan Gualberto Gómez,** *therefore frequently emphasized the great distance between their efforts and the Haitian experience.*

*The author of this satirical travel narrative, Tomás Carrión Maduro, took a different approach. A Black journalist from Puerto Rico who lived in Cuba in the early 1890s, Carrión recounted his own visit to Haiti as an explicit rebuke to racist stereotypes that "others" deployed when discussing the "Black republic." Once there, the spirits of the revolutionary heroes Jean-Jacques Dessalines and Toussaint Louverture manifested themselves to him, correcting his memory of the Haitian struggle for independence and allowing the Black traveler, abandoned by his own society, to understand the "solemn majesty" of a country in which Black people occupied every profession and social rank. Similarly, Carrión suggested, a firsthand experience of the unpretentious, but not uncivilized, Haitian Republic provided a useful comparative frame for understanding the flaws of the pretentious and corrupt colonies of Cuba and Puerto Rico. Maduro later became a member of the Puerto Rican House of Delegates (1900–06).*[8]

## I

Battered like a castaway by an ocean of misfortunes, tossed by the brutish tempests of adversity upon the reefs of a neighboring shore – in such a condition, I arrived on the morning of this past July 28 in Haiti, the

[8] On Carrión Maduro, see Fusté, "Unsettling Citizenship."

Black republic, as some call it, the country, others say, where there are
people who eat people.

I have no fatherland.

Without one, I have been an orphan from the cradle.

My mother gave birth to me in a field, not like Mary giving life to Christ
in a doorway, but like a beast with her cubs.

A black crow squawked a savage welcome that unlucky day, greeting
a new son of **Ham** as he arrived in this stupid and childish world. If this is
not the truth, it seems so to me.

The day I arrived in the fiefdom of Hyppolite[9] was a day without sun,
a day as cloudy and dark as the conscience of a tyrant.

The black shadows seemed to have gathered to witness the arrival of
the obscure traveler.[10]

The scene was bursting with darkness.
Black, the crew of the ship that carried me aboard.
Black, the day of my landing.
Black, I myself.
Black, even the soil that I tread for the first time.
How much darkness!

It could be called the Apocalypse of my life
A sinister orgy of all that is dark:

There are more Blacks there than there are prejudices in Cuba.

Blacks who come and Blacks who go.
Blacks in commerce.
Blacks working in the arts.
Blacks working in industries.
Blacks in the militia.

---

[9] Louis Mondestin Florvil Hyppolite, president of Haiti from 1889 to 1896.
[10] In Spanish, *oscuro* means not only unknown or shadowy but also literally dark.

Blacks serving in the civilian government.
Blacks performing delicate official assignments.
Black diplomats.
Black scientists.
Black writers.
Black artists.
Black everything, in sum.

To me, this scene had the solemn majesty of a great novelty.

But swiftly the great names of Toussaint and Dessalines sprang to my mind, as if called forth by a spirit of veneration and respect. And when these two august shadows took shape within the shrine of my memory, I thought:

These buildings that stand out before my gaze without artistic audacity or aesthetic pretension;

Here where there are no Corinthian capitals or Doric columns;
Here where such architectural orders do not enjoy the fictitious value assigned to them in other countries, countries enervated by vanity and made abject by a grandeur poorly understood and terribly practiced.

Here where there are Generals who walk about in modest dress, because they do not live by larceny or fraud, and nevertheless, they serve their country as best they can and with what they can.

Here where there are not so many high-ranking scoundrels nor so many tycoons who deserve shackles around their ankles as in some other countries that have the audacity to call themselves civilized.

On this soil, where morality has been placed before material questions; where the hygiene of the body is neglected, but not the hygiene of the soul. Here one understands that self-respect has won out over arrogance.

Instead of clowns there have been men.
Instead of **Cains** there have been Christs.
Instead of men who are dogs, worthy men.

## II

Port-au-Prince, the capital of Haiti, resembles a giant fair. The natives gather in motley groups along avenues and in plazas to display to shoppers all of the outpouring of products from that bountiful land. There are doorways in which business owners set up crates as makeshift displays or hang long ropes, and with these they exhibit all the novelties for sale in their establishments; but there are no doorways where women go, as in other, pseudo-enlightened countries, to offer themselves to passersby, for the price of ten or twelve cents.

There are wide streets shaded by the thick foliage of giant trees; streets that are somewhat abandoned, because, on rainy days the constant coming and going of carriages creates deep ruts. It occurs to these good people to conceal this flaw by tossing large quantities of straw over these potholes, with this pretense the authorities consider that they have done their duty. But the innocent traveler, who has no prior experience, runs the risk of submerging himself up to the ears in a spot where he had thought he saw a yellow carpet worthy of being trodden by foreign soles.

Nevertheless, there are no distinguished rulers who cheat their subjects out of distinguished sums for the purposes of their grandiose urbanism. There are high-ranking public officials and dignitaries who walk about in humble dress, but there are no officials or dignitaries who present constant threats to the interests of the national treasury.

They, like swords of Damocles, eternally suspended over the wealth of the public purse!

There are wives of Ministers who carry a basket to the market to buy what is needed in their homes; but there are no wives of Ministers who keep appointments at the cheap dance halls and thus ruin the honor of their husbands.

There are gentlemen of dark color who belong to the noble lineage of men of virtue and talent; but there are no Black men of White color who belong to the noble lineage of disgusting debauchery.

There are delicate and cultured *negritos* who always dress in tails and top hat, luxuries that they attain with the product of their honest labor;

but there are no *blanquitos*[11] who like to make themselves out to be high and mighty but are actually living a pipe dream and are great friends of the miserable whores.

There are those who say that the Haitians eat human flesh.[12] Be that as it may, I would dare to walk through the most tangled jungles of Haiti with no fear of being devoured by anyone, not even the wild beasts, though I travel cautiously through the most crowded places in countries, seemingly more cultured, for fear of being eaten by some White negrophile.

Tomás Carrión

(Puerto Rican)

## 7.5 "GRAVE ERROR!" O BANDEIRANTE (SÃO PAULO, BRAZIL: SEPT. 1918)

*Throughout Latin America, the United States was well known to be a society characterized by extreme racial oppression and exclusion. In response to reports of segregation and lynching in the American South, Black writers in Latin America measured their own societies against the United States and often found a favorable comparison that could be useful to their political arguments. In this article, O Bandeirante used the United States as a foil to demonstrate Brazil's racial openness, and to place blame on Black Brazilians for their own marginalization. While African Americans were brutally excluded from national life, in Brazil, "wherever a White person is, a Black person may easily be there as well." The article argued that, by working together to build and defend Brazil, Blacks and Whites had forged strong and unbreakable ties of racial brotherhood.[13] Like "Black Letters" (6.3), the article also rejected the idea of Afro-Brazilian identification with Africa and urged readers to "not seek to perpetuate our race, but rather to infiltrate ourselves into the*

---

[11] The use of the diminutive "little Black man" or "Black boy" is notable here. Though frequently used as a term of endearment, the word *negrito* was also used to describe stereotyped characters in blackface plays of the era and could be belittling or insulting, similar to "darky" in the United States in that era. Here it is paired with *blanquito*, "White boy" or "Whitey," which was a derogatory term for White men who wielded unmerited power.

[12] This is probably a reference to the White Puerto Rican author José Rodríguez-Castro, who claimed in his 1894 book, *Cosas de Haití: Notas de un viaje a este país*, to have been served human flesh while visiting Haiti. Fusté, "Possible Republics."

[13] On "racial fraternity," see Alberto, *Terms of Inclusion*, pp. 69–109.

*bosom of the privileged race – the White race, because, we repeat, we are not Africans but purely Brazilians." This endorsement of the idea that Brazil was characterized by racial fraternity and race mixture prefigured and anticipated arguments later made famous by Brazilian sociologist* **Gilberto Freyre.**

There are many among us who form a mistaken idea of what it means to raise up our **class**; there are many who, completely adulterating the elevated goal that we should all have in view, think and preach, with no basis whatsoever, simply the separation of races, setting our race apart from the White race!

This is the height of foolishness. It is a grave error, if not a true crime against the nation.

To attempt to establish a parallel equivalence between us and the North American Blacks is to ignore completely the atmosphere of prejudice, hatred, scorn, and persecution in which our [North American] brothers of color live; it is to demonstrate the crassest ignorance on the subject.

If our ancestors had as their cradle the lands of Africa, it is necessary to note, we have as our cradle and our fatherland this great country. We are not Africans, we are Brazilians!

Twenty-one states constitute this colossus, Brazil, under a single flag. To undertake the separation of races, to promote that absurdity of absurdities, is to preach discord and to provoke hatred and possible fratricidal struggles.

If in the United States there does exist race prejudice, here, fortunately, we do not have that terrible scourge. Do we need to demonstrate it?

In North America, the Black is a detested, hated element at the margins of White society: schools and government offices, civic and social organizations, drugstores and shops, theaters and places of recreation, barbershops and railroad cars exist exclusively for the Whites; Black people's entry [to those places] is completely barred. In certain cities where hatred against people of our color is more accentuated, Whites walk on the sidewalks and Blacks ... in the middle of the street. If any of those miserable wretches step on the paved walkways, they are arrested and fined, they are beaten or, as frequently happens, they are lynched and hung from the lampposts!

Does any of that exist here?

Where is the hate, the persecution, the war to the death against us?

Where are the lynchings and the prejudice? If anyone feels ready with arguments that contradict us, let them give testimony.

Here the Black is employed in government offices, he is a trusted assistant in the most important commercial houses of the country, he is a servant in the most highly regarded homes of the Brazilian aristocracy; he can enter the academies where the Whites study, he enjoys the same rights and privileges and is a Brazilian citizen.

Wherever a White person is, a Black person may easily be there as well. Therefore, to try to provoke the Utopian separation of races would be to bring down on us war without quarter, in which we will be fatally defeated and covered with disgrace.

In pursuing the impossible and unnecessary separation of races, we will deny our beloved country, which is this one!

Let us remember that Blacks and Whites, made brothers by the same love for this land, have been fighting for its growth and advancement, in business as in private and public life, in politics as in industry, in war as in peace. In all these instances, always next to the Black man is a White man!

So what are we complaining about?

We should complain about ourselves, about our own negligence, about our own lack of a common vision, about living the way we do in a vast cosmopolitan milieu such as this one. In this capital city [São Paulo], the national element mixes with the foreigners and, as the latter have their centers for mutual aid and general assistance, we, the nationals [Brazilians], each in their sphere, must mobilize to provide ourselves with mutual assistance.

That is what we must do, along with the following:

Not seek to perpetuate our race, but rather to infiltrate ourselves into the bosom of the privileged race – the White race, because, we repeat, we are not Africans but purely Brazilians.

In order to achieve this more quickly, it is necessary for us to seek, by every means, to elevate the character of our men, to obligate our sons, brothers, and friends to go to school, to inculcate in the spirit of our daughters, sisters, or wives the exact understanding of what constitutes honor and self-respect. This is what we need to do. This is the uplift of our class as we understand it!

We see all around us many Black men living from vice, large numbers of dirty, disheveled women, and vagabond children wandering through the streets, instead of seeing people searching for honorable work, others valuing cleanliness, and others going to schools where one pays nothing, created by the Whites, for us and for them, in intimate communion.

Is this all that we see!? No, unfortunately not. The rest ... the pen refuses to describe.

As long as these ills that we mention are not remedied, we will never achieve all the goals that we long for. The blame does not belong to Whites – it is ours! For the means are there within our reach and at our disposition.

This is a very difficult task; very few are those who take this question seriously. Unfortunately, many among us, the majority, think only of entertainments and nothing more. The day will come when their repentance will be too late.

Let us mobilize, let us raise ourselves up before all, let us be severe judges of ourselves, let us solidify the brotherhood that makes us indistinguishable from the Whites born under the Brazilian flag. Let us seek out work and search for the enlightenment of our intelligence, so that we will no longer present the unedifying spectacle that we offer today.

Brazil is our country. Let us be Brazilians and remember the words of [Theodore] Roosevelt on the occasion of his visit to our country.[14]

To elevate our character, to constitute lawful and legitimate families, to create men of worth – this is our mission.

To preach the madness of the separation of races, establishing tremendous prejudices between us and the Whites, is simply to commit a crime of treason against the country.

Brazil above all, first and foremost!

D'Alencastro

## 7.6 EVARISTO DE MORAES, "BLACKS IN THE UNITED STATES AND IN BRAZIL," GETULINO (CAMPINAS, BRAZIL: JAN. 13, 1924)

*In 1923 Congressman Fidélis Reis[15] introduced a bill into the Chamber of Deputies barring immigration into Brazil by "settlers of the Black race."*

---

[14] In 1913–14 former President Theodore Roosevelt visited Brazil as part of an exploratory expedition to the Rio da Dúvida (today the Rio Roosevelt). Upon his return to the United States he publicly applauded Brazil's tolerance of race mixture. Roosevelt, "Brazil and the Negro."

[15] Fidélis Reis (1880–1962), White Brazilian politician who served in the Chamber of Deputies from 1921 to 1930, representing the state of Minas Gerais.

*He was reacting to reports that companies in the United States were making plans to buy large tracts of land in central Brazil, to be distributed among African American immigrant settlers. Black newspapers in São Paulo were horrified by the bill and argued strenuously against it. In this article, Afro-Brazilian lawyer and journalist **Evaristo de Moraes** focused on one particular argument made by the bill's supporters: that African American immigrants were intensely anti-White and would import race hatred with them into Brazil. Summarizing the conclusions of Whites and Blacks in the United States and Brazil,[16] a short book that he had published in 1922, Moraes agreed that African Americans were barbarously oppressed in the United States and were appropriately resentful of that treatment. Once they arrived in Brazil, however, and saw the racial openness and harmony that prevailed there, they would lose those resentments and would join in the work of constructing the Brazilian nation.*

*At the beginning of the article, Moraes also called out Reis's racist language and presumptions, arguing that his condemnation of Black and Asian people's physical unattractiveness could just as easily be applied to the European immigrants Brazil had received.*

*Reis's bill ultimately was not approved.*

In a previous article, which initiated this brief analysis of the bill recently presented in the Chamber [of Deputies] by Dr. Fidélis Reis, we made clear the inappropriateness of our compatriots supporting [their arguments] by using foreign authors – like Gobineau and Lapouge[17] – who, full of prejudices, defamed Brazil through their complete ignorance of the phenomena of ethnic fusion that have taken place here and through not foreseeing the soaring achievements of our civilization.

Today, we will try to correct one of the mistakes most frequently made by the enemies, among us, of North Americans of the Black race.

First, however, let us emphasize, even if briefly, a concern of the deputy who wrote the bill.

He is moved, it seems, not only by the fear of an increase in the [number of] degenerates – who, in his understanding, are all the people of mixed race. He does not only fear the undermining of Brazil through new arrivals of inferior people; he is afflicted as well by an artistic anxiety, as a lover of

---

[16] Moraes, *Brancos e negros*.
[17] Joseph Arthur de Gobineau (1816–82) and Georges Vacher de Lapouge (1854–1936) were French **scientific racists** who wrote in very negative terms about the mixed racial composition of Brazil and other Latin American countries.

Beauty. And that anxiety expressed itself in words that it would be a crime to hide from the eyes of readers who are probably strangers to the *Diário do Congresso Nacional*, an attachment of the *Diário Oficial*.[18]

Here they are:

Besides the ethnic, moral, political, social, and perhaps even economic reasons that lead us to reject, at the very outset, the entry of the yellow person and the Black into the process of amalgamation that is taking place under our skies, upon our immense stage, there is another [reason] that perhaps should be considered, "which is the aesthetic point of view and that our Hellenic conception of beauty could never be brought into harmony with the features produced by such a racial fusion."[19]

As for the fusion of White and Black, we will say to the talented deputy that not all lovers of Beauty share his conception.

The criterion of "taste" is, in this case as in others, varied and relative.

Do you want proof?

The extremely unimpeachable Sílvio Romero,[20] one of the most authentic "Whites of Brazil," after praising the Black race as the producer of our wealth [and the] indirect creator of our mental culture, said:

Race mixture modified the relations of master and slave, brought more sweetness to [our] customs and produced the person of mixed race, who constitutes the mass of our population and, to a certain degree, the beauty of our race. Even today our prettiest women are those agile, strong, lively young maidens, with skin the color of caramel candy, with black eyes, voluminous black hair – healthy young women in whose veins flow, surely quite diluted, many drops of African blood.

Aesthetic for aesthetic, there will be some who prefer that of Sílvio Romero. Especially because, if we accept "the Hellenic concept of beauty," we will run the risk of finding undesirable the thousands of immigrants of the White race who absolutely do not conform to that concept, not even in terms of cleanliness.

* * *

Let's attend to more serious subjects.

---

[18] These two *Diários* are publications of the federal government, in which official actions, decrees, legislation, etc. are recorded. Moraes was suggesting that relatively few Brazilians read the *Diários*, which was undoubtedly true.

[19] We do not know who Reis was quoting here. It is possible that quotation marks were used, here and elsewhere in this article, for emphasis rather than to signal a direct quotation.

[20] Sílvio Romero (1851–1914) was a prominent literary critic and poet.

One of the frequently used arguments against the entry into Brazil of settlers of the Black race, coming from North America, consists of frightening us with their anti-White prejudices.

It is claimed, with the appearance of conviction, that they will bring race struggle here in their luggage.

Dr. Fidélis Reis acknowledges that our African Black man fought alongside us in the harshest battles that formed our nationality; he worked, suffered, and, with his dedication, helped us to create the Brazil that is here today.

But [Fidélis Reis] is horrified by the coming of the North American Black, who, in his view, will disturb our domestic peace.

For its part, the newspaper *O Jornal* argues, in an article that is extremely cruel to the Black race:

Of the disadvantages of African immigration, only one did not take root among us, because of the servile condition in which it arrived: race struggle. It would be precisely that new problem that the immigration of the American Blacks would bring here.

One will easily understand how unfounded this fear is, if we reflect on the causes, in the United States, of the prejudice among North Americans of the Black race against those of the White race.

How is it possible to respect those who scorn us?

To wish well to those who mistreat us?

To treat with affection those who persecute us, insult us, revile us?

To ask the representatives of the Black race in the United States to show favor and affection toward the Whites; to try to dissipate, in their aching souls, the bitterness of the insults they have suffered, would be to demand from them a saintly patience that is incompatible with human nature. It would seek to transform them into supernatural beings of infinite goodness.

Victims of monstrous prejudice, "which was not dismantled even by the recent proofs of loyalty in the trenches,"[21] they – who constitute the minority of the nation – saw and see themselves coerced in every social relation; and mainly in the southern states, and even after the ending of slavery, they were even more hated than before. Their notable progress is not pardoned, nor are their efforts to raise themselves, more and more, from their former abjection.

---

[21] We do not know who Moraes was quoting here, or if this is a direct quotation. The reference, however, is to African American military service in World War I.

In the past, their White compatriots only saw them as being useful as slaves. Today, they only accept Blacks' proximity if those of the Black race limit themselves to servile occupations in which, on principle, all intimacy is prohibited.

Observe: among their servant staff, the rich Yankees prefer the darkest-skinned Blacks to *mulatos* of all shades, as if to dig a large, deep abyss that must always separate the two races.

Don't think that the separation imposed by the Whites declined in intensity in recent years. Even now, after the welcoming actions of [Theodore] Roosevelt and the humanitarian and civilizing words of [Woodrow] Wilson, imperious and unbending prejudice rules.

What does it matter that the 11 million North Americans of the Black race contributed to the prosperity of their country, and even more, to develop the agriculture of almost the entire South?

Of what help is the evidence of their mental capacity in the reduction of illiteracy to less than 30 percent of their people, when it is certain that in 1872 that proportion was around 90 percent?

What importance is given to the fact of the "colored people" (as is said there [in the United States]) having contributed with almost 400,000 men and 225 million dollars to the last war, in which the United States answered the European call and the objectives of its industrial imperialism?

Of what value are their many universities, their schools, their 50,000 college graduates, their farms, their banks, their large factories, their newspapers, their magazines?

So many remarkable demonstrations of perfect adaptation to all the forms of human progress do not succeed in modifying, in the United States, the attitude of the White race toward the Black race.

Prejudice affects equally, from those who have truly dark skin to those who, three or four generations back, were connected to the scorned race but whose skin color is, in reality, White.

Blacks, openly declared *mulatos*, and disguised *mulatos* are not admitted to the hotels, the vehicles, the majority of high schools, the churches where Whites live, travel, study, and pray.

There are states, and not a few, in which marriage between people of different races is absolutely forbidden. In some of those states, not only are there severe penalties of fines and imprisonment for infractions, but the marriages are annulled, even when there are children. (See our pamphlet, "Whites and Blacks," pp. 24–27.)

The men of color are underhandedly deprived of their voting rights, despite the 14th and 15th amendments of the North American Constitution. And when no underhanded maneuver takes place, the barbarous secret society Ku Klux Klan enters the scene, threatening, coercing, separating by force the non-White voters from the polls.

The system of agricultural labor is different for the two races: for the representatives of the Black race, there still persists a kind of slavery, peonage, that chains them to the ground through an extremely complicated system of debts, killing them in poverty and servile abasement.

There is also no justice for the "colored people," it having been cynically confessed to an extremely impartial French writer that, when two Blacks or *mulatos* appear before certain courts, bringing charges against each other, both are punished, even though one of them is correct. And if a lawyer of color argues against a White, the victory of the latter is inevitable.

Everywhere and in everything terrible prejudice reveals itself, even in the savage application of the so-called "lynch law." Statistics show that, from 1889 to 1918, there were 3,224 lynchings in the United States, of which only 702 were of White people.

\* \* \*

Is the animosity of the more or less Black North Americans against their White compatriots justified, or is it not?

As we see, it is a simple effect of the environment, the result of the conditions in which they live, vexed, degraded, tortured by the others.

Under different conditions, in which the victims of brutal prejudice are transferred to another environment, in which opportunities for work combine with an effective welcome, the animosity will promptly cease.

The wisdom of the proverbs teaches that "two don't fight, when one doesn't want to."

There [in the United States], the one who provokes the fight is the one who believes himself to be, up until now, the stronger. Here [in Brazil], the stronger, the national majority, is undeniably comprised of racially mixed people, who, not being imbued with racial prejudice, will give no motive for rejection by, or ill will from, the foreigners.

Unless, that is, our few prejudiced ones (like the author of a report rejected by the Institute of Lawyers) convince the people here that all the men of color who migrate from the United States to Brazil are "undesirable," making them believe what those newspapers that oppose [their coming] say.

But to those [newspapers] we can reply with what is documented in the [US] Black press – newspapers and magazines – reflecting the moral, intellectual, and industrial worth of those admirable descendants of enslaved Africans.

### 7.7 "A COLOSSAL CONVENTION OF BLACK PEOPLE," GETULINO (CAMPINAS, BRAZIL: OCT. 26, 1924)

*One of the first and most important Black internationalist organizations in the Americas was the* **Universal Negro Improvement Association** *(UNIA), founded in 1914 by Jamaican businessman and activist* **Marcus Garvey***. By the mid 1920s, the UNIA comprised over 1,000 local affiliates in more than 40 countries. Its newspaper,* The Negro World, *circulated widely in the United States and the Caribbean region, and Black periodicals in Brazil regularly reprinted articles from its pages. This short article reported on the UNIA's Fourth International Convention, held in New York in August 1924. Its description of the thousands of delegates marching along the parade route is borne out by James Van Der Zee's celebrated photographs of the event.[22] Getulino's reporting reflected the aspirations of some Afro-Brazilian activists to be represented in this historic event (through the gift of a bound collection of their newspaper, among the most important in Brazil's Black press at the time) and to be able to hold similar events in São Paulo.*

A colossal convention of Black people has just gotten underway in New York. Posters placed along all the [city's] streets in the last few days announce it as the "largest Black convention in the world."

This conference, organized by the **Universal Negro Improvement Association** and headed by Mr. **Marcus Garvey**, comprises a thousand delegations from all over the world, primarily the United States, the West Indies, and Northern Africa. Its goal is to forge a vast political union aimed at protecting and demanding respect for the rights of the Black race. Its inauguration consisted principally of a parade, along the streets of New York,

[22] On Van Der Zee's photos, see Boone, "Reproducing the New Negro."

made up of close to thirty thousand Black delegates heralded by six orchestras.

At the front of it all marched Marcus Garvey, surrounded by Black soldiers who were magnificently attired.

The convention will draw to a close in February of next year with a large exhibition, which will feature a complete collection of *Getulino*, bound in morocco leather, to attest to the degree of advancement of our people in Brazil.

### 7.8 HORÁCIO DA CUNHA, "THE BLACKS OF NORTH AMERICA AND THE BLACKS OF SOUTH AMERICA," O CLARIM DA ALVORADA (SÃO PAULO, BRAZIL: FEB. 5, 1928)

*Although writers in the Black press typically found exchanges with counterparts in the United States to be empowering, in this article Horácio da Cunha expressed concern over the inequality and cultural insensitivity that sometimes characterized these relationships. When Black Brazilians talked or thought about the United States, da Cunha found, they were appropriately admiring of that country's extraordinary technological and industrial achievements and of African Americans' participation in those achievements. However, he went on to observe, in identifying with their country's power and status, African Americans sometimes assumed an air of superiority and condescension toward their "Black brothers" in the South American countries, including Brazil. While North Americans expected immigrants in the United States to learn and speak English, many African Americans living in São Paulo did not speak Portuguese and stayed within their own small community, not socializing with Black Brazilians. Da Cunha's comments suggest how strongly held national identifications, among both Black Brazilians and Black North Americans, could impede feelings of racial and diasporic unity.*

From where I stand, I've noticed that when my brothers of color in this capital city [São Paulo], in the course of their conversations, speak enthusiastically about the progress of our brothers of color in North America, they have a lot to say: that they [Black North Americans] are the inventors of telephones, radios, player pianos, and so forth.

That should come as no surprise, since the United States of North America is fundamentally an industrial nation in every way; we can see that they have already overtaken England.

Brazil is a young nation, only now, strictly speaking, beginning its evolution.

I can confidently say this to my Black brothers: a few years from now, once we reach the peak of our progress, we will see our Brazil running parallel to North America in everything and for everything.

The sun rises for everyone.

And intelligence is the [exclusive] privilege of no one.

In light of North America's formidable progress, Black North Americans display a racial pride, even judging themselves superior to the Blacks of South America. Perhaps they consider us to be the dregs of society because we lack money.

Would my countrymen like proof? There exist, in this capital city, many Black North Americans who associate only with their compatriots, keeping to themselves.

And many of them do not speak Portuguese, because of racial pride, when they should do so in homage to the land that hosts them.

Meanwhile, we know full well that anyone who wishes to go try his luck in their land has a strict obligation to speak English or American.

We have endless enthusiasm for what is done in other countries; we ceaselessly valorize anything that comes from abroad while disdaining what is ours.

That is not right.

To overcome this difficulty, we need to carry our nation's textbooks in our right hand, and in the other, the workman's tools that represent the formidable progress of our glorious state of São Paulo, pinnacle of our Union.

I do not seek to malign a race, our brothers in color, but neither do we want to be maligned by them. Thank God we are Brazilians and are in our land. And so I say with enthusiasm, "let us go forth together as one, separate in nothing" – the words of Dr. Sáenz Peña.[23]

## 7.9 FRANCISCO RONDEAU, "THE WORD OF DR. RONDEAU," LA VANGUARDIA (MONTEVIDEO, URUGUAY: FEB. 15, 1928)

*Francisco Rondeau was a leading figure in Montevideo's Black community. He received his law degree from the Universidad de la República in*

---

[23] The author refers to a speech given by Roque Sáenz Peña (1852–1914), president of Argentina (1910–14), during an official visit to Brazil in August 1910. The original quotation, in reference to Argentine–Brazilian relations, is "Everything unites us, nothing separates us." Preuss, *Transnational South America*, p. 119.

*1901 and was one of only a handful of Black lawyers in the city. In this article Rondeau congratulated La Vanguardia on its first issue and went on to list important historical and literary figures of the African diaspora. By doing so, he achieved three goals: demonstrating his own erudition, refuting those racists who dismissed the achievements of members of the Black race, and giving "encouragement and stimulus" to Black Uruguayans in their own projects of self-improvement. Rondeau surveyed eminent Africans and Afrodescendants from around the globe, including Germany and Russia; in his own country of Uruguay, he focused on Black military officers who had fought in the country's civil wars, a recurrent theme in the Afro-Uruguayan press. His admitted reliance on "many writers better equipped than I" highlights the network of intellectuals across the hemisphere who collected and shared, often through the medium of the Black press, information about Black achievement that was excluded from textbooks and academic histories.*

We received with gratitude the following letter from Dr. **Francisco Rondeau,** which with deep pleasure we hasten to publish.

To the Editor of La Vanguardia, Dr. **Salvador Betervide.**

Esteemed friend and colleague:

If my sincere thoughts might find a place (as I believe they might) in your spirit, always so open to noble initiatives, then please accept, yourself and the other members of the editorial staff, my warmest congratulations for the longed-for debut of *La Vanguardia.*

Your well-known talent and learning are qualities more than sufficient to guarantee the success of the enterprise, the goal of which is that our race continue to enlighten itself, in whatever way may be most feasible, in order to stand out and impose itself by developing its own intellectual abilities in all the spheres of human endeavor. Toward that end, I believe it necessary to pause for a moment to investigate the history of a distant past that offers us a brilliant group of men of color, of such outstanding intellectual achievement that they astonish, [especially] if one notes that in those times they had to live in a political and social setting completely averse to their legitimate aspirations.

It is certain that racial prejudice has existed and exists, but such prejudice only finds space in the poverty-stricken spirit of lazy, ignorant people, or in the mental imbalances of cretins, or in the stupid pretensions of those complainers who, of all these, are the fewest. [These last] make the absurd claim that talent and enlightenment are and will be the exclusive patrimony of the White race, demonstrating that those who are

prejudiced against the Black race live at the margins of the most fundamental principles of justice, proclaimed in irrefutable form by the erudite
writer Jean Finot.[24]

But as a word of encouragement and stimulus for those who are
undecided, unbelieving, or unaware of the distant and recent past, I will
mention a few cases.

Referring to the talent of Black people, the celebrated writer Rubén
Darío[25] published in a Paris newspaper in 1912 an article on "the intel-
lectuality of some men of the Black race.["] Among the many cases he
cited was that of Hannibal,[26] whose education was overseen by Czar Peter
I of Russia. Ascending to the rank of Lieutenant General, he wrote various
works on engineering and was decorated with the red ribbon of the Order
of Saint Alexander.

Anton Wilhelm Amo,[27] a native of Guinea, was a slave, studied at the
Universities of Saxony and of Wittenberg, and became an astronomer. He
spoke Latin, Greek, Hebrew, French, Dutch, and German and published
several philosophical works, inspiring admiration from the rectors of
those universities.

Jacob Daisan,[28] a slave in Philadelphia, was one of the most noteworthy physicians in New Orleans, and wrote various works on medicine
and other no less important subjects.

In the Congo lived **René Maran**, who wrote his literary jewel *Batouala*
on the life and customs of the Black people in that region, so brilliantly
that he won the prestigious Goncourt Prize.

In the United States, where implacable hatred of the Black race still
exists as an outrage to civilization, **Booker T. Washington** left *Up from
Slavery* as a demonstration of his solid talent. Upon his death he was

---

[24] Jean Finot (born Jean Finckelhaus, 1858–1922), French-Polish intellectual and author of
*Race Prejudice* (1906).
[25] Rubén Darío (born Félix Rubén García Sarmiento, 1867–1916), renowned Nicaraguan
poet. Leonel Delgado Aburto, "Darío, Rubén," in Knight and Gates, *Dictionary*, vol. II,
pp. 290–93.
[26] Abram Petrovich Hannibal (1696–1781?), an enslaved African from Cameroon who
became a military engineer and general in the Russian army. He was the great-
grandfather of the Russian author, Alexander Pushkin.
[27] Anton Wilhelm Amo (1703–59), an accomplished scientist and philosopher, born in what
is now Ghana. During Amo's lifetime, Europeans used the word "Guinea" in reference to
the entire coast of West Africa south of the Senegal river, including Amo's birthplace.
Rondeau seems to have adopted this usage from historical sources.
[28] Rondeau appears to be referring to James Durham (1762–1802?), who practiced medicine
in New Orleans. He is believed to be the first African American physician in the United
States.

succeeded [as principal of the **Tuskegee Institute**] by Robert R. Moton,[29] of great prestige and rare talents. Moton was a military man, a university graduate, lecturer, sociologist, and a complete and peerless intellectual.

In the great French Republic there existed such prestigious talents as Alexandre Dumas, Sr.,[30] Gratien Candace,[31] who brilliantly occupied a seat in the parliament of his native land, and many other men, still living, of outstanding intellectual attributes.

In the Republic of Cuba, the lamented **Gabriel de la Concepción Vald[és]**, who was a poet of high inspiration and unstained patriotism; Generals **[Antonio] Maceo** and Quintín Bandera,[32] who in defending the independence of their country astonished the world with their intrepid valor and military skill, to such an extreme that the High Command of the Spanish army recognized their high military gifts. Today a grateful nation perpetuates in bronze the memory of its great liberator [Maceo].

In South America, among others there was **José do Patrocínio**, who stands out as a fearsome polemicist and great leader of the Brazilian Parliament,[33] and whose lofty figure inspired the admiration of Brazilians and foreigners.

In the Argentine Republic there were great and selfless servants of the nation, among them Colonels **[Lorenzo] Barcala** and **[José María] Morales** and Sergeant **Falucho**. There are also notaries public and writers, all of well-known competence.[34]

In my own country there have been valiant and selfless servants of the nation who through their indisputable merits rose to high military rank; I recall General Luna,[35] Colonels Marcelino Sosa,[36] Feliciano González,[37]

[29] Robert R. Moton (1867–1940), writer and educator who served as principal of the Tuskegee Institute from 1915 to 1935.

[30] Alexandre Dumas (1802–70), author of *The Count of Monte Cristo*, *The Three Musketeers*, and other works.

[31] Gratien Candace (1873–1953), born in Guadeloupe, served in the French Chamber of Deputies from 1912 to 1942. Leslie R. James, "Candace, Gratien," in Knight and Gates, *Dictionary*, vol. II, pp. 30–31.

[32] Quintín Bandera (1834–1906), general in the Cuban independence forces, died in the Liberal uprising of 1906. Gregg French, "Bandera Betancourt, José Quintín," in Knight and Gates, *Dictionary*, vol. I, pp. 198–200.

[33] Despite Rondeau's assertion, Patrocínio never served in the Brazilian Parliament.

[34] Rondeau probably had in mind here Tomás Platero (1857–1925), Argentina's first Black notary public and a founding member of the Radical Party; poets Horacio Mendizábal (1847–71) and **Casildo Gervasio Thompson**; painter and essayist **Juan Blanco de Aguirre**; and others.

[35] José María Luna (?–1846).   [36] Marcelino Sosa (1808–44).

[37] Feliciano González (1820–1901). Mario Ángel Silva Castro, "González, Feliciano," in Knight and Gates, *Dictionary*, vol. III, pp. 178–79.

Isidoro Carrión,[38] and Captain Pedro Pérez.[39] In other spheres there are lawyers, architects, and journalists, who through their talent and enlightenment have succeeded in occupying a high intellectual plane.

Such examples make very clear what is further confirmed by science and by experience, that regardless of what race a man belongs to, and according to the environment in which he lives and develops, he will [either] evolve or remain stationary.

Of course, I don't claim to have revealed anything new on this topic, given that many writers better equipped than I, with a larger stock of scientific knowledge than mine, have already laid out what can only be news for men of my race who, for multiple reasons, are not aware of these facts. I have been guided solely by the sincere desire to lend my little grain of sand to the realization of the good work [that you have] undertaken.

Affectionate greetings,

F. RONDEAU

### 7.10 SALVADOR GARCÍA AGÜERO, "BLACK BROTHER," ADELANTE (HAVANA, CUBA: SEPT. 1935)

*In 1930, the Cuban poet **Nicolás Guillén** published an interview with the African American poet **Langston Hughes**, introducing Cuban readers to one of the leaders of the literary movement known as the **Harlem Renaissance**. The two discussed the brutality of European colonialism in Africa as well as the poems that Hughes based on jazz, blues, and African American spirituals. Hughes suggested that getting to know Black people from outside the United States had helped him to understand his own identity more fully. He explained that his travels to colonial Africa had inspired him to become a "Black poet." This, he told Guillén, was the meaning of the refrain "I am Negro: Black as the night is black" in the poem "Negro."*

*Hughes's travels to Cuba seem to have had a similar effect. According to Guillén, Hughes peppered his host with questions about the situation of Black Cubans and with requests to visit spaces of working-class Black social life. In one such venue, while observing a Cuban bongo player, Hughes reportedly exclaimed "black as the night" before sighing, "I would like to be Black. Really Black. Truly Black."[40] In the poem,*

---

[38] Isidoro Carrión does appear in military records and in the Afro-Uruguayan newspapers, but we have not been able to recover much information about his life.

[39] Pedro Pérez (1872–1931) retired from the armed forces in 1924 at the rank of major.

[40] Nicolás Guillén, "Conversación con Langston Hughes," *Diario de la Marina* (Havana, Cuba: Mar. 9, 1930).

*"Black Brother," **Salvador García Agüero** reflected these sentiments back at Hughes. Coming to know Hughes, a Black "brother" from elsewhere in the diaspora, who also happened to be a fellow communist, could help Black Cubans come to know themselves as well.*

> Black Brother
>   (to Langston Hughes)
>
> Brother, Black brother, I salute you.
> For you, I play and sing, my spirits back.
> Seeing you, my heart emerges naked
> No rhetoric or falsehoods, open, honest: Black.
>
> Though from afar and in a foreign tongue,
> Your message, when it reached me, left no doubts.
> Your *blues*, so eloquent – in rhythm and in essence –
> Is like a brother to my bongo's shouts.
>
> In me, do not your pain and yearnings quiver?
> My soul is also free just "like the rivers"[41]
> and, like a brother, full of pride to call your name.
>
> Black man, let us join hands with one another.
> "I want to be Black," so you say, my brother.
> "Black as the shadow," and I feel just the same.

## 7.11 NORA TABARES, "BLACK BROTHERS OF URUGUAY!", NUESTRA RAZA (MONTEVIDEO, URUGUAY: JAN. 1938)

*In November 1937 President **Getúlio Vargas** of Brazil suspended the Constitution of 1934 and imposed a fascist-inspired dictatorship, the **Estado Novo**, on the country (see 1.12). In this article Brazilian writer Nora Tabares reported to the anti-fascist Uruguayan newspaper* Nuestra Raza *on the wave of repression that had swept Brazil. This topic was especially important to Black Uruguayans, she argued, because nearly all Brazilians were Black, and because of specific measures targeting the "collectivity of color." "The Brazilian people are suffering all the tortures and persecutions of a Nazi regime," which, she feared, might spill over the border into Uruguay. Opposing the Vargas regime was thus both "a*

---

[41] The reference seems to be to Hughes's poem "The Negro Speaks of Rivers," which includes the refrain "My soul has grown deep like the rivers."

*moral obligation of racial solidarity for all Blacks" and a matter of national self-defense for Uruguay.*

It was our intention to write today on the role that the Blacks of our country [Brazil] took in their own liberation. But the complete lack of information on our comrades in prison, and of names and concrete facts that could support our article, prevents our making an actual report on the situation of those individuals arrested in Brazil. Furthermore, when one speaks of Brazilians, or of the Brazilian people, one is speaking, even if indirectly, about the Black race, since even those Brazilians who appear more White carry in their veins the generous blood of the martyrs of slavery.

So please understand, my Black Uruguayan friends: Brazilians are Black. Eighty percent, if they are not totally Black, are at least *mulatos* or *mestizos* or disguised Whites. The Brazilian people are suffering all the tortures and persecutions of a Nazi regime. There are thousands of Blacks who need help from their Uruguayan brothers. It is not important to know individual names, it is enough to know that there are thousands of comrades who have been arrested, persecuted, and tortured, and that only with a great movement across the entire continent will it be possible to prevent this regime of terror and barbarism from implanting itself in Brazil.

In Brazil, Congress is closed and the freedoms of the press, religion, and individual freedoms are all suppressed. The **Spiritist** temples that in Brazil are the religion of the poor were forced to close their doors. **Macumba**, reminiscent of the African rites, is prohibited.[42] Individuals are arrested for no cause, on any pretext. All the organizations that campaigned for the rights of the collectivity of color were dissolved. Agricultural colonies and concentration camps have been created. The children of those people arrested can be ripped away from their families and sent to Boy Scout camps.

This, in a few words, is what is occurring in Brazil, just a few steps from Uruguay. It is not necessary to say what the consolidation of such a regime, almost inside your own country, means for the entire continent, and especially for all of you [Uruguayans]. Where does Brazil end and Uruguay begin? It would be difficult to say. The frontiers are porous and mixed.

In the Brazilian navy, the officers are aristocratic reactionaries, while the enlisted men are almost entirely Blacks and *mestizos*. The percentage of sailors and marines in the prisons is noteworthy. Some of them I saw in

---

[42] On constitutional protections for African-based religions in Brazil, see 6.9.

1935 and 1936.[43] They were the preferred victims: the most frequently beaten, the most tortured; heroic and great. I saw them enter [the prisons] healthy, strong, young, happy. And I saw them – a horrible picture, worthy of Dante – come out invalids, some blind, others deaf, many with tuberculosis or on crutches.

For this reason, fighting against a regime that sows terror and torture, that kills and annihilates everything that is great and pure in civilization, is not just a duty of humanity, not just a moral obligation of racial solidarity for all Blacks. It is above all a question of self-defense. We must prevent the monster that is feeding on the martyred body of my poor Brazil from extending his claws toward the country of the generous Uruguayan people.

### 7.12 "MARGINAL NOTES ON A JUDGMENT," NUESTRA RAZA (MONTEVIDEO, URUGUAY: JAN. 1947)

*Ellen Irene Diggs was an African American anthropologist who received her PhD in 1943 from the University of Havana and devoted her career to researching and teaching the history and culture of the New World African diaspora. In 1946 and 1947 she traveled to Argentina, Brazil, and Uruguay, supported by a fellowship from the US Department of State. While spending several months in Montevideo, she gave an interview to the Argentine magazine,* Qué sucedió en 7 días, *to which this article was a response. The editors of* Nuestra Raza *expressed agreement with Diggs's judgment that "the Black race in Uruguay, in general, displays a visible cultural poverty" but were quite pained that she chose to make those comments to media outside the Black community. This reflected a problem common both to Uruguay and to the United States, they suggested, in which educated Black elites withdrew from working-class Black communities and criticized them from a distance, rather than joining in the work of helping them advance. The paper particularly deplored Diggs's public criticisms of a community that had welcomed her so enthusiastically and with open arms. Note the contrast between* Nuestra Raza*'s comments on Diggs and its coverage of another diasporic*

---

[43] In November 1935 units of the Brazilian army rose against the federal government of Getúlio Vargas. The rebellion was quickly defeated, and was followed by a wave of repression that continued through 1936 and swept up thousands of suspects, many of whom were imprisoned and tortured. Levine, *Father of the Poor?*, pp. 41–47.

*visitor,* **Nicolás Guillén,** *who arrived in Montevideo shortly after Diggs had left (7.13).*

Dr. **Ellen Irene Diggs,** living among us for the last few months on a research trip, and holding a fellowship, has made statements in a specialized intellectual milieu, one alien to our own, on the cultural capacity of our collectivity. She has said that "the Black race in Uruguay, in general, displays a visible cultural poverty."

Dr. Diggs says nothing new, nor is her judgment untrue. Her opinion coincides with that held by the *Nuestra Raza* group, with the fundamental difference that, obeying a spirit of brotherhood and struggle that does not derive from school or from methods other than those created by practice, and following a progressive and constructive line, we communicate our criticisms within the setting to which they apply, that is to say, among the Blacks themselves. For if we wish to correct such obvious failings, it is within that milieu, whose improvement we seek, where those criticisms must be heard, along with the guidance that, from our point of view, can rationally correct those deficiencies.

Self-taught, with fourteen years[44] of uninterrupted preaching in which we address all the problems facing the Black race, with no sectarianism or pretensions, our sermons, spoken and written, arrive directly to that sector of the Uruguayan people, of admitted "cultural poverty," while the university-educated withdraw and look on from afar. We, in contrast, assume responsibility for that struggle with a simple load of knowledge acquired through basic elementary-school education and the efforts of the "gauchos" who, for more than thirty years,[45] have roamed the countryside spreading ideas and searching for the road to solutions for problems as complex as that cultural poverty and its consequences, which have surprised and are criticized by those who, despite being able to, do not contribute [even] a grain of sand to the guidance that could eliminate that evil.

We agree in our evaluation of the same problem with Dr. Diggs, who, out of context, has expressed her opinion, which, though entirely legitimate, has some debatable aspects.

---

[44] A reference to *Nuestra Raza*'s years of publication up to that point, 1933–47. The newspaper ceased publication in 1948.
[45] A reference to *Nuestra Raza*'s origins in the rural town of San Carlos, in eastern Uruguay ("gauchos" were rural ranch hands). The paper published ten issues there in 1917 before closing and eventually re-opening in 1933 in Montevideo.

The Black North American intellectual arrived in our country in August, 1946, on a mission from her government. The guest of a milieu that is poor but welcoming, the Black community, perhaps enamored of novelty, a logical consequence of that depressing cultural condition, surrounded her from her first day [in Uruguay]. And having listened to and diagnosed the environment, she has gathered the impressions that she divulged in the intellectual circles of Buenos Aires.

Where we do not agree with the Afro-Indo-American sociologist is that that opinion should be expressed to the same group that she is criticizing, of whose needs she is ignorant. We do not agree, because we maintain that that negative aspect displayed by our collectivity is explained by two determining factors: first, the racial discrimination denied by the Blacks themselves, which obviously survives [and exercises] permanent action and influence; disloyal opposition to our rights as citizens, legally recognized but ripped to pieces in the application, the consequence of the corrupt pseudo-democracy in which we live. And second, the traditional isolation of the educated members of our race, who, save for the brave and responsible position of Dr. Juan Crisóstomo Díaz and the notary Hipólito Martínez (at the end of the last century), and of **Dr. Francisco Rondeau** and the never forgotten **Salvador Betervide**,[46] an outstanding figure at the university, who only in death abandoned his race – the graduates of the university and the teaching institutes – a considerable number – when they did not change their pigmentation, nevertheless deliberately cut themselves off and took up residence in an artificial milieu, created for their own convenience, leaving to the good will of others the future of their race.

Furthermore, Dr. Diggs, in complete ignorance, told the Argentine magazine *Qué*, [in the issue of] December 26, 1946, that "in Montevideo there is only one Black professional who practices medicine."

Does she know the trial and punishment of racial prejudice applied to that graduate on the occasion of his final examination? Does she know that that artist and professional, who could contribute so much to the cultural advancement of the [Black] collectivity, is [one of those] withdrawn in isolation?[47]

---

[46] Juan Crisóstomo Díaz (?–1884), **Francisco Rondeau**, and **Salvador Betervide** were graduates of the Law School at the Universidad de la República; Hipólito Martínez (?–1894) was a student at the school who died before completing his degree.

[47] The lone Black physician was **José María Rodríguez Arraga**. On the racism that he encountered in his medical studies, see "Nuevo médico," *Nuestra Raza* (May 25, 1935), 2.

Given all this, we are inclined to think that the North American emissary, who once affirmed to us that she had never felt the effects of racial discrimination in her country, lives there in the [same] artificial environment [as] some of the university-educated Blacks and *mulatos* of Uruguay.

### 7.13 "CIAPEN PAID WARM HOMAGE TO THE POET NICOLÁS GUILLÉN AND TO NUESTRA RAZA ON ITS 15TH ANNIVERSARY," NUESTRA RAZA (MONTEVIDEO, URUGUAY: JUNE 1947)

*In 1947 the renowned Cuban poet **Nicolás Guillén** (see 8.8) took up residence in Montevideo for several months, using the city as a base for his travels through southern South America. Guillén was a great celebrity in the region, and he was warmly welcomed with artistic and literary events wherever he went. This article reports on one such event, organized by* Nuestra Raza *and the Círculo de Intelectuales, Artistas, Periodistas, y Escritores Negros (CIAPEN), an organization of Afro-Uruguayan artists and intellectuals established the previous year. In addition to welcoming Guillén, the evening also celebrated* Nuestra Raza*'s fifteen years of continuous publication, an unprecedented achievement in the history of Uruguay's Black press. It included introductory presentations by journalists and community figures, performances by local musicians, and a public address by Guillén, who discussed conditions of Black life in Cuba and in Uruguay. The evening was representative both of the artistic and literary events regularly reported in the Black press and of the diasporic conversations and connections that developed in Montevideo and other Latin American cities.*

CIAPEN has recently justified, with real actions, the reason for its existence. And it has done so without fuss, with no inappropriate pomposity – to which it had no reason to resort – revealing only the intrinsic artistic and intellectual values that it carries in the marrow of its bones. Apart from its larger resonance, the ceremony carried out on the night of June 5, at [CIAPEN's] headquarters on Joaquín de Salterain Street, in homage to the formidable poet **Nicolás Guillén** and to our publication, celebrating fifteen years of journalistic life, evidences the spirit of equity and justice that animates this group of young Black people who fight, work and strive to make headway in the face of indifference, of repudiation, when not of the perverse intentions, of some who, calling themselves Black, work to impede any project that seeks to raise the low cultural and social level on which the Black man himself lives.

\*

Before a large and select audience that overflowed the room, Mr. César Techera[48] began the event by introducing the honorees and saying, among other things:

"Today CIAPEN pays homage to Nicolás Guillén and to the magazine *Nuestra Raza*, together in the same tribute. Anyone who has followed the career of *Nuestra Raza* knows that it has always been alongside Guillén and that, if within Uruguay's Black race Guillén is well known or popular, it is [through] the work of this champion of the community.

"When CIAPEN thought about this tribute to Nuestra Raza, it did so in the belief that those who work selflessly and generously for the good of others deserve an expression of gratitude and a lasting memory in the intimacy of that shrine called the heart. And this truth had to be said, from gratitude and for encouragement, so that it would serve at least as a moral reward and as instruction."

Alberto Noé Méndez, newly elected president of CIAPEN, then took the podium to give a witty speech outlining the goals and purposes of the institution over which he will preside jointly with Pedrito Ferreira,[49] offering warm words of praise to the Cuban poet and to *Nuestra Raza*.

After some guitar interpretations by Pedrito Ferreira, who was accompanied by the young Santiago Luz,[50] and recitations by the poet José Roberto Suárez, Sra. de Zeballos,[51] etc., the program proceeded to the main event, which was the previously announced talk by Nicolás Guillén. With precision of expression and command of the subject, he spoke for an hour on the Cuban Black race, ranging from its beginnings to its social and economic development, its participation in political life, its contribution to the wars of independence, and its co-existence with the White race. At the end of his erudite lecture, Guillén touched on very interesting aspects of what he has been able to observe during his stay in Uruguay,

---

[48] From 1938 to 1945 César Techera edited the Black newspaper *Rumbos* in the coastal city of Rocha. He closed the newspaper in 1945 and moved to Montevideo, where he became a contributor to *Nuestra Raza* and *Revista Uruguay*. From 1948 to 1950 he published occasional issues of *Rumbos* in Montevideo.

[49] Pedro Ferreira was the stage name of Pedro Rafael Tabares (1910–80), a renowned musician, composer, and bandleader who helped shape the Afro-Uruguayan musical genre of **candombe**. Eduardo Palermo, "Tabares, Pedro Rafael 'Pedro Ferreira'," in Knight and Gates, *Dictionary*, vol. VI, pp. 151–52.

[50] Santiago Luz (1914–83) was a well-known clarinetist, specializing in jazz and swing. Mario Ángel Silva Castro, "Luz, Santiago," in Knight and Gates, *Dictionary*, vol. IV, pp. 148–49.

[51] José Roberto Suárez (1902–64) and Cledia Núñez de Zevallos (1906–?) contributed occasional poems to *Nuestra Raza* and *Revista Uruguay*.

with regard to the [Black] collectivity. With clarity and psychological insight, he raised problems that affect Uruguayan Blacks, accurately presenting the road that we must take if we truly want to stand as a collective entity in partnership with the other societies of the American continent.

\*

We cannot finish this brief report without expressing our gratitude to the painter Ramón Pereyra,[52] who was kind enough to present us that night with a portrait of the famous Cuban violinist **Claudio José Domingo Brindis de Salas**,[53] and also to Dr. Modesto de Abreu, for the donation of his book, *The Black Race and its Contribution to Brazilian Culture*,[54] to the library of *Nuestra Raza*.

### 7.14 ABDIAS DO NASCIMENTO, "US," QUILOMBO (RIO DE JANEIRO, BRAZIL: DEC. 9, 1948)

*In this introduction to the first issue of* Quilombo, **Abdias do Nascimento** *laid out the magazine's mission in explicitly internationalist terms. Referring to the creation and initial meetings of the United Nations, and to recent elections in the United States and South Africa, in both of which race had played a central role, Nascimento positioned Brazil as a multiracial society poised to play a leadership role in the global politics of anti-racism. (For similar points by other writers in* Quilombo, *see 1.14 and 2.16.) Before it could do so, however, Brazil would have to put its own house in order by fully incorporating Black people into the country's recently restored democracy. Only by doing so could Brazil hope to conquer both the "foreign Ku Klux Klans" and its own "home-grown Ku Klux Klans of mentalities and attitudes." To support his assertions about Brazilian society, Nascimento chose to include parenthetical citations to leading scholars and politicians.*

We set out – vigorously and with pride – to engage in dialogue all those who believe, sincerely or maliciously, that we aim to create a problem in this country. Discrimination by color and race in Brazil is a matter of fact

[52] Ramón Pereyra (1919–54) was an Afro-Uruguayan painter.
[53] On Brindis de Salas, see 8.8.
[54] Modesto de Abreu, *La raza negra y su contribución a la cultura brasileña* (Montevideo: Alianza Cultural Uruguay-Brasil, 1947).

(Senator Hamilton Nogueira).[55] Yet *Quilombo*'s struggle is not specifically against those who deny our rights, but rather in favor, especially, of helping the Black himself to remember or acquaint himself with his rights to life and to culture.

A culture that is African in its intuition and accents – art, poetry, thought, fiction, music – as the ethnic expression of the darkest-skinned group of Brazilians, is slowly being relegated to neglect, ridiculed by the leaders of "Whitening." These "aristocrats" forget that ethnic, cultural, religious, and political pluralism infuse our national organisms with vitality, for they are the very blood of democracy (**Gilberto Freyre**). We could say that ignorance of the Black as a creative and receptive force dates back to **May 13, 1888** (**Arthur Ramos**).

Our case relates to the larger problem by which one economically powerful race or ethnic group asserts political predominance over another ethnic group or race lacking in means. Even though before the conquest of the Americas, Pope Pius II, Silvio Enéas Picolomini, imposed theological restrictions on the Portuguese traffic in Africans; despite the Civil War in the United States, which was motivated by the [question of] slave emancipation; and [even] in the wake of struggles for freedom [from slavery] in Cuba and Brazil, the problem remains much the same.[56] When it is no longer possible to speak of servitude and military submission, they want to tear from the Black the economic and political control over his land, as in South Africa; they violently strip him of his rights in the country that he helped to form and build, as in the United States; or they cunningly deprive him of the psychological and mental tools that would train him to acquire consciousness of his true condition despite a legal equality, as in Brazil.

The situation barely sketched [here] becomes even clearer when we observe Haiti demanding and obtaining, at the **San Francisco Conference**, the condemnation of all forms of racial discrimination. In the last US elections, Strom Thurmond appeared as the candidate of the old South, with a belligerently racist and abusive platform that received more than

---

[55] Hamilton Nogueira (1897–1981) was a White, center-right politician who served in the Senate and the Chamber of Deputies. His acknowledgment that racial discrimination did exist in Brazil would have been viewed by many readers of *Quilombo* as particularly conclusive, since he was not affiliated with Black movements.

[56] Pius II's papal declaration of 1462 condemned the enslavement of newly baptized Christians, a relatively small number of trafficked Africans; it did not condemn the slave trade as a whole.

a million votes, while [Harry S.] Truman's own victory was based on the campaign to bring civil rights to all of the North American people, including Blacks.[57] India, in the United Nations Assembly that took place in Paris, informed that body of the problem of discrimination in South Africa, where the reactionary descendants of Boer smugglers, who comprise only one and half million people against a native population of nine million, won the elections against the party of General [Jan] Smuts, favorable to Blacks.[58]

This is a clear historical truth: the Black man won his liberty not through the philanthropy or kindliness of Whites, but through his own struggle and through the unsustainability of the slaveholding system (Caio Prado Jr).[59] [This is true] here, or in any country where slavery once existed. The Black man rejects debasing pity and philanthropism and fights for his right to Rights.

The Black Brazilian has already conquered his theoretical and codified rights, but he still needs the active exercise of those rights. As Brazilians we protest against the existence not just of foreign Ku Klux Klans, but also of the home-grown Ku Klux Klans of mentalities and attitudes.

Our work, *Quilombo*'s effort, is to help the Black man breach the dam of present-day oppositions with his human and cultural worth, within a climate of democratic lawfulness that guarantees all Brazilians equality of opportunities and obligations. Assaults against that legal equality, which indeed frequently take place among us, are anti-democratic, separatist, and prejudicial to the [process of] national integration, of which the Black man is a principal protagonist. We refuse the "ghetto," the "color line" that, day by day, becomes more conspicuous in our social relations, attempting to make us exiles in our own land and in our spirits.

---

[57] Strom Thurmond (1902–2003) was a segregationist politician who served as governor of South Carolina and senator from that state. In 1948 he ran for president on the States Rights Democratic Party ticket, winning the electoral votes of four states.

[58] Nascimento was referring here to the 1948 elections in South Africa, in which the National Party, led by D. F. Malan, narrowly defeated the United Party, led by incumbent Prime Minister Jan Smuts. Once in power, the National Party created the system of racial segregation known as *apartheid* and ruled the country until the historic elections of 1994, won by the African National Congress.

[59] Caio Prado Jr. (1907–90) was an important Brazilian historian; his many books, particularly *Formação do Brasil contemporâneo* (1942) and *História econômica do Brasil* (1945), greatly influenced Brazilians' understandings of their country's past.

We have nothing to do with parties, neither the so-called democratic ones, nor [those] of the right, nor of the left, which always exploit Blacks in electoral terms (**Édison Carneiro**). Even less do we advocate a Black politics, but we do [advocate] a Black will to be Brazilians with the same responsibilities as all Brazilians.

## 7.15 "OUR NEIGHBORS TO THE NORTH," AMANECER (HAVANA, CUBA: JAN. 1953)

*Cold War politics began to reshape conversations about diaspora in the Cuban Black press in the 1950s. When this article appeared, less than a year had passed since a military coup had installed* **Fulgencio Batista** *as dictator in Cuba. Batista had quickly asserted himself as an ally of the United States and an enemy of communism, while using violence and patronage to exercise influence over Black clubs (1.16). The period saw a marked shift in the magazine* Amanecer *from demands for legislative action against discrimination in the workplace, a struggle that had been led by communists, toward a focus on Black entrepreneurship. In this context, this anonymous author recast the familiar comparison with the United States. Rather than suffering under the worst possible forms of racial violence, Black North Americans were thriving. They were becoming educated, gaining higher incomes, and choosing better housing.*

*This was a highly selective view of North American society, one year before the Supreme Court decision in* Brown v. Board of Education, *a moment when racial discrimination in education, employment, housing, voting rights, and criminal justice was both overt and rampant. This essay nevertheless serves as an example of a new current of Black diasporic politics that emerged in the context of anti-communism and Cold War diplomacy. The author argued that Black Cubans should imitate their neighbors to the North, who had triumphed because of their zeal for "economic liberation." He also revealed that the United States Embassy in Cuba was the source of some of his rose-colored information about the progress of African Americans.*

Undoubtedly, if we make an inventory of the progress that our Black neighbors to the North have attained, we will observe that, from the year 1900 to today, the population of color in the United States has achieved more social advancement than any other group in the land of Uncle Sam.

This affirmation is based not only on social statistics. It also represents the opinion of those leaders of the race who are directly involved in the struggle for equality, according to the information that we have in our possession. We see that in an article published in *Ebony Magazine,* one of the two most important illustrated magazines of the USA, whose writers and editors are of color, Dr. Joseph R. Houchins, a specialist in statistics about the Black race in the Federal Census Bureau, states that the census conducted in 1950 constitutes, in all its parts, real evidence of the triumph of the Black American.[60]

The aforementioned article expresses that the census results reflect a hopeful, rosy picture, in concrete numbers. These translate into the elevation of the status of the Black man in the social panorama.

It can be confirmed that Black Americans have not only increased astonishingly in number but also with respect to the distinct phases of life, including everything from employment and income to sanitary levels and educational opportunities.

Education is perhaps the most significant index of the general progress of the Black American. (And we Cubans should come to understand this well.) As long as he keeps himself ignorant and illiterate, the Black man will have the doors closed to holding the best jobs. Without the rise in the level of his income that would come from better jobs, he will encounter obstacles to finding better housing. [He will remain in an] unhealthy environment that engenders illness, crime, and discouragement.

When he acquires a better education, the Black man is in a position to defend his rights. He increases the prestige of his community and his self-respect, and he can, for this reason, demand his rights with integrity and honor.

The Black North American, according to information that we offer thanks to the valuable statistics published by the Embassy of the United States in Cuba, has risen to attain 90 percent literacy in that country. The aforementioned statistics, which are for the year 1950, record that nine of every ten Black people of school age attend a school, and 86 percent of those attend regularly. [Statistics for] the university level are greater still, if we note that there are currently 128,000 Black students attending

[60] Joseph R. Houchins was an economist and former member of Roosevelt's "Black Cabinet," who worked for the Commerce Department and the Bureau of the Census over several subsequent administrations. His summary of statistics from the 1950 census relating to the Black population, published in *Ebony*, highlighted deep inequities, and became the factual basis for much of the civil rights litigation of the 1950s. Green and Houchins, "Black Progress through Business Improvement."

universities. More than seventy universities in the United States employ professors of color and we notice a very curious fact. There exist in North America some seventy-eight universities for Black people, mostly situated in the South.

Some fifty years ago, the majority of White Americans accepted the inferiority of the Black man. They were of the opinion that the Black man was ignorant, lazy, irresponsible, and "too fun-loving" (the attitude in Cuba is currently more or less the same, even though [the Black man here] has also risen notably in the area of cultural progress). Today, however, the White Americans have begun to understand that it is necessary to view the Black citizen from another point of view.

To be sure, there exist in the USA, as in Cuba, the sorts of Black people we would call "common" (despite being a minority), on behalf of whom the leaders of the race undertake initiatives and demand better treatment and opportunity. Black American leaders raise issues concretely in order to move toward immediate solutions.

So that our readers may know, among others, the most distinguished Black leaders, we mention Walter White, of the NAACP (National Association for the Advancement of Colored People), Lester Granger, of the National Urban League of New York, [A.] Phillip Randolph, President of the International Brotherhood of Sleeping Car Porters, Doctor Mary McLeod Bethune, an eminent educator who, through her abnegation and force of will, sustains the College that bears her name in Daytona Beach. We who have seen for ourselves can say that it is marvelous and worthy of imitation by our compatriots, here.

[We also mention] Dr. Charles S. Johnson, sociologist and university dean; Channing H. Tobias, a great social worker; Dr. F. D. Patterson, educator; Doctor Mordecai S. Johnson, President of Howard University (another first-rate educational facility, located in the capital); Congressmen Adam Clayton [Powell] and William Dawson. All of these men have the devoted support of the members of both races and many of them have access to constant consultation from men of journalism of the highest caliber, legal experts, employers, educators, bankers, etc.

It is logical that we should observe that the Black American maintains his zeal for economic liberation as the cornerstone of his progressive aspirations. And we see that he has, in great measure, succeeded in this. Those of us who have visited the United States can see that the American Blacks manage banks, run important companies, occupy prominent government posts, etc.

In Cuba, we can attain all of this too. But it would be necessary to come together, to forget old quarrels, eliminate jealousies and think only that we are Black and that our ancestors, in large proportion, made an offering of their lives in pursuit of the freedoms of our homeland, and that the same privileges belong to us as to other [Cubans].

Let us imitate our neighbors to the North. Let us come to understand that in Cuba we enjoy a great advantage to achieve our aspirations.

# CHAPTER 8

# Arts and Literature

## INTRODUCTION

Latin America's Black newspapers and magazines were sites for both dissemination and extensive discussion of literature and the arts. Culture was no less important to Black editors and writers than politics or social commentary. The papers published numerous stories, poems, and serializations of novels, by both White and Black authors. They wrote profiles of important Black artists, writers, and musicians, and debated the quality of their work. Their efforts to alert readers to the existence and the achievements of Black cultural creators simultaneously created space for the development of Black cultural theory and arts criticism.

The chapter's first three articles, all taken from Argentina, are perfect examples of that mission. In 1878, *La Broma* published a review by musician and writer Manuel T. Posadas of **Casildo Gervasio Thompson**'s landmark poem, "Canto al África" (8.1). A dramatic portrayal of the crimes of the slave trade, the poem "give[s] off a sort of magnetic current that goes straight to the heart," Posadas concluded. Three years later, however, the paper lamented that public attention to works by Black writers was almost non-existent (8.2). While White authors were regularly feted by the Buenos Aires press, Black ones "remain obscure, and so by extension do their works ... which lie forgotten in the dark corner that harbors this community called *of color*." The following year *La Broma* briefly profiled the young musicians of the Espinosa family and expressed the hope that they would someday receive the attention and acclaim that they deserved (8.3).

Two pieces from the 1920s and 1930s show Black writers at work on their craft. Cuban author Enrique Andreu offered a richly textured account of his stroll with a friend through downtown Havana and their encounter with the Marine Corps Band playing "a *pot-pourri* of Cuban tunes" at an outdoor concert (8.4). As the band ran through the various genres of Afro-Cuban dance music, the well-dressed audience responded with visceral enthusiasm, leading Andreu to ask, with more than a hint of irony: how could people so open to Black music and dance ever be racist? Young Uruguayan writer **Iris María Cabral** contributed a lyrical account of a bus trip from Montevideo to her childhood home on the Atlantic coast to spend Easter with her family and friends (8.5).

Cuban authors **Gustavo Urrutia**, **Nicolás Guillén**, and Teodoro Ramos Blanco wrote probing reflections on the relationship of Blackness to artistic expression, and on what it meant to be a Black artist. Urrutia posed the question of why Afro-Cubans as cultural producers, and Blackness as a topic, were so under-represented in Cuban painting, sculpture, and art, and so over-represented in music (8.6). Focusing on the renowned Cuban violinist **Claudio José Domingo Brindis de Salas**, **Nicolás Guillén** asked whether, given his vast success in Europe and his embrace of European musical forms, we should consider him to be a Black artist (8.8). Observing that "every work of art is ... an answer the artist gives to a reality that injures his sensibility," Ramos Blanco argued that the centuries-long injuries of enslavement and racism endowed Black artists with the ability to express "the universal sentiment of all the oppressed of the world," making Black art genuinely transcendental (8.11).

The death of Uruguayan writer **Isabelino José Gares** in 1940 prompted *Nuestra Raza* to reflect on the recent passing of other Black authors, including Iris María Cabral, tragically deceased at the age of 21 (8.9). The Brazilian paper *Senzala* pondered "the bitter life of Lucila," a cook whose aspirations to be a poet were never realized (8.10).

### DISCUSSION QUESTIONS

- What, according to these articles, did it mean to be a Black artist in Latin America? Was it enough for the artist to identify, and be identified, as racially Black? Or did it imply practicing the arts in certain ways, and not in others? Did it mean addressing certain themes or topics in one's art, and not others? How did such considerations change when artists achieved recognition or fame? What do you think? What makes someone a Black artist? What is Black art?

- These articles return repeatedly to the relationship between European art and African or African-influenced art. How did the articles present that relationship? How did they see the influences of European forms on Black artists, and the influences of African and Black forms on White and European artists? Did they believe it was possible for Black artists to master European art forms? Did they believe it was possible for European or White artists to master Black or African-influenced art forms?

- As in Chapter 2, on Racism and Anti-Racism, emotion is a recurrent theme in this chapter – hardly surprising, in a selection of articles dedicated to artistic expression. What emotions do you notice in the articles and in the works or genres being discussed? And how did Black artists and critics connect to, or express, or embody, that range of emotions?

- In Latin America, as in other parts of the African diaspora, the arts (including music, dance, literature, the plastic arts, and others) stand out as a space in which people of African descent have excelled and earned the recognition of their societies. How might one explain that pattern? Was this equally true for all the arts – why, or why not? Drawing on these writings (see also 4.5, 4.6, 4.14), how do you think that different types of artistic recognition affected Afro-Latin American projects for civil, social, and political equality?

## 8.1 MANUEL T. POSADAS, "THE POETRY OF YOUNG THOMPSON," LA JUVENTUD (BUENOS AIRES, ARGENTINA: JUNE 10, 1878)[1]

*In this article, Afro-Argentine musician, journalist, editor, and soldier Manuel T. Posadas (1841–97)[2] gave readers of the Afro-Argentine press a preview of what would become one of the best-known works of literature by an Afro-Argentine writer:* **Casildo G. Thompson**'s *"Song of Africa" (Canto al África). The poem was, by the standards of Buenos Aires' Black press, an unusually explicit account of the crimes of the slave trade and of White people's collective responsibility for its horrors (on this point, see 2.1). It was also a rare invocation of Africa – an empathetic and*

---

[1] This article has been abridged for length, with omissions in the text marked by ellipses inside brackets.

[2] María de Lourdes Ghidoli, "Posadas, Manuel," in Knight and Gates, *Dictionary*, vol. V, pp. 202–3.

*nostalgic re-imagining of family life on the continent – in a press over-*
*whelmingly focused on Argentine realities.*

*Posadas' review offers a glimpse of an early stage in the poem's*
*development, as well as insight into the process by which Afro-*
*Argentine cultural creators critiqued and shaped each other's work.*
*Writers in the Black press often noted that cultivating success among*
*aspiring Black authors and artists depended not only on innate*
*talent and educational opportunities but also on access to well-*
*informed and frank criticism (see 8.2). After downplaying his quali-*
*fications to criticize a writer of Thompson's stature, Posadas*
*engaged in precisely that task: praising certain qualities of the*
*piece and pointing out the shortcomings of others – especially the*
*ending. Before publishing the "Song" in full in 1899, Thompson*
*edited and expanded it, and gave it a much more conciliatory*
*ending. The published version ends not (as in this version) with*
*the narrator damning Whites, but with the rise of the "sun of*
*Redemption," following which "slaves and tyrants, free and*
*oppressed" "link hands in the name of love," becoming "commin-*
*gled in an embrace" of equality and justice.[3]*

It may have been truly presumptuous of me to have made the commitment, to some friends I esteem and who esteem me in turn, to publicly air
my opinions regarding the literary importance of the poetic compositions
of the intelligent young D[on] **Casildo G. Thompson.** For, in truth, my
intellectual capacities lag many leagues behind his renowned talents.

This brief and simple clarification furnishes me with enough authority
to beg the poet's indulgence, especially since he is the only [potential]
victim of my error or ignorance.

Those who honor me by reading this modest and simple piece do so
also out of interest in my personal opinion, and it is, therefore, precisely on
those grounds that I claim their attention.

This is not, then, a critical assessment, nor do I in any way presume to
elevate it to that category. On the contrary, these are merely individual
opinions that belong to me by right, and for which I gladly assume full
responsibility.

[...]

I do not believe young Thompson to be a luminous constellation that
appears in our midst to show us the path of redemption, nor a towering

---

[3] Ford, *Beneméritos de mi estirpe*, pp. 113–17.

figure who may be permitted to occupy the first place among those who, through their talents and their compositions, have demonstrated their profound literary knowledge. But it is my heartfelt conviction that his is a fresh and robust intelligence, and that not a few run-of-the-mill versifiers would be honored to sign their names at the end of some of his brilliant compositions.

His "Song of Africa," which in my view is but the beginning of a magnificent poem, is, insofar as the plot is concerned, a composition full of novelty and interest.

What is worthy of notice is the scrupulous care the poet has taken with rhyme, and the prudent use he has made of the imagery that represents the composition's philosophical truth.

Is there anyone among us who has described, with more simplicity and elegance, the beautiful African land than the author of the "Song of Africa"?

Here is what he tells us:

> Beneath a radiant sky
> Of clearest blue and clouds of white
> A vision glimpsed through cherub's eyes;
> Sky of a million stars
> That shine forth in nights of bliss
> With lover's zeal
> And the world do adorn and kiss.
>
> Under a sun fiery and awesome
> That sets all aglow in beams of gold,
> With perfumed breeze and riches untold
> In the rubies and pearls of its blossoms,
> Lies a virgin land that was the womb
> By blessed fortune
> Of a race martyred in history:
> Destined by God, perhaps, to glory
> Which was, one fateful night,
> Hurled into infamy's abyss
> With criminal scorn, with icy hand
> By the cruel villainy of a fellow man!

I do not believe anyone could expect verses to rhyme any better than these, nor a description better accomplished.

But where Thompson shows himself to be a true poet, full of inspiration and life – for his ease of diction, greatness of concepts, elegance of style, and for the fact that, as even an ear untrained for poetry can perceive, the verse flows spontaneously, the poet has not strained unduly for rhymes nor become constrained by meter – is in the following verses, which I consider a veritable literary jewel for more reasons than one.

> Knowest thou the name
> Of that divine and blessed soil
> That jewel bequeathed by God
> That chaste virgin despoiled
>     Who humiliated stands?
> Africa is that lovely land.
> It is the Black man's cradle, the home
> Of the eternal exile, his fate bemoaned,
>     Of the eternal orphan
> Who from foreign shores, a song intoned
>     Dreaming of his hearth.
>     It is the Black man's cradle,
> That universal pariah! The ardent sun that smiled
> Upon his proud brow as a child
> Saw him mournfully depart,
>     With bloodied soles
> Shackles dragged, eyes heaven-turned,
> Witnessed his affront, saw the vile brand
> Seared on his neck by hangman's hand.

Although it is true that these verses will bring to mind, for those who suffered such cruel humiliation, the sad and painful memory of a torment as barbaric as it was unjust, it is also true that those of us who from that virile race descend feel, thanks to these [verses], strong enough to curse tyranny a thousand times over, and to sing the praises of liberty a thousand times more.

Undoubtedly, these [verses] give off a sort of magnetic current that goes straight to the heart.

Absorbed in a melancholic meditation, the poet is surprised by the memory of the iniquities committed against the unhappy dwellers of the African jungles, and the pain he feels in his heart pulls forth this beautiful declaration:

> Ever since that day
>     Of tears and dismay
> The sky was bereft of the rays
>     Of the Sun of justice.
> The hut cut from baobab tree,
>     A hundred generations' shelter,
> A home made of nature's bounty
> That neither tigers nor lions dared enter

From the African wilds,
To the hangman's axe fell.
     And as it pleased him well,
Out, amid screams, came boy and maiden,
She of coral lips and flaming eyes
Of flashing gaze, of plaintive cries.

The verses I reproduce below recommend themselves on their own; any further recommendation would therefore seem futile.

Thus did the Black man see him arrive
At the ancient step of his domain
(That eternal sanctuary of joy)
          As yet unprofaned,
And seeing him stand so menacingly
          One hand gripping iron,
          He bends his head in entreaty
Hoping to calm the sinister ire,
And a gentle plea he speaks
As tears of fire sear his cheeks
Such as cannot but pity inspire:
"Stop," the Black man says, "this is the house
Where dwells the memory of my spouse
That doth my life with love perfume,
          Light of my eyes
That kept me company in my gloom.
Stop! I beg you, for here were born
          Two pieces of my soul
Who did with blessed calm console
                    [me],
Two stars . . . . two pearls . . . my two children,
          The kindly lifeblood that imparts
Vigor to a tired life
And is ever dear to a father's heart."
          Yet the inhuman White man
Steps forth with scornful smile.
"Stop," the Black man says, "do not defile
The happiness of my life."
          And the relentless White
Spits upon the face of the Black so brave
And says, with unbearable disdain,
"Get away, vile Black, away, thou slave!"

                    V

Accursed be thou, a thousand times
Be cursed, o faithless White; may your memory
Forever be a foul stain on history[.]
May it dishonor the sons of your sons

> And on their brow may they display
> The legacy of infamy you bore
> Just as the Black will carry always
> The wounds in the soul that you tore.
> Accursed be thou, yes, and may the very earth
>     Cast you from its embrace
> When you sleep, and may venom replace
> The air you draw, forevermore.

The way in which the poet Thompson concludes his "Song of Africa" does not seem to me to be entirely suitable or fitting, because we see him [Thompson] mingled among the four characters who appear in the composition.

The dénouement would have been more apt had it culminated [either] in the suicide of the Black man, out of despair for failing to impede the White man from entering his hut, or in the death of the latter by the former.

However, this circumstance in no way affects its true literary merit.

Let us congratulate ourselves, then, that the poet has gifted us a poem in the belief that he was sending us a *song*.

The benefit redounds entirely to us.

Manuel T. Posadas

## 8.2 "THINGS THAT ARE BORN AND DIE UNKNOWN," LA BROMA (BUENOS AIRES, ARGENTINA: JULY 20, 1881)

*Writers in the Black press across Latin America worked diligently to record and celebrate the triumphs of Black writers and artists who achieved national and international reputations. This writer in* La Broma *took a different approach, reflecting instead on the social prejudice and marginalization that prevented most Afro-Latin American artists from ever achieving such fame. Poverty and lack of access to formal education were real barriers. But when, against all odds, "stray lights" flickered in the "shadows of misfortune" or "wildflowers" managed to flourish among the "weeds," the work of these budding Afro-Argentine artists was rarely recognized outside of a small circle of Black writers and readers. While the "arrogance," "vanity," and "ostentation" of Whites were the primary obstacles to the success of Black artists, the author suggested that experienced Black cultural creators could be part of the solution. Offering "stern critique, learned advice, and beneficial correction" to younger generations could help strengthen their work and ensure that it reached broader audiences.*

Why do so many brilliant sparks remain hidden behind the dense and arrogant cloud that, in this life, divides human societies?

Why do genius, intelligence, and talent not always shine forth at their own level, to their fullest expanse, to their natural heights?

Ah! It is because mankind has distorted that divine and immutable law that makes all beings on Earth equal, creating distinctions of race [and] establishing social hierarchies that humiliate and debase men before the vanity and ostentation that shroud this world.

A brother does not hear the cries of pain of another brother who struggles desperately from the depths of the sad situation in which the misfortunes of fate have placed him!

Such misery, such injustice! In this way, societies live in eternal antagonism, divided, some subjugated by others that have acquired greater predominance.

Thus are extinguished, without ever being known, the stray lights that, like fireflies shining in the night, emerge from the shadows of misfortune.

These minor digressions slip from my humble pen when I contemplate the sad situation to which our men appear to be condemned in the haphazard twists and turns of life.

From time to time, a name comes to resound in our social circles: obscure names, devoid of pedigree and with no more titles to recommend them than the intelligence or the genius that shines, radiant, upon brows drenched by the sweat of toil.

They are born into humble laps, rocked by the cradle of poverty, and, endowed by nature, appear like the wildflowers that spring up among weeds offering their sweet perfume, shedding the light of their privileged minds among the ill-fated sphere in which they were born.

Yet it is a great pity. In fact, these minds are sterilized and drowned without bearing any kind of beneficial fruit, for lack of the sap of learning and of the stimulus that invigorates them and gives them life, [allowing them to] spread their roots and create new shoots.

Across the many careers to which a man might dedicate himself, we find men who have belonged to the bosom of our community, and who have distinguished themselves by more than one quality, yet today it is as if they had never existed.

In the military career, [whose members] have earned such splendor by achieving glory for the Fatherland, we will surely find many [men of our community] who figure among the best of the best, for their talent, bravery, and daring in difficult ventures.

But who still remembers [Lorenzo] **Barcala**, [Domingo] **Sosa**, [Felipe] Mansilla,[4] and many others who spilled their generous blood and died as heroes on the battlefields?

National history is ungrateful, forgetting to record in its glorious pages the names of those who sacrificed themselves for the Fatherland.

So too in literature, beautiful productions remain in obscurity because the fruits of the labor and study of our young men who embark upon that path circulate only among us, without ever reaching the hands of those who occupy a higher sphere.

There are many young poets – García Mérou, Navarro Viola, Adolfo Mitre, and Rivarola doubtlessly head the list.[5] But it is not just because they were born with the gift of lovely inspirations, but also because from their earliest attempts, they have been nurtured with encouragement, stimulus, and incentive, [which] motivate them to continue to display the most delicate and sublime fruit of their vigorous imaginations.

And day by day they receive more encouragement, and their reputation extends further each time, inspiring respect and great confidence in their futures.

But something very distant from this occurs with our poets – which we do, in fact, have. No one knows them, they remain obscure, and by extension so do their works, many of which rise almost to the level of those of the above-cited [poets].

Other than us, who knows of the "Song of Africa,"[6] the "Cradle of Infancy," or "The Dreamer," by **Casildo G. Thompson?**

It is true that they were published, but in an Almanac that, it could also be said, was written expressly for us, and has thus not moved beyond our social circle.[7]

---

[4] Felipe Mansilla (1814–79), born in Buenos Aires, fought in Argentina's civil wars and in wars of expansion against Indigenous peoples in Patagonia, and attained the rank of sergeant major.

[5] Martín García Mérou, Miguel Navarro Viola, Adolfo Mitre, and Pantaleón Rivarola were renowned poets, writers, and thinkers from the late eighteenth and the nineteenth centuries. All were White, well-connected figures, influential in national politics.

[6] See 8.1.

[7] Garzón, ed., *Almanaque del progreso*. The almanac was produced by writers from the Afro-**Porteño** press, particularly *La Broma*, which sponsored the publication. Ghidoli, *Estereotipos en negro*, pp. 239–42.

Who, besides us, reads the frequent productions with which Mateo Elejalde[8] continually adorns the columns of our humble newspapers, which also never move outside of our social faction?

What encouragement, what incentive can a young man receive, when he launches his first works precisely among a *public* that, in addition to being small, generally lacks the aptitudes necessary to enhance those [works] that are moderately adequate, or to advise, correct, or approve those considered good?

I do not wish only applause for the young men who try out any branch [of the arts], because I am convinced that while it is true that applause and flattery can stimulate and embolden, it is no less [true] that they make young men vain and can often lead them to ruin.

As proof, then, of the appreciation and esteem I feel for them, I do not wish them applause for works that do not deserve it. What I do [wish for them] is stern critique, learned advice, and beneficial correction that will serve as an incentive, will encourage them and place them on the path first cut by the trailblazers. [This will] make known to everyone their unknown names and their works, which lie forgotten in the dark corner that harbors this community called *of color.*

We have painters, like **[Juan] Blanco de Aguirre** and Bernardino Posadas.[9]

Of the first, it can be said that he is already known by all our public; he teaches drawing at the Colegio Nacional, and he is the only one who has made any progress in terms of making a name for himself. His works, although they have never stood out for their artistic perfection, have been regularly appreciated, sometimes with biased judgment, and other times, with impartiality.

The second is an *adolescent* still learning his craft, but his first works begin to surprise pleasantly.

---

[8] Mateo Elejalde (1862–?) was an Afro-Porteño poet and writer who frequently published his compositions in the Afro-Porteño press. María de Lourdes Ghidoli, "Elejalde, Santiago and Mateo," in Knight and Gates, *Dictionary*, vol. II, pp. 444–45.

[9] Bernardino Posadas (1861–?), who trained with Blanco de Aguirre, was only 19 years old at the time of this piece, and already an artist of promise. He went on to contribute many illustrations to mainstream magazines, and to co-found his own publication, *El Eco Artístico*. María de Lourdes Ghidoli, "Posadas, Bernardino," in Knight and Gates, *Dictionary*, vol. V, pp. 199–200.

He has much promise, and if the government took inspiration from true justice, it would send him to Europe to continue his studies, as it has done with Mendilahurso and Ballerini.[10]

In terms of music, there are many young men who dedicate themselves to it, with some of them being notable persons who are recognized by competent authorities.[11]

I desist from expounding further on this topic, saving myself for another occasion, of which I hope to take advantage soon in order to focus exclusively on this branch of art.

Many are there, then, who live and die in the shadows, unknown to a world that turns engulfed in the earth's vanity and ostentation, but not [unknown] to the righteous God who sees the weaknesses and frailties of humanity.

So much injustice in this miserable world!

## 8.3 "THE USUAL ODDS AND ENDS," LA BROMA (BUENOS AIRES, ARGENTINA: NOV. 10, 1882)

*In Argentina, as in other parts of Latin America, it was not uncommon for several generations of Afrodescendant families to become accomplished and renowned musicians. Music was a cornerstone of community life (4.5, 4.6, 4.14, 6.1, 8.4) and one of the few paths through which Afro-Latin Americans could make a living while earning the acclaim of their co-nationals (8.6, 8.7, 8.8). The Argentine Black press often sang the praises of Afro-Argentine musicians, like* Casildo G. Thompson *or* Zenón Rolón, *who achieved local and international fame. This tidbit from one of* La Broma's *social sections featured the musicians of the Espinosa family, who remained largely unknown beyond the Afro-*Porteño *community and press, despite being among "the most excellent musicians born and living in this capital." Brothers Lorenzo and Juan Espinosa were church organists and piano composers. The third brother, Pedro, played and taught violin and brass instruments, and ran a dance hall. The Espinosa brothers*

---

[10] Graciano Mendilaharzu [sic] (1856–94) and Augusto Ballerini (1857–1902) were White Argentine painters who benefited from scholarships to live and study in Europe.

[11] Most notably, the pianist and composer Zenón Rolón (3.5, 3.6), and Gabino Ezeiza (1858–1916), famous for singing and playing guitar in the *payada* counterpoint style of Argentina's rural interior. María de Lourdes Ghidoli, "Ezeiza, Gabino Jacinto," in Knight and Gates, *Dictionary*, vol. II, pp. 484–87.

*often played together at community festivities. One of the Espinosa sisters, Rita, was a piano instructor. The note also hinted at the ways that families passed musical training down across generations. The author witnessed a private performance of Pedro's young children and expressed the hope that they might someday share their musical talents more broadly. It seems he got his wish; La Broma later reported that the children held a concert at a local venue.*

Everyone has heard of, or what is more, personally knows [members of] the distinguished Espinosa family [who are] among the most excellent musicians born and living in this capital.

Pedro, Andrés, Lorenzo, and Juan are well known, as is [the fact] that even their adult sisters practice the musical arts. But what is to me a surprise, a pleasant surprise, is to hear little ones perform the way that Pedro's three children do (his eldest daughter is barely eleven years old), when they play no less than the trumpet, bass, and violin with such bearing and pleasure. We congratulate Don Pedro Espinosa, offering our wishes that his children should prosper in his family's favorite art, and that he might someday grant our society the opportunity to come to know the talents of his three jewels.

## 8.4 ENRIQUE ANDREU, "THE THURSDAY CONCERT," LABOR NUEVA (HAVANA, CUBA: JULY 30, 1916)

*In this literary essay, writer Enrique Andreu[12] adopted the persona of the* flâneur, *a detached wanderer observing the modern city and its inhabitants. On an adventure to Havana's seaside promenade, two Black men effortlessly occupied public space on a streetcar and among a heterogeneous crowd on an elegant boulevard of the city. Their conversation was peppered with French phrases, classical allusions, and references to contemporary psychological and sociological theories. Andreu's frank discussion of their attraction to women and of appetites "of every physical kind" was unusual for writers in the Black press, who usually avoided any mention of sexuality.*

*Arriving at a public concert, the two found themselves in the middle of a crowd dancing to a performance of "scandalous" rhythms, including* Rumba del Solar *and* Toques de Santo, *which the narrator first describes*

---

[12] Enrique Andreu y Larrinaga (1892–?), writer, scholar, and activist. See biographical note in Andreu, *Cosas que Usted debe conocer*, pp. 119–21.

as "*hysterical convulsions*" and "*brutal atavistic lust.*" He and his companion were astonished, reflecting that if White Cubans are so enamored of African music, there must not be any racism in Cuba.

On first reading, this might seem a straightforward adoption of the language that White contemporaries deployed to justify public outrage, mob violence, and police repression against Afro-Cuban cultural expressions, while also denying the existence of racism in Cuba. But the narrator's innocent perplexity can also read as sarcasm, an interpretation supported by Andreu's other writings denouncing the "ethnosociological apostolate," and by the giant eye that his narrator imagined "winking ironically about the events of the night." The narrator finally retreated to his room, where he shifted from aimless wanderer to sleepless writer, wrestling with the notes that would become this stylized account of the evening and his reflections on the puzzling complications of Cuban society. How could something both be barbarous and criminal and also part of an "authentically Cuban musical mosaic, in its rhapsodic, democratic heterogeneity"? What did it mean to live in a society that belittled Black people as uncivilized while enthusiastically consuming Black culture? These questions informed Andreu's writings, two decades later, when he was an editor of the journal of the **Sociedad de Estudios Afrocubanos**.

My spirits [were] in a rare state, combining nervous impatience and mental exhaustion. Mechanically, I boarded the first streetcar I found. I felt a desire to be carried along by a rapid and unusual force. Were I the owner of an automobile, I believe I would launch myself down the highway at two hundred miles per hour; devouring the road, and devouring whatever I might find in my way. But as this is impossible, where should I go? Well ... I will pay five cents for the electric engine of a humble, unspecified streetcar and go to whatever destination it leads me.[13] I pondered this as I occupied a seat. Presently the conductor arrived, and as he collected the fares, he pretended not to notice me as he walked past. He was already moving along when I called to him, "Listen, sir," I said, "you did not charge me. If a secret inspector is traveling among us, he will notice your forgetfulness and they will throw you out of the Company." The good man responded, "I did not charge you because your ticket is already paid for." Pointing to another seat [he explained],

---

[13] This interplay between human emotion and the speed of motorized conveyance may be an allusion to Filippo Tommaso Marinetti's *The Futurist Manifesto*, published in 1909.

"That gentleman purchased it." I turned my face and I could see my dear friend Julián González who sat calmly with a smile, satisfied with the incident.[14] I moved to sit next to him. I had not seen him because my incursion into the car had been too hasty.

After greeting one another, I told him about my state of mind and we began to chat. We spoke of useful arts and of fine arts, of science, of politics, and of that eternal subject which could not be left out, the feminine. When we reached this point, he said to me, "Come with me tonight. Today is Thursday. Accompany me to the Malecón, today is *día de moda*.[15] You will see a fair that is impossible to detail in a description. There, all of the senses are entranced. After two hours among the delights of the setting and the scenes lit up as bright as day, and after taking a turn through the finery on display, which is no more than elegance and luxury taken to their farthest extreme by the throng that assails the avenue, after all of this one suffers a perverse and sibylline[16] torture, so refined as to be very delicately agreeable.

"The ear perceives the pleasing lyrical tones of the Marine Corps Band, which bequeaths a concert from the bandstand. The asphalt, the inebriating fragrances of suggestive perfumes that allow us to divine the secrets of Venus who, represented in all of her forms, passes us by. The gaze flits like a butterfly from female to female as if wanting to drink up the nectar of the contours that each and every one has half-covered with those light and almost transparent arrangements prescribed by the summer's *dernier cri*.[17] And taste and touch, these, these my friend, are the tyrants that torment our desires, because they cannot join the priesthood of the task that Nature has imposed upon them. In such a hyperesthesia of the senses, we arrive at a vertigo stemming from the vortex of pleasant titillating sensations; appreciated much more because discrete circumspection prohibits any violent gesture; and the contrast works like the torment of Tantalus, which in this case is an agreeable torment.[18] Come, my friend, let us go to the concert on the Malecón. It will be a shame if you do not accompany me; you will see . . ."

---

[14] Julián González was a co-founder and frequent contributor to *Labor Nueva*.

[15] The Malecón is a seaside promenade in central Havana. The *día de moda* is a day of the week when tickets to theaters and cinemas are discounted for the general public. Here it seems to refer to a free public concert.

[16] Mysterious or cryptic. A reference to sibyls, as female oracles were called in ancient Greece.

[17] A French phrase meaning the latest fashion.

[18] Hyperesthesia is a clinical term, meaning excessive sensitivity of the senses. In Greek mythology, Tantalus was tortured by thirst. Though able to see a refreshing pool, he could not drink from it because every time he approached, the level of the water would recede.

And my good friend Julián did everything he could to convince me. At last, he succeeded in his attempt. He convinced me. I accepted because I had to leave behind my unpleasant gloom in some place or other. We were already at the Parque de Martí. We got off of the streetcar. We started to walk along the Paseo de Martí. All along this *boulevard* such a large public was taking the air that it was nearly impossible to take a step. Down the two rows of poplars, we pass through two rows of small palaces belonging to tycoons, and we reach the end of the street, where, on colonial foundations, as if in a silent protest of sarcastic spite, the ancient and decrepit prison rises up on the same grounds as the Ministry of Public Education. We walk a little more, and we are at the spot. González did not deceive me. Impossible to reproduce such a splendorous and sizzling scene. Good tone, good taste raised up to its quintessence. The private vehicles and even cars for hire are fabulous, crowding the loop around the park. One can see, seated and strolling, everyone from the stuck-up ladies of ancient lineage to the highly paid women of the underworld; from the cretin to the intellectual, from the brilliant representative of the high circles to the obscure [individual] unfit for any circle. All well-mannered, almost adopting the gestures of polite society.

The pedestrians around the bandstand search this way and that for nearby harmonies. The tired and lazy sit down in iron chairs provided by the city. And every one of them, both male and female, the lovers, those whose gaze seduces and those who gaze back, seduced, whisper sweet nothings, offer false compliments, and wait for or promise favorable opportunities for passionate intermingling. The eyes of each and every one shine in the night like burning coals while, to the left, in the garden of the Miramar Cabaret, their stomachs are invited to consume a dinner or some trifle. And that is reasonable: the wear and tear on the nervous system are significant. We are at the seashore, our neighbors are the port, the bay, the gulf. So it is logical that the tides and the movements of the undertow, impregnating the atmosphere with marine iodine, awaken and accentuate the appetites for a general gluttony of every physical kind ... These were my volitions when I was surprised by the sound of a kettle drum.

Now, only moments after our arrival the concert was ending. Without a doubt, we arrived on the late side. They play the last score: It is a *pot-pourri* of Cuban tunes. Every living creature pays the greatest attention possible and listens with the greatest absorption. No one walks or speaks. They only listen to the cadences of the authentically Creole musical mosaic, in its rhapsodic, democratic heterogeneity.[19] The notes of a Habanera ring out, bringing to mind the grace of the Cuban woman of the high ballrooms who, like all women, is a turtledove when she whispers sweet nothings and a panther when she feels desire. One hears the Punto Guajiro and the classic Zapateo, which express so much because they bring to the city a small bit of the countryside and the history of the riches, the poverty, the exodus, the heroisms, and the simple life of our peasants. The Canción and the Bolero (sentimental, storybook melodies), come next and stir our poetic souls. But what comes now is a whirlwind. Resonances flow that are more national than provincial. The voluptuous rhythms of the **Danzón** fill the atmosphere. It is no more than a moment. They degenerate right away into a Rumba. The sharp polyphony of the Rumba is a scalpel that removes the muscles from the bones of the listening multitude. Now it is the roar of the African Toque de Santos, in the fetishist cult populated by hysterical convulsions. Now it is the red, black, white, and yellow vision of the **Ñáñigo** rituals, whose music produces the feeling of infinite shivers in the marrow.

Its power of suggestion is horrible. One can make out eurythmic voices, almost human. It is the arrival of the Clave. The chorus sings, then, like a firework, a Toque de Cajón shoots up and a scandalous Rumba de Solar arises. Here all of the shades of the *pot-pourri* mix together. The cadences begin slowly. As each measure advances, the movement accelerates. Singing, dancing, music, all at once, this is the Rumba del Solar; nothing exists that awakens a more brutal atavistic lust, nor a more sensual unleashing of the ancestral, sentimental contents of the sensorium. Afterwards, the Band shifted to the meter of a Contradanza that ended in a Danza Loca; and the *pot-pourri* of Cuban airs came to an end.

The public then rewarded the musicians with unanimous acclamation. Frenetic applause thundered through the space for more than ten minutes. That well-groomed crowd, momentarily transformed into a clamorous, adoring throng, asked for a reprise of the *pot-pourri*. And it was gratified with an encore of the culminating moments. The tumultuous applause returned. Then the [homeward] procession began. A few (we among them) remained there in the place where the warm African sun had caused such a great effect.

Julián González and I began to philosophize; one after the other, taking turns. And each of us, more or less, said the following: Surely, it is impossible for a crowd that is so epileptically carried away by African

---

[19] This paragraph and the next list a number of popular Cuban musical and dance forms; for definitions and descriptions of them, see Orovio, *Cuban Music*.

things to have racial prejudices. From what was seen and heard, one deduces that it must be inaccurate that there are ethnic prejudices or preconceptions of other kinds. Did you see? They were almost holding their breath. Their hearts, almost paralyzed. The shoulders and backs of one person or another, were shaking, quivering. One or two waists flew out of alignment. Some more and some less, they jumped the rails, they gasped for breath, and they lost their level or equilibrium. It is as if most palates like a bit of spice, and for this reason they prefer "Guinea" pepper, which is the best ... in summary, if Nelson Page, the great sociologist, were to witness this, surely he would add a chapter to the *Psychology of Crowds*, which is by the French author Le Bon.[20] And he would also find it strange that our National Anthem is *La Bayamesa*, which very few pay attention to while it is played, and not a good Danzón or a stunning Rumba ... And speaking thus, we decided to depart.

Going out to the right, we passed alongside the Castillo de la Punta, the headquarters of the Marine Corps Band. We rested our elbows on the wall a while, to watch the reflections on the sea, the effects of the moon on the large half-circle of the bay, replete with vessels. On the opposite shore, across from us, there are two old and decayed fortresses: la Cabaña y el Morro; and in the second of these there is a semaphore. And to mark the entry to the bay, a monumental lamp, whose flashing light seems to me to be the giant eye of a roguish cyclops, winking ironically about the events of the night. González and I remained silent for a long while, without articulating a word, but mentally conversing, remembering that the Greeks were very wise when they gave Pallas Athena, the goddess of wisdom, the owl as her divine emblem, a repulsive little bird that feeds itself by hunting and eating mice ... And finally, taking my leave, I broke the silence.

My friend Julián González, who is something of a poet, something of a dreamer, did not follow my brusque decision. He remained in the midnight hours, enjoying, with his soul, the moon as it was savored by the earth and sea. I, prosaic, simple, with my pen like the knife of a common assassin, spend the early hours doing battle with these restless notes; leaving their murdered corpses on the white sheets of

[20] Thomas Nelson Page, a White writer who argued, in *The Negro: The Southerner's Problem* (1906), that since it was not possible to remove Black Americans from the South, White people should work for their "elevation" and moral "improvement" through education. The title of Gustave Le Bon's 1895 book is typically translated into English as *The Crowd: A Study of the Popular Mind*. He argued that individuals lost their capacity for rational action when in the presence of crowds.

paper that perhaps someday will become the vulgar pages of a pretentious glossary that speaks of this problematic life that God has granted us.

## 8.5 IRIS MARÍA CABRAL, "IMPRESSIONS OF A TRIP," NUESTRA RAZA (MONTEVIDEO, URUGUAY: MAY 1934)

*Many of the writers in the Afro-Uruguayan press were migrants to Montevideo from smaller provincial towns and cities. This was the case with* **Iris María Cabral**, *one of the few female members of the* Nuestra Raza *staff. Here Cabral wrote about a trip to spend Easter with her family in the Atlantic coastal city of Rocha. The article provided descriptions of the countryside from Montevideo to the coast, as seen through the eyes of an imaginative 19-year-old. After daydreaming through the landscape and arriving in Rocha, Cabral observed the cemetery, near the train station, and wondered: would she some day be laid to rest there? Sadly, the answer was yes. Two years later, Cabral died unexpectedly in Montevideo, and her body was brought back to Rocha for burial.*[21]

It is morning, an autumn morning, a little cool, the sky orange-colored, almost red, above the fields still darkened by the shadows of the night. The highway, like a silver ribbon extended to its full length, is being devoured by one of those modern monsters. The bus goes fast, but I don't feel it. I go in comfort, asking who put so many marvels on the earth, for the amusement of these poor mortals. Here and there one glimpses pretty little cottages, with their houses and gardens. One also sees some vineyards.

We pass Pando, a growing little town. It is 8:00 am on Good Friday, and the church is open. The faithful leave and enter. This natural detail, which will be repeated in every town we pass, makes me think of the church of my own town; I would like to fly to get there. We arrive at Empalme Olmos and ask, what time does the train leave? At 8:50, they reply. Is it going with a motor coach or a locomotive? No sir, a locomotive. The employee has no idea how his reply saddened me, since it will take longer for me to arrive.

[21] See "La fatalidad ronda nuestra casa: Ha muerto Iris Cabral," and other articles in *Nuestra Raza* (June 26, 1936). The articles did not state the cause of death.

. . . . . . . . . . . . . . . . . . .

The rush of passengers running late, vendors, goodbyes, a bell, a green kerchief, a long whistle . . . and here I am, on my way again. One more parcel that this giant rocket will launch to the station at Rocha!

While I wait, I take pleasure in contemplating the landscape: La Sierra, a sugar beet plantation. All of its fields are plowed, and the beets spread about in little piles, little white piles like snowflakes! I pass stations, country houses, farms, and I marvel at how settled and well tilled our national territory is. In the distance I make out La Floresta, a well-known beach on our coast, known especially for its large island of eucalyptus trees. The strong sun, softened by the cool breeze, invites me to dream, and I seem to find myself at the edge of the sea, in one of those Arab countries, with blue sky and golden sand. But I'm not dreaming; we too have marvels. Atlántida, an important seaside resort with great resources to attract tourists, its beauty further heightened by that labor that the hand of man has imprinted [on the town], is suggestive and enchanting. Mainly that clean and solitary sand, which gives the impression of being at the edge of a desert oasis, expecting to see a camel carrying a traveler who wears a white burnoose.

. . . . . . . . . . . . . . . . . . .

How many stations have we passed? I'm not counting, but now I am in Sauce, in [the department of] Rocha. Everything I see is a piece of my native land; I seem to feel the same particular gift I felt when I used to run through the countryside. I see trees, hills, and I avidly look at the prettiest forms and colors, which surprise me more and more. Behind one of the ridges appears the city of Rocha, resting on the hills of the same name and [under] a white cloud that rises up gracefully, a plume reigning over the fields. Seen from afar it looks like a big village, with light-colored houses and dark roofs that highlight the church tower, which shows that one is entering a Christian and cultured town. To the right, the stockyards of the public market, which every day provide meat to the population. To the left the cemetery, very white with cypress trees, tall and elegant as fairies' fingers, imposing silence on the town's most sacred place. And I think, will I be able to rest under that earth? Will those cypresses watch over my ashes? Who knows where this pilgrim's life will take me?

The fairgrounds, where livestock and industrial fairs are held, include several pastures, one in particular where they show the tourists and the city folk how one ropes a steer or tames a colt. A few more meters and

I am rejoicing in the train station. Many people I know, greetings, handshakes; no one awaits me in the station. I want to pretend that I never left my town, and I get in a car that takes me speeding to my house, to live for a few days what I will later relive as a sweet memory in Montevideo.

## 8.6–8.7 GUSTAVO E. URRUTIA, "CUBA, THE ARTS, AND THE BLACK," INSTALLMENTS I–II

*The journalist **Gustavo Urrutia**, a university-trained architect, began writing and editing a weekly feature on Black themes in the conservative newspaper* Diario de la Marina *in 1928. Though not affiliated with any political party, he was widely recognized as a spokesman for Black Cubans and received several government appointments in the mid 1930s. He also contributed articles to the monthly magazine* Adelante.

*In his series on Black arts and artists, Urrutia reflected on the changing cultural landscape in Cuba. He sought to articulate what Black arts might look like given, on the one hand, persistent racism in cultural institutions and among White Cuban audiences, and on the other, a growing fascination for primitive and folkloric themes among European modernists. Could Black artists, denied the right to embody "universal" or "civilized" aesthetics, become primitivists, a European creation? Could they articulate a literary style of their own, akin to the work of North American writers in the **Harlem Renaissance**? What was the significance of the "preconceptions favorable to the Black" in the field of music? What is the relationship between Black art and African art?*

### 8.6 Gustavo E. Urrutia, "Cuba, the Arts, and the Black, I," *Adelante* (Havana, Cuba: Oct. 1935)

Mr. Bonifacio López, in his literary letter that we published here last Wednesday, notes the absence of any influence of the Black Cuban in our literature. Although our music acknowledges its markedly African origins, and the influence of the Black man on our present-day painting and sculpture has been revealed, he writes, "Other than the extremely original *Motivos de son*, by our [**Nicolás**] **Guillén**, and one or two other poems published in *El Mundo* and [*Diario de*] *la Marina*,[22] I do not know

---

[22] A reference to Urrutia's regular feature and to a similar Sunday feature in *El Mundo*, edited by **Lino D'ou**.

of any other literary works that have sought inspiration in genuinely Black themes." B[onifacio] L[ópez] finds Blacks as characters, as members of society, in all the Cuban literature of everyday life,[23] but he does not find Blacks represented "as ones who possess their own particular culture." He asks, "Why, in Cuba, has there not been a more direct imitation of Black literature?"

This matter lends itself to a magnificent study, which will appear one day, somewhere. For now, I am only concerned to show what I have been thinking through since I received Mr. López's letter, to explain how this influence has worked among us. I will climb the hill on the gentlest slope: Sculpture and Painting first, then Music, and then Literature last, since this is the order in which our milieu presents, stepwise, its resistance to the penetration of African art. In each of these sectors, the influence of Black art follows a well-defined pattern: unnoticed influence in the plastic and pictorial; welcome influence in the musical; and rejected influence in the literary.

- - - - - - - - - - - - - -

It seems an intuitive truth that the majority of our artists do not know that the avant-garde is the godchild of African sculpture. It is certain that the most familiar art history texts say nothing of this, and that only a few eccentric specialists, possessors of the secret, have begun to divulge it to the world, to the great disgust of certain masters who would rather continue passing as elemental geniuses. The ignorance of the clientele is more forgivable. In any case, artists and public in our small circle would have accepted the influence of African art obsequiously, since it came by way of Paris, which is "definitive." But their lack of understanding of avant-garde content has spared them this deference.

This influence on Cuban painting and sculpture has been foreign to our will, our comprehension, and our discernment. Even Black artists, reduced to mediocrity in academies here and in Europe, like the others, did not see any beauty other than in the shepherds of Segovia, the landscapes of the Seine, or in the Italian piazzas. And if they now paint and sculpt like the avant-garde, or about some Black theme, it must be credited to fashion. If ever the ancestor cried out in their spirit, they carefully quieted him so as not to clash. There is no need to ridicule them for this. The time when people of color felt provoked if they were called Black is still very recent.

---

[23] Literature of everyday life (*costumbre*), popular in many Spanish-speaking contexts in the nineteenth century, took as its primary theme the careful depiction of local customs or manners.

In Cuba we have a certain usable representation of African sculpture, but who would be the artist, White or Black, with sufficient courage and artistry to proclaim the richness in plasticity and rhythm contained in a Changó, in the Jimaguas, and in other idols of the African religions that surround us?[24] They have the same sentiment and rhythm as the African sculptures exhibited by Paul Guillaume in Paris.[25] However, our unpublished Guillaume, though he knows as much as the other one, would have to be impervious to the taunt that he is a witch, which would be hurled at him because of the religious disrepute carried by these figures. And this would be too much to ask.

This rhythm and this sentiment, translated into vanguardism, returned to Cuba with an unforeseen halo of sympathy for the topic of Blacks. This has inspired our artists to try out the Afro-Cuban motif, although without comprehension, without the deep and elemental understanding of a true discovery, like one who applies formulas without understanding the principles. As a result, all their works are anecdotic. I cannot recall a single case in which our people have dealt with the Black man except with academic discernment, although, to be sure, mingled with pseudo-vanguardist lengthening and distortion. It is to be expected, despite everything, that when the essences of Black arts are noted and incorporated, the results will be most brilliant, given that the relationship to Africa is primordial among us.

We know that Sculpture, Painting, and Literature are three fine arts that are considered representational and complex, in contrast to Music and Architecture, which are pure arts. The first three send multiple messages that reach the individual spirit on the intellectual, the sentimental, and the emotional levels. So, for example, literary prose and poetry are pleasing in part because of their ideological meaning, in part because of their sonority and in part because of the emotion that accompanies them.

The same is not true of Architecture or Music, pure arts that speak only to sentiment.

For this reason we have just seen that the evolving influence of Black art on our sculpture and our painting encountered an inert and unconscious opposition in the social prejudices that disqualified African sculpture

---

[24] Changó and the Jimaguas are deities in the Afro-Cuban spiritual practice known as **Regla de Ocha**.

[25] Paul Guillaume (1891–1933) was a French art dealer who organized the First Exposition of Black and Oceanic Art in Paris in 1919 and published *Sculptures Nègres* in 1917, both of which had a major influence on European modernism.

because of its identification with witchcraft, and that this art has only been able to make its way, slowly and surreptitiously, disguised as vanguardism and protected by the masterful prestige of the French, like a new dogma.

Latent within this inferiority complex lies the embryo of the intellectual, ideological element that is a factor in the representational fine arts. In another essay we will show that this factor is active, predominant, and carries a wholly political meaning in the strident opposition to Black arts that can be observed in our literature.

By contrast, in Music, a purely emotional artform in which intellectual reactions have no place, Black influence is necessary and welcome, for interesting reasons that I will try to lay out in my next article.

Courtesy of *Diario de la Marina*, "Armonías" Section

### 8.7 Gustavo E. Urrutia, "Cuba, the Arts, and the Black, II," *Adelante* (Havana, Cuba: Nov. 1935)

Why does Black art have so much influence in our music, despite its absence in our literature and scarcely any hint in our painting and sculpture? The primary-school answer, which the student on his bench offers feebly, hoping to be promoted to the head of the class, is this: "Because the Black man has a marvelous musical talent, which predominates among all his aptitudes, which saturates him, and which expands through the air he breathes."

All this is true, but it is also an old adage that does not explain the phenomenon fully. This commonplace reduces the judgment even of many persons with a willingness to consider the matter. It creates in music a preconception favorable to the Black man, just as exaggerated as the thousand prejudices against him in other areas of his ability. The Black is supposed always to have a privileged musical organization, no matter that our **Juan Gualberto [Gómez]** has declared honestly from the public tribune, that his friend, the tremendous **[Claudio José Domingo] Brindis de Salas**, could not bear to listen to his [Gómez's] disastrously semi-tonal singing.

In my opinion, it is not the true musicality of the Black man that determines his influence over our Music, but rather Music's status as pure and exclusively emotional art. This allows it to thrill to the marrow the Black man who produces it, without leaving, in his soul, any kind of ideological complex that might force him to elude it, to ignore it, or to forget it, as happens in Cuba with Painting and Sculpture, in part, and with Literature, entirely.

If the great African influence in our music were to be measured only by the musical aptitude of the Black man, logically one would have to attribute the nullity of such influence in literature to his lack of capacity in that realm. And well we all know that the Black race has a very rich literary tradition, romantic, religious, and martial in nature, able to compete with other ancient civilizations. It is necessary, therefore, to insist that it is not only or primarily the subjective ability of the Black interpreter that has imposed and spread the influence we are analyzing, but rather also – and to a great degree – the essential objective condition of MUSIC in the abstract, and at the same time, the melodic and rhythmic fullness of Black music.

There is also a very important historical cause. Ancient African culture was eminently social and religious, while ours is principally economic and scientific. Social organization into castes was prevalent, as was a religious structure headed by a priestly class who were assisted in worship by other auxiliary classes, among whom were included the sculptors of religious images. Sculpture was a profession tied to a social class. So was literature, represented by the troubadours – "griots" – the poets, reciters, narrators, etc., who, similar to our academies of language, safeguarded the purity of their oral literature to cleanse it, order it, and give it splendor. Sculpture and literature were not, for this reason, popular arts. The average man did not participate in them except as a spectator or listener.

In contrast, music was in the public domain. African rituals were governed by choral music and dance, in which all of the worshippers participated, and for this reason, while only professionals could sculpt or compose poems, everyone was allowed and knew how to sing and dance.

When the African was installed in America, with the confusion of the slave ship, which did not transport, in parallel, his social and religious organization, professionals [in the fields of] sculpture and literature must have been made scarce. And for the precarious plastic and literary traditions transported by the average Black man to have flourished, as they did in the United States, the impetus of social, economic, and political agents would have been needed. These, though favorable in the United States, were adverse, in Cuba, to this development, as we will see in the next article on the "rejected influence" of Black arts in our literature.

When the Black man absorbed the White civilization of America, his mind, which only contained traces of the aristocratic arts of African sculpture and literature, was almost like a blank record on which the artistic ideas of the dominant race were imprinted. For the influence of these branches of Black arts to be felt, it would have been necessary that the slaves overcome two powerful obstacles: their lack of mastery in the corresponding vernacular artforms, on the one hand, and, on the other, their lack of understanding of the meaning of those White arts. And they practiced these for a White public; the Black public was not conversant with them.

With music just the opposite occurred. The Black masses arrived endowed with a long musical experience, because music, in their homeland, was a popular art deeply rooted in the intimacy of their souls. They did not have to submit themselves to the influence of any foreign instruction. The Black man had composers, performers, and audience among his own people: a market of his own. So Black music became stronger in America, and into its rhythms and its melody it incorporated, and reshaped, the spirit of the New World. It became a prevailing and dominant art whose allure thrills and compels the White man just the same as the Black man; whether in the "**náñigo**" rhythm or in the "witch" rhythm, despite social injunctions against these religious and fraternal institutions, which are distorted and maligned among us.

Because of its origin, Black music is essentially choral and multitudinous. The power of the ancestor is so strong in it that, even acclimatized through the natural modifications of the environment, it is still "sung" and with no other genuine instrumental accompaniment than the ineffable harmony of the drums. Its gregarious character is made more conspicuous by the fact that our authors – who have utilized this music so lovingly in their modern symphonic poems[26] – have not yet achieved the universal and fully realized triumph that awaits once they decide to compose these with percussion and large choirs as dominant elements.

We see, then, that for aesthetic and historical reasons the Black man could express himself with more freedom in music than in the other artforms of his ancient civilization. This explains the "welcome influence" of his music on ours. In another article I will explain why Black art has

---

[26] Here the author is referring to several Cuban composers in the Grupo Minorista, especially Amadeo Roldán (himself a man of mixed European and African origin) and Alejandro García Caturla, who began to produce major symphonic works based on Afro-Cuban themes, often combined with literary texts by **Nicolás Guillén** and Alejo Carpentier (1904–80), a preeminent White novelist, essayist, and cultural figure.

wielded no influence over our literature, despite having achieved such prestige in North American literature.[27]

Courtesy of Diario de la Marina

## 8.8 NICOLÁS GUILLÉN, "BRINDIS DE SALAS, A ROMANTIC," ADELANTE (HAVANA, CUBA: FEB. 1936)

*Of the dozens of Black intellectuals and literary figures who contributed to the magazine* Adelante *in the 1930s, none was more widely celebrated than poet* **Nicolás Guillén** *(7.13). Guillén came from a preeminent Afro-Cuban family. His father, a journalist and politician affiliated with the Liberal Party, had edited the newspaper* La Libertad *and served in the Cuban Senate before being killed in political violence in 1917. By 1936, when the essay translated below appeared, Guillén had already held high-ranking government posts and had been an editor of left-wing publications. He had also published several highly acclaimed books of poems that incorporated Afro-Cuban rhythms and discussed Black themes.*

*In this article, Guillén offered a biographical sketch of one of the most famous Cuban artists of the nineteenth century, the violinist* **Claudio José Domingo Brindis de Salas**. *In Guillén's account, Brindis was a dashing and peripatetic Romantic who triumphed in Europe. As other authors in* Adelante *sometimes did, Guillén poked fun at Parisians' fascination with artistic figures whom they regarded as coming from "a mysterious country – the distant Island, lost in the waters of the Tropics." But Guillén then posed a surprising question: "Was Brindis Black?" The answer provides fascinating insight into how Guillén understood Blackness, as both a status ascribed by others and a form of solidarity that can be expressed "sentimentally." Guillén took Brindis as an entry point for exploring a theme with which he was personally familiar, the challenge of being a famous Black artist. He glossed over the exoticization of Blackness in Europe in order to highlight the particular cruelty of Cuban attitudes toward Black artistic achievement.*

Few lives offer such piercing interest as that of the great Black violinist, **Claudio [José Domingo] Brindis de Salas,** who was born in Havana on August 4, 1852, and died in Buenos Aires on June 2, 1911.

---

[27] Urrutia published two more articles in this series, which appeared in *Adelante* in December 1935 and January 1936.

In contrast to that other great figure of universal artistic significance, the Matanzas-born violinist **José Silvestre White** – erudite, sensible, professorial, technical – Brindis represents an unrestrained and overflowing temperament; an overwhelming "force" that hurtles itself toward life and has the quality of a natural phenomenon.

This does not mean, not remotely, that Brindis was an improvisation. Rather, he fed his spirit with enduring musical knowledge, acquired in the highest centers of Europe, among them the Paris Conservatory, where he was the disciple of professors such as Danclás and Leonard. But it is beyond doubt that he differed greatly from the type of genius that **Buffon** wished to see as nothing more than patience.[28] Wrapped up in the whirlwind of his present, he never worried about the future, nor benefited from the lessons of the past. He lived his moment, he drained his cup to the dregs and hurled it away when it was empty, though the next day his tongue might torture him with thirst.

There was someone he resembled. His father, famous in his time, also a violinist, can be included – acknowledging the limits of the colonial context and those that resulted from his race in a pro-slavery milieu – among the group of those fiery Romantic figures, whose brilliance ran neck and neck with chaos. He made and spent his money lavishly. He mingled, as an artist, with the leading families of Havana. He married two times, once with extraordinary luxury. He always dressed with princely elegance and, after coming to know the whip, imprisonment, and exile,[29] he died and was buried in poverty, without, for this reason, ever abandoning the ridiculous idea that he was a different kind of Black man from his racial brothers, almost nobility, with his back turned toward his past and his eyes blind to the future.

How much did José Domingo share the same spiritual roots? He shared them. Like his father, he distinguished himself as a child in the art that would make him famous. They say that he composed a piece and dedicated it to a Havana lady at the age of eight. And like his father, he was always enthusiastic about ornamentation and luxury. Beyond that, he had much more talent than his father, or perhaps he found himself in a better circumstance to improve his natural gifts than [his father], who was forced to limit himself to a rudimentary artistic milieu.

---

[28] The quote typically attributed to Georges-Louis Leclerc, Comte de Buffon, is "Genius is nothing else than a great aptitude for patience."

[29] Claudio Brindis de Salas (1800–72) was tortured, imprisoned, and exiled during the brutal **Year of the Lash**, a wave of repression inspired by a suspected racial uprising in 1844.

What is certain is that Brindis had not yet turned ten years old when he debuted with clamorous success in the Artistic and Literary Lyceum, and that at the age of seventeen he sailed for Paris, for Europe, where his sensibility and culture would take definitive shape. It was in that year (1869) that the paths of the father and son diverged, to such a degree that they would never meet again. But there is no doubt that the former made sure that his heir, whom he liked to refer to as the "musical hope of Cuba," would reach a superior artistic destiny; and that, escaping the cultural prison of his fatherland – a factory without personality, without profile – [he] would achieve the perfect contour of an exceptional figure.

Brindis accomplished this. His arrival in the French capital produced curiosity at first, soon followed by expectation and, later, admiration. Profound, clamorous admiration. And when, having graduated from the Conservatory, he presented himself to the great public, he became one of the most interesting celebrities in Paris. They pointed at him and applauded him on the boulevards. "Brindis! That is Brindis!" Love devised its storylines, constructed from easy adventures, from satisfied curiosities, and from deep passions. He attained glory. Black, tall, beautiful as an Apollo carved from ebony, with brilliant eyes and speech like his eyes. Master of his art and son of a mysterious country – the distant Island, lost in the waters of the Tropics – Brindis was an irresistible attraction for a city that always favored geniuses, and much more so if they, as was the case with the Cuban, were endowed with characteristics that were unusual in that setting.

Unlike White, who settled permanently in Paris and who even became a professor at the Conservatory and a substitute for the director, José Domingo embarked on a tour of Europe, with no other weapon than his violin, from which he wrested incredible tones. He leaps to Italy and debuts in Milan. "He feels," a critic wrote the day after hearing him at La Scala, "and he feels with a passion that sends sparks from his pupils, which have an electrifying expression." They baptize him anew. Now they will call him "The Black Paganini" or the "King of the Octaves." From Italy, he travels to Central Europe. He tours much of Germany. He plays in Berlin, before the Emperor [Kaiser Wilhelm II], who decorates him, as the government of France had already done.[30] He visits Saint Petersburg

---

[30] Wilhelm II reigned from 1888 to 1918. In Germany Brindis was named Baron of Salas and awarded the Cross of the Black Eagle; in France he was named a knight of the Legion of Honor.

[Russia], he flies to London and, after another visit to France, he leaves for America with the title of Director of the Conservatory of Haiti.

But there is little hope that this tireless spirit will rest! He resigns his post and, abandoning Port-au-Prince, travels through all of Central America and Venezuela, before returning, finally, to Cuba, at the end of 1877, eight years after abandoning her and five years after the death of his father. He debuted in Havana at the Payret Theater, and then he traveled throughout the island. A year later, he had made it all the way to the easternmost province, appearing in Santiago de Cuba. Rest? Never. Return to Havana. Travel to Mexico. Return to Europe ... And so on, to the point of vertigo: this artistic Sinbad[31] never adapted to any climate, nor did any one view capture his fancy, nor did he set down roots in any soil. Married in Germany to a woman of high society; in the musical instruments business, after his triumphant trip to Buenos Aires, from which he returned a rich man, he abandoned his business and his wife to once again head out on the dusty road. Romantic, bohemian, quarrel-some, free-spending, he was a figure escaped from that restless canvas that was the first half of the nineteenth century, like Byron and Espronceda.[32] And his death was just as romantic as his life, in a dark garret in Buenos Aires, where he arrived poor, defeated, and with his lungs rotted out by tuberculosis, on the doorstep of his sixtieth year.

Was Brindis Black? If to answer this question we contemplate the portraits that remain of the great artist, or if we ask what he seemed to those who knew him and interacted with him, the answer cannot be anything but affirmative. Very Black. A formidable Black. *Negrísimo.*

But if we do not content ourselves with this superficial investigation and we try to go a bit deeper into the spirit of the "King of the Octaves," the result must be very different. Brindis ... was White. A paradox? No. Reality. In this, as with his art, there was someone he took after. He resembled his father. Educated in Europe, where the Black man does not exist, and even less so from an economic perspective, where the color of an artist's skin was a reason for admiration rather than contempt, José Domingo could never feel the pains, the sufferings, and the longings of the Blacks: only when he returned to Cuba – six times in forty-two years – did Brindis have the sensation of his color and of his race. Though famous,

[31] Sinbad the Sailor, the subject of seven tales in *A Thousand and One Nights*, set out on his many adventures because of a spirit of restlessness and a desire for travel.

[32] George Gordon "Lord" Byron (1788–1824), English Romantic poet; José Ignacio Javier Oriol Encarnación de Espronceda y Delgado (1808–42), Spanish Romantic poet.

he found himself insulted by a bumpkin, by a servant in a Havana café. The same ones who listened to him, the ones who delighted in his marvelous technique, never got used to seeing him as a pure and singular artist, but rather also as "the Black man" who by setting foot in the land where he was born fell prisoner to the sticky web of prejudice and misery that comprise our impoverished social organization. This is why he always took care to highlight his status as a German subject, his title as baron and his knighthood, all of that ornamentation that he liked to surround himself with, and that in Cuba was useful as a kind of insulation against rudeness, injustice, and brutality.

But if Brindis was not sentimentally Black; if he did not have, to some degree, the occasion to be Black in the wholeness of this concept, we should still consider him as such, because he is a glorious exponent of the high degree of culture and refinement that a race can attain when it matures in an environment that is favorable to its expansion and development.

### 8.9 "ANOTHER OF OUR ESTEEMED WRITERS HAS DISAPPEARED," NUESTRA RAZA (MONTEVIDEO, URUGUAY: JUNE 1940)

*This article marked the passing of **Isabelino José Gares**, a journalist, playwright, and long-time contributor to the Afro-Uruguayan press. Gares died relatively young, in his early 40s, and the article links his passing to that of other contributors to* Nuestra Raza *who had died in recent years, most of them young adults. Clearly it was as difficult to sustain the lives of individual Black writers as it was to sustain the papers for which they wrote.*

In this capital city on June 20, the ***conrazáneo*** writer **José I. Gares** [*sic*] passed away. He had been suffering for some time from a persistent illness, which in the last few days caused a crisis, despite the efforts of science.

Like most of the Black and ***mulato*** neo-intellectuals of our country, José Gares was an autodidact who, from an early age and absorbed by the racial problem, sought with firmness and persistence to contribute to a solution of said complex. He collaborated with tact and skill in the periodical press or writing plays about social problems, in which, with true high-mindedness and in a constructive sense, he presented those problems and his vision of the future.

Following a natural law, and even more that of mortality, which has sunk its claws cruelly in our ranks, *Nuestra Raza* has watched the most esteemed group of our collaborators disappear. First was that youthful spirit, all light and femininity, **Iris [María] Cabral,** who unexpectedly left us on a May morning;[33] then the death of **Salvador Betervide** snuffed out the purest talent of our times; later, almost recently, disappeared Marcelino Bottaro,[34] a tenacious and sincere journalist; and today, with José I. Gares, another of those vigorous fighters who, as a group, made a cult of the race and offered it everything they were able to give: talent, self-sacrifice, and vigilance.

At the tomb of the author of "The Road to Redemption,"[35] the sorrowful voice of *Nuestra Raza* should have been heard, but reasons beyond his control prevented our editor from arriving on time. He had been designated to say farewell to that eclectic spirit who, together with the three companions who preceded him on the journey with no return, contributed with his enthusiasm and his thoughtfulness to the work of dissemination and the cultural advancement of the people.

Facing the disappearance of this great lover of the holy cause of the advancement of Black people, we respectfully doff our hats and leave at his tomb the unfading gift of memory, which will live always in this house to which he was such an important contributor.

## 8.10 ELOÁ, "THE BITTER LIFE OF LUCILA," SENZALA (SÃO PAULO, BRAZIL: JAN. 1946)

*In this article the pseudonymous author Eloá presented the cautionary tale of Lucila (it is unclear whether Lucila was a real person or a fictional character), a working-class woman who was enraptured by the study of poetry and sought to be a poet in her own right. According to Eloá, Lucila lacked the "cultural capital" to pursue such a calling, and her artistic pretensions ultimately alienated and repelled her friends and suitors. Although the Black press frequently celebrated self-taught Black male writers from extremely modest backgrounds, Eloá suggested that Black women should not give themselves such airs and should instead pursue the practical vocational training that would enable them to earn a living and*

---

[33] See Cabral's essay, 8.5.
[34] Marcelino Horacio Bottaro (1883–1940), journalist, activist, and editor of *La Propaganda*.
[35] The title of one of Gares' plays, performed at a 1935 benefit for *Nuestra Raza*.

*support themselves financially. Only with that vocational preparation should they allow themselves the luxury of pursuing the fine arts.*

*This story of Lucila recalls (unintentionally) the famous writer Carolina Maria de Jesus, who during the 1950s, while living in the São Paulo favela of Canindé, was reading the work of major Brazilian authors and filling her own notebooks with poems, short stories, and journal entries.[36] Had Carolina followed Eloá's advice, she would never have attained international fame and renown.*

A delicate little Black woman, displaying good taste in her style of dress and in the topics of her public talks, she appeared to have a level of erudition that she was far from possessing. An avowed admirer of Castro Alves, Bilac, and Casimiro de Abreu, she never missed an opportunity to recite, at intimate little parties, the most popular poems of those three poets.[37]

So it was that the Black woman Lucila, so delicate, so distinguished, with a cultural capital of only six months of study in Dona Jacira's little school, was invariably selected as the official club orator for the solemn festivities of New Year's, Holy Saturday, and May 13. But if these honors truly flattered her self-esteem, they had the disadvantage of provoking resentments. She appeared pretentious and pedantic. The young women and men avoided her, pejoratively calling her "teacher" [*professora*].

Little by little, her intuitive intelligence made her see, "behind the mask of the faces," the hostility in the hearts of the people who rejected her.[38] She isolated herself and gave herself over, almost fanatically, to reading her favorite authors. And principally influenced by the virile poet who had as a lyre "a bronzed trumpet," she began to produce.[39] She wrote notebooks and notebooks of inspired verses, emptying into them all her bitterness, all her resentment.

And so the years passed. And the little Black woman Lucila entered her thirties, and her forties, finally turning fifty years of age.

She died alone, disillusioned, working until the end in her sad job as a cook, and leaving in the care of a nephew, who had been somewhat enlightened by the example of his heroic aunt, her complete poetic works.

---

[36] José Carlos Sebe Bom Meihy, "Jesus, Carolina Maria de," in Knight and Gates, *Dictionary*, vol. III, pp. 405–9.

[37] Antônio Frederico de Castro Alves (1847–71), Olavo Bilac (1865–1918), and Casimiro de Abreu (1839–60) were important Brazilian poets.

[38] "Através da máscara da face" is a line from "Mal secreto," a poem by Raimundo Correa (1859–1911), who was a colleague and associate of Olavo Bilac (see previous note).

[39] Castro Alves used this phrase in his poem, "Deusa incruenta."

In the meantime, it was the madness of the muses that embittered, all the way to the end, Lucila's life. That madness pushed away her friends, puzzled her relatives, frightened away her suitors, and provoked the derision of the ignorant mistresses [employers] who never forgave the fifty-year-old cook who sought to be a poet: "Professora Lucila."

\* \* \*

Even today, dear female reader, I insist on seeing, in Lucila's embittered life, the drama of my countrywomen who dream of an education.

But, you will ask me, how to avoid these intimate conflicts? And my answer will be:

Young Black women must begin, for now, with the practical professions like sewing and tailoring, flowers, embroidering and – why not say it? – the culinary arts, properly said, with special courses in snacks and sweets.

Once in possession of a technical profession and, consequently, with an independent spirit, then yes, take up the worship of literature, painting, music, etc., and you will find no one who, in good conscience, dares to call you, pejoratively, "professora."

## 8.11 TEODORO RAMOS BLANCO, "THE CONTRIBUTION OF THE BLACK FORM TO THE PLASTIC ARTS," ATENAS (HAVANA, CUBA: DEC. 1951)

*Along with those of his contemporary* **Nicolás Guillén**, *the many artistic triumphs of sculptor Teodoro Ramos Blanco (1902–72)[40] were a frequent topic in Cuba's Black press. Known for sculpture depicting Black subjects, Ramos Blanco reflected, in this rare written work, on the representation of Black bodies in contemporary art.*

*He began by distinguishing the "sterile" renderings of Black people that had become a fad in modernist artistic circles from other works that took into account the interior lives of Black subjects. He then argued for an expanded idea of beauty to take into account the full diversity of the natural world, including Black beauty. Next, he shifted to the question of Black expression. Ramos Blanco insisted that the "primitive" motifs and representational styles understood within the art world as "Negroid," or typical of Black artists, were not universally Black. They were, rather,*

---

[40] Anna Kaganiec-Kamienska, "Ramos Blanco, Teodoro," in Knight and Gates, *Dictionary*, vol. V, pp. 255–56.

*specific to the social development of a particular moment of the African past, appropriated and transformed by a specific moment in European cultural development.*

*Ramos Blanco's vision of African societies as devoid of economic dynamism and commercial exchange, and isolated from external contact, is no longer widely held by historians of Africa. Nevertheless, by explaining the historical origins of stereotypes about Black artistic expression, he was able to articulate a powerful alternative argument for the universality of contemporary Black arts. The contribution of the Black artist to the plastic arts, he concluded, was a "revolutionary" response to "the social injustice that he has suffered ever since he was ripped from his native land."*

It is not our purpose, here, to say anything new, surprising, or original about a topic that has been fully, even exhaustively, discussed by specialists in this discipline. We are only moved by the wish to express here, to the degree that we are able, the enthusiasm that we feel for the plastic arts, and especially for sculpture, to which, due to an irresistible impulse of our soul and with profound devotion, we have dedicated the fervor of our youth, worshiping form in all of its various and multiple aspects. A passionate lover of all artistic expression, I believe that I am obliged to declare that my soul is nourished by all that is artistic in nature and life. And although it is true that my art is, specifically, sculpting hard stone, aristocratic marble, or carving noble and precious wood, and modeling malleable clay, I now resort to the art of the word to express my impressions regarding an interesting topic, discussed at length in the current moment, which we only propose to discuss in terms of plastic arts: the contribution of the Black form to universal arts.

Our effort will not be stayed by the fact that such a thought-provoking issue has already been thoroughly discussed by the most conspicuous authorities on this subject, including by writers like Professor [Elie] Faure,[41] who because of their devotion to these studies, enjoy a solid international reputation. Given that, in all places and at all times, a great deal of respect has been reserved for the [human] form, it seems worthwhile to concern ourselves here exclusively with that which has to do with the Black form.

---

[41] French art historian (1873–1937) whose multivolume *Histoire de l'art* was published in Spanish translation in the early 1940s.

To begin, it is worth highlighting a fact that is very useful for informing a thorough understanding of the problem we are considering. The fact is that if, over the years, the most respectable artists have taken up the Black form, in truth, in most cases, they have only managed to capture the external part, the purely superficial or peripheral, without having been able to penetrate to the deepest and innermost part of its being, to give us its essence, its most intimate and vital content. They have given us a vessel, but it is totally empty. Profound emotion, without which every authentic work of art turns out to be castrated, sterile, and cold, has been missing. If ever these artists believed themselves to be moved by [the Black form], at the end of the day the work has turned out to be insincere, like all those that have not been truly felt and lived; that is, like a work created only in response to the imperative command of a fad or to a simple and fleeting snobbery, no matter the caliber and creative power of the artists who attempted it.

But how different the achieved effect has been when this form has been interpreted – and now the word is appropriate – by sincere artists who felt, without shame, proud to be inspired by it, and whose spirits were not burdened, consciously or unconsciously, by those preoccupations of artistic movements or those social prejudices that deform [the artists'] expression and distort their content. The truly valid creative enterprise is not to make a White or *amarillo* [Asian][42] form that is painted black; what is important is to feel [the form] in order to give shape to its expression, its rhythm, its beauty, and more important still, its interior. Only in this way, even when it is made of white marble, will the form be Black, and its essence will also be integrally Black.

In the first case, as is natural, the artist will give us nothing more than a mutilated, apocryphal, and lifeless expression of Blackness, that which is least important because it is least transcendent; that is, the purely superficial. In the second case, Blackness will be achieved to its fullness, because with the form will come, esoterically, in all of its splendor, the genuine Black soul. The subjective and the objective will come together in a happy marriage to give us Blackness in its full expression.

\*

In the arts – and outside of them – Black expression, as a spiritual manifestation, is not and cannot be a simple question of fashion,

---

[42] The word *amarillo*, literally meaning yellow, has frequently been used to designate people from Asia in many Latin American contexts.

a decorative topic suitable for humor, as some determined spirits influenced by racist views would have it. After the discovery of African art and its invasion of the Western world, so-called Black art emerged, which was then nothing more than a fad. Some French artists, and by contamination, some Latin American [artists], took it upon themselves to make things of Africanoid lineage, such as fetishes, nudes, and symbolic figures typical of the natural art of primitive peoples, but without any critical intention or even a minimal attempt to penetrate their inner sentiments, to discover how much humanity is contained there.

As with every social and historical phenomenon that is ecumenical in character, truth quickly made itself apparent, thanks to the opportune intervention of learned and scholarly persons uncontaminated by the virus of racism. The incorporation of the Black form in universal art was far from being an insignificant phenomenon, an episode without historical importance in the evolution of art, a simple, accidental incident stemming from the collision between ancient African culture and Western civilization. Rather, to the contrary, it had to do with an inevitable and necessary phenomenon determined by the dialectic that governs the evolutionary process of society and of life. Neither art nor any manifestation of the cosmos can be outside this dialectic. The Black art that had injected itself into Western culture, to make it viable, had to fulfill a great historical mission.

In effect, the Black form is, like it or not, a living and breathing reality, a product of nature and, therefore, a motif that tends toward artistic feeling, a quality that is a *sine qua non* present in all of nature's manifestations. We always find, within each distinct species of the zoological scale, along with chromatic variation of the epidermis, impeccably beautiful types alongside those that are strange and ugly. We establish our aesthetic concepts on these contrasts without one or the other ceasing to belong to the same biological group. There are, in the same way, distinct types within the different human groupings, for telluric and geographic reasons, differing in both pigmentary coloration and physiological features. [These types] have qualities that either by themselves or by means of contrast, when considered all together, give the whole a special and evocative harmony and establish its beauty. If all this is true, how is it possible to reject or despise the Black form? Can it be that the Black form does not contain within itself its own natural and particular beauty? Is it not a part of this world as much as the White, the *amarilla*, and the *cobriza*

[Indigenous]?[43] Do not each have their uglinesses and their beauty? Why should we not appreciate them, seeking properly to capture their beauty exactly as nature gives it to us, since this is art's noble mission?

\*

As with all that exists in this world, art has evolved from its most primitive and rudimentary forms, elevating itself progressively, following the rhythm of economic development in [each] society. This development has given rise, throughout [each society's] history, to distinct ideological superstructures, of which art is a principal element. As was the case for peoples of the old and new worlds, Black art, which could not but reflect the low economic development of African communities, could only have a typically Negroid character before coming into contact with Occidental civilization. Given its incipient development and the rudimentary state of its civilization, Black art, confined to the narrow limits of African tribes and clans, lacked the expansive power that emerged in other peoples thanks to commercial exchange. Nourished only by its own substance, living its own life, it was able to keep itself, for many centuries, free of all foreign contamination.

"Black civilization is the oldest civilization, although it is not contained within books," says Ramón Gómez de la Serna, "because it has not wanted to be corrupted or limited. All of this very ancient experience is like a silent secret that is transmitted by means of its idols, and from one generation to the next. Tired, searching for something on a different path from those on which it had already reached the definitive limit, [Western] art has gone towards Blackness in order to take the first steps, and there at the starting point, follow other paths that only depart from there, the main square of all of the jungles of the world."[44]

Indeed, one day the Black form was discovered by the avid curiosity and the adventurous spirit of the European man, who was attracted by the fantastical artistic treasures buried in this African world he scarcely knew, which offered a sharp contrast with the predominant aesthetic norms in old Europe. But the White man had gone to the African continent to "civilize" the Black through conquest, imposing on him a harsh form of

---

[43] The term *raza cobriza,* literally "copper-colored race," was used in Latin America to refer to the Indigenous peoples of the Americas.

[44] Ramón Gómez de la Serna (1888–1963), Spanish author and critic. This quotation is from his book *Ismos* (1931), which argued that the fascination with Black themes in European primitivism was a fad, an idea that became broadly influential in Cuban artistic circles. García Yero, "To Whom It Belongs."

servitude under the pretext that he was from an inferior race in which everything was despicable, even his spiritual expressions. It is often claimed that the historical force of a moral, political, or aesthetic principle is measured by its power of attraction. For this reason, the European, surprised by the discovery of this new art, despite its pronounced primitivism, was so influenced by it that he wished to remove it from its native land to incorporate it into universal culture. In this conflict, the African may have been defeated physically, but not spiritually. He took revenge on his oppressors by concealing, in the deepest recesses of his being, the secret mechanism of his aesthetic conceptions.

"The Blacks are isolated and deeply individualistic beings," notes R. G. de la S. "The Whites blend with others. The Blacks, to the contrary, live isolated to themselves, their own masters, tormented and problematic, starkly silhouetted in any light. It makes sense that the slaves should have had so much life of their own, such personality. This is why they could be slaves. Slavery would have absorbed and extinguished a White man."

But from the moment that Black art was inserted in universal culture, it would become a transplanted art, in which the typical Black form, through inevitable and inescapable osmosis, would lose its pristine and natural beauty, commencing the process of its de-Africanization to adapt it to the reality of the new environment and the demands of the new era. Every work of art is nothing more, when it is honest, than an answer the artist gives to a reality that injures his sensibility. Therefore, when the stimuli that inspired the Black man's artistic creations changed, when he was reduced to slavery, this is what would imprint, going forward, all his aesthetic expressions. If in the early stages the Black, finding refuge in himself, fought to conserve his cultural traditions under his new civil status, later, as he becomes more and more oppressed, materially and morally, as he is flayed, his instinct becomes sharper, his sensitivity develops, and a new and profound sentiment germinates within him, and overpowers all others: the universal sentiment of all the oppressed of the world.

Maybe – no, not maybe – it is on this very human point, more than in some other plastic expression, that the universalist meaning and historical significance of the Black contribution to the arts is to be found. To the great social turmoil of the world, he adds his bitter cry, renewed over long ages, revolutionary, an expression of the social injustice that he has suffered ever since he was ripped from his native land.

We know of the cultures of many ancient peoples by the works of art left behind by extinct generations, which were later rescued from the bowels of the earth. We are working so that the future, when it studies us, will know about the contribution made by the diverse human treasures who populated and gave their brilliance to this new world in which we live. A great wealth of Black forms enriches America. And even that diligent mixing of some forms with others – an experiment that can be fertile – will be seen, if interpreted with our own local criteria, to achieve with those ingredients a true model that can guarantee the durability of our arts, through the original and sincere expression of the artists of our time. The promoters of the arts are now beginning to appreciate the beauty of the Black form in a functional sense, as [Rafael] Suárez Solís[45] would say. In North America, the Harmon Foundation of New York organizes annual expositions of Black painting and sculpture, awarding various prizes and extending its influence through all of the states of the union.[46]

"Elvira y Tiverio," a notable image of Black forms painted by the Spaniard Hipólito Hidalgo Caciedes, won first prize (a thousand dollars) in the international painting competitions of the Carnegie Institute. The Black genius conquers and wins credit in all fields. Lately, a new Black gem, J[esse] Owen[s],[47] has earned for his nation – as utilitarian as it is prejudiced – a resounding victory by winning first place in the Olympic Games in Berlin, just as **Claudio José Domingo Brindis de Salas, José White**, Lico Jiménez[48] had done in other fields in Cuba in the past, and how very recently **Paul Robeson** triumphed in London in the most modern of the arts: cinema.

Black because of the pigmentation of our skin, Black in form, our blood is red, it is human blood, and our sensibility is noble and deep. Let us love our color, our family, our essence. Let us feel pride. Let us nurture and affirm our morals. Let us raise our spirits with energetic faith, supported by culture, which perfects [us] and provides us a weapon, and by the natural and robust purity of our origin. Let us prepare to fight for our spiritual and physical existence, but let us incorporate ourselves into the

---

[45] Rafael Suárez Solís (1881–1968), Spanish-born journalist, art critic, and editor-in-chief of the Havana newspaper *Diario de la Marina*.

[46] Ramos Blanco's work was displayed at a Harmon Foundation exhibition of "Negro Art" in 1933.

[47] Jesse Owens (1913–80), Olympic track champion who made a highly publicized visit to Havana in 1936. In the 1950s, Owens traveled the world as a goodwill ambassador, sponsored by the US State Department.

[48] José Manuel Jiménez Berroa (1851–1917), Afro-Cuban classical pianist and composer who studied in Paris as a young man and later settled in Germany.

worldwide spirit of transformation, proudly taking our rightful place alongside other human values in universal civilization.

And now, we will recall the words of the Yankee sculptor [Lorado T] aft, "It has not been vouchsafed us [sculptors] to be masters of articulate speech, but we would tell you in words of bronze and marble the things that seem to us most worthwhile, most enduring, most exalted, or most poignant."[49]

Likewise, if I have not known how to express my thoughts well in these pages, I refer readers to the works that I have produced, hoping that they will speak for me with greater clarity.

---

[49] Quoted in "Lorado Taft," *Bulletin of the Pan American Union* 48, 1 (1919), 50, which was also published in Spanish translation.

# APPENDIX

## Black Periodicals in Argentina, Brazil, Cuba, and Uruguay, 1856–1960

This appendix offers readers a listing of publicly available historical Black newspapers and magazines in the four countries covered by this volume. The list is complete to the best of our knowledge, though we hope and expect that researchers will discover additional titles and collections of Black periodicals in the future, not just in these countries but in others as well.

In Argentina, Brazil, and Uruguay, almost all of the titles listed are available in digital form through those countries' national libraries and/ or other websites. In Cuba, identifying and accessing Black publications is more complicated. Very few archival resources in the country have been digitized, and we have not had the opportunity to consult directly all, or even most, of the Cuban titles listed here. We identified them by cross-referencing titles listed in Cervantes, "Publicaciones de la raza de color," with digital library catalogues, or by searching under the subject heading "*negros*" in catalogues at the BNCJM and the UM-CHC. We also consulted two important bibliographies of works by Black Cuban authors: Deschamps Chapeaux, *Periodismo negro*, and Trelles, "Bibliografía de autores de la raza de color." Those sources include titles that, while edited and written by Black journalists, may not strictly fit the definition of the Black press we have adopted (publications that spoke openly for and to a Black community). However, some of the most prominent Black newspapers and magazines in Cuba also did not name themselves as such; the line between a Black newspaper and a general interest newspaper or partisan organ was often intentionally blurry. As a stimulus to further research on the Black press, it seemed to us more useful to include titles about which we are unsure than to exclude them. Items identified in Deschamps Chapeaux are marked with an asterisk (*) and items identified in Trelles with two asterisks (**).

Readers will find a great deal of additional material in Black-themed columns or inserts, edited by Black journalists, that were regular features of mainstream newspapers in Cuba. Some key examples are:

"Palpitaciones de la raza de color" in *La Prensa* (1916); "Armonías" and "Ideales de una raza" in *Diario de la Marina* (1928–36); "Marcha de una raza," *El Mundo* (1930s); "La situación del elemento de color," *Unión Nacionalista*; "Motivos sociales," *El País* (1930s–40s); and under various titles in *El Tiempo*.[1]

For each country, publications are listed in chronological order, with places and dates of publication and the websites or repositories where they can be consulted. Dates indicate years for which known issues exist; actual periods of publication may have been longer. We have not attempted to update or standardize the spelling, orthography, and diacritical marks of titles and subtitles (as they appear in the original papers or, when those are unavailable, in source citations). Subtitles sometimes changed over the course of a publication's lifetime; for purposes of consistency, we list the earliest known subtitle for each publication that had one.

### ARGENTINA

*La Raza Africana, o sea El Demócrata Negro.* Buenos Aires, 1858. UNC.

*El Proletario. Periodico semanal, politico, literario y de variedades.* Buenos Aires, 1858. BPUNLP.

*La Igualdad. Semanario de intereses generales.* Buenos Aires, 1872–74. BNMM.

*La Broma. Periodico semanal.* Buenos Aires, 1876–82. BNMM.

*La Juventud. Periodico semanal.* Buenos Aires, 1876–79. BNMM.

*El Unionista. Periodico semanal. Organo de las clases obreras.* Buenos Aires, 1877–78. BNMM.

*La Perla.* Buenos Aires, 1878–79. BNMM.

*El Aspirante. Periodico semanal.* Buenos Aires, 1882. BNMM.

*La Palabra. Organo defensor de la clase obrera.* Buenos Aires, 1888, 1917–30. BNMM.

### BRAZIL

*O Homem. Realidade constitucional ou dissolução social.* Recife, 1876. APEJE, BNB.

*A Pátria. Orgam dos homens de cor.* São Paulo, 1889. BNB.

*O Exemplo. Propriedade de uma associação.* Porto Alegre, 1893–1919. BNB.

[1] de la Fuente, "La 'raza' y los silencios de la cubanidad."

*O Baluarte. Orgam oficial do "Centro Litterario dos Homens de Côr."*
*Dedicado á defeza da classe.* Campinas, 1903–4. APESP, BNB, USP.

*A Alvorada. Periodico litterario, noticioso e critico.* Pelotas, 1911–19,
1926, 1935–38, 1943–57. BNB, BPP.

*O Menelik. Orgam mensal, noticioso, literario e critico dedicado aos*
*homens de cor.* São Paulo, 1917. BNB.

*A Rua. Literario, critico e humoristico.* São Paulo, 1916. BNB, USP.

*O Xauter. Jornal independente.* São Paulo, 1916. BNB.

*O Bandeirante. Orgam de combate em prol do reerguimento geral da*
*classe dos homens de cor.* São Paulo, 1918–19. APESP, BNB, USP.

*O Alfinete. Orgão literario, critico e recreativo dedicado aos homens de*
*cor.* São Paulo, 1918–21. APESP, BNB, USP.

*A Liberdade. Orgam dedicado á classe de côr, critico, literario*
*e noticioso.* São Paulo, 1919–20. APESP, BNB, USP.

*A Sentinella. Orgão critico – literario e noticioso.* São Paulo, 1920.
USP.

*O Kosmos. Orgam do Gremio Dramatico e Recreativo "Kosmos."* São
Paulo, 1922–25. BNB.

*Elite. Orgam oficial do Gremio Dramatico, Recreativo e Literario*
*"Elite da Liberdade."* São Paulo, 1923–24. BNB, USP.

*Getulino. Orgam para a defesa dos interesses dos homens pretos.*
Campinas, 1923–24; São Paulo, 1924–26. BNB.

*O Clarim da Alvorada. Orgam literario, noticioso e humoristico.* São
Paulo, 1924–33, 1940. BNB, USP.

*Auriverde. Litterario, humoristico e noticioso.* São Paulo, 1928.
APESP, BNB, USP.

*O Patrocínio. Orgam literario, critico e humoristico.* Piracicaba, 1928–
30. BNB.

*Progresso.* São Paulo, 1928–32. BNB, USP.

*Chibata.* São Paulo, 1932. AESP, BNB, USP.

*Evolução. Revista dos homens pretos de São Paulo.* São Paulo, 1933.
BNB, USP.

*A Voz da Raça. Orgam oficial da "Frente Negra Brasileira."* São Paulo,
1933–37. BNB, USP.

*Tribuna Negra. Pela união social e política dos descendentes da raça*
*negra.* São Paulo, 1935. AESP, BNB, USP.

*O Clarim. Publicação mensal da mocidade negra. Editado pelo depar-*
*tamento intelectual do C.N.C.S. [Clube Negro de Cultura Social].*
São Paulo, 1935. BNB, USP.

*O Estímulo. Semanario independente, litterario e noticioso.* São Carlos, 1935. BNB, USP.

*A Raça. Orgam da Legião Negra de Uberlandia.* Uberlândia, 1935. BNB.

*Alvorada. Orgão de propaganda cívica.* São Paulo, 1945–48. APESP, BNB, USP.

*O Novo Horizonte. Órgão de propaganda unificadora.* São Paulo, 1946–61. BNB, USP.

*Senzala. Revista mensal para o negro.* São Paulo, 1946. BNB, USP.

*Quilombo. Vida, problemas e aspirações do negro.* Rio de Janeiro, 1948–50. BNB, IPEAFRO. See also the facsimile edition, *Quilombo. Vida, problemas e aspirações do negro* (São Paulo: Editora 34, 2003).

*Mundo Novo.* São Paulo, 1950. BNB, USP.

*Redenção. Trabalhemos unidos por um Brasil melhor.* Rio de Janeiro, 1950. BNB.

*Cruzada Cultural. Orgão oficial da Cruzada Social e Cultural do Preto Brasileiro.* São Paulo, 1950–60. BNB.

*Notícias de Ébano. Órgão noticioso do "Ébano Atlético Clube."* Santos, 1957. BNB, USP.

*O Mutirão. Orgão da Associação Cultural do Negro.* São Paulo, 1958. BNB, USP.

*Hífen. O traço de união da elite.* Campinas, 1960–62. BNB, USP.

*Niger. Publicação a serviço da coletividade negra.* São Paulo, 1960. BNB, USP.

CUBA

*El Rocío.* Havana, 1856. BNCJM.*

*La Fraternidad. Periodico politico independiente consagrado a la defensa de los intereses generales de la raza de color.* Havana, 1879–93. BNCJM.

*El Pueblo. Semanario literario y de intereses generales. Órgano de la clase de color.* Matanzas, 1880. BNCJM.

*La Antorcha. Periódico político independiente y de intereses generales.* Trinidad, 1887–90. BNCJM.*

*La Revista Popular. Periodico quincenal, politica, literatura, ciencias, [etc].* Key West, 1888. IISH.*

*Minerva. Revista quincenal dedicada a la mujer de color.* Havana, 1888–89, 1913–15. BNCJM, and on microfiche at many libraries in the United States.

*La Nueva Eva. Revista quincenal cubana.* Havana, 1892–95. BNCJM.*

*La Verdad. Político, biográfico, literario y de intereses generales.* New York, 1894. BNCJM.*

*La Estrella Solitaria. Industrias, comercio, literatura, ciencias, variedades, noticias y avisos.* Caracas, 1895. BNCJM.*

*La Doctrina de Martí. Periódico biográfico, político, literario, de intereses generales y anuncios.* New York, 1896–98. APHHC, BNCJM, NHAN.

*El Sport. Seminario politico y literario.* Tampa, 1897. BNCJM.*

*La Voz de la Razón. Periódico político y de intereses generales.* Havana, 1900. BNCJM.**

*La República Cubana.* Havana, 1901. BNCJM.**

*El Nuevo Criollo. Semanario politico moderado.* Havana, 1904–5. BNCJM.

*La Estrella Refulgente. Semanario literario, humorístico, sports e ilustrado. Dedicado a las damas que forman los Comités de las Sociedades de la República y órgano oficial de los mismos.* Havana, 1905–6. BNJCM.**

*Previsión. Periodico politico independiente.* Havana, 1908–10. BNCJM.

*Juvenil.* Havana, 1912–13. BNCJM.

*Aurora. Revista quincenal.* Havana, 1914. BNCJM.

*Albores. Revista cubana ilustrada.* Camagüey, 1914–16. UM-CHC.**

*Labor Nueva. Revista literaria ilustrada.* Havana, 1916. BNCJM, UCONN-LDC.

*La Antorcha. Periódico independiente y de intereses generales.* Havana, 1917–20. BNCJM.**

*Destellos. Revista literaria quincenal ilustrada.* Cárdenas, 1918. BNCJM.

*Albores.* Güines, 1921. BNCJM.

*Luz de Oriente.* Santiago de Cuba, 1922–25. BNCJM.**

*Fraternidad y Amor. Revista quincenal de ideas progresistas, literaria y de intereses generales.* Guanabacoa, 1923–25. BNCJM.

*Cultura. Revista literaria de la Sociedad Centro La Luz.* San Antonio de los Baños, 1926. BNCJM.

*El Demócrata. Periódico político independiente.* Guanabacoa, 1926. BNCJM.

*El Veterano. Organo oficial de la Delegación de Veteranos de Guanabacoa.* Guanabacoa, 1928. BNCJM.

*El Cometa. Periódico quincenal de intereses generales.* Havana, 1929. BNCJM.

*Baraguá. Quincenario nacional y de reafirmación patriótica.* Havana, 1930. BNCJM.

*Evolución. Semanario de intereses generales.* Havana, 1930. BNCJM.

*Boletín Oficial del Club Atenas.* Havana, 1930–31. BNCJM, UM-CHC.

*Renacimiento. Publicación nacional de identificación patriótica.* Havana, 1933. BNCJM.

*Adelante. Revista mensual.* Havana, 1935–39. BNCJM, CRL-DDS.

*Atomo. Revista mensual.* Havana, 1936. BNCJM, UM-CHC.

*Unión Fraternal. Revista de avance.* Havana, 1936–37. BNCJM, UM-CHC.

*Ibarra. Órgano oficial de la Sección de Cultura de la Sociedad Juan G. Gómez.* Regla, 1938. BNCJM.

*Rumbos. Órgano de la Unión Maceista.* Havana, 1939–41; 1943–48. BNCJM, NYPL.

*Fragua de la Libertad.* Havana, 1942. BNCJM.

*Orientación. Semanario de información e intereses generales. Editado por la Federación Nacional de Periodistas Negros de Cuba y la América, defensores de la democracia y su sociedad.* Havana, 1942. BNCJM.

*Fraternidad.* Havana, 1942. BNCJM.

*¡Somos!* Havana, 1943. BNCJM.

*Nuevos Rumbos.* Havana, 1945–49, 1959. BNCJM.

*Ateniense. Revista mensual.* Havana, 1950. UM-CHC.

*Atenas. Organo oficial del Club Atenas. Mensuario cultural de afirmación cubana.* Havana, 1951–54. BNCJM, UM-CHC.

*Amanecer. Revista social independiente.* Havana, 1952–54. BNCJM.

URUGUAY

*La Conservación. Organo de la sociedad de color.* Montevideo, 1872. BNU.

*El Progresista. Organo de los intereses de la sociedad de color.* Montevideo, 1873. BNU.

*La Regeneración.* Montevideo, 1884–85. BNU.

*El Periódico. Órgano de las clases obreras.* Montevideo, 1889. BNU.

*La Propaganda. Periódico político-social.* Montevideo, 1893–95, 1911–12. BNU.

*El Eco del Porvenir.* Montevideo, 1901. BNU.

*La Verdad. Organo defensor de los intereses generales de esta colectividad.* Montevideo, 1911–14. BNU.

*Nuestra Raza. Periodico social, noticioso. Organo de la colectividad de color.* San Carlos, 1917; Montevideo, 1933–48. AU, BNU.

*La Vanguardia. Órgano defensor de los intereses de la raza negra.* Montevideo, 1928–29. BNU.

*Acción. Organo del Comité Pro-Edificio del "Centro Uruguay."* Melo, 1934–35, 1944–52. BNU.

*Rumbos!! Periódico independiente de la raza de color.* Rocha, 1938–45; Montevideo, 1948–50. BNU.

*Ansina. Manuel Antonio Ledesma.* Montevideo, 1939–42. BNU.

*Orientación. Organo de la colectividad de color.* Melo, 1941–45. BNU.

*Democracia. Organo racial independiente.* Rocha, 1942–46. BNU.

*Rumbo Cierto. Un rumbo cierto de progreso, cultura y libertad bajo el cielo del Uruguay.* Montevideo, 1944–45. BNU.

*Revista Uruguay. Organo de la colectividad, editado por el Centro Cultural y Social "Uruguay."* Montevideo, 1945–48. AU, BNU.

*Bahia-Hulan Yack. Organo adherido al "Ateneo Pro-Cultura del Negro: R. Bunche – A. Reboucas."* Montevideo, 1958–92. BNU.

## LIBRARIES AND DIGITAL REPOSITORIES

APEJE – Arquivo Público Estadual Jordão Emerenciano, Recife.

APESP – Arquivo Público do Estado de São Paulo, São Paulo. www.arquivoestado.sp.gov.br/site/acervo/repositorio_digital/jornais_revistas

APHHC – Arte Público Hispanic Historical Collection (EBSCO). www.ebsco.com/products/digital-archives/arte-publico-hispanic-historical-collection-series-1

AU – Autores de Uruguay. https://autores.uy/obra

BNB – Biblioteca Nacional (Brasil), Rio de Janeiro. http://bndigital.bn.gov.br/hemeroteca-digital/

BNCJM – Biblioteca Nacional de Cuba José Martí, Havana. www.bnjm.cu

BNMM – Biblioteca Nacional Mariano Moreno, Buenos Aires. https://catalogo.bn.gov.ar/F?func=find-m

BNU – Biblioteca Nacional de Uruguay, Montevideo. http://bibliotecadigital.bibna.gub.uy:8080/jspui/

BPP – Bibliotheca Pública Pelotense, Pelotas. http://acervobibliotheca
.com.br

BPUNLP – Biblioteca Pública de la Universidad Nacional de La Plata,
La Plata. www.biblio.unlp.edu.ar/hemeroteca/hemeroteca-14489

CRL-DDS – Center for Research Libraries Digital Delivery System,
Chicago. www.crl.edu/services/digital-services/digital-delivery

IISH – International Institute of Social History, Amsterdam. https://iisg
.amsterdam/en/collections

IPEAFRO – Instituto de Pesquisa e Estudos Afro-Brasileiros, Rio de
Janeiro. https://ipeafro.org.br/acervo-digital/leituras/ten-
publicacoes/jornal-quilombo-no-01/

NHAN – Newsbank Hispanic American Newspapers. www.readex
.com/products/hispanic-american-newspapers-1808-1980

NYPL – New York Public Library, New York.

UCONN-LDC – University of Connecticut Library Digital Collections,
Storrs. https://lib.uconn.edu/location/asc/

UM-CHC – University of Miami-Cuban Heritage Collection, Miami.
www.library.miami.edu/chc/

UNC – Universidad Nacional de Córdoba, Córdoba (Argentina).

USP – Universidade de São Paulo, Imprensa Negra Paulista, São Paulo.
http://biton.uspnet.usp.br/imprensanegra/

# Glossary

Except where otherwise noted, all individuals listed were self-identified or identified by their society as being of African ancestry. All references to *Dictionary* are to Franklin W. Knight and Henry Louis Gates, Jr., eds., *Dictionary of Caribbean and Afro-Latin American Biography*, 6 vols. (New York: Oxford University Press, 2016).

**Abakuá.** An all-male Afro-Cuban secret society with distinctive philosophical, musical, and dance traditions related to those of similar organizations in the Cross River Delta region of West Africa.

*Academias.* In nineteenth- and early twentieth-century Buenos Aires, lower-class dance halls, often cited as the birthplaces of tango as a musical and dance form.

**Andes, Crossing of the.** A military campaign during January–February 1817, in which Argentine General **José de San Martín** led his troops over that mountain range to help liberate Chile from Spanish rule. Half of those soldiers were formerly enslaved.

**Barcala, Lorenzo (1793–1835).** Argentine military officer who served in the country's independence and civil wars. María de Lourdes Ghidoli, "Barcala, Lorenzo," *Dictionary*, vol. I, pp. 220–23.

**Barrios, Pilar (1889–1974).** Uruguayan poet, founding editor of *Nuestra Raza*, and one of the founders of the **Partido Autóctono Negro.** Eduardo Palermo, "Barrios, Pilar," *Dictionary*, vol. I, pp. 235–36.

**Bastille.** Notorious fortress and state prison in Paris that was attacked and destroyed during the French Revolution, in 1789.

**Batista, Fulgencio (1901–73).** Cuban soldier, officer, and politician who served as elected president from 1940 to 1944 and then as dictator from 1952 to 1959. Overthrown by the Revolution of 1959, he died in exile in Spain.

**Betervide, Salvador (1903–36).** Uruguayan lawyer and activist, editor of *La Vanguardia*, and the founding president of the **Partido Autóctono Negro**. Eduardo Palermo, "Betervide, Salvador," *Dictionary*, vol. I, pp. 321–23.

**Black Mother.** In Brazil, the symbolic representative of the African and Afrodescendant women who nursed and cared for the children of their White enslavers (in the case of enslaved women) or employers (in the case of free workers). In the 1920s several journalists and activists proposed that a statue of her be erected in the national capital; a statue was eventually erected in São Paulo in 1955. Micol Seigel, "Mãe Preta (Black Mother)," *Dictionary*, vol. IV, pp. 165–66.

**Blanco de Aguirre, Juan (c. 1855–?).** Afro-**Porteño** illustrator and painter who received artistic training in Florence with financial support from the Argentine government. In addition to working as a drawing instructor at the Colegio Nacional, he became known for his attempts, beginning in 1899, to construct a monument honoring **Antonio Ruiz (Falucho)**. María de Lourdes Ghidoli, "Blanco de Aguirre, Juan," *Dictionary*, vol. I, pp. 349–50.

**Blanco Party.** One of the two principal political parties in nineteenth- and twentieth-century Uruguay, also known as the National Party.

**Brindis de Salas, Claudio José Domingo (1851–1911).** A world-renowned Cuban violinist, Brindis de Salas performed throughout Europe and the Americas. After a series of career reversals in the early 1900s, he died in poverty in Buenos Aires. Bárbara Francisca Danzie León, "Brindis de Salas, Claudio José Domingo," *Dictionary*, vol. I, pp. 401–2.

**Buffon, Comte de, Georges-Louis Leclerc (1707–88).** Prolific French (and racially White) naturalist, mathematician, and author.

*Caboclo/a.* In Brazil, an Indigenous person, or a person of mixed Black and Indigenous ancestry.

**Cabral, Elemo** (1887–1969). Uruguayan journalist, an editor of *Nuestra Raza*, and a founder of the **Partido Autóctono Negro**.

**Cabral, Iris María** (1915–36). Uruguayan journalist who wrote for *Nuestra Raza* and who died tragically young.

*Cafuso/a*. In Brazil, a person of mixed Black and Indigenous ancestry.

**Cain, sons of.** Along with Ham, a Biblical figure cursed for having committed crimes (Cain murdered his brother Abel, and Ham saw his father Noah naked). The phrase "sons of Cain" (alongside "sons of Ham") refers to African people. Over time, different Christian traditions have read the curses of Cain (sometimes interpreted as the "mark" of dark skin) or of Ham (the condemnation to servitude of his descendancy) as justifications for African slavery.

**Candombe.** In nineteenth-century Argentina and Uruguay, (a) an African-based form of music and dance, and (b) the places and occasions at which that music and dance were performed. In the 1900s candombe evolved to become one of the most popular musical genres in Uruguay, and important as well in Argentina.

**Candomblé.** Widely practiced religion combining elements of Catholicism and of the Orisha-based religions of West Africa. Originating in northeastern Brazil, Candomblé subsequently spread to Uruguay, Argentina, and other countries.

**Carneiro, Édison** (1912–72). Brazilian journalist, author, and ethnographer, and one of the foundational figures of Afro-Brazilian studies. The federal Museu de Folclore Édison Carneiro, founded in 1968, is named in his honor. Stefania Capone, "Carneiro, Édison," *Dictionary*, vol. II, pp. 52–54.

**Carnival.** In Latin American countries, the period of celebration and merrymaking immediately preceding the forty days of Lent. Over the course of the 1900s Carnival became increasingly regulated and promoted by municipal and national governments, which oversaw public dances, parades, and other events. Today it is a major tourist attraction in Brazil, Colombia, Uruguay, and other countries.

**Centro Cívico Palmares.** Afro-Brazilian social and civic organization founded in São Paulo in 1926. Some members and leaders of the organization went on to found the **Frente Negra Brasileira**.

**Class of color** (also **"the class"**). In the late 1800s and early 1900s, a term used by writers in Latin America's Black press to refer to Afrodescendants or people of the Black race.

**Club Atenas.** Afro-Cuban social club and cultural institution in Havana from 1917 through the 1950s. Club members tended to enjoy relatively high social status as professionals, government employees, and elected officials.

**Coimbra de Valverde, Úrsula** (?–?). Cuban pianist, teacher, and journalist who wrote under the pen name Cecilia. She was the acknowledged leader of the group of women who helped create the magazine *Minerva*.

**Colorado Party.** One of the two principal political parties in nineteenth- and twentieth-century Uruguay.

*Compadrito.* In Buenos Aires, a street tough, brawler, idler, and flashy dresser, usually from the popular classes.

*Comparsa.* Musical group created to sing, parade, and dance through the streets during **Carnival.**

**Complementary laws.** Laws intended to implement broad constitutional principles by listing specific actions that violate those principles, and punishments for those actions.

**Congressos Afro-Brasileiros.** Two conferences, held in 1934 in Recife, and in 1937 in Bahia, at which academic researchers and cultural practitioners presented papers and "communications" on Afro-Brazilian history and culture.

*Conrazáneo/a.* A word used in the Uruguayan newspaper *Nuestra Raza* to refer to people of African ancestry. Grammatically analogous to "comrade" or "compatriot," it conveyed that the person so designated shared Black racial status with the writer.

**Constitution of 1940 (Cuba).** A broadly progressive document, written in the wake of a popular revolution in 1933. Black activists and the Communist Party successfully mobilized to insert provisions guaranteeing labor rights, social rights, and naming racial and gender discrimination as crimes.

**Copacabana.** A wealthy, mostly White, beachfront neighborhood in Rio de Janeiro.

**Cuéllar Vizcaíno, Manuel (1899–1988).** Cuban journalist, writer, social worker, and long-time member, beginning in the 1930s, of the Communist Party.

**Danzón.** Popular musical and dance style developed by Afro-Cuban musicians and dancers in Havana and Matanzas.

**Diggs, Ellen Irene (1906–98).** North American anthropologist who received her PhD from the University of Havana in 1943 and devoted her career to researching and teaching the history and culture of the African diaspora.

**Directorio Central de las Sociedades de la Raza de Color.** In Cuba, a national federation of Black social clubs and community organizations, founded in 1886. **Juan Gualberto Gómez** served as its president and also edited its newspaper, *La Igualdad.*

**Dom Pedro II.** See **Pedro II.**

**D'ou, Lino (1871–1939).** Cuban journalist, civil rights activist, and lieutenant-colonel in the independence army. D'ou was elected to the Cuban House of Representatives in 1908. Ana Rodríguez Navas, "D'ou Ayllón, Lino," in *Dictionary*, vol. II, pp. 388–89.

**England, role in abolition of the slave trade.** Between 1849 and 1851 the United Kingdom intervened forcefully to end the African slave trade to Brazil, capturing over ninety slaving vessels and threatening to invade Brazilian ports. Under British pressure, in 1850 the Brazilian Parliament approved legislation criminalizing the slave trade, and over the next two years the government effectively suppressed the trade.

**Estado Novo.** Authoritarian regime that ruled Brazil from 1937 to 1945, headed by President **Getúlio Vargas.**

**Estenoz, Evaristo (c. 1870–1912).** Soldier in Cuba's last independence war and in the Liberal uprising of 1906, and co-founder (with Gregorio Surín) of the **Partido Independiente de Color.** Estenoz was killed in the government's violent repression of the party. Takkara Keosha Brunson, "Estenoz Corominas, Evaristo," *Dictionary*, vol. II, pp. 474–75.

**Falucho.** *See* Ruiz, Antonio.

**Favelas.** Shantytown neighborhoods built within, or on the outskirts of, Brazilian cities. Afro-Brazilians are overrepresented among the residents of favelas.

**Ferreyra, Benedicto** (c. 1850–1912). Brazilian-born journalist and founding editor of the Argentine newspaper *La Verdad*; noted orator and leader of the Afro-Argentine community in the early 1900s.

**Ferreyra, Oscar** (c. 1889–?). Argentine journalist and son of **Benedicto Ferreyra**; became editor of *La Verdad* immediately following his father's death in 1912, and again during the paper's second phase in the 1930s.

**Florêncio, Benedicto** (?–?). Co-editor of *O Baluarte* and occasional contributor to *Getulino* and *Progresso*.

**Free Womb Law.** Officially known as the Rio Branco Law, the Free Womb Law was passed by the Brazilian Parliament in 1871. Under its provisions, children born to slave mothers were considered legally free but were required to serve their mother's owner until the age of 21. Similar laws were enacted in Cuba in 1870 and in the Spanish American republics during the 1810s and 1820s.

**Frente Negra Brasileira.** Civic organization and political party founded in São Paulo in 1931. The dictatorship of **Getúlio Vargas** banned all political parties in Brazil in 1937, and the organization formally dissolved the following year.

**Freyre, Gilberto** (1900–89). White Brazilian sociologist and public intellectual who popularized the idea of Brazil as a racially harmonious and egalitarian society. Jeffrey D. Needell, "Freyre, Gilberto (de Mello)," *Dictionary*, vol. III, pp. 68–70.

**Gama, Luiz** (1830–82). Brazilian lawyer, poet, journalist, and leading abolitionist. Lamonte Aidoo, "Gama, Luiz Gonzaga Pinto da," *Dictionary*, vol. III, pp. 85–87.

**García Agüero, Salvador** (1907–65). Cuban teacher, activist, writer, and long-time member of the Communist Party. Following the Revolution of 1959 he served as Cuba's ambassador to Guinea and to Bulgaria, where he died in 1965.

**Gares, Isabelino José** (?–1940). Uruguayan journalist and playwright, editor of *La Propaganda* and frequent contributor to *Nuestra Raza*.

**Garvey, Marcus Mosiah** (1887–1940). Jamaican-born publisher, businessman, and activist, best known as the founder of the **Universal Negro Improvement Association**. D. A. Dunkley, "Garvey, Marcus Mosiah," *Dictionary*, vol. III, pp. 11–15.

**Gómez, Juan Gualberto** (1854–1933). Cuban journalist, politician, and independence and anti-racist activist. Gómez founded and edited *La Fraternidad* and *La Igualdad*, and also headed the **Directorio Central de las Sociedades de la Raza de Color**. After Cuba won its independence from Spain, he served in the Constitutional Convention of 1901, the House of Representatives, and the Senate. Bárbara Danzie, "Gómez Ferrer, Juan Gualberto," *Dictionary*, vol. III, pp. 167–70.

**Guillén, Nicolás** (1902–89). Cuban journalist and internationally acclaimed poet. Because of his membership in the Communist Party, Guillén spent prolonged periods in the 1930s, 1940s, and 1950s outside of Cuba. Following the Revolution of 1959, he was appointed president of the Unión de Escritores y Artistas de Cuba, a position he held until his death. Anna Kaganiec-Kamienska, "Guillén Bautista, Nicolás Cristobal," *Dictionary*, vol. III, pp. 231–33.

**Ham, sons of.** *See* Cain.

**Harlem Renaissance.** A period of intense artistic, literary, and intellectual production among African American writers, artists, and musicians in New York City from the late 1910s through the 1930s.

**Hughes, Langston** (1901–67). Internationally acclaimed North American writer and anti-racist activist. Translated versions of his poems and other writings were widely read and admired in Latin America.

**Integralism.** Brazilian political movement partially inspired by Italian fascism. The Ação Integralista Brasileira was founded in 1931 and banned by **Getúlio Vargas'** government in 1938 following its attempted assault on the presidential palace.

**Law of Association, Cuba.** The law that regulated the creation of clubs, labor unions, and other social organizations in Cuba from 1888 to 1976. Prior to 1960, Cuban governments did not apply prohibitions against racial discrimination to private social clubs registered under this law.

**Leite, José Correia** (1900–89). Brazilian journalist and activist, founding editor of *O Clarim da Alvorada*, *Alvorada*, and other newspapers. Michael Hanchard, "Leite, José Correia," *Dictionary*, vol. IV, pp. 62–64.

**Maceo, Antonio** (1845–96). Commander-in-chief of Cuba's rebel army in the independence wars of the late 1800s. Anna Clayfield, "Maceo, Antonio," *Dictionary*, vol. IV, pp. 152–55.

**Machado, Gerardo** (1869–1939). White Cuban businessman and politician, and president of Cuba from 1925 to 1933.

**Macumba.** A broad term referring to several different variants of African-based religious practice in Brazil.

*Mãe Preta.* *See* Black Mother.

**Maran, René** (1887–1960). Novelist from French Guiana and the first Black winner of the Prix Goncourt, for his novel *Batouala* (1921). James E. Genova, "Maran, René," *Dictionary*, vol. IV, pp. 210–11.

**Martí, José** (1853–95). White Cuban writer, poet, and journalist, and a national hero of Cuban independence. Sentenced to prison and then exile by the Spanish colonial government, Martí returned to Cuba in 1895 and was killed in battle.

**May 13, 1888.** The date on which Princess Isabel signed the Lei Áurea (the Golden Law) that abolished slavery in Brazil.

**Méndez, Mario Rufino** (1888–1942). A Uruguayan artist and activist, Méndez supplied much of the cover art for *Nuestra Raza* and served as president of the **Partido Autóctono Negro** after the death of **Salvador Betervide**.

*Mestiço/a.* In Brazil, a person of mixed race.

*Mestizo/a.* In Spanish America, a person of mixed race. The word usually refers to people of mixed European and Indigenous ancestry but is sometimes applied to people with African ancestry as well.

**Moraes, Evaristo de** (1871–1939). Brazilian lawyer, journalist, and author. Moraes was closely associated with Brazil's early union movement and during the 1930s helped draft the Consolidação das Leis do Trabalho, the legislation that still governs Brazil's labor relations today.

**Morales, José María** (1818–94). Argentine military officer who served in Argentina's civil wars and in the **War of the Triple Alliance**. He later served in Buenos Aires' provincial legislature. María de Lourdes Ghidoli, "Morales, José María," *Dictionary*, vol. IV, pp. 397–400.

*Moreno/a.* A racial term in both Spanish and Portuguese, originally (in the colonial period) referring to a person with dark-brown skin, and considered a more polite term than *negro*. During the 1900s the word's usage broadened to become a racial term that mediates between Black and White. It can be applied both to darker-skinned White people and to racially mixed people.

**Morúa Delgado, Martín (1857–1910).** Cuban journalist, novelist, and politician. Morúa Delgado edited a number of newspapers and served both in Cuba's first Constitutional Convention (1901) and in the Senate. As Senator, he wrote the Morúa Amendment, which outlawed the **Partido Independiente de Color**. Emilio Jorge Rodríguez, "Morúa Delgado, Martín," *Dictionary*, vol. IV, pp. 422–24.

*Mulato/a.* A term in both Spanish and Portuguese for a person of racially mixed ancestry or an Afro-descendant person with a lighter complexion. The female form, mulata, is often invoked in Latin American societies as a symbol of strong female sexuality, sometimes celebrated and other times vilified. Otherwise, these terms do not have the same negative connotation as "mulatto" in English.

*Ñáñigo.* In Cuba, an initiate in the all-male **Abakuá** secret societies.

**Nascimento, Abdias do (1914–2011).** Prominent Brazilian activist and intellectual, founder of the **Teatro Experimental do Negro** and of *Quilombo* magazine. Exiled from Brazil from 1968 to 1983, he later served in the Chamber of Deputies and, from 1994 to 1999, in the Senate. Elisa Larkin Nascimento, "Abdias Nascimento," *Dictionary*, vol. IV, pp. 454–57.

**Nascimento, Maria [de Lourdes Vale] (1924–95).** Brazilian social worker, teacher, journalist, and activist. Founder, along with **Abdias do Nascimento** and others, of *Quilombo*, and managing director of the paper.

**Occupation of Cuba by the United States.** Following the defeat of Spain in 1898, US military forces occupied and governed Cuba until 1902, and then again from 1906 to 1909.

**Paraguayan War.** *See* **War of the Triple Alliance.**

**Partido Autóctono Negro.** Uruguayan political party created in 1936 by activists associated with *Nuestra Raza*. After running a list of candidates in the Congressional elections of 1938, the party withdrew from electoral competition and officially disbanded in 1944.

**Partido Independiente de Color.** Cuban political party created in 1908 by Black veterans of the independence army and the Liberal uprising of

1906. The party was effectively outlawed by the Morúa Amendment in 1910 and violently repressed by the Cuban government in 1912.

**Patrocínio, José do (1853–1905).** Brazilian journalist and leading abolitionist. Jeffrey D. Needell, "Patrocínio, José Carlos do," *Dictionary*, vol. V, pp. 90–92.

**Pedro II (1825–91).** Emperor of Brazil from 1840 to 1889, considered racially White. His overthrow by the armed forces ended monarchical rule in Brazil; he died in exile in Paris.

**Plácido.** *See* Valdés, Gabriel de la Concepción.

*Porteño/a.* Native to the city of Buenos Aires.

**Princess Isabel (1846–1921).** Isabel was the daughter of Emperor **Pedro II** and the presumptive heir to his throne. As Princess Regent while Pedro was traveling abroad, she signed the **Free Womb Law** in 1871 and the Golden Law of final emancipation in 1888.

**Racial democracy.** The idea that Brazilian society (and that of other Latin American countries as well) is characterized by high levels of racial harmony and egalitarianism, especially when compared with the United States.

**Ramos, Alberto Guerreiro (1915–82).** Brazilian sociologist and public intellectual. A member of the **Teatro Experimental do Negro** and of *Quilombo*'s editorial board, he left Brazil in 1966 and taught at the University of Southern California until his death in 1982.

**Ramos, Arthur (1903–49).** White Brazilian psychiatrist, anthropologist, and ethnographer. Ramos is considered to be one of the founding fathers of Afro-Brazilian studies; he originated the term "**racial democracy.**"

**Regla de Ocha.** Afro-Cuban spiritual practice developed by Lucumí, or **Yoruba**-speaking, people. Also sometimes called Santería.

**Robeson, Paul Leroy (1898–1976).** Internationally renowned North American singer, actor, and activist.

**Rodríguez Arraga, José María (?–?).** To the best of our knowledge, the only Black medical-school graduate in Uruguay during the first half of the 1900s.

**Rolón, Zenón (1856–1902).** Argentine musician, composer, and conductor. Supported by a government fellowship, Rolón studied composition and conducting in Italy; returning to Argentina in 1879, he composed a number of symphonic works and earned his living teaching music in high schools and colleges. María de Lourdes Ghidoli, "Rolón, Zenón," *Dictionary*, vol. V, pp. 366–68.

**Rondeau, Francisco (c. 1870–c. 1940).** Uruguayan lawyer and occasional contributor to Afro-Uruguayan newspapers.

**Ruiz, Antonio (?–1824).** Soldier, commonly known as **Falucho,** who served in Argentina's independence armies and was allegedly killed while defending the Argentine flag in a military uprising in Peru. María de Lourdes Ghidoli, "Ruiz, Antonio 'Falucho'," *Dictionary*, vol. V, pp. 403–5.

**San Francisco Conference.** The United Nations Conference on International Organization, held in San Francisco from April through June 1945. Delegates from fifty Allied and neutral nations gathered to write and approve the UN Charter.

**San Martín, José de (1778–1850).** White Argentine commander of the Army of the Andes, which invaded Chile in 1817, winning the independence of that country and, in 1821, of Peru.

**Santos, Arlindo [J.] Veiga dos (1902–78).** Brazilian activist and journalist, member of the **Centro Cívico Palmares,** and a founder and first president of the **Frente Negra Brasileira.**

**Scientific racism.** A body of racist ideology, supposedly based on scientific findings, that was hegemonic in Western academic and intellectual life from the second half of the 1800s through the 1930s. Scientific racism posited that humans were biologically divided into clearly defined racial groups, ranked in an equally clearly defined racial hierarchy, with White people at the top.

**Senghor, Léopold Sédar (1906–2001).** Poet and politician who served as Senegal's first president (1960–80).

**Serra, Rafael (1858–1909).** Cuban journalist and activist, editor of a number of newspapers, including *La Verdad*, *La Doctrina de Martí*, and *El Nuevo Criollo*. Bonni Lucero, "Serra y Montalvo, Rafael," *Dictionary*, vol. VI, pp. 49–50.

**Sociedad de Estudios Afrocubanos.** Organization founded in 1937 to support the study of Afro-Cuban folklore and anthropology. Many Black intellectuals, including Enrique Andreu, **Manuel Cuéllar**

Vizcaíno, and **Salvador García Agüero**, were members of the Society or contributed to its publication, *Estudios Afrocubanos*.

**Sosa, Domingo (1784–1866).** Argentine military officer who served in that country's independence and civil wars, and in the Buenos Aires provincial legislature. María Lourdes de Ghidoli, "Sosa, Domingo," *Dictionary*, vol. VI, pp. 107–9.

**Spiritism.** In Brazil, a form of religious practice incorporating elements from French spiritism and from African and Indigenous religions.

**Suárez Peña, Aguedo (c. 1890–1948).** Uruguayan journalist who contributed to *Nuestra Raza* and edited *Revista Uruguay*.

**Teatro Experimental do Negro.** Afro-Brazilian cultural and civic organization founded in Rio de Janeiro in 1944 by **Abdias do Nascimento** and closely linked to *Quilombo* magazine. The organization continued its activities until Nascimento was forced into exile by the Brazilian dictatorship in 1968.

**Ten Years' War (1868–78).** The first of three wars that Cuba fought for national independence from Spain. The treaty that ended the war granted freedom to slaves who had fought for either side; during the war Spain also decreed a **Free Womb Law** (1870) that spelled the eventual end of slavery in Cuba.

**Thompson, Casildo Gervasio (1856–1928).** Argentine musician, poet, journalist, and co-editor (with Froilán P. Bello) of *El Unionista*. María de Lourdes Ghidoli, "Thompson, Casildo Gervasio," *Dictionary*, vol. VI, pp. 180–82.

*Trigueño/a* (in Portuguese, *trigueiro/a*). Like *moreno/a*, *trigueño/a* (literally, "wheat-colored") is a racial term that mediates between Black and White. It can be applied both to darker-skinned White people and to racially mixed people.

**Tuskegee Institute.** Founded in 1881 as the Tuskegee Normal School for Colored Teachers, under the direction of **Booker T. Washington** the college (and later university) became a national leader in the education of African Americans. During the 1890s and early 1900s, it enrolled many Black students from Cuba and Puerto Rico.

**Ubarne [Mansilla] de Espinosa, Margarita (?–?).** Uruguayan schoolteacher and occasional contributor to *La Verdad*.

**Universal Negro Improvement Association (UNIA).** Founded in Jamaica in 1914 by **Marcus Garvey**, the UNIA was one of the earliest and most important Black internationalist organizations. At its height, in the 1920s and 1930s, it comprised over 1,000 local chapters in more than 40 countries.

**Urrutia, Gustavo (1881–1958).** Cuban architect, journalist, and public intellectual. He edited the "Ideales de una raza" column in *Diario de la Marina* and actively promoted intellectual and literary contacts between Afro-Cuban and African American authors. Andrés Fletch, "Urrutia, Gustavo," *Dictionary*, vol. VI, pp. 227–28.

**Valdés, Gabriel de la Concepción (1809–44).** Cuban poet who wrote under the pseudonym Plácido. In 1844, during the **Year of the Lash**, he was charged with participating in an anti-colonial conspiracy and was executed by firing squad. Matthew Pettway, "Valdés, Diego Gabriel de la Concepción (Plácido)," *Dictionary*, vol. VI, pp. 235–38.

**Vargas, Getúlio Dornelles (1882–1954).** White Brazilian politician, governor of Rio Grande do Sul, and president of Brazil from 1930 to 1945 and 1951 to 1954.

**War of the Triple Alliance.** South America's largest international war, fought from 1864 to 1870 between Paraguay and the Triple Alliance of Argentina, Brazil, and Uruguay. Many Black soldiers served in the Triple Alliance armies, and the Brazilian Parliament decreed the gradual abolition of slavery in 1871, shortly after the end of the war.

**Washington, Booker T. (1856–1915).** North American educator, writer, and public figure; the Spanish translation of his autobiography, *De esclavo a catedrático* (1908), was widely read in Latin America.

**White, José Silvestre (1835–1918).** Internationally celebrated Cuban violinist and composer. Aimara Magana, "White Lafitte, José Silvestre de los Dolores," *Dictionary*, vol. VI, pp. 356–57.

**Year of the Lash (1844).** A brutal investigation and repression of a suspected conspiracy to a racial uprising. Colonial officials in Cuba imprisoned, banished, and executed hundreds of free and enslaved Afro-Cubans, including the poet **Plácido**.

**Yoruba.** One of the largest ethnic groups in Africa, living today in Nigeria, Benin, and Togo. The word also refers to the group's language and to its religious practices.

# Bibliography

Acree, William G., and Alex Borucki, eds. *Jacinto Ventura de Molina y los caminos de la escritura negra en el Río de la Plata*. Montevideo: Linardi y Risso, 2008.

Adamovsky, Ezequiel. "Un periódico afroargentino desconocido: La Palabra (1888–1930)," *PerspectivasAfro*, 1–2 (2022): 181–88.

Alberto, Paulina L. *Black Legend: The Many Lives of Raúl Grigera and the Power of Racial Storytelling in Argentina*. New York: Cambridge University Press, 2022.

*Terms of Inclusion: Black Intellectuals in Twentieth-Century Brazil*. Chapel Hill: University of North Carolina Press, 2011.

and Eduardo Elena, eds. *Rethinking Race in Modern Argentina*. New York: Cambridge University Press, 2016.

Andreu, Enrique. *Cosas que Usted debe conocer*. Havana: Editorial Nuevo Rumbo, 1950.

Andrews, George Reid. *The Afro-Argentines of Buenos Aires, 1800–1900*. Madison: University of Wisconsin Press, 1980.

*Afro-Latin America, 1800–2000*. New York: Oxford University Press, 2004.

*Blackness in the White Nation: A History of Afro-Uruguay*. Chapel Hill: University of North Carolina Press, 2010.

*Blacks and Whites in São Paulo, Brazil, 1888–1988*. Madison: University of Wisconsin Press, 1991.

"Epilogue: Whiteness and Its Discontents." In *Rethinking Race in Modern Argentina*, ed. Paulina Alberto and Eduardo Elena. New York: Cambridge University Press, 2016: 318–26.

Barbosa, Rui. *Embaixada a Buenos Aires*. Rio de Janeiro: Fundação Casa de Rui Barbosa, 1981.

Bastide, Roger. *The African Religions of Brazil: Toward a Sociology of the Interpenetration of Civilizations*, trans. Helen Sebba. Baltimore: Johns Hopkins University Press, 2007.

Batrell, Ricardo. *A Black Soldier's Story: The Narrative of Ricardo Batrell and the Cuban Wars of Independence*, ed. and trans. Mark Sanders. Minneapolis: University of Minnesota Press, 2010.

Benson, Devyn Spence. *Antiracism in Cuba: The Unfinished Revolution*. Chapel Hill: University of North Carolina Press, 2016.

Boone, Emilie. "Reproducing the New Negro: James Van Der Zee's Photographic Vision in Newsprint," *American Art* 34, 2 (2020): 4–25.

Borucki, Alex. *From Shipmates to Soldiers: Emerging Black Identities in the Río de la Plata*. Albuquerque: University of New Mexico Press, 2015.

Bronfman, Alejandra. "Más allá del color: clientelismo y conflict en Cienfuegos, 1912." In *Espacios, silencios y los sentidos de la libertad: Cuba entre 1878 y 1912*, ed. Fernando Martínez Heredia, Rebecca J. Scott, and Orlando F. García Martínez. Havana: Ediciones Unión, 2001: 285–94.

*Measures of Equality: Social Science, Citizenship, and Race in Cuba, 1902–1940*. Chapel Hill: University of North Carolina Press, 2005.

Brunson, Takkara K. *Black Women, Citizenship, and the Making of Modern Cuba*. Gainesville: University of Florida Press, 2021.

"'Writing' Black Womanhood in the Early Cuban Republic, 1904–1916," *Gender and History* 28, 2 (2016): 480–500.

Bucheli, Marisa, and Wanda Cabela. *Perfil demográfico y socioeconómico de la población uruguaya según su ascendencia racial*. Montevideo: Instituto Nacional de Estadística, 2007.

Burgueño, María Cristina. *Mario Rufino Méndez y la caricatura política en Nuestra Raza*. Montevideo: Biblioteca Nacional de Uruguay, 2015.

Butler, Kim. *Freedoms Given, Freedoms Won: Afro-Brazilians in Post-Abolition São Paulo and Salvador*. New Brunswick: Rutgers University Press, 1998.

Cabella, Wanda, Mathías Nathan, and Mariana Tenenbaum. *La población afro-uruguaya en el Censo 2011*. Montevideo: Universidad de la República, 2013.

Castilho, Celso Thomas. "A 'Gallery of Illustrious Men of Color': Recife's *O Homem*, the Black Press, and Transatlantic Literary Genres." In *Press, Power, and Culture in Imperial Brazil*, ed. Hendrik Kraay, Celso Thomas Castilho, and Teresa Cribelli. Albuquerque: University of New Mexico Press, 2021: 242–60.

and Rafaella Valença de Andrade Galvão. "Breaking the Silence: Racial Subjectivities, Abolitionism, and Public Life in mid-1870s Recife." In *The Boundaries of Freedom: Slavery, Abolition and the Making of Modern Brazil*, ed. Brodwyn Fischer and Keila Grinberg. New York: Cambridge University Press, 2022: 241–63.

Castillo Bueno, María de los Reyes. *Reyita: The Life of a Black Cuban Woman in the Twentieth Century*, trans. Anne McLean. Durham: Duke University Press, 2000.

Chagas, Karla, and Natalia Stalla. *Recuperando la memoria: afrodescendientes en la frontera uruguayo brasileña a mediados del siglo XX*. Montevideo: Ministerio de Educación y Cultura, 2009.

Chalhoub, Sidney, and Ana Flávia Magalhães Pinto, eds. *Pensadores negros, pensadoras negras: Brasil séculos XIX e XX*. Belo Horizonte: Fino Traço, 2020.

Cirio, Norberto Pablo. *Tinta negra en el gris del ayer: los afroporteños a través de sus periódicos entre 1873 y 1882*. Buenos Aires: Editorial Teseo, 2009.

"Indización de los periódicos afroporteños (1858 a principios del siglo XX)," *Revista Electrónica de Fuentes y Archivos* 12 (2021): 30–70.

Danky, James P., and Maureen E. Hady, eds. *African-American Newspapers and Periodicals: A National Bibliography.* Cambridge, MA: Harvard University Press, 1999.

de la Fuente, Alejandro. *A Nation for All: Race, Inequality, and Politics in Twentieth-Century Cuba.* Chapel Hill: University of North Carolina Press, 2001.

"La '*raza*' y los silencios de la cubanidad," *Revista Encuentro* 20 (2001): 107–18.

Delmont, Matthew F., ed. *Black Quotidian: Everyday History in African-American Newspapers.* Stanford: Stanford University Press, 2019.

Deschamps Chapeaux, Pedro. *El negro en el periodismo cubano en el siglo XIX.* Havana: Ediciones Revolución, 1963.

Diagne, Bachir Souleymane. "Négritude." In *The Stanford Encyclopedia of Philosophy*, ed. Edward N. Zalta. https://plato.stanford.edu/entries/negritude/. Accessed July 23, 2021.

Domingues, Petrônio José. *Uma história não contada: Negro, racismo, e branqueamento em São Paulo no pós-abolição.* São Paulo: SENAC, 2004.

"A insurgência de ébano: A história da Frente Negra Brasileira (1931–1937)." PhD diss., Universidade de São Paulo, 2005.

Edwards, Brent Hayes. *The Practice of Diaspora: Literature, Translation, and the Rise of Black Internationalism.* Cambridge, MA: Harvard University Press, 2003.

Fernández Calderón, Alejandro Leonardo. *Páginas en conflict: debate racial en la prensa cubana (1912–1930).* Havana: Editorial Universidad de La Habana, 2014.

Fernández Robaina, Tomás. "La bibliografía de autores de la raza de color, de Carlos M. Trelles," *Boletín del Instituto de Investigaciones Bibliográficas* 3 (1989): 94–102.

*El negro en Cuba: apuntes para la historia de la lucha contra la discriminación racial.* Havana: Editorial de Ciencias Sociales, 1990.

Ferrara, Miriam Nicolau, ed. *Imprensa negra.* São Paulo: Imprensa Oficial do Estado, 1984.

*A imprensa negra paulista (1915–1963).* São Paulo: FFLCH/USP, 1986.

Ferrer, Ada. *Insurgent Cuba: Race, Nation, and Revolution, 1868–1898.* Chapel Hill: University of North Carolina Press, 1999.

Flórez-Bolívar, Francisco Javier. "Opino, luego existo: prensa artesanal/obrera, raza y ciudadanía en Cartagena, 1910–1930," *Boletín Cultural y Bibliográfico* 52, 94 (2018): 22–39.

Ford, Jorje Miguel. *Beneméritos de mi estirpe: esbozos sociales.* Buenos Aires: Catálogos, 2002.

Foster, Frances Smith. "A Narrative of the Interesting Origins and (Somewhat) Surprising Developments of African-American Print Culture," *American Literary History* 17, 4 (2005): 714–40.

Frigerio, Alejandro. *Cultura negra en el cono sur: representaciones en conflicto.* Buenos Aires: Universidad Católica Argentina, 2000.

"'Sin otro delito que el color de su piel': imágenes del 'negro' en la revista *Caras y Caretas* (1900–1910)." In *Cartografías afrolatinoamericanas: perspectivas* *situadas para análisis transfronterizo*s, ed. Florencia Guzmán and Lea Geler. Buenos Aires: Biblos, 2013: 151–74.

Fusté, José I. "Possible Republics: Tracing the 'Entanglements' of Race and Nation in Afro-*Latina/o* Caribbean Thought and Activism, 1870–1930." PhD diss., University of California, San Diego, 2012.

"Unsettling Citizenship/Circumventing Sovereignty: Reexamining the Quandaries of Contemporary Anti-Colonialism in the US through Black Puerto Rican Anti-Racist Thought," *American Quarterly*, 65, 4 (2014): 161–69.

García Yero, Cary. "To Whom It Belongs: The Aftermaths of *Afrocubanismo* and the Power over *Lo Negro* in Cuban Arts, 1938–1958." Work in Progress.

Garzón, Luis, ed. *Almanaque del progreso.* Buenos Aires: Imprenta de la Escuela de Artes y Oficios de San Carlos, 1880.

Geler, Lea. *Andares negros, caminos blancos. Afroporteños, Estado y Nación Argentina a fines del siglo XIX.* Rosario: Prohistoria Ediciones, 2010.

and María de Lourdes Ghidoli. "Falucho, paradojas de un héroe negro en una nación blanca: raza, clase y género en Argentina (1875–1930)," *Avances del Cesor* 16, 20 (2019): 1–27.

Geler, Lea, Carmen Yannone, and Alejandra Egido. "Constructing the White City: Urban Trajectories of the Afro-Argentines of Buenos Aires during the Twentieth Century." In *Scenes from the Shadows: Afro-Argentine Life in the Twentieth Century*, ed. Lea Geler and Robert Cottrol. Athens: Ohio University Press, forthcoming.

Ghidoli, María de Lourdes. *Estereotipos en negro: representaciones y autorrepresentaciones visuales de afroporteños en el siglo XIX.* Buenos Aires: Prohistoria Ediciones, 2016.

Godoi, Rodrigo Camargo de, and Henry Pratt. "Printers, Typographers, and Readers: Slavery and Print Culture." In *Press, Power, and Culture in Imperial Brazil*, ed. Hendrik Kraay, Celso Thomas Castilho, and Teresa Cribelli. Albuquerque: University of New Mexico Press, 2021: 72–89.

Goldman, Gustavo. *Negros modernos: asociacionismo político, mutual y cultural en el Río de la Plata a fines del siglo XIX.* Montevideo: Perro Andaluz Ediciones, 2019.

Goldthree, Reena. "Afro-Cuban Intellectuals and the New Negro Renaissance in Harlem." In *New Perspectives on the Black Intellectual Tradition*, ed Keisha N. Blain, Christopher Cameron, and Ashley D. Farmer. Evanston: Northwestern University Press, 2018: 41–58.

Gomes, Flávio. *Negros e política (1888–1937).* São Paulo: Zahar, 2005.

and Petrônio Domingues. *Da nitidez e invisibilidade: Legados do pós-emancipação no Brasil.* Belo Horizonte: Fino Traço, 2013.

Graham, Jessica L. *Shifting the Meaning of Democracy: Race, Politics, and Culture in the United States and Brazil.* Oakland: University of California Press, 2019.

Green, Rodney D., and Sue E. Houchins. "Black Progress through Business Improvement: Two Articles by Joseph R. Houchins, 1900–1989," *Review of Black Political Economy* 44 (2017): 421–33.

Guimarães, Antonio Sérgio Alfredo. *Classes, raças e democracia.* São Paulo: Editora 34, 2009.

Guridy, Frank Andre. *Forging Diaspora: Afro-Cubans and African Americans in a World of Empire and Jim Crow*. Chapel Hill: University of North Carolina Press, 2010.

and Juliet Hooker. "Currents in Afro-Latin American Political and Social Thought." In *Afro-Latin American Studies: An Introduction*, ed. Alejandro de la Fuente and George Reid Andrews. New York: Cambridge University Press, 2018: 179–221.

Guzmán, Florencia. "¿Quienes son los trigueños? Análisis de una categoría racial intersticial (1810–1830)," *Archivos* 29, 1 (2021): 77–98.

Helg, Aline. *Our Rightful Share: The Afro-Cuban Struggle for Equality, 1886–1912*. Chapel Hill: University of North Carolina Press, 1995.

"Race in Argentina and Cuba, 1880–1930: Theory, Policy, and Popular Reaction." In *The Idea of Race in Latin America, 1870–1940*, ed. Richard Graham. Austin: University of Texas Press, 1990: 37–70.

Hellwig, David J., ed. *African-American Reflections on Brazil's Racial Paradise*. Philadelphia: Temple University Press, 1992.

Higginbotham, Evelyn Brooks. *Righteous Discontent: The Women's Movement in the Black Baptist Church, 1880–1920*. Cambridge: Harvard University Press, 1994.

Hoffnung-Garskof, Jesse. *Racial Migrations: New York City and the Revolutionary Politics of the Spanish Caribbean*. Princeton: Princeton University Press, 2019.

"To Abolish the Law of Castes: Merit, Manhood and the Problem of Colour in the Puerto Rican Liberal Movement," *Social History* 36, 3 (2011): 312–42.

Hordge-Freeman, Elizabeth. *Second-Class Daughters: Black Brazilian Women and Informal Adoption as Modern Slavery*. New York: Cambridge University Press, 2022.

Ibarra Cuesta, Jorge. "Caciquismo, racismo y actitudes en relación con el status político en la Isla en la provincia de Santa Clara (1906–1909)." In *Espacios, silencios y los sentidos de la libertad: Cuba entre 1878 y 1912*, ed. Fernando Martínez Heredia, Rebecca J. Scott, and Orlando F. García Martínez. Havana: Ediciones Unión, 2001: 270–84.

International Monetary Fund. *Annual Report ... 1949* (Washington, DC: International Monetary Fund, 1949).

Jesús, Úrsula de. *The Spiritual Diary of a Seventeenth-Century Afro-Peruvian Mystic, Ursula de Jesús*, ed. and trans. Nancy E. van Deusen. Albuquerque: University of New Mexico Press, 2004.

Knight, Franklin W., and Henry Louis Gates, Jr., eds. *Dictionary of Caribbean and Afro-Latin American Biography*. 6 vols. New York: Oxford University Press, 2016.

Kynaston, David, and Francis Green. *Engines of Privilege: Britain's Private School Problem*. London: Bloomsbury Publishing, 2019.

Lamadrid, C. C., C. O. Lamadrid, and N. Cirio. "Primer censo autogestionado de afroargentinos del tronco colonial," *Identidades* 2, 6 (2015): 72–89.

Lanier, Oilda Hevia. *El directorio central de las sociedades negras de Cuba (1886–1894)*. Havana: Editorial de Ciencias Sociales, 1996.

Law, Robin. "The Evolution of the Brazilian Community in Ouidah," *Slavery & Abolition*, 22, 1 (2001), 3–21.

Leal, Maria das Graças de Andrade. *Manuel Querino entre letras e lutas: Bahia, 1851–1923*. São Paulo: Annablume, 2009.

Leite, José Correia, and Cuti [Luiz Silva]. *. . . E disse o velho militante José Correia Leite*. São Paulo: Secretaria Municipal de Cultura, 1992.

Levine, Robert M. *Father of the Poor?: Vargas and His Era*. New York: Cambridge University Press, 1998.

Lunn, Joe. "Tirailleurs Sénégalais." In *The Encyclopedia of War*, ed. Gordon Martel. Blackwell Publishing, 2011.

Manzano, Juan Francisco. *Autobiography of a Slave*, ed. Ivan Schulman, trans. Evelyn Picon Garfield. Detroit: Wayne State University Press, 1996.

Matory, J. Lorand. "The English Professors of Brazil: On the Diasporic Roots of the Yoruba Nation," *Comparative Studies in Society and History* 41, 1 (1999): 72–103.

McKnight, Kathryn Joy, and Leo Garofalo, eds. *Afro-Latino Voices: Narratives from the Early Modern Ibero-Atlantic World, 1550–1812*. Indianapolis: Hackett, 2009.

Mirabal, Nancy Raquel. *Suspect Freedoms: The Racial and Sexual Politics of Cubanidad in New York, 1823–1957*. New York: New York University Press, 2017.

Montejo Arrechea, Carmen. "*Minerva*: A Magazine for Women (and Men) of Color." In *Between Race and Empire: African-Americans and Cubans before the Cuban Revolution*, ed. Lisa Brock and Digna Castañeda Fuertes. Philadelphia: Temple University Press, 1998: 33–48.

Moraes, Evaristo de. *Brancos e negros: Nos Estados Unidos e no Brasil*. Rio de Janeiro: Miccolis, 1922.

Nascimento, Abdias do, ed. *O negro revoltado*. Rio de Janeiro: Grupo GRD, 1968.

Olivares Sánchez, Carlos. *Relato de una gran contienda*. Guantánamo: Editorial El Mar y la Montaña, 2005.

Orovio, Helio. *Cuban Music from A to Z*. Durham: Duke University Press, 2004.

Pappademos, Melina. *Black Political Activism and the Cuban Republic*. Chapel Hill: University of North Carolina Press, 2011.

Pereda Valdés, Ildefonso. *El negro en el Uruguay pasado y presente*. Montevideo: Revista del Instituto Histórico y Geográfico del Uruguay, 1965.

Pérez, Louis A. "Politics, Peasants, and People of Color: The 1912 'Race War' in Cuba Reconsidered," *Hispanic American Historical Review* 66, 3 (1986): 509–39.

Pinto, Ana Flávia Magalhães. *Escritos de liberdade: Literatos negros, racismo e cidadania no Brasil oitocentista*. Campinas: Editora da UNICAMP, 2018.

*Imprensa negra no Brasil do século XIX*. São Paulo: Selo Negro, 2010.

Platero, Tomás A. *Piedra libre para nuestros negros: La Broma y otros periódicos de la comunidad afroargentina, 1873–1882*. Buenos Aires: Instituto Histórico de la Ciudad de Buenos Aires, 2004.

Portuondo Linares, Serafín. *Los Independientes de Color: Historia del Partido Independiente de Color*. Havana: Librería Selecta, 1950.

Poumier, María, ed. *La cuestión tabú: el pensamiento negro cubano de 1840 a 1959*. Tenerife: Ediciones Idea, 2007.

Preuss, Ori. *Transnational South America: Experiences, Ideas, and Identities, 1860s–1900s*. New York: Routledge, 2019.

Putnam, Lara. *Radical Moves: Caribbean Migrants and the Politics of Race in the Jazz Age*. Chapel Hill: University of North Carolina Press, 2013.

*Quilombo. Vida, problemas e aspirações do negro*. São Paulo: Editora 34, 2003.

Ramos, Ana Flávia Cernic, and Ana Flávia Magalhães Pinto, eds. *A imprensa negra e sua intelectualidade*. Special issue of *Intellèctus* 17, 1 (2018).

Ramos Perea, Roberto, ed. *Literatura puertorriqueña negra del siglo XIX escrita por negros*. San Juan: Editorial LEAP, 2011.

Reis, João José. *Slave Rebellion in Brazil: The Muslim Uprising of 1835 in Bahia*, trans. Arthur Brakel. Baltimore: Johns Hopkins University Press, 1995.

Rodríguez, Romero Jorge. *Mbundo malungo a mundele: historia del movimiento afrouruguayo y sus alternativas de desarrollo*. Montevideo: Rosebud Ediciones, 2006.

Roosevelt, Theodore. "Brazil and the Negro," *Outlook* (Feb. 21, 1914): 409–11.

Santos, José Antônio dos. *Raiou a Alvorada: Intelectuais negros e imprensa, Pelotas (1907–1957)*. Pelotas: Editora da Universidade Federal de Pelotas, 2003.

Sartorius, David. *Ever Faithful: Race, Loyalty, and the Ends of Empire in Spanish Cuba*. Durham: Duke University Press, 2014.

Scott, Rebecca J. *Degrees of Freedom: Louisiana and Cuba after Slavery*. Cambridge: Harvard University Press, 2005.

*Slave Emancipation in Cuba: The Transition to Free Labor, 1860–1899*. Princeton: Princeton University Press, 1985.

Seigel, Micol. *Uneven Encounters: Making Race and Nation in Brazil and the United States*. Durham: Duke University Press, 2009.

Stubbs, Josefina, and Hiska N. Reyes, eds. *Más allá de los promedios: afrodescendientes en América Latina*. Washington, DC: World Bank, 2006.

Tinajero, Araceli. *El Lector: A History of the Cigar Factory Reader*, trans. Judith E. Grasberg. Austin: University of Texas Press, 2010.

Torres-Saillant, Silvio. "The Tribulations of Blackness: Stages in Dominican Racial Identity," *Callaloo* 23, 3 (2000): 1086–1111.

Trelles, Carlos M. "La bibliografía de autores de la raza de color," *Cuba Contemporánea* 43, 169 (Jan.–Apr. 1927): 30–78.

United States, Department of the Treasury. *Treasury Decisions under Customs and Other Laws*, vol. LVI. Washington, DC: Government Printing Office, 1930.

Vallejo de Paredes, Magarita. *Apuntes biográficos y bibliográficos de algunos escritores dominicanos del siglo XIX*. Santo Domingo: Publicaciones ONAP, 1995.

Vogel, Todd, ed. *The Black Press: New Literary and Historical Essays*. New Brunswick: Rutgers University Press, 2001.

Von Eschen, Penny M. *Race against Empire: Black Americans and Anticolonialism, 1937–1957*. Ithaca: Cornell University Press, 1997.

Wright, Winthrop R. "The Todd Duncan Affair: Acción Democrática and the Myth of Racial Democracy in Venezuela," *The Americas* 44, 4 (1988): 441–59.

Xavier, Giovana. *Maria de Lourdes Vale Nascimento: Uma intelectual negra do pós-abolição*. Niterói: EDUFF, 2020.

# Index

Lightning Source UK Ltd.
Milton Keynes UK
UKHW030431041122
411620UK00010B/612